Public Personnel Management: Current Concerns, Future Challenges

Second Edition

Edited by

Carolyn Ban

University of Pittsburgh

Norma M. Riccucci

University at Albany, State University of New York

LONGMAN

An imprint of Addison Wesley Longman, Inc.

New York • Reading, Massachusetts • Menlo Park, California • Harlow, England
Don Mills, Ontario • Sydney • Mexico City • Madrid • Amsterdam

Public Personnel Management: Current Concerns, Future Challenges, Second Edition

Copyright © 1997, 1991 by Longman Publishers USA,
A Division of Addison Wesley Longman, Inc.

Longman, 10 Bank Street, White Plains, N.Y. 10606

Executive editor: Pamela A. Gordon
Associate editor: Hillary B. Henderson
Editorial assistant: Chia Ling
Production editor: Linda Moser
Production supervisor: Edith Pullman
Cover design: Anne M. Pompeo
Compositor: ExecuStaff

Library of Congress Cataloging-in-Publication Data

Public personnel management : current concerns, future challenges / by
   Carolyn Ban, Norma M. Riccucci.—2nd ed.
       p.   cm.
   Includes bibliographical references and index.
   ISBN 0-8013-1699-5
   1. Civil service—United States—Personnel management   I. Ban,
   Carolyn.   II. Riccucci, Norma.
JK765.P947   1997
353.001—dc20   96-25492
                                                              CIP

1 2 3 4 5 6 7 8 9 10-MA-0099989796

Contents

Contributors

Carolyn Ban is Dean of the Graduate School of Public and International Affairs at the University of Pittsburgh. Her research focuses on civil service and administrative reforms, ranging from the Civil Service Reform Act to the National Performance Review. She is the author or coauthor of three books, including *How Do Public Managers Manage? Bureaucratic Constraints, Organizational Culture, and the Potential for Reform*, as well as numerous articles. She has served as a consultant to federal and state agencies and to the World Bank. She served in 1994 as chair of the Section on Personnel and Labor Relations of the American Society of Public Administration.

Evan M. Berman is a faculty member of the Department of Public Administration at the University of Central Florida in Orlando. His research focuses on public personnel management, public productivity, and local government. He is the author and coauthor of articles that have appeared in *Public Administration Review, Administration & Society, American Review of Public Administration, Journal of Public Administration Research and Theory, Review of Public Personnel Administration, Public Productivity & Management Review, State and Local Government Review, Policy Studies Journal, Policy Studies Review,* and other scholarly journals.

Willa Marie Bruce is a Professor in the Department of Public Administration at the University of Nebraska at Omaha. Her research interests include administrative ethics, job performance and satisfaction, spirituality of work, environmental issues, and dual-career couples. Since 1990 she has authored or coauthored four books, including *Problem Employee Management: Proactive Strategies for Human Resources Managers,* as well as numerous articles and book chapters. She is a co-winner, with Dr. Christine Reed, of the James E. Webb Award for best paper at the 1992 national conference of the American Society for Public Administration.

N. Joseph Cayer is Professor of Public Affairs at Arizona State University. He is author or coauthor of several books and numerous chapters and articles on public management and policy, with emphasis on public sector human resources management issues. Books he has authored or coauthored include *Public Personnel Administration in the United States, Public Administration: Social Change and Adaptive Management, Managing Human Resources, Handbook of Training and Development for the Public Sector,* and *Supervision for Success in Government.*

Tamu Chambers is an education specialist at Hudson Valley Community College and Executive Director of the Diversity Enrichment Institute. She is an adjunct faculty member at Russell Sage College and the University at Albany, State University of New York. She is the author of the Cultural and Social Enrichment curriculum and various diversity training materials for public and private businesses. She is a contributor to many business journals and has been recognized as an African American Woman of Distinction by the NAACP.

Charles J. Fox is a Professor of Political Science and Director of the Center for Public Service at Texas Tech University. He writes in the areas of public administration theory, ethics and public administration, public personnel administration, and public policy implementation. He is coauthor with Hugh Miller of *Postmodern Public Administration: Toward Discourse.* His work has appeared in *Administration & Society, Public Administration Review, American Review of Public Administration, Western Political Quarterly, Public Policy Review, Administrative Theory and Praxis, International Journal of Public Administration,* and various book chapters.

Charles W. Gossett is Assistant Professor of Political Science and Director of the Bureau of Public Affairs at Georgia Southern University. He is the author of several journal articles, including "Domestic Partnership Benefits: Public Sector Patterns," and coauthor with Norma Riccucci of "Employment Discrimination in State and Local Government: The Lesbian and Gay Male Experience." He holds a B.A. from Hope College and an M.A. and Ph.D. from Stanford University.

Paul S. Greenlaw received his Ph.D. with a major in public personnel administration from the Maxwell School of Citizenship and Public Affairs, Syracuse University. He has taught American government at Duke University and worked in the personnel field in industry. He is a Professor of Management at Penn State, where he specializes in computer educational simulation and equal employment opportunity law. He is the author or coauthor of 12 books and over 50 articles.

Patricia W. Ingraham is Professor of Public Administration and Political Science and Director of the Campbell Institute for Public Affairs at the Maxwell School, Syracuse University. She is the author of *The Foundation of Merit: Public Service in American Democracy,* the coauthor of *Making Government Work: Reforming the Civil Service,* and the editor or co-editor of six other books. Her research interests are in public management reform and change and in the relationships between political officials and members of the higher public service.

Donald F. Kettl is Director of the Robert M. La Follette Institute of Public Affairs at the University of Wisconsin—Madison and Professor of Public Affairs and Political Science. He is also a Nonresident Senior Fellow in the Brookings Institution's Center for Public Management. He is the author of and contributor to, among other works, *Civil Service Reform: Building a Government That Works, Inside the Reinvention Machine: Appraising the National Performance Review, Sharing Power: Public Governance and Private Markets,* and *Deficit Politics.*

Robert D. Lee Jr. is Professor of Public Administration and Professor of Hotel, Restaurant, and Recreation Management at the Pennsylvania State University, University Park. He is coauthor of *Public Budgeting Systems,* 5th ed., and author of *Public Personnel Systems,* 3rd ed.

Debra J. Mesch is Associate Professor at Indiana University in the School of Public and Environmental Affairs. She received both her M.B.A. and Ph.D. in management from Indiana University, School of Business. Previously, she has taught at Simmons College and Northeastern University, College of Business Administration. Her primary area of research is in dispute resolution—specifically, the arbitration and grievance process. She has published over 20 articles in such journals as *Administrative Science Quarterly, Journal of Applied Psychology, Human Relations, Academy of Management Journal, International Journal of Conflict Management, Labor Studies Journal, Journal of Applied Behavioral Science, Review of Public Personnel Management,* and *Journal of Public Administration Research and Theory.*

Katherine C. Naff is Assistant Professor of Public Administration at San Francisco State University. Prior to joining the faculty at SFSU, she spent eight years with the U.S. Merit Systems Protection Board in Washington, D.C., as a Senior Research Analyst. Her work there focused on issues pertaining to the employment of women and minorities in the federal government. She has a Ph.D. in Government from Georgetown University and an M.P.A. from San Francisco State University.

James L. Perry is Professor in the School of Public and Environmental Affairs, Indiana University, Bloomington. His research focuses on public management and public personnel administration. Perry's research has appeared in such journals as the *Academy of Management Journal, Administrative Science Quarterly, American Political Science Review,* and *Public Administration Review.* He has coauthored or edited six books, including the *Handbook of Public Administration,* 2nd ed. Perry is a recipient of Fulbright and NASPAA Fellowships, the Yoder-Honeman Award for innovative personnel research, and the Charles H. Levine Memorial Award for Excellence in Public Administration.

Beryl A. Radin is Professor of Public Administration and Policy in the Graduate School of Public Affairs at Rockefeller College of the State University of New York at Albany. Currently the president of the Association for Public Policy Analysis and Management, she has focused on public management, intergovernmental, and federalism issues in a number of policy areas. She has been involved in studies of federal systems in India and Australia. Professor Radin has been a consultant to a wide range of government agencies, including the Office of Management and Budget, and U.S. Department of Agriculture, the World Bank, the Department of Health and Human Services, and NASA. She has received research support from the Ford Foundation, the Aspen Institute, the Fulbright Foundation, the National Science Foundation, and a number of other organizations.

T. Zane Reeves is Professor of Public Administration in the School of Public Administration at the University of New Mexico. He is author or coauthor of *Managing Human Resources, The Politics of Peace Corps and VISTA, Personnel Management in the Public Sector,* and *Collective Bargaining in the Public Sector.* Reeves serves as an arbitrator on a number of arbitration panels, including the Federal Mediation and Conciliation Service and the American Arbitration Association.

Norma M. Riccucci is Associate Professor of Public Administration and Policy at Rockefeller College of the University at Albany, State University of New York at Albany. She has published extensively in the areas of public personnel management, affirmative action, and public sector labor relations. She is the author of *Unsung Heroes: Federal Execucrats Making a Difference* and *Promoting and Managing Diversity in Municipal Government Work Forces,* and a coauthor of *Personnel Management in Government,* 4th ed.

Barbara S. Romzek is Professor of Public Administration at the University of Kansas, where her work has included a five-year term as department chair. Her research and teaching interests include public management, accountability, employee commitment, and intergovernmental relations. Her work has been published in various social science journals. She is the coauthor of *Public Administration: Politics and the Management of Expectations* (with M. Dubnick) and *New Governance for Rural America: Creating Intergovernmental Partnerships* (with B. Radin and Associates). She is coeditor of *New Paradigms for Government: Issues for the Changing Public Service* (with P. Ingraham).

David H. Rosenbloom is Distinguished Professor of Public Administration at American University, Washington, D.C. He was Editor-in-Chief of *Public Administration Review* from 1991 through 1996. Rosenbloom has a longstanding interest in the constitutional law of public personnel management, has published widely on the subject, and was appointed to the Clinton-Gore 1992 Presidential Transition Team for the U.S. Office of Personnel Management. He was elected to the National Academy of Public Administration in 1986.

Kurt A. Shirkey is an ABD Ph.D. student at Texas Tech University specializing in both American government and politics, and public policy and administration.

James D. Slack is Professor of Public Administration and Director of the Public Policy and Administration Institute in the School of Business and Public Administration at California State University at Bakersfield. His research focuses on the workplace and policy ramifications of HIV/AIDS.

George T. Sulzner is Professor of Political Science at the University of Massachusetts, Amherst, where he is also Director of the Masters Program in Public Administration. He has published extensively on the subject of public sector labor relations in both the United States and Canada. Currently he is researching the implementation of the 1992 Public Service Reform Act of Canada.

Frank J. Thompson is Dean of the Graduate School of Public Affairs and Associate Provost of Rockefeller College at the State University of New York at Albany. He also serves as Executive Director of the National Commission on the State and Local Public Service. He has published extensively on issues of health policy, policy implementation, public personnel policy, and administrative politics. His books include *Personnel Policy in the City, Health Policy and the Bureaucracy, Public Administration: Challenges, Choices and Consequences,* and, most recently, an edited volume, *Revitalizing State and Local Public Service.*

INTRODUCTION

Public Personnel Management in a Time of Rapid Reform

Carolyn Ban and Norma M. Riccucci

In the time since the first edition of this book appeared in 1991, much has changed. There have been ferment and rapid reform in public management as well as in the larger social and political environment. The premise of this book is that public personnel management is an integral part of public management; thus reforms in public personnel management often reflect broader changes in public management and, indeed, changes in society as a whole.

Hence the focus of this book is not on personnel management techniques. Look elsewhere if you want detailed instructions on how to classify a position or to develop an affirmative action plan. This book approaches public personnel management from a policy perspective. It has two main goals: (1) to provide students of public personnel management with the most up-to-date information possible on the debates and issues currently shaping the field, and (2) to help students understand the process of change.

This introduction provides a framework within which all the issues discussed in the book can be placed. We begin by examining the cycles of reform in public personnel management and in public management as a whole. We then focus on current reform efforts at the federal, state, and local levels. Next we present the range of political, economic, and social changes that provide the impetus for reform; we also discuss the nature of the reform process and impediments to change. Finally we conclude with a brief description of what human resources management may look like in the future.

CYCLES OF REFORM IN PERSONNEL ADMINISTRATION

Because personnel management is an integral part of public management, reforms in personnel management have paralleled development in public management generally. The creation of the merit system, with passage of the Pendleton Act in 1883, reflected societal rejection of the spoils system and acceptance of the value of a stable professional public service. Personnel techniques, such as position classification systems, sprang from the scientific management theories that were dominant in the 1920s and 1930s.

Reforms have also focused on two key themes: strengthening presidential control and improving management efficiency. Early reformers, from the Keep Commission (in 1905) through the Brownlow Commission (in 1937), saw them as linked—an efficient but harnessed bureaucracy would provide the vehicle for political control (Garvey, 1995). By the late 1970s, popular views of government as a force for positive change were increasingly being replaced by distrust, reflected in the "bureaucrat bashing" of Presidents Carter and Reagan. Carter's Civil Service Reform Act (CSRA) of 1978 reflects a tension between the goals of strengthening presidential control of the bureaucracy (through creation of the Senior Executive Service and simplified methods for firing federal workers) and increasing managerial efficiency.

That tension is even more evident in the recent proposals of the National Performance Review (NPR), with its emphasis on deregulation both of personnel and of other highly regulated areas of management, decentralization and devolution of authority, participative management or shared power (including Total Quality Management), and an increased focus on giving managers more authority and holding them accountable for results. Taken together, these new approaches have been called "the New Public Management." Like many of the CSRA reforms, the New Public Management reflects the tendency to attempt to graft private sector management techniques onto the public sector. But doing so may actually undermine centralized control by the president. Indeed, Garvey argues that "[t]he NPR is mainly about governmental capacity—to the point, indeed, of carelessness about the value of control" (1995: 101). Chapter 1 addresses the NPR reforms in detail.

The recommendations of the National Commission on the State and Local Public Service (or Winter Commission), also discussed in Chapter 1, place more stress on increasing centralized administrative control while also calling for improved managerial capacity.

IMPETUS FOR REFORM

As noted earlier, the current and future challenges of public personnel administration are marked by reform. The field is constantly seeking to reform—and sometimes even reinvent—itself in order to keep pace with the prevailing political, social, legal, and economic tides in this nation. At every level of government we are seeing reforms in public personnel in response to permutations in resource availability, the nature of the work force, approaches to managing the work force, and the power and role of public sector unions, to mention a few. For example, Draconian cuts in federal, state, and local budgets have created pressures for governments to be more efficient in the spending and redistribution of tax dollars. These pressures, in turn, necessitate a personnel or human resources function that is capable of managing environments that are debilitated by resource scarcity, and that at the same time is able to attract and retain the best and brightest government workers. In short, public personnel administration, like its genitor, public administration, must embrace as a fundamental value managerial or economic efficiency (Rosenbloom, 1983).

In addition, we have already begun to see, as a result of overall shifts in this nation's demography, changes in the demographics of public sector work forces. Despite political, social, and legal trends that have greatly hampered the reaches of such equity policies as affirmative action, changing economic and demographic winds have compelled the business community as well as the government to develop personnel management programs and policies that enhance and promote diversity.

Moreover, new management approaches and technologies aimed at empowering government employees as well as citizens spur significant reforms to public personnel administration at the federal, state, and local levels of government. As President Bill Clinton stated in announcing the National Performance Review in March 1993, "Our goal is . . . to change the culture of our national bureaucracy away from complacency and entitlement toward initiative and empowerment" (National Performance Review 1993: 1). The National (Winter) Commission on the State and Local Public Service made similar proclamations. Monumental pressure for reform is being placed on public personnel and human resources management in that they are the purveyors of the tools, techniques, and strategies for reinventing and redesigning government service. In many public sector jurisdictions across the country, new approaches to hiring, firing, compensating, and appraising employees are emerging. Efforts to manage and improve the quality of government services also continue to remain on the agendas of public personnelists and human resources managers. And labor-management partnerships are being forged so that governments can pursue the path of least resistance in their struggles to reinvent themselves. These partnerships are changing the role that unions play in the governance of public employees.

THE NATURE OF THE REFORM PROCESS

There are several characteristics of the reform process that are important to keep in mind as one reads this book. First, the issues that reformers are facing are complex and interrelated, and they sometimes pull reformers in contradictory directions. For example, how can we deregulate the hiring process and still ensure that we protect equity and diversity? How can we attract and motivate high-quality government employees while cutting the size and costs of government? How can we empower employees without disempowering either managers or union representatives?

Second, the process of reform is complex, involving both administrative and political processes. Some reforms can be put in place via executive action, but many others require legislative approval or must be bargained over with unions. And, as Norma Riccucci makes clear in Chapter 4, the courts also play a major role in approving, or undoing, reforms. Further, many public personnel issues are also political issues; debates over affirmative action, gay and lesbian rights, the role of unions, and pay and benefits of government workers are at the center of current political debates in our country.

Given the political nature of the debates, most of the reforms have both strong supporters and opponents. Supporters of the approaches referred to as the New Public Management see the opportunity to increase government efficiency and responsiveness. Opponents may resist change because they see their own power or interests as potentially harmed. But there is genuine opposition to such reforms as Total Quality Management (TQM; discussed in several chapters, but particularly by Evan Berman in Chapter 18) from those who see the focus on the "customer" as an inappropriate way to view the relationship between the government and citizens.

Because change is difficult and the issues are complex, the rate of change is uneven. Most of the reforms discussed in this book have been implemented in some locations. Indeed, several chapters highlight examples of successful reform. But across the 50 states and thousands of local governments, reform has proceeded at different rates, reflecting both the difficulty of securing agreement for reforms and the challenges of successfully implementing the changes. This means that our state and local governments provide a natural laboratory for studying the reform process.

HUMAN RESOURCES MANAGEMENT OF THE FUTURE

It is clear that as personnel policies change, the role of the Human Resources Office must also change. On the one hand, some reformers have called for the Human Resources Office to continue its traditional role of administering the merit system, managing the usual personnel functions of hiring, classification, administration of pay, and so forth, but to emphasize service to managers (seen as "customers" in TQM terms) and to deemphasize its traditional role of oversight and protection of the merit system (Ban, 1995).

Others have argued for a more radical redefinition of the Human Resources Office's role, seeing it as taking on new functions such as organizational development and internal consulting within the organization. Chapter 2 of this volume offers an argument for even more drastic reform. James Perry and Debra

Mesch present a model of strategic human resources management in which organizations move from a personnel unit that is isolated from the mainstream of the organization, with a focus on the technical minutiae of hiring, classification, and benefits, to a strategic human resources unit, integrated into the management of the organization, where management of human resources is seen as making a difference for the effectiveness of the organization. Many other chapters reflect both positive goals for the field and the conflicts that make studying public personnel so interesting.

Trying to keep up with a field that is changing so rapidly is a challenge for scholar and student. As we move into the next century, the one thing we can be sure of is that public personnel administration will continue to reform and reinvent itself. One would expect no less from a field that is dynamic and mutable, especially in its ability to keep up with the changing political, social, legal, and economic demands of this nation.

REFERENCES

Ban, Carolyn. 1995. *How Do Public Managers Manage? Bureaucratic Constraints, Organizational Culture, and the Potential for Reform.* San Francisco: Jossey-Bass.

Garvey, Gerald. 1995. "False Promises: The NPR in Historical Perspective," in Donald F. Kettl and John J. DiIulio Jr., eds., *Inside the Reinvention Machine: Appraising Governmental Reform.* Washington, D.C.: Brookings Institution.

National Performance Review. 1993. *From Red Tape to Results: Creating a Government That Works Better and Costs Less.* Washington, D.C.: U.S. Government Printing Office.

Rosenbloom, David H. 1983. "Public Administrative Theory and the Separation of Powers." *Public Administration Review* 43, no. 3: 219–227.

Acknowledgments

Many students and colleagues have helped in the production of this book. In particular, students in our advanced public personnel administration course were extremely helpful in reviewing both the first and second editions of *Public Personnel Management: Current Concerns, Future Challenges.* Special thanks are also extended to the following individuals, who reviewed the manuscript and made helpful suggestions:

Linda DeLeon, University of Colorado at Denver
J. Edward Kellough, University of Georgia
Fred A. Kramer, University of Massachusetts, Amherst
Linda Richter, Kansas State University
Lois R. Wise, Indiana University

Reform: Politics and Prospects

This section explores the major theme of this book: the efforts to reform civil service systems, linked closely to broader efforts at reforming public management. It sets the stage for many of the other chapters by exploring the impetus for reform, the specific reforms called for, and some of the broader implications of the reform effort.

Chapter 1 begins the discussion of reform by profiling two important calls for reform. The first, the report of the National Commission on the State and Local Public Service, exhorted state and local governments to reform their approaches to public management. Many of the recommended reforms were related to human resources issues. The second, the National Performance Review, headed by Vice-President Gore, proposed sweeping reforms in public management for the federal government with the goal of achieving a government system that "works better and costs less." As Frank Thompson and Beryl Radin make clear, the two reports share many common themes, in particular the recommendations for deregulation of personnel functions, increased delegation of authority to line managers, delayering (i.e., reducing the number of middle managers), and increased labor-management cooperation.

Chapter 2, "Strategic Human Resource Management," broadens the discussion of reform; it explores a very different concept of the role and functions of a personnel office. In the new public management, deregulation should give organizations more discretion but also hold them (and individual managers) responsible for results. In this environment, the role of the personnel office will need to shift from the traditional control function to a broader human resources focus, linking human resources management to the goals and strategy of the organization. James Perry and Debra Mesch argue convincingly that it is probably essential for the future success of public organizations.

Current reform efforts propose moving away from the traditional hierarchical style with a focus on formal systems of control toward a deregulated, decentralized management system. As Barbara Romzek makes clear in Chapter 3, "Accountability and Challenges of Deregulation," the assumption is that removing constraints on management will increase both efficiency and responsiveness. But these new approaches to public management raise difficult issues of accountability. Romzek also raises the critical question of whether the American people will accept giving their public servants the level of discretion and flexibility that the reforms propose.

As you read these chapters, look particularly for common themes. Many of the themes will recur, from different perspectives, in later chapters of the book. How realistic are these reform efforts? What might be the unintended consequences of reform?

chapter **1**

Reinventing Public Personnel Management: The Winter and Gore Initiatives

Frank J. Thompson and Beryl A. Radin

The 1990s witnessed new ferment over the performance of governmental institutions in the United States and the call for "reinvention." As part of this initiative, analysts put the structures, cultures, policies, and procedures of personnel administration under the microscope and quickly diagnosed infirmities.

In their popular book *Reinventing Government*, David Osborne, a journalist, and Ted Gaebler, a former city manager, argued that governments needed "the flexibility to respond to complex and rapidly changing conditions" but that they could "do none of these things easily thanks to their civil service regulations and tenure systems" (1992: 34). They went on to assert that "the only thing more destructive than a line-item budget system is a personnel system built around civil service." Although acknowledging that the system was "well intended" and had checked the abuses brought on by "patronage hiring and political mani-pulation of public employees," Osborne and Gaebler concluded that "like a howitzer brought out to shoot ants, it left us with other problems. Designed for a government of clerks, civil service became a straightjacket in an era of knowledge workers" (124–125).

The thematic flavor of this book subsequently permeated the findings of two major reports released in 1993 that together focused on all levels of government in the United States.[1] The first of these reports, *Hard Truths/Tough Choices: An Agenda for State and Local Reform*, emerged from the work of the National Commission on the State and Local Public Service (often called the Winter Commission after its chair, William F. Winter). This commission released its primary report at a White House meeting with President Clinton in late June 1993. The second volume, *From Red Tape to Results: Creating a Government That Works Better and Costs Less*, grew from an intensive six-month study of the federal government under the banner of the National Performance Review

(NPR). Headed by Vice-President Al Gore, the NPR report was released at a White House ceremony in early September 1993. Like *Reinventing Government,* these initiatives provided a diagnosis and treatment for a wide range of governmental practices and cast a critical eye on public personnel administration in particular.

This chapter briefly analyzes the origins of each report, the vision and recommendations each had for public personnel management, and any evidence of change in the direction espoused by the Winter Commission and NPR. A concluding section compares and assesses the contributions of the two reports and their implications for the future of public personnel management.

WINTER: *HARD TRUTHS/TOUGH CHOICES*

Established in 1991, the Winter Commission in part reflected efforts to extend the work of an earlier commission, the National Commission on the Public Service (otherwise known as the Volcker Commission after its chair, Paul Volcker). The Volcker Commission had emerged in the late 1980s largely in response to concerns that the capacity of the federal government—especially its ability to attract and retain top-flight personnel—had eroded during the years of the Reagan presidency. After the presentation of its report, *Leadership for America: Rebuilding the Public Service,* to President Bush in 1989, several individuals who had been involved with the Volcker Commission remained convinced of the need for additional work. They believed that in its understandable concern with the national government, the Volcker Commission had not devoted sufficient attention to those levels of the federal system where the great majority of public servants work. The nearly 87,000 state and local governments in the United States grapple with an abundance of issues: education, health, public safety, social services, and much, much more. These levels of the federal system employ approximately 15.5 million workers, compared to roughly 2 million civilian employees in the case of the federal government.

A group working through the Rockefeller Institute of Government in Albany, New York, subsequently obtained private funding to support the Winter Commission. William F. Winter, a former governor of Mississippi, agreed to chair the 28-member commission. Following considerable research (Thompson, 1993) and hearings all across the country, the Winter Commission released *Hard Truths/ Tough Choices.* Although the report covered a broad range of topics, issues of public personnel administration ranked high on the agenda of concerns.

The Core Personnel Themes

The Winter Commission's basic personnel recommendations emerge in three of the report's five major sections. The first of these focuses on removing the barriers to stronger executive leadership. By bolstering the authority of the chief executive—governors, mayors, city managers, county executives—the Winter Commission hoped to enhance prospects for political accountability and more efficient and effective performance by state and local governments. In this regard the Commission called for enhancing the ability of the chief executive to shape his or her top management team by reducing the number of independently elected executive officers. For instance, the Commission noted that 36 states elected a secretary of state and 12 an agricultural commissioner. The Winter Commission believed that giving the chief executive more appointment power to top posts would enable that executive to delegate authority to subordinates he or she considered trustworthy and to avoid the impulse to microman-age administrative agencies. This concern that chief executives possess suf-ficient appointment authority stands in sharp contrast to the Volcker Com-mission's findings concerning the federal government. This commission had found excessive politicization of top-level jobs in the national government and called for scaling back the number of exempt positions.

Second, the Winter Commission set forth a series of recommendations under the general banner of reducing the barriers to lean and responsive government via the deregulation of personnel systems. The commission's commitment to augmenting agency and managerial discretion over key aspects of person-nel management manifested itself in many ways. Structurally, the commission affirmed "that states and localities are best served by a decentralized merit system" that assigned line agencies and departments pivotal roles (National Commission, 1993: 25). Beyond this, the commission focused its reform spotlight on such critical personnel arenas as the hiring, transfer, and removal of person-nel, work-force structure, and compensation packages. Most of its recom-mendations sought to give managers more discretion.

In terms of hiring, the Winter Commission urged less reliance on written tests for entry-level jobs or promotions, seeing this traditional merit tool as all too frequently "biased, out-of-date, poor in predicting performance and expensive to construct" (p. 26). The ranking of candidates for positions should not only depend less on written tests but less on veterans preference and seniority as well. The Winter Commission further sought to elevate the role of management judgment in personnel decisions by giving these officials more discretion to pick from eligible lists (i.e., the lists of those deemed qualified to perform a job). Rather than the conventional "rule of three," which limits the manager to selecting from the top three names on the eligible list who remain interested in the position, the commission wanted managers to be able to interview and pick from a longer list (e.g., five or ten applicants). Managers could use this discretion to hire the most competent applicants and foster a more demographically representative work force in terms of gender and race. The commission also urged managers to support special intern programs designed to fast-track the best students into government.

The personnel systems conducive to "lean, responsive government" would also showcase a certain work-force structure—one with fewer job classifications and managers. Rather than the 7,300 different job families or classifications found in such states as New York, the Winter Commission called for "no more than a few dozen" (p. 27). These broad classifications would facilitate managerial flexibility in work assignments and salary determination. Beyond this, the Winter Commission called for thinning the ranks of managers and reducing the layers between the top and bottom of the hierarchy. In the view of the commission, the cuts in managerial jobs "should improve accountability and save money." But the commission did not see this approach as the fast track to downsizing. Instead, the commission suggested that the savings achieved by cutting managers would allow "most agencies to shift personnel dollars to the front line," where demands on such workers as job counselors, social service case workers, and public health nurses were often "excessive and unrealistic" (p. 24).

The quest for lean, responsive, flexible government also prompted the Winter Commission to take a stand on certain compensation issues. It urged that state and local governments reevaluate the pay-for-performance plans that existed (mostly on paper) in many jurisdictions. Claiming that these plans were often based on "unbelievably complicated" and "poorly administered" processes that led to the allocation of small bonuses, the commission urged abandonment of such plans if employees did not perceive them as fair or if they were under-funded. Instead, the Winter Commission urged team-based pay-for-performance systems, such as gainsharing, that "make it every employee's business to assure the overall success of the organization" (p. 30).[2] To facilitate mobility in and out of government, the Winter Commission also called for reform in "antiquated, nonportable pension systems." It recommended that states and localities at a bare minimum honor the same five-year vesting period required of private firms under federal law. This would ensure that employees would have rights to the pension contribution of their government employer after five years and would not be penalized for taking a job with another government or in the private sector.

Third, the Winter Commission called for removing barriers to a high-performance work force by creating a learning government. Pointing to a "knowledge gap" rooted in "a decade of cuts and narrow thinking about the government's human capital" (p. 40), the commission called on states and localities to set aside 3 percent of total personnel costs for employee training and education. The commission recommended that these funds be assigned to employees as individual accounts. Operating within general guidelines established by his or her employer, the individual could purchase a course from a training unit or a college or university. States and localities would reward workers by designing systems that linked pay increases to skills acquisition by the employee. Although recognizing a vast array of different training needs, the commission set forth skills packages that employees and a new type of public manager would need to operate in a high-performance organization where, among other things, there would be fewer managers and broader spans of control.[3] As part of this new approach, the commission stressed that managers must work with unions to engender a less adversarial, more cooperative relationship.

The Response of States and Localities

Assaying the exact impact of a commission report targeted at 87,000 units of government is a staggering task. Huge variation exists in the practices of these governments. We lack handy report cards that detail key features of their personnel systems and practices and that would allow us to monitor change. At times, officials even have an incentive to obfuscate what they do. Top executives know, for instance, that they must often hide training money in various budget accounts to shield it from cuts. This makes it very difficult to ascertain just what state and local governments invest in training and educating their employees. Ultimately, the monitoring task we face is somewhat akin to flying an airplane low over ground covered by dense, patchy fog. Much of the ground remains blocked from view, but we occasionally get a glimpse of what is occurring. On balance, this spotty evidence suggests that many jurisdictions have adopted at least some of the practices endorsed by the Winter Commission.

The Winter Commission's plea to reduce the number of independently elected executive officials in the cabinets of chief executives no doubt faces tough sledding. In the case of state governments, for instance, the number of popularly elected executives has changed little over the past four decades—from 514 in 1955 to 511 in 1994. Given the addition of Alaska and Hawaii over that period, the average number of separately elected officials per state declined from 10.7 to 10.2 (Beyle, 1995).

Yet aside from issues of the number of popularly elected executive officers, occasional breakthroughs do occur in strengthening the chief executive's appointment authority. For instance, a scandal in the South Carolina legislature in the early 1990s fueled efforts to strengthen the appointment powers of the governor in that state. In 1991 the state government in South Carolina consisted of more than 145 agencies, including 123 under the formal control of part-time independent boards and commissions. The state legislature, rather than the governor, appointed many of the board members. With Governor Campbell's strong backing, compromise legislation surfaced in 1993 that consolidated 75 agencies into 17. The governor for the first time gained the authority to hire and fire 11 of the directors of these agencies and to hire (but not fire) the directors of 2 others. All appointments were subject to senate confirmation (Durning, 1995).

Furthermore, governors in general have increased their appointment powers through the exemption of more positions from civil service coverage. Since 1970 at least 28 states have moved to increase the number of exempt top managers (Roberts, 1993). The Winter Commission is silent on exactly how much appointment authority chief executives should have beyond the cabinet level. The degree to which this trend constitutes "reform" remains an open question. Analyses comparable to those conducted at the state level should be targeted at local governments to gauge the appointment powers wielded by their chief executives.

The Winter Commission's support for the deregulation of personnel systems on behalf of greater administrative flexibility also finds expression in many states and localities. In part this is because some state and local personnel systems never achieved the level of centralized, rule-bound inflexibility depicted by the commission. States such as Texas and local governments such as that of Indianapolis (Perry et al., 1994) had never moved to the highly centralized and regulated systems evident in so many jurisdictions. On balance, however, we detect some movement in the direction advocated by the Winter Commission. Many governments have attempted to streamline their hiring processes and to give managers more discretion to interview and select personnel (Ban and Riccucci, 1993). For instance, a survey conducted in 1993 (Suffolk County Personnel Department, 1993) found that the great majority of state governments no longer narrowed managerial discretion by imposing a rule of three; instead, state officials can interview the top 5 individuals on the eligible list (e.g., in Alaska), the top 10 (e.g., in Georgia), the top 20 (e.g., in Minnesota), or even more. Furthermore, genuinely innovative approaches to personnel recruitment and selection abound in states and localities. Citing the Winter Commission's *Hard Truths/Tough Choices* as one source of inspiration for its efforts, the state of Wisconsin launched an initiative to reform its hiring systems. In 1995 the state's program (described in Chapter 12 of this volume) was named one of 30 finalists in the prestigious innovation awards program of the Ford Foundation and Kennedy School of Government at Harvard.

State and local efforts to improve work-force structure have also surfaced. Many jurisdictions have succeeded in reducing the number of job classifications. From 1991 to 1995, for instance, 62 percent of state governments decreased the number of job classifications whereas 34 percent increased them. The three states with the greatest number of job classifications all trended downward—New York from 7,300 to 6,200; New Jersey from 6,400 to 4,653; and California from 4,324 to 4,000 (National Commission, 1993; Council of State Governments, 1995). Interest in broad-banding pay scales has often accompanied efforts to cut the number of classifications. For instance, the state of California has launched a "pioneer project" aimed at broad-banding. The Department of Personnel Administration in that state is currently testing the plan and hopes to extend the system to other units of state government (Walters, 1995a).

The Winter Commission's theme of pruning managerial layers also has supporters in local and state governments. The City of Dallas won a special award for excellence in 1993 from the International Personnel Management Association in part for its efforts to flatten the organizational structures of several departments, reducing the number of layers of management. In the early 1990s the Iowa legislature passed a bill that called for increasing the ratio of employees to supervisors by 50 percent and for halving the layers of management in state agencies (Walters, 1992).

Innovation in the compensation arena appears to be much less frequent. In 1993 the South Carolina state legislature passed the State Government Accountability Act; among other things, it called for agencies to develop procedures to reward work groups for their efforts. But the legislature provided no extra funds for this program, and agencies got off to a slow start in implementing it. Although gainsharing has attracted the attention of many state and local officials, very few jurisdictions have adopted the approach (Walters, 1995b). Whether focused on groups or individuals, pay-for-performance initiatives tend to be very long on talk and very short on delivery. Broadly viewed, the best hope for greater flexibility in pay decisions resides in efforts to broad-band classification systems.

We could also find little evidence of states and localities breaking down the barriers to intergovernmental mobility via shortened vesting periods. It deserves note, however, that a survey conducted by the Government Finance Officers Association found that over one-third of the sampled state and local jurisdictions had vesting periods of five years or less in fiscal year 1992 (Zorn, 1995).[4] Moreover, the modest trend from defined-benefit (the dominant approach) to defined-contribution pension plans in state and local governments may open the door to greater interemployer mobility among workers. Defined-contribution plans are usually portable and frequently have shorter vesting periods than do defined-benefit plans (Cranford, 1993).

Scattered examples of movement forward in efforts to deregulate and change civil service systems in ways consistent with the themes of the Winter Commission beg the question of whether some jurisdictions have experienced backsliding toward more rules and inflexibility. Clearly, strong opposition to the types of reforms espoused by the Winter Commission exists in some settings. For instance, efforts in New York State to add flexibility to the screening process by adopting zone scoring of exams prompted a lawsuit by two of the state's largest public employee unions. New York's highest state court subsequently ordered the Civil Service Commission to narrow the range of test scores encompassed by the zones. More recently, a state legislator introduced a bill to expand the rule of three only to encounter a union threat to push for legislation requiring a rule of one if the legislator continued in his efforts (Ban and Riccucci, 1994). Attempts to deregulate personnel administration in New York City have met similarly stiff resistance (Cohen and Eimicke, 1994). Although prospects for change seem dim in many jurisdictions, nevertheless the fragmentary evidence readily available to us suggests significant movement in the direction espoused by *Hard Truths/Tough Choices.*

The degree to which state and local governments have invested more in training of high quality remains unclear. No institution routinely gathers valid and reliable data on how much these levels of government invest in employee education and training, let alone the quality of such initiatives. However, the message that such training is highly desirable, especially in a period of rapid technological change and organizational restructuring, is getting through to many state and local officials. Some of this impetus comes from the experience of the private sector, especially the Fortune 500 companies. As IBM executive David Miller emphasized to a forum of government officials in Illinois in 1994, if that company could have changed one thing in its restructuring efforts, "we would have allocated more resources to education. . . . So I encourage you to learn from IBM and others, and ensure a robust training program as part of each of your reinvention and transformation efforts" (Walters, 1995a: 40).

In view of such sentiments, one can readily comprehend how a conference of officials from Oklahoma reached the conclusion that the 3 percent expenditure target set by the Winter Commission was too low and that 5 percent would be a better goal (Walters, 1995a). By all accounts, some agencies, such as the California Franchise Tax Board, have spent more than 3 percent and to very good effect (Thompson, 1993). Innovative efforts to demonstrate the value of employee education and training to skeptical elected officials have also surfaced. For instance, the Minnesota Department of Employee Relations persuaded the state legislature to provide $200,000 for the retraining of staff who faced the risk of being laid off. A joint labor-management committee set up a competitive grant process and eventually selected the proposals of eight departments for funding. The purpose of the grant is to examine the argument that it will cost less to retrain and retain state employees than to lay them off. The project also seeks to identify the best training practices (Walters, 1995b).

Although examples such as these provide hope that states and localities will do more to invest in employee education and training, a period marked by the downsizing of government and the slashing of public budgets may well overwhelm the impetus to create a more committed, knowledgeable, and skilled work force. In the face of hard budgetary trade-offs, the gutting of training budgets may become an irresistible siren call to elected officials.

GORE: *FROM RED TAPE TO RESULTS*

Unlike the Winter Commission report, which had a clear antecedent in the work of the Volcker Commission, the NPR's origins are less obvious. In part the NPR reflected ideas found in earlier administrative reform efforts that had surfaced sporadically since the dawn of the twentieth century. Indeed, American administrative reformers have behaved much like the purveyors of the fashion world. They move from one costume to another. They have a short attention span, substituting one set of reform attempts for another. The various initiatives typically leave some imprint on administrative procedures before passing but seldom deliver fully on the promises of their supporters.

Several important factors set the stage for President Clinton's foray into reinventing the federal government. The 1980s and 1990s featured considerable ferment in the private sector over how to keep American businesses "quality conscious" and competitive in an international economy. The quality management movement, with its emphasis on sensitivity to customers and continuous effort to improve the products and efficiency of American firms, became the subject of much discussion and occasional action in the private sector. Other popular management experts emphasized the need for experimentation, innovation, and a new entrepreneurial spirit (e.g., Peters and Waterman, 1982). By 1992, Osborne and Gaebler (1992) had built upon many of these private sector themes in their call for the reinvention of government at all levels. Osborne in particular had personally expressed his views to several governors, including Governor Bill Clinton of Arkansas.

This ferment mingled with survey data showing a relentless decline in the public's esteem for government over the last 30 years. Although suspicion and skepticism about the efficacy of government have been part of the nation's culture since its birth, the mounting lack of trust in government's ability to perform reached epidemic proportions by the early 1990s (Thompson, 1993).

For President Clinton, therefore, a reinvention initiative brought several benefits. It reflected a genuine opportunity to introduce the latest management thinking from the private sector into government. It also offered a political opportunity to score points with the public by appearing "tough" with the "bureaucracy" without simply indulging in the bash-the-bureaucrat rhetoric of the Reagan years. Under the best of circumstances, the initiative might help government turn the corner on its trust deficit. If citizens began to have more confidence that public programs could be conducted efficiently and effectively, prospects would improve for the kind of government initiatives that President Clinton planned to propose.

Unlike most administrative reforms of the past, the NPR became a public issue from its earliest days. The first stages of the NPR resembled a political campaign— fast-paced, intense, and controlled by generalists. It drew on direct communication with citizens (including an appearance by Vice-President Gore on the David Letterman show), face-to-face exchanges with career executives, and the work of teams of experienced federal employees who assessed various administrative practices and offered advice. The effort was launched soon after President Clinton assumed office; its first report, *From Red Tape to Results: Creating a Government That Works Better and Costs Less,* came out in September 1993. The 168-page report contained four major sections—"Cutting Red Tape," "Putting Customers First," "Empowering Employees to Get Results," and "Cutting Back to Basics." The Gore report dealt with a vast range of administrative and policy matters that extended well beyond issues of personnel policy and management. Still, much of the report intersected with the personnel arena in one way or another.

Key Personnel Themes

The preface to the Gore report set forth a prescription that would profoundly shape the context for the other changes it espoused. Unlike the Winter and Volcker reports, the NPR (1993: iii–iv) squarely committed itself to downsizing the government's work force. It asserted that "the reinvention we propose will allow us to reduce the size of the civilian, non-postal workforce by 12 percent over the next 5 years. This will bring the federal workforce below two million employees for the first time since 1967. This reduction in workforce will total 252,000 positions." In pursuing these reductions, the NPR singled out personnel concentrated "in the structures of overcontrol and micromanagement"— "supervisory, headquarters staffs, personnel specialists, budget analysts, procurement specialists, accountants, and auditors." Eliminating these "unnecessary layers of management and non-essential staff" would in the view of the Gore report open up new opportunities for higher productivity and lower costs.[5]

With this downsizing thrust established, the first section of *From Red Tape to Results* offered five major recommendations aimed at personnel policy. First, it recommended phasing out the Federal Personnel Manual. The NPR noted that the accumulation of rules involving federal personnel amounted to 850 pages of law; 1,300 pages of regulations from the Office of Personnel Management

(OPM); and 10,000 pages of guidelines from the Federal Personnel Manual. The NPR urged that this system be replaced by a decentralized one in which line agencies and their managers would assume much more control over the personnel function. The OPM would work with agencies to replace the existing system with manuals tailored to user needs, automated personnel processes, and electronic decision support systems.

Second, the Gore report specifically recommended that departments and agencies be given the authority to conduct recruitment and examinations. It called for the abolition of central registers and standard application forms—hallmarks of the system that the OPM had administered. Under the proposed structure agencies could ask the OPM to screen candidates but would also have the ability to perform these tasks themselves. In place of a central register listing individuals certified for employment, the NPR recommended that the OPM create a government-wide employment information system that would allow a citizen to go to one place for information about all federal job opportunities.

Third, the NPR touted the virtues of simplifying the position classification system and giving agencies more discretion over this area. The report challenged agencies to continue experiments in broad-banding jobs, such as the initiative at the Naval Weapons Center in China Lake, California, and the Naval Oceans Systems Center in San Diego. It pointed out that reducing the number of classifications and broadening them would give agencies greater flexibility in hiring, retaining, and rewarding staff. It would help these agencies flatten their hierarchies and "remove OPM from its role as 'classification police'" (National Performance Review, 1993: 24).

Fourth, the report suggested that agencies be provided with authority to design their own performance management and reward systems. Noting that the current performance appraisal system often amounted to a "meaningless exercise in which most federal employees are given above-average ratings," the NPR called for the development of appraisal systems focused on a single goal: to improve the performance of individuals and organizations (p. 25). Turning this task over to agencies would allow them to meet their particular needs and to reflect their particular cultures.

Fifth, the Gore report stressed the need to reduce the time required to terminate managers and employees for poor performance. It observed that although it was possible to fire inept workers in the federal government, the time it took to accomplish this task undermined good management. In order to halve the time required for terminating employees for cause, it called for legislation to be drafted lowering the requirement for advance notice of termination from 30 to 15 days. It also endorsed extending the waiting period for a within-grade pay increase if an employee failed to meet expectations for job performance.

The next three sections of the Gore report made fewer and less obvious personnel pronouncements. In general, these sections called for the transplantation of aspects of the business world into the public sector. They emphasized, for instance, the need for federal employees to treat citizens as customers and the virtues of forcing various governmental agencies to compete with other entities to provide service. These and other admonitions had general implications for personnel management, but only a few recommendations directly targeted the traditional concerns of the field. These more specific recommendations included two themes of particular note:

- Insistence that agencies have the flexibility to finance employee training and that the federal government focus particular attention on upgrading information technology training for employees. Agencies would have license to invest in training a "substantial portion of the savings" they realized from decentralizing staff and reducing operating costs under other reinvention initiatives (p. 79). By persuading Congress to amend the Government Employees Training Act, the federal government would expand training options for its employees.
- An assertion that federal employee unions and management would surmount "the adversarial relationship that binds them to noncooperation" through the establishment of a National Partnership Council. Membership on the council would include top federal executives as well as the presidents of major federal employee unions and a representative of the Public Employees Department of the AFL-CIO. (See Chapter 10 in this volume.)

The Implementation of the NPR

The Gore report promised a dramatically new context for public personnel policy *FROM* and management in the federal government. Among other things, this context *CONTRG* featured a new role for the Office of Personnel Management—one that would *TO* shift it from a central control agency to an organization primarily involved with *ASSISTANCE* technical assistance functions.

The heavy emphasis on downsizing in the Gore report ensured that implementation efforts would occur in a context marked by high levels of employee anxiety over their job futures. Many middle managers believed that the report singled them out for cuts and that if they survived they would experience a more stressful work setting. Action by Congress did little to allay these anxieties. Encouraged by the tone of the NPR, Congress moved quickly to increase the number of employees that would be cut from the proposed 252,000 to nearly 273,000. By mid-1995, the NPR proudly reported that the federal government had already been slimmed down by more than 160,000 workers and that civilian federal positions now made up a smaller share of all jobs in the country than at any time since the eve of World War II. It claimed that in just two years the NPR had managed to reduce supervisory personnel by 30 percent so that there was 1 supervisor for every 10 federal workers. It affirmed the goal of reducing this ratio to 1 in 15 by 1999. Through these and other actions, the NPR claimed budget savings of $58 billion (National Performance Review, 1995: 75–76). However much the Clinton administration wished to pursue a balanced strategy with respect to reinvention, the commitment to downsizing and budget savings quickly became the dominant, driving force in the initiative. Ultimately the downsizing targets advanced by the NPR and increased by Congress were essentially arbitrary. No one could produce credible evidence, one way or the other, as to how the cuts would affect governmental efficiency and effectiveness (Kettl, 1995).

Although downsizing assumed center stage, the executive branch also moved to implement some of the other recommendations of the Gore report. The 10,000-page Federal Personnel Manual was thrown out at a January 1994 ceremony at the OPM in which employees moved the document in a wheelbarrow to a waiting recycling truck. Supporters of the NPR claimed that the OPM had scrapped 86 percent of the manual in one fell swoop. In addition, the OPM abolished Standard Form 171, the long-standing job application form, in December 1994. The OPM also initiated action on other fronts. By mid-1995, for instance, the agency had requested public comment on a proposal to consolidate approximately 450 General Schedule job series titles into 74 (National Performance Review, 1995). The Clinton administration also moved quickly to cement its relationship with federal employee unions. In response to Executive Order 12871, which President Clinton issued in October 1993, agencies and unions signed on to some 400 labor-management partnership agreements. Officials hoped this would be the first step toward labor-management cooperation in carrying out the NPR's program for change.

Progress in achieving other recommended actions came much more slowly. After generating publicity to focus attention on the report, the White House assigned the difficult job of implementation to the executive departments and agencies. The success or failure of the reinvention initiative rested substantially on their shoulders. The NPR office in the White House primarily played the role of "cheerleader" as the departments went to work on the critical management details. The line agencies varied greatly in terms of the commitment and skill they evinced in approaching the reinvention task. Some of them took the process very seriously, creating NPR offices that became ongoing institutional structures. Others relied on short-term task forces to work on reinvention (Radin, 1995). The implications of the different approaches and the degree to which they fostered changes in personnel management have yet to be evaluated systematically.

Some evidence suggests that human resource specialists in the line agencies reacted favorably to the NPR. A survey of officials in 37 offices of six large agencies found considerable support for the personnel provisions of the NPR (U.S. General Accounting Office, 1995). However, these administrators believed that the additional workload that would result from decentralization presented nagging challenges in an environment marked by downsizing. Nor did they concur with all the recommendations. Officials in most of these offices opposed abolishing the SF-171 on grounds that nonstandard job applications would take more time to process and assess.

Many of the NPR recommendations required Congress to modify existing statutes. By 1995, the Clinton administration had made very little progress in securing needed legislation. To be sure, Congress did enact legislation in late 1993 that terminated the government-wide performance management system for federal managers and supervisors. However, the legislation did not authorize agencies to design their own programs. The Federal Workforce Restructuring Act of 1994 broadened agency authority to pay for employee training. However, budget stringencies made it unlikely that a substantial investment in such training would occur.

From the start, the relentless pressures to downsize the federal government threatened to crowd out other reinvention concerns. These pressures intensified after the Republicans seized control of Congress in the 1994 election. In the wake of this dramatic development, the NPR increasingly shifted its emphasis from the processes of administration—the "how" of government—to the appropriate scope of public intervention in the private sector—the "what" of government. This second phase of the NPR demanded that agencies scrutinize whether the national government ought to be performing certain functions at all. It magnified and buttressed the commitment to contracting out more services to the private sector and to finding alternative forms of organization, such as government-sponsored corporations, to improve the management of federal programs. By so doing, the second phase of the NPR moved issues of public personnel policy to the back burner. As the 1996 presidential campaign heated up, management reform—particularly those aspects dealing with personnel issues—appeared to be on a burner that might not even be turned on to "low."

COMPARISON AND ASSESSMENT

The Winter and Gore reports share many common themes with respect to public personnel management. Table 1.1, which compares the Winter Commission's perspective on key personnel matters with those of the NPR, indicates substantial agreement in the major areas of concern. For instance, both initiatives favor the decentralization of authority over critical personnel decisions to line agencies, the deregulation of many aspects of public personnel management, a reduction in the number of middle managers and job titles, and a more cooperative relationship between managers and unions.

Although they are more similar than different, the reports do vary in specificity and emphases. The Winter Commission, for example, deals more extensively with ways of enhancing the authority of chief executives in personnel processes and sets a more specific benchmark for investments in training (3 percent of personnel expenditures). For its part, the Gore report sets forth a more detailed timetable and procedure for firing employees. In the final analysis, however, the most fundamental difference between the Winter and Gore reports involves their orientation toward downsizing. The Gore report sees reinvention as a vehicle for reducing the number of federal employees and saving money, whereas the Winter report offers no such prescription for state and local governments.

TABLE 1.1 Comparison of Winter and Gore reports on selected issues of public personnel administration.

Topic Area	Winter Report	Gore Report
Chief Executive Authority	Favors enhancing authority of chief executive to appoint top-level cabinet officers.	Does not address executive authority explicitly but implicitly accentuates the role of the executive branch. Seeks increased presidential authority to change the organizational structures of federal government.
General Responsibility for Civil Service System	Favors decentralization of authority over critical personnel decisions to line agencies and departments.	Same as Winter Commission
Recruitment, Mobility, and Removal	Generally favors deregulation; supports less reliance on written tests and greater managerial discretion to select from lists of eligible applicants; backs reduced emphasis on seniority and veterans preference in personnel decisions but urges renewed focus on fostering work-force diversity; endorses fast-track intern programs to bring the best students into government.	Accentuates decentralization of decision-making authority to agencies. Focuses on discretion of managers rather than OPM to make hiring decisions.
	Sees firing as a last resort but supports streamlined procedures involving binding arbitration.	Focuses on the reduction in time required for termination of employees.
Work-Force Structure	Supports reducing layers of the bureaucracy, as well as the number of middle managers, and job classifications; emphasizes redeployment of positions to the front lines rather than downsizing.	Strongly emphasizes reducing the number of federal employees. Calls for reducing classifications and middle management positions, and increasing span of managerial control.
Compensation	Expresses doubts about pay-for-performance plans targeted at individuals but praises those targeted at groups such as gainsharing; supports five-year vesting period for pension systems to foster employee mobility.	Recommends a linkage between agency reward systems and performance measures. Calls for authority for agencies to design their own systems.

Education and Training	Urges governments to commit 3 percent of personnel expenditures to employee education and training and to link pay increases to skills acquisition by the employee; sets forth new skills packages that employees and managers must acquire.	Suggests increase in training and emphasizes importance of improved information technology and management information systems. Additional money for training to come from savings that result from implementing other recommendations.
Labor-Management Relations	Generally favors less adversarial, more cooperative relationship, and input from front-line employees in key decisions.	Calls for partnership between management and labor through the National Partnership Council and similar councils at departmental levels.

SOURCE: National Commission on the State and Local Public Service, *Hard Truths/Tough Choices: An Agenda for State and Local Reform* (Albany, N.Y.: Nelson A. Rockefeller Institute of Government, 1993); National Performance Review, *From Red Tape to Results: Creating a Government That Works Better and Costs Less* (Washington, D.C.: Government Printing Office, 1993).

In reviewing the recommendations embedded in the Winter and Gore reports, two questions come to mind. First, did the reformers get it right? If enacted, will the proposed changes in personnel administration foster more efficient, effective, and democratically accountable government that stands a better chance of winning the confidence of the citizenry? Second, whatever their merits, are the proposals likely to attract the support needed to implement and sustain them?

We believe that the reinvention movement in general, and the Winter and Gore initiatives in particular, have pumped some adrenaline into an administrative arena that all too often has evinced more torpor than creative energy. Many personnel institutions and practices found in government have in fact ceased to add value. This is not to argue that the prescriptions of the Winter and Gore reports will yield positive results in all settings. One size almost never fits all in public administration. The staggering degree of variation among federal, state, and local governments virtually ensures that the Winter and Gore recommendations will not be universally applicable. Viewed broadly, however, we believe that most of the recommendations contained in these reports represent plausible working hypotheses. That is, they derive from a reasonable assessment of currently available evidence but clearly need to be evaluated carefully, employing clearly specified criteria in those jurisdictions that adopt them. The good news is that in a political system with close to 87,000 different governments, we can be sure that one government or another has tried or will try these reforms. Those specializing in public personnel administration should be vigilant in assessing the results of the many natural experiments that occur in the country's laboratories of democracy.

Knowing that some governments and agencies will adopt practices endorsed by the Winter and Gore initiatives, of course, begs the question of whether these practices will gain a foothold in most jurisdictions. Here the picture remains cloudy. Inertial forces remain strong. Officials typically must invest considerable time and energy to obtain change. They must often be willing to joust with the supporters of the status quo. Even when they prevail, it may bring them little, if any, recognition or acclaim, since the details of personnel management reform are hardly the stuff of high political or administrative drama.

But if the barriers to change loom large, so do the pressures of the mid-1990s to recast government's role and its modus operandi. Diminished citizen confidence in the public sector, the fervor for restructuring in the corporate world, the reluctance of taxpayers to maintain (let alone increase) funding for public services, and other forces make it harder for governmental officials to rest content with a business-as-usual approach. Nonetheless, it remains an open question whether the stress induced by these forces will accelerate or dampen administrative reform. By the mid-1990s, discussions and debates about public administration had moved from a "R" to a "D" phase. The former featured the dominance of such concepts as reinvention, revitalization, and rejuvenation. The latter has emphasized such notions as downsizing, dismantling, and deinventing. The two emphases do not fit easily together. For instance, the efforts of the NPR to reinvent and downsize simultaneously proved to be an extraordinarily tricky balancing act and shows evidence of blocking that initiative from greater success in transforming the culture of management in the federal government.

Evidence from the private and public sector drives home the same point— that poorly managed downsizing often yields demoralized employees who mistrust their bosses; it undermines organizational efficiency and effectiveness (Wysocki, 1995; Kettl and DiIulio, 1995). Funding for training and other initiatives aimed at improving personnel management often become more difficult than ever to obtain. In fact, any reform that requires an initial investment to realize long-term benefits tends to fall by the wayside. The stress induced by downsizing may spur some of the changes in personnel systems and practices endorsed by the Winter and Gore reports. Some of the reforms, such as enhanced hiring and recruitment flexibility for managers, appear to have gained substantial momentum. But it would be Panglossian to assume that the "D" phase so dominant in the late 1990s will automatically provide fertile ground for the changes advocated by the Winter and Gore reports.

NOTES

1. David Osborne testified before the Winter Commission at its hearing in Jackson, Mississippi, in 1992 and served actively as an advisor to the National Performance Review.
2. Under gainsharing, awards go to members of work groups that have achieved outstanding performance.
3. The Winter Commission recommended that every public employee should have competence in team building, communication, and involving others in performing

tasks, as well as a commitment to cultural awareness and quality. It envisioned the new public managers as coaches, benchmarkers, listeners, mentors, and champions.
4. The data do not derive from a random sample of all state and local governmental pension systems. But the survey did systematically sample from the largest pension systems (about 800), which cover roughly 75 to 80 percent of all state and local employees with retirement benefits (Zorn, 1995).
5. Although treated as a budget reform, the NPR (1993: 19) also called for another step that would enlarge agency flexibility in the personnel arena: the elimination of full-time equivalent position ceilings imposed by the Office of Management and Budget. These ceilings imposed a control mechanism over and beyond budget limits on an agency's operating costs.

REFERENCES

Ban, C., and N. M. Riccucci. 1993. "Personnel Systems and Labor Relations: Steps toward a Quiet Revitalization," in F. J. Thompson, ed., *Revitalizing State and Local Public Service.* San Francisco: Jossey-Bass, pp. 71-103.
——— . 1994. "New York State: Civil Service Reform in a Complex Political Environment." *Review of Public Personnel Administration* 14: 28-39.
Beyle, T. L. 1995. "Enhancing Executive Leadership in the States." *State and Local Government Review* 27: 18-35.
Cohen, S., and W. Eimicke. 1994. "The Overregulated Civil Service: The Case of New York City's Public Personnel System." *Review of Public Personnel Administration* 14: 10-27.
Council of State Governments. 1995. "More or Less Classes." *State Trends* 1, no. 3: 6-7.
Cranford, J. 1993. "Providing Cover: A Look at Public Employee Benefits." *Governing* 7, no. 3: 45-53.
Durning, D. 1995. "Governors and Administrative Reform in the 1990s." *State and Local Government Review* 27: 36-54.
Kettl, D.F. 1995. "Building Lasting Reform: Enduring Questions, Missing Answers," in D.F. Kettl and J.J. DiIulio Jr., eds., *Inside the Reinvention Machine.* Washington, D.C.: Brookings Institution.
Kettl, D.F., and J.J. DiIulio Jr. 1995. *Cutting Government.* Washington, D.C.: Center for Public Management, Brookings Institution.
National Commission on the State and Local Public Service. 1993. *Hard Truths/Tough Choices: An Agenda for State and Local Reform.* Albany, N.Y.: Rockefeller Institute of Government.
National Performance Review. 1993. *From Red Tape to Results: Creating a Government That Works Better and Costs Less.* Washington, D.C.: U.S. Government Printing Office.
——— . 1995. *Common Sense Government Works Better and Costs Less.* Washington, D.C.: U.S. Government Printing Office.
Osborne, D., and T. Gaebler. 1992. *Reinventing Government.* Reading, Mass: Addison-Wesley.
Perry, J., L.R. Wise, and M. Martin. 1994. "Breaking the Civil Service Mold: The Case of Indianapolis." *Review of Public Personnel Administration* 14: 40-54.
Peters, T.J., and R.H. Waterman Jr. 1982. *In Search of Excellence.* New York: Warner.
Radin, B.A. 1995. "Varieties of Reinvention: Six NPR Success Stories," in D.F. Kettl and J.J. DiIulio Jr., eds., *Inside the Reinvention Machine.* Washington, D.C.: Brookings Institution.

Roberts, D.D. 1993. "The Governor as Leader: Strengthening Public Service through Executive Leadership," in F.J. Thompson, ed., *Revitalizing State and Local Public Service.* San Francisco: Jossey-Bass, pp. 41–70.

Suffolk County Personnel Department. 1993. "State Narratives." Hauppauge, N.Y.: Unpublished study.

Thompson, F.J., ed. 1993. *Revitalizing State and Local Public Service.* San Francisco: Jossey-Bass.

U.S. General Accounting Office. 1995. *Federal Personnel Management: Views on Selected NPR Human Resource Recommendations.* Washington, D.C.: GAO, no. IGGO-95 221 BR.

Walters, J. 1992. "The Many Lives of Civil Service." *Governing* 6, no. 2: 30–34.

———. 1995a. *Paths to Performance: A Seven State Focus.* Report for the National Commission on the State and Local Public Service. Albany, N.Y.: Rockefeller Institute of Government.

———. 1995b. "The Gainsharing Gambit." *Governing* 8, no. 10: 63–64.

Wysocki, B., Jr., 1995. "Some Companies Cut Costs Too Far, Suffer 'Corporate Anorexia.'" *Wall Street Journal,* July 5, p. A1.

Zorn, P. 1995. Interview and table showing selected data. Washington, D.C.: Government Finance Officers Association.

chapter **2**

Strategic Human Resource Management

James L. Perry and Debra J. Mesch

Despite repeated reform efforts, human resource management in government remains a focus for intense criticism, as reflected in the following illustrations:

- In fiscal 1989 the U.S. Department of Health and Human Services issued $58 billion in grants, but the federal personnel system provided no formal training or career development for the grants management work force (U.S. Department of Health and Human Services, 1990).
- In 1991 the state of Florida experienced high rates of turnover in its 120,000-person civil service, but the Florida Department of Administration had no mechanisms for assessing the role of the pay system on turnover, employee morale, or performance (Wechsler, 1994).
- In 1993 the National Commission on the State and Local Public Service concluded that state and local government managers struggle to assemble work forces to accomplish their missions in the face of antiquated entry tests and rigid limits on the number of candidates whose names may be forwarded for interviews (National Commission on the State and Local Public Service, 1993).

Are these problems inherent in the enterprise, or can something be done about them? Advocates of strategic human resource management (SHRM) contend that the human resource function can contribute more effectively to mission accomplishment and the achievement of organizational goals (Devanna, Fombrun, and Tichy, 1984; Lengnick-Hall and Lengnick-Hall, 1988; Schuler, 1992; Perry, 1993). SHRM seeks to align personnel practices with the strategy of the organization and integrate them into the everyday work of line managers and employees (Schuler, 1992). A U.S. Department of Health and Human Services (HHS) study (Secretary of Health and Human Services, 1995) associated SHRM with attributes such as mission and customer responsiveness, speed, cost effectiveness, flexibility and simplicity, empowered and entrepreneurial clients, and productivity through people.

Powerful economic, demographic, and technological forces have arisen that are radically reshaping longstanding assumptions about organization and management. These forces represent the challenges that will be driving human resource management in the future. The most significant economic force is globalization of economic activity. A direct effect of globalization has been to stimulate the search for new organizational forms that can accommodate the imperatives of the changing environment (Naisbitt and Aburdene, 1985).

Interwoven with global economic changes is a technological revolution. The pace and scope of technological change, particularly the revolution in information technologies, bears great relevance for human resource management (Perry and Kraemer, 1993). Increasing technology allows organizations to maximize performance through the optimal combination of human and automated capabilities (Offermann and Gowing, 1993). Information technologies are incrementally transforming the ways governments at all levels are organized, the activities they perform, how they perform them, and the nature of the work itself (Perry and Kraemer, 1993).

The implications of changing technology are complicated by dramatic demographic shifts in the work force. Among key demographic trends are a declining rate of growth of youth entering the labor force; aging of the work force; multiple wage earner families; and increasing proportions of women, minorities, and immigrants in the U.S. national work force (Johnson, 1988; U.S. General Accounting Office, 1992). Accompanying these trends are increased demands for technological competence, educational levels, and skills involving teamwork and autonomy (Shin and Mesch, 1996).

These economic, technological, and demographic challenges have created the need for more attention to human resources, a longer time perspective in thinking strategically about people as resources, and consideration of people as assets rather than as variable costs (Beer et al., 1985). This conclusion follows logically from the general principle that human capital has become a strategic resource. The shift in the conceptual status of human resources, however, does not ensure changes in organizational realities. Although many analysts believe that human resources have taken on new importance, it is less clear that the management of human resources has attained a status equal to its enhanced importance.

This chapter begins by contrasting a general model of SHRM with traditional public personnel systems. As part of our discussion of the SHRM approach we identify practical implementing concepts that organizations are using to create more strategic systems. Finally, we provide illustrations of SHRM in three government organizations and conclude with a prognosis for SHRM in the public sector.

CONTRASTING MODELS OF HUMAN RESOURCE MANAGEMENT SYSTEMS

Human resource management systems can be differentiated along four dimensions: (1) centralization/decentralization, (2) uniformity/customization, (3) specialist/generalist, and (4) process/results (Mesch, Perry, and Wise, 1995). The anchors of each dimension represent the archetype of two contrasting human resource management models: bureaucratic and strategic. These are represented by polar configurations of the organizing principles represented in Figure 2.1.

The centralization/decentralization dimension involves the extent to which decision-making power about human resource management is delegated down the chain of authority and rests with single or multiple control centers (Daley, 1990; Ingraham, 1992; Mintzberg, 1983). Mintzberg (1983) calls this organization design parameter "vertical decentralization." Decisions regarding centralization/decentralization depend upon differences in the size, mission, and culture of individual agencies (Hyde and Rosenbloom, 1993). The key question policy makers and managers must address is: How much responsibility, authority, and power should the organization delegate and to whom? Under a decentralized human resources system, agencies and their subunits are required to take more responsibility for classification, recruitment, selection, discipline, training, compensation, and retention (Hyde and Rosenbloom, 1993).

The second dimension, uniformity/customization, indicates the extent to which human resource management policies are uniform across organizational units or are customized to the needs and environment of a specific agency (Ingraham, 1992; National Academy of Public Administration, 1993; Perry, 1993).

FIGURE 2.1   A human resource management model.

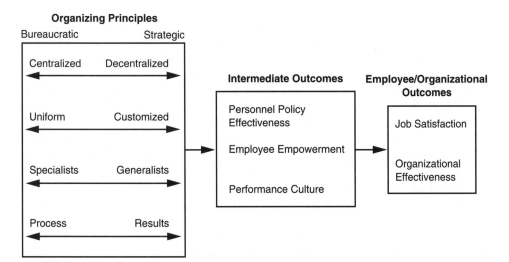

The way in which an organization is structured and designed controls this human resources decision. Given the mission and structure of the organization, the choice becomes whether a "one size fits all" policy is best or whether a more flexible set of policies is appropriate. For example, if an organization designs its work force into self-managed teams, human resources policies need to reflect the needs of employees by designing the recruitment, selection, promotion, reward, and evaluation policies to match the requirements of this design. Under this personnel system, rules and procedures would be limited largely to enforcing statutory requirements (rather than prescribing uniform personnel policy or practice) (Hyde and Rosenbloom, 1993).

The third dimension, locus of authority, refers to the extent to which personnel specialists (through their knowledge of rules and regulations and their authority to approve or deny), rather than line managers, control personnel actions (Klingner, 1990; Perry, 1993). The issue here is to what extent the human resources function is integrated into management responsibilities. Is the personnel function made an integral part of the organization's activities by decentralizing and deregulating it, or are these activities seen as buffered from the central mission of the organization (U.S. GAO, 1995)?

The fourth dimension concerns the degree of emphasis on the personnel process itself in contrast to organization results (NAPA, 1993). A process emphasis focuses on maintaining the integrity of the personnel process for its own sake. A results-oriented approach focuses on customer outcomes and employee accountability for performance.

Mesch, Perry, and Wise (1995) discuss the differences between bureaucratic and strategic models. At one extreme, the bureaucratic model is characterized as centralized, prescriptive, and uniform (Newland, 1976). It places authority for personnel actions in a single, central agency and attempts to make personnel management uniform and consistent across an entire jurisdiction, viewing government as a single employer. Extensive rules and regulations and centralized oversight agencies enforce consistency.

The bureaucratic model is hierarchical and relies on personnel specialists to manage the human resource function. It limits the amount of discretion available to line managers, who might introduce inconsistency or favoritism into the system. Oversight commissions and boards monitor adherence to stated practices and regulations. The primary focus of human resource management is to protect the integrity of the process, which is seen as fundamental to limiting inequitable treatment in the employment relationship, unfair distribution of organizational rewards, or politicization. Within a bureaucratic culture, few line managers perceive their primary role as that of a human resources manager. The relationship between the two is often adversarial; line managers perceive personnel specialists as obstructionists, and personnelists perceive line managers as uncooperative and uninterested.

In contrast, the strategic human resource management model emphasizes decentralization and devolution of authority. It seeks not uniformity but variety in personnel policies and practices. Flexibility is a key component of strategic organization and involves not only flexibility in decision making but also flexible roles for employees and an emphasis on cross training, multiple skills, and compensation for skill development (Kanter, 1983). Power is channeled to line managers and employees as partners in determining workplace policy. SHRM attempts to pare down excessive rules and regulations, thereby enabling managers to function more efficiently and to focus on achieving their organization's mission. An emphasis is placed on measuring outcomes within a results-oriented philosophy. Results-oriented organizations track performance against mission-related goals in such areas as product quality, service delivery, and customer satisfaction (U.S. GAO, 1995). SHRM's definition varies among writers, but at its core is a system that attempts to enhance organizational performance (NAPA, 1993; Lengnick-Hall and Lengnick-Hall, 1988; Perry, 1993).

The model presented in Figure 2.1 describes a linear relationship among these human resource management design attributes and two other components: intermediate outcomes, and organizational and employee outcomes. The four dimensions of human resource management systems are depicted as influencing both organizational processes and outcomes. Three intermediate outcomes and two employee and organizational outcomes are identified. Among the intermediate outcomes are personnel policy effectiveness, employee empowerment, and performance culture. Employee and organizational outcomes include job satisfaction and organizational effectiveness.

IMPLEMENTING CONCEPTS

Some cautions should be sounded at this point. We expect that the organizing principles outlined above will be operationalized differently in different organizations. It is important that the dimensions outlined here not be embraced in a "one size fits all" fashion. Some organizations will appropriately remain traditional and more bureaucratic because their missions, environments, or other key contingencies necessitate higher levels of organization and stability. For example, high reliability organizations (e.g., nuclear power plants, aircraft carriers, air traffic control centers) (Roberts, 1990) might be ill advised to embrace SHRM as outlined above. On the whole, however, the ideas about SHRM can be adapted to the needs of a wide range of organizations.

We turn now to the issue of how public human resource managers can effectively implement the general principles of SHRM. We suggest concrete ways, what we call implementing concepts, for achieving better ties between human resource management and organizational mission: (1) linking human resources to the strategic planning process; (2) aligning human resources policies with organizational strategies; (3) developing personnel generalists; (4) delegating personnel administration and management responsibility; (5) training personnelists and managers; (6) developing results-oriented measurement systems; and (7) creating information systems.

Linking Human Resources to Strategic Planning

One means for making the human resource function more supportive of mission accomplishment is to integrate human resources considerations into the strategic planning process. In order to accomplish this, human resources managers must become strategic partners with management and play an integral part on the strategic team in the initial stages of planning (NAPA, 1995b). This means senior management must recognize the importance of the human resources contribution to the organization's strategic goals and must allow the human resources senior manager the same status and power as other top team players.

Buller (1988) identifies four types of linkages between strategic planning and human resources: administrative linkage, one-way linkage, two-way linkage, and integrative linkage. The integrative linkage, characterized as close interactions between the strategic planning and human resources senior executives, is described as a dynamic, interactive relationship wherein the senior human resources executive is viewed as a true strategic partner with other senior executives (p. 34). Buller's study identifies several important factors that can foster the strategic planning–human resources integration, including requiring senior human resources executives to have substantial line experience, involving them in top-level decisions, and giving line management a major planning role (p. 41).

Aligning Human Resources Policies with Organizational Strategies

The goals and results that human resources achieve must be synonymous with organizational success. This means that human resources policy and practice should be relevant and connected to the organization's mission (NAPA, 1995b). When the "one size fits all" model is eliminated and agencies are allowed to design and customize human resources policies to fit their organizational strategy, human resources activities are more likely to be aligned with agency goals. Through decentralization, differences among agencies in their mission and culture would be supported by removing constraints on innovation and flexibility and by shifting responsibility for managing people from personnel staff to agency managers (NAPA, 1995b). This strategy of decentralization is accomplished by devolving authority from agency personnel officials to line managers in the human resources decision-making process.

A current impetus for strategic realignment is total quality management (TQM). Pursuit of quality as an organizational strategy requires substantial change (see Chapter 18 of this book for a discussion of TQM). Lawler and Bowen (1992) argue that total quality management necessitates a corresponding realignment in the way organizations conceive of human resource management by focusing on the organization, rather than the job, and supporting group rather than individual performance.

Compensation is another arena in which to align organizational strategy and human resources policy and practice (Lawler, 1990). Strategic compensation programs are designed to match organizational goals with pay strategies. For example, compensation systems that reward senior line and function managers for organizational performance are ways to focus organizational efforts on results.

Developing Personnel Generalists

The goal of integrating human resource management into the mission of the organization cannot be accomplished without training line managers to be personnel generalists and expanding the roles of personnel specialists. Typically, personnelists function in such common roles as benefits administration, compensation and pay processing, training, records management, or job analysis. Line managers are not involved in these activities, nor do they have the skills to function in these roles. Expanding the functional roles of personnelists to take on multiple personnel tasks will contribute to simpler and more effective support to line managers. Essentially, a SHRM approach would encourage the personnelist to be transformed from specialist to human resources generalist/consultant for service delivery while, simultaneously, training managers in personnel skills.

Enlarging and enriching the roles of personnel specialists provide a way to integrate functional activities. Other initiatives such as job rotation, cross training, and job redesign are also means to increase the integration of specialists and generalists and to broaden personnel roles. For example, rotating line managers through human resources functions and having human resources specialists in line positions as part of their career development would help to reduce existing organizational barriers and develop greater competence for all roles.

Delegating Personnel Administration and Management Responsibility

Delegating responsibilities is a way to achieve both greater vertical decentralization and generalist involvement. Such delegation can occur while simultaneously ensuring the accountability of line and staff roles. Managers can be held accountable for human resource management results, and human resources staff can become accountable for achieving mission results (NAPA, 1995b).

There are at least two ways in which delegation with accountability can be pursued. One involves retaining a traditional public law framework, which statutorily specifies personnel administration and management responsibilities and grants authorities for delegating them. An alternative involves the use of performance contracting (Perry, 1993). Performance contracts would permit departments to articulate goals for human resources management, identify objectives, and measure progress using appropriate indicators such as productivity levels, employee satisfaction, and skill development (p. 62).

Training Personnelists and Managers

Providing adequate training and information is essential to prepare managers for their new and expanded roles (Perry, 1993). The only way to accomplish this goal is by training managers in new leadership roles such as career counseling, teamwork, and job design skills (NAPA, 1995b; Perry, 1993). Critical competencies for line managers in this new environment emphasize supervisory and leadership skills as well as data analysis and statistical techniques so that they can evaluate program results (NAPA, 1995b:33). If human resources senior management is expected to achieve the status of strategic partner, competence in the strategic planning process is required as well. Organizations must invest in developing human resources staff competence to function in all role requirements. Breaking out of the traditional functional orientation of personnel administration requires extensive training.

Developing Results-Oriented Measurement Systems

Measurement is important for assessing the efficiency and effectiveness of human resource management in relation to an organization's mission (NAPA, 1995b). Taking regular measures such as costs and servicing ratios, return on investment, employee and human resources service satisfaction, and customer needs are ways to measure organizational success. When human resources goals are tied to desired mission results, line managers are held accountable for these outcomes. Line managers must be involved in this process, however, to ensure that human resource management measurement captures information that is important to agency mission results (NAPA, 1995b: 33).

To achieve a results-oriented focus, managers need to evaluate organizational effectiveness by measuring outcomes and by using benchmark measures for human resources efficiency. Some of these mechanisms are already in place at the federal level. For example, the Government Performance and Results Act of 1993 (GPRA) was passed to improve the effectiveness of federal programs by establishing a system to set goals and measure performance (NAPA, 1995b). The GPRA requires federal agencies to describe how they will use human resources to meet goals established in their strategic plans (NAPA, 1995b).

Creating Information Systems

Information technology is critical to successful management of the work force (NAPA, 1995b). Technology plays an important part in decentralization and in achieving a results-oriented strategy (Perry, 1993). When managers are given direct access to systems that provide work-force information, they are empowered to make more informed decisions at lower levels of the organization and are more competent to handle personnel tasks. Automated systems allow human resources departments to transform themselves from transaction processors to advisors, consultants, and strategic partners (NAPA, 1995b:13). Human resources online information technology also allows managers to accomplish more complex tasks such as succession planning and staffing projections. Without this type of technology, human resources specialists are not capable of handling large quantities of information. Increased use of information technology serves to develop and promote the concept of "management generalist" while improving services and reducing costs. Finally, improved technology will allow a greater number of human resources services to be performed by the customer.

EXAMPLES OF STRATEGIC HUMAN RESOURCE MANAGEMENT

The model and implementing concepts provide an indication of the direction in which we expect public sector human resource management to evolve in the future. Are there current examples of strategic human resource management in the public sector? Yes, but they are relatively new and not very common. Three are briefly discussed here: the city of Hampton, Virginia; the state of Washington, and the National Institutes of Health (NIH).

City of Hampton, Virginia

In 1984 the city of Hampton, Virginia, faced daunting urban problems. Its real estate tax rate was among the highest in Virginia. The annual budget was being balanced with reserve funds. Population growth was stagnant, and school enrollments were declining. To make matters worse, Hampton was losing businesses to neighboring cities and was facing significant reductions in federal aid.

Under a new chief executive, Hampton sought to turn around the bleak state of affairs. Its turnaround strategy focused on five targets of change: its environment, organizational structures, work design, employee behaviors, and organizational systems. In pursuing change, Hampton sought to reshape itself as what has become known as a "high-performance organization." Among the characteristics the city leadership attempted to build into the organization were clarity of purpose, shared power, flexibility, customer and employee focus, and a results orientation.

During the course of Hampton's transformation, the human resource function was itself transformed. Tharon Greene, director of human resources for Hampton, describes the transformation:

> We had eighteen people in our office when we started this trans-
> formation ten years ago, and now we do just as much work—probably
> a lot more work and more effectively—with nine people. We attribute
> that to the reengineering of work, the elimination of the mid-
> management level of supervision, and the reduction of handoffs from
> one branch to another. We've eliminated the overhead costs associated

with the extra layer of supervision and shortened cycle time by eliminating handoffs. (U.S. GAO, 1995: 22)

The transformation of human resources in Hampton involved more than streamlining processes and eliminating positions. Another result was the creation of personnel generalists, one of the implementing concepts discussed earlier. Greene describes this aspect of the shift to strategic human resource management:

> Our department used to be structured along the same specialized lines as traditional personnel offices with branches of recruitment, placement, employee relations, training, and so forth, with branch chiefs and technicians and secretaries assigned to those branches. That system served us well enough, but over the years we found we had to make it more flexible. So we took out a level of supervision—the branch chief level—and we collapsed the organization into two self-directed work teams. The professional teams are fully cross-trained in all human resource functions and offer one-stop shopping to a set of customers. All the work comes into one place, the team members decide how it will get done, and the team manages its resources to see the job through. (U.S. GAO, 1995: 21–22)

Hampton's organizational transformation has been supported by significant changes in organizational systems that accompanied the structural changes noted above. Hampton eliminated its classification system. The pay philosophy adopted by the city council provides incentives so that high performers are paid above market. Over two hundred employees participate in various self-directed teams. For these employees, pay is based on results, demonstrated skills, group accomplishments, customer satisfaction ratings, and budget performance.

Hampton's high-performance strategy has succeeded. Tax rates, debt service, and work-force size have declined. Human resource management has been an integral part of the city's success.

State of Washington

The state of Washington is in the early stages of transition from a functional to a strategic human resource management system. The state employs about 70,000 people, 50,000 of whom are in state agencies and 20,000 of whom are nonfaculty employees at higher education institutions. Among its first steps to introduce flexibility into the civil service system, the state created the Washington Management Service (WMS) as part of its 1993 civil service reform legislation. The WMS covers about 2,000 top-level managers who have supervisory, personnel administration, and budgetary responsibilities.

The WMS introduces substantive changes in personnel policy that have been widely discussed, but infrequently adopted, in the public sector. These include simplified classification, broad-banding, a performance management system that emphasizes program results and management skills, and strengthened management training and career development. The WMS also provides flexible recruitment and hiring procedures, including an option for managers to hire a research firm to locate candidates rather than using the services of the Washington State Department of Personnel (DOP).

The DOP's role has also begun to shift. The director reports to the governor as a member of the governor's cabinet. This facilitates consideration of personnel implications of new legislative and administrative initiatives. Thus the close working relationship between the governor and director of personnel promotes the consideration of human resource issues in strategy making. The DOP has also sought to champion employee interests. One illustration is Workforce 2000, which systematically gathered data from employees and translated it into 121 improvement initiatives. The DOP has also played the role of change agent as reflected in several initiatives, most notably the WMS implementation.

Another step in the DOP's evolution is its effort to develop and enhance human resources information systems (HRIS) throughout the state. In September 1994, the DOP completed an HRIS feasibility study. The DOP's customers place a high priority on flexible access to human resource information. The effort to satisfy this priority is presently under way.

National Institutes of Health

In October 1995, the secretary of the Department of Health and Human Services (HHS) authorized an experiment in the National Institutes of Health (NIH) (a subunit of the Public Health Service) as part of the broader effort of the National Performance Review. The HHS initiative had its origins in a National Academy of Public Administration report (1993) that called for reinventing federal human resource systems so that they became the responsibility of all organization members and units, not just the functional responsibility of personnel offices.

The express goals of the experiment are to simplify personnel management and administration and make it more responsive to the NIH strategic plan. The experiment makes use of several implementing concepts. First, it is governed by a formal, written performance agreement (1995a) between the secretary of HHS and the director of NIH. Second, the performance agreement delegates to the director those personnel management and administration authorities historically held by the secretary. These delegations also include responsibility for setting policies with respect to work schedules, recruitment and retention bonuses, market salary surveys, and other specified areas. Restrictions on redelegations have been eliminated so that program managers can be given direct responsibility for human resource management. Third, requirements that authorities redelegated to line managers be approved by a servicing personnel office have been lifted. Finally, the performance agreement calls for an external evaluation that must "link the use of the delegated authorities to the NIH Strategic Plan and to two of the five goals that form the framework for accomplishing its mission" (p. 3).

The NIH experiment is in its infancy, but it illustrates one way that human resource management can be implemented within a public law framework. The performance agreement between the secretary and director redefines responsibility within existing legal structures. The changes simultaneously decentralize and retain clear accountability. Thus SHRM does not inherently assume departures from principles of democratic accountability.

CONCLUSION

Like the NIH example, SHRM is a new and evolving approach to human resource management in the public sector. It is more a way of thinking about the human resource function in organizations than a prescribed set of techniques. In fact, the logic of SHRM is intended to avoid Wallace Sayre's (1948) oft-repeated criticism of personnel management as the triumph of technique over purpose. Whether the SHRM approach becomes the norm in public jurisdictions will depend on a variety of factors, among them its ability to achieve results, achieve public acceptance, and avoid threats to political neutrality.

REFERENCES

Beer, Michael, Bert Spector, Paul R. Lawrence, Quinn Mills, and Richard E. Walton. 1985. *Human Resource Management: A General Manager's Perspective.* New York: Free Press.

Buller, P. 1988. "Successful Partnerships: Human Resources and Strategic Planning at Eight Top Firms." *Organizational Dynamics* 27: 27–43.

Daley, Dennis. 1990. "Organization of the Personnel Function: The New Patronage and Decentralization," in Steven W. Hays and Richard C. Kearney, eds., *Public Personnel Administration.* Englewood Cliffs, N.J.: Prentice Hall, pp. 20–28.

Devanna, Mary Anne, Charles Fombrun, and Noel Tichy. 1984. "A Framework for Strategic Human Resource Management," in Charles Fombrun, Noel Tichy, and Mary Anne Devanna, eds., *Strategic Human Resource Management.* New York: John Wiley.

Hyde, A.C., and David Rosenbloom. 1993. "Design of Federal Personnel Management." *Public Manager* (Summer): 9–14.

Ingraham, Patricia W. 1992. "The Design of Civil Service Reform: Good Politics or Good Management?" in Patricia W. Ingraham and David H. Rosenbloom, eds., *The Promise and Paradox of Civil Service Reform.* Pittsburgh: University of Pittsburgh Press.

Johnston, William B. 1988. *Civil Service 2000.* Washington, D.C.: U.S. Office of Personnel Management.

Kanter, Rosabeth Moss. 1983. "Frontiers for Strategic Human Resource Planning and Management." *Human Resource Management* 22 (Spring/Summer): 9–21.

Klingner, Donald E. 1990. "Variables Affecting the Design of State and Local Personnel Systems," in Steven W. Hays and Richard C. Kearney, eds., *Public Personnel Administration.* Englewood Cliffs, N.J.: Prentice-Hall.

Lawler, Edward. 1990. *Strategic Pay: Aligning Organizational Strategies and Pay Systems.* San Francisco: Jossey-Bass.

Lawler, Edward, and David Bowen. 1992. "Total Quality-Oriented Human Resources Management." *Organizational Dynamics* 21: 29–41.

Lengnick-Hall, Cynthia A., and Mark A. Lengnick-Hall. 1988. "Strategic Human Resource Management: A Review of the Literature and a Proposed Typology." *Academy of Management Review* 13, no. 3: 454–470.

Mesch, Debra J., James L. Perry, and Lois R. Wise. 1995. "Bureaucratic and Strategic Human Resource Management: An Empirical Comparison in the Federal Government." *Journal of Public Administration Research and Theory* 5: 385–402.

Mintzberg, Henry. 1983. *Structure in Fives: Designing Effective Organizations.* Englewood Cliffs, N.J.: Prentice-Hall.

Naisbitt, John, and Patricia Aburdene. 1985. *Re-Inventing the Corporation.* New York: Warner Books.

National Academy of Public Administration. 1993. *Leading People in Change: Empowerment, Commitment, Accountability.* Washington, D.C.: NAPA.

———.1995a. *Innovative Approaches to Human Resources Management.* Washington, D.C.: NAPA.

———. 1995b. *Strategies and Alternatives for Transforming Human Resources Management.* Washington, D.C.: NAPA.

National Commission on the State and Local Public Service. 1993. *Hard Truths/Tough Choices: An Agenda for State and Local Reform.* Albany: Nelson A. Rockefeller Institute of Government, State University of New York.

National Performance Review. 1993. *Creating a Government That Works Better and Costs Less.* Washington, D.C.: U.S. Government Printing Office.

Newland, Chester A. 1976. "Public Personnel Administration: Legalist Reforms vs. Effectiveness, Efficiency, and Economy." *Public Administration Review* 36 (Sept./Oct.): 529–537.

Offermann, L.R. and M.K. Gowing. 1993. "Personnel Selection in the Future: The Impact of Changing Demographics and the Nature of Work," in N. Schmitt et al., eds., *Personnel Selection in Organizations.* San Francisco: Jossey-Bass, pp. 385–412.

Osborne, David, and Ted Gaebler. 1992. *Reinventing Government: How the Entrepreneurial Spirit Is Transforming the Public Sector.* Reading, Mass.: Addison-Wesley.

Perry, James L. 1993. "Strategic Human Resource Management." *Review of Public Personnel Administration* 13: 59–71.

Perry, James L., and Kenneth L. Kraemer. 1993. "The Implications of Changing Technology," in Frank Thompson, ed., *Revitalizing the State and Local Public Service: Strengthening Performance, Accountability, and Citizen Confidence.* San Francisco: Jossey-Bass, pp. 225–245.

Roberts, Karlene H. 1990. "Managing High Reliability Organizations." *California Management Review* (Summer): 101–113.

Sayre, Wallace. 1948. "The Triumph of Techniques over Purpose." *Public Administration Review* 8: 134–137.

Schuler, Randall S. 1992. "Strategic Human Resource Management: Linking the People with the Strategic Needs of the Business." *Organizational Dynamics* 21: 18–23.

Secretary of Health and Human Services. 1995. "Performance Agreement between the Secretary of Health and Human Services and the Director of the National Institutes of Health." Mimeo. Washington, D.C.: U.S. HHS.

Shin, Roy W., and Debra J. Mesch. 1996. "The Changing Workforce: Issues and Challenges." *International Journal of Public Administration* 19, no. 3: 291–298.

U.S. Department of Health and Human Services. 1990. *Occupational Study of Grants Management Profession, Phase One: Final Report.* Washington, D.C.: Office of the Secretary, March 1990.

U.S. General Accounting Office. 1992. *The Changing Workforce: Demographic Issues Facing the Federal Government* (GAO/GGD-92-38). Washington, D.C.: U.S. GAO.
———. 1995. *Transforming the Civil Service: Building the Workforce of the Future* (GAO/GGD-95). Washington, D.C.: U.S. GAO.
Wechsler, Barton. 1994. "Reinventing Florida's Civil Service System: The Failure of Reform." *Review of Public Personnel Administration* 14, no. 2: 64–76.

chapter 3

Accountability Challenges of Deregulation

Barbara S. Romzek

$\mathbf{T}$alk of deregulation and government reform is much in the wind these days. In the broadest policy arenas, devolution of many government programs and functions to lower levels of the federal system is under consideration (DiIulio, 1994; Kettl and DiIulio, 1995; Radin et al., 1996). Efforts at reforms of operations within federal and state governments are widespread, as are changes in intergovernmental relationships (DiIulio and Kettl, 1995; Ingraham and Romzek, 1994). Many of these reforms include reductions in the scope of government activities and expansion of flexibility and discretion of public managers. At the federal level both the president and Congress are considering fundamental revisions in what government does and how government goes about its business. Most of these initiatives reflect a recognition that government operations are cumbersome and unwieldy and a perception that government simply is not as effective as the American public would like (Gore, 1995). The expectation is that these reforms will increase government's effectiveness and accountability.

Criticism of government and public employees' performance is often couched in terms of a need for greater accountability. Oftentimes calls for "more accountability" are really somewhat imprecise calls for different accountability relationships—ones that utilize the kinds of incentives, represent the degree of control, and promote the underlying behavioral expectation that the critic prefers. The fact of the matter is that the American public sector has a great deal of accountability at all levels. Public employees typically work enmeshed within several different accountability relationships simultaneously (Romzek and Dubnick, 1987). Among these various kinds of accountability relationships utilized in the public sector in this country, some are better suited to the current managerial reforms than are others (Romzek and Dubnick, 1994). Critics who deplore the lack of accountability of public employees would be more accurate if they deplored the lack of a "preferred" accountability relationship—the lack of the one that the critic(s) would prefer to see used to hold public employees answerable for their performance.

Most of the deregulatory and reform efforts currently under consideration emphasize increasing responsiveness and effectiveness by removing layers of regulations and constraints on how governments operate and increasing the discretion, autonomy, and responsiveness of public employees. The presumption is that removing layers of constraints—on how public employees are hired and fired and on how they do their jobs—will increase the chances that government employees will do what is expected of them. These trends reflect a widespread recognition that the pendulum in the United States has swung too far in the direction of control and rigidity and needs to swing toward greater discretion and flexibility. This dynamic is possible because one era's essential accountability mechanism is another's bureaucratic "red tape" (Kaufman, 1977). Calls for eliminating red tape, streamlining procedures, adopting a customer service orientation, and engaging in entrepreneurial management are consistent with this trend.

This chapter examines the accountability implications of government reforms in public personnel management. The public management arena is in a considerable state of flux these days. Calls for reform have been widespread and urgent (National Academy for Public Administration, 1994; Volcker Commission, 1989; Winter Commission, 1993). Some reforms are already under way and others are currently under consideration. With changes in what government does come changes in the expectations the American polity has for government performance. These changes have implications for the accountability relationships under which public employees must answer for their performance. And they present substantial challenges for human resource managers. Indeed, human resource managers need to be cognizant of the accountability dynamics that are characteristic of their agencies. If they are to be responsive to the current reforms, human resource managers must develop and sustain repertoires of accountability techniques that are well suited to the reforms and can be utilized with relative ease by themselves and by employees who work within their domain of influence. Before exploring the accountability implications of these reforms, let us briefly review the dynamics of accountability as a governance issue in the American political system.

ACCOUNTABILITY

Accountability is a relationship in which an individual or agency is held to answer for performance that involves some delegation of authority to act. Accountability in the public sector is a fundamental concern of the American political system. Indeed, a recent analysis identified three significant issues in public management: micromanagement, motivation, and measurement (Behn, 1995). In their own way, each of these issues relates to issues of accountability. The cultural norm of distrust of government is deep-seated in the United States.

Such sentiment preceded the writing of the Articles of Confederation and is currently embodied in the separation of powers principle that underlies our nation's governmental structures. This distrust magnifies our interest in government accountability.

In Search of Accountability: Weaving a Web

Although everyone agrees that governments and their employees should be accountable, there is not a great deal of consensus about which kind(s) of accountability relationships are preferred. The debate was engaged in earnest in the mid twentieth century (Friedrich, 1940; Finer, 1941) and has yet to be definitively resolved. One perspective emphasizes extensive oversight by democratic institutions (Finer, 1941; Gruber, 1987). Another perspective emphasizes self-control by professionals (Friedrich, 1940; Burke, 1986). The lack of consensus can be seen in the general dynamic that the American political system has followed regarding accountability relationships for public employees.

The pattern has been to design accountability relationships in reaction to undesirable situations that have arisen. For example, in the personnel arena, the infamous spoils system used during the mid nineteenth century (Mosher, 1982) was a reaction to a sense that government had not been sufficiently responsive to changes in electoral will. The spoils system relies on accountability relationships based on the responsiveness of employees to external actors (the elected officials who made the appointment). The merit system, instituted in the late nineteenth century, was a reaction to excesses of responsiveness under the spoils system and a sense that there had been insufficient attention given to the knowledge, skills, and abilities of job holders. The merit system relies on accountability relationships that emphasize obedience to internal organizational and supervisory directives, not responsiveness to external actors. In instituting the merit system, initiated in the federal government with the Pendleton Act of 1883, a political appointee system was retained for the highest-level positions of government. So although the merit system established new accountability relationships (which emphasized obedience to rules), the spoils system and its accountability relationships (which emphasized responsiveness to elected officials) were not discarded entirely.

This early pattern of layering accountability relationships has been repeated time and again. As a management problem or scandal arises, new accountability relationships are instituted to prevent such a circumstance from arising in the future. These new accountability relationships are not substituted for the accountability relationships that were in place at the time of the problem (which are now perceived to be inadequate) but are simply added to accountability relationships already in place. The result is the weaving of a thick web of multiple, overlapping accountability relationships within which public employees must work.

The metaphor of a web of accountability relationships captures the situation for public employees fairly well. Different strands of the web of accountability represent different relationships with actors or institutions that have legitimate performance expectations for public employees. These relationships vary in how they hold public employees accountable and what performance standards are used.

The presence of these webs of accountability relationships reflects the American pragmatic approach to governance. Although the use of multiple accountability relationships does not reflect any elegance of design, the multiplicity of relationships provides numerous opportunities for holding public employees answerable for their performance. The problem that arises from this pragmatic approach is an ironic one: the more accountability relationships there are available for holding public employees answerable for their performance, and the more goals and expectations there are for which they are accountable, the greater latitude employees have in managing their accountability relationships and performance expectations (Kettl, 1995: 56–57; Romzek, 1996). When public employees work within multiple accountability relationships and face numerous expectations for their performance, they can always make a claim to being accountable to some legitimate source of expectations. From the critic's point of view, it may not be the "preferred" or most important source or expectation.

A few scholars seek to understand the implications of this complex accountability context for public managers (Kearns, 1994; Romzek, 1996; Romzek and Dubnick, 1994). There are numerous governance problems related to accountability issues, including establishing expectations, verifying performance, maintaining responsiveness of agents, assessing blame, sorting out responsibility, determining the master(s), and managing under conditions of multiple accountability systems (Romzek and Dubnick, 1997). Although all these problems are interrelated parts of the accountability challenges facing governments, some have particular relevance to the issue of accountability in an era of deregulation.

Multiple Sources of Legitimate Control

The American constitution establishes a system of separation of powers that designates (1) the executive branch as responsible for implementing government programs, and (2) Congress and the president jointly with responsibility for establishing tasks and delegating them to public employees for implementation. Similar institutional arrangements exist at state levels. As elements of a democratic society, government institutions and processes in the United States are expected to be answerable to the citizenry for their performance. Yet as a pluralistic nation we recognize a wide variety of legitimate sources of expectations for public agencies and employees' performance. These sources include the Constitution, elected chief executives, legislatures, courts, other government agencies, organizational supervisors, professional groups, interest groups, clientele, citizens, as well as the public employees themselves (Dubnick and Romzek, 1991). Each of these groups has its own expectations about what public employees should be doing and how they are supposed to do it. Two noted observers of the public management scene describe this context as follows. "As governance becomes increasingly complex and the crossplay of interests more dynamic, the harried public official yearns for refuge from hostile litigators, importunate lobbyists, and investigators from Congress and from the home department's inspector general. The official retreats to some rule to cover for his or her official acts" (Garvey and DiIulio, 1994: 23).

Multiple Expectations

The notion of expectations for performance is a central feature of accountability relationships (Dubnick and Romzek, 1993). Holding public employees answer-able for their performance implies some prior expectations regarding their performance. The American political system is so complex and the tasks that government undertakes are sufficiently complicated that the situations facing public employees typically involve multiple expectations that are diverse, changing, and often contradictory. Some of these are expectations for com-mitments to fundamental institutions, such as to uphold the Constitution, to maintain democracy through openness and access to government decisions, and to seek to discover and achieve the public good. Other expectations are more obvious and explicit, such as to obey organizational directives and comply with laws, fulfill agency goals, uphold professional standards, provide clientele services efficiently and effectively, achieve programmatic ends of political leadership, satisfy the demands of active supporters, and achieve one's personal goals and career objectives (Dubnick and Romzek, 1991). If they are lucky, staff and agencies find these multiple expectations mutually reinforcing and com-patible. More typically, they find these multiple expectations to be a challenge to accommodate.

Various reform efforts currently proposed also embody conflicting expectations. Don Kettl (1995: 47) notes that "The three strategies send contradictory signals, raise different expectations, and often create radically different motivations for the workers who have to do the hard work of reinventing." The reinvention movement seeks downsizing and lower expenditures; reengineering seeks efficiency through dis-continuous, breakthrough strategies; and continuous improvement reforms seek responsiveness to customers through cooperation.

A common example of this situation in the world of public personnel management is the expectation that public managers hire individuals on the basis of merit, make some efforts at diversity in the work force, protect employees' individual rights, and operate as efficiently as possible (Klingner and Nalbandian, 1993). The challenge for managers is to reconcile responsiveness, merit, diversity, employee rights, and efficiency—expectations that are multiple, diverse, con-flicting, and changing. As anyone who has worked even a short while in the public sector can attest, protecting employee rights is a very time-consuming and, hence, expensive managerial task. The grievance and hearings processes that protect individual rights are notoriously inefficient. In short, individual rights, efficiency, and merit principles often conflict. Public managers face the challenge of trying to meet these conflicting expectations.

Beyond reconciling conflicting expectations, managers must accommodate changes in those expectations. Affirmative action programs provide an example of how expectations for public managers change. The 1990s has seen a dramatic shift away from the public and institutional support that existed in the 1970s and 1980s for affirmative action programs. By the mid-1990s affirmative action was under serious attack (see Chapter 4 in this book). Although some portion of affirmative action has been redefined as work-force diversity issues, other aspects (such as minority set-aside programs in contracting and education) have much less support. As a consequence, the relative importance of this expectation has changed for public managers.

Multiple Accountability Relationships

Under our basic constitutional principles, all government employees work for elected officials, who in turn work for the citizenry as expressed by the will of the voters (Mosher, 1982). Under this system of government, public employees are held accountable for their performance through oversight, monitoring, and executive appointments originating with external democratic institutions (e.g., elected chief executives, courts, and legislatures). These are the accountability relationships on which Finer (1941) and Gruber (1987) focus their attention. But the reality of public administration, and the fact that the nature of the work of public employees affords them many opportunities to exercise discretion in the course of their work (Lipsky, 1980), gives rise to concerns for control from internal sources (Friedrich, 1940; Burke, 1986).

As noted earlier, the pattern in the United States has been a web of numerous accountability relationships. These relationships reflect both internal and external sources of control and differing degrees of control and scrutiny over administrative actions. The multiple relationships fall into four different types: hierarchical, legal, political, and professional (Romzek and Dubnick, 1987). The differences in these types are illustrated in Figure 3.1.

Before exploring these dynamics, let us first briefly summarize the nature of these various accountability relationships.

FIGURE 3.1   Types of accountability relationships.

SOURCE OF CONTROL

		Internal	External
DEGREE OF CONTROL	**High**	Hierarchical	Legal
	Low	Professional	Political

Hierarchical accountability relationships are those most readily recognized by administrators and the general public because these relationships are closest to popular conceptions of accountability. Under hierarchical[1] accountability relationships, the individual being held accountable is not in a position to exercise much discretion about his or her performance. Instead, the emphasis is on obedience to supervisory and organizational directives, following standard operating procedures and adhering to rules. The source of control is from within the organization, from hierarchical superiors, and the degree of control is high.

Annual performance evaluations are one example of typical hierarchical relationships. In this instance, an individual's supervisor scrutinizes the employee's accomplishments in great detail for whether or not the individual has met performance expectations. The source of control is from within the organization, from a hierarchical superior, and the degree of control is high. Another common example of a hierarchical accountability relationship is the use of time sheets to report subordinates' work hours to supervisors. Employees typically do not have discretion about completing the time sheets. In this instance, an individual's supervisor receives the employee's time sheet, which reveals in detail whether the individual has met performance expectations (rules) regarding hours of work.

Legal accountability relationships are used in circumstances where the source of control is external and the degree of control or scrutiny is high. The high control means that individuals working under legal accountability relationships do not have a great deal of discretion about whether or not to comply with whatever external expectations are relevant. Typically these externally set standards carry some force of law. Under a legal accountability relationship the behavioral expectation is compliance with some externally derived standard.

An example of a legal accountability relationship can be seen in the kind of control and scrutiny police performance receives from a judge (a source of control external to the police department) when issues of suspects' constitutional rights are in question. Except under certain conditions, police must seek a search warrant from a judge (an external actor). The judge scrutinizes the request to be sure that the police have complied with all constitutional and statutory safeguards. The judge has control over whether a search warrant is issued. When a judge dismisses a lawsuit because of an invalid search, the judge has closely scrutinized police performance to determine whether the officer has complied with expectations regarding the rights of the accused—in this instance, for compliance with expectations regarding the necessary probable cause for a search or an arrest. More visible instances of legal accountability relationships in action are (1) legislative oversight hearings wherein Congress investigates whether a particular government program or policy has been administered in compliance with legislative mandates, or (2) a court appointment of a special master to oversee an agency's compliance with court-mandated standards.

Personnel-related examples of legal accountability relationships can be seen in externally mandated personnel ceilings and in the typical monitoring undertaken by an Office of Affirmative Action, the Equal Employment Opportunity

Commission, or a Merit System Protection Board when they investigate employee complaints regarding workplace rights. Similarly, when the Office of Personnel Management reviews agency compliance with various civil service laws and regulations under its personnel management evaluation program, it is party to a legal accountability relationship (Merit Systems Protection Board, November 1992).

Professional accountability relationships emphasize the exercise of discretion on the part of the employee in a manner that is consistent with internalized standards of performance, typically those of one's professional or peer work group. Trust and confidence are the foundations of professional accountability systems, reflecting the belief that employees will monitor and regulate themselves through adherence to professional norms and peer-based review (Burke, 1986). The source of control is internal, and the degree of control is low. Under professional accountability relationships the behavioral expectation is that discretion will be responsibly exercised. Under this kind of accountability relationship the organization defers to the expertise of the employee. The organization relies on the experience and judgment of the employee and trusts that the judgment will be made in a responsible manner—a manner that is consistent with prevailing practice. The exercise of discretion—whether it is about welfare benefits, medical treatment, or firefighting—is expected to result in responsible behavior that is within the boundaries of accepted practice.

The Senior Executive Service is an example of a public management program that was intended to afford substantial discretion to managers in staff assignments; unfortunately it has not lived up to early hopes for success (Sanders, 1994). Another personnel-related example of professional accountability relationships can be seen in programs that allow managers to manage their work force under payroll limits rather than with personnel ceilings. "Managing to payroll" allows administrators considerable discretion in determining the credentials, skills, and pay levels appropriate for their work group. The expectation is that the manager is the best judge of what kind of staff are needed to produce the desired outcomes (Romzek and Dubnick, 1994).

Political accountability relationships are based on the exercise of discretion by individuals in response to expectations from some external source. Under political accountability relationships, the public employee focuses on responsiveness to an external group's expectations and has some discretion about whether and how to respond. This is in contrast to legal accountability relationships wherein the individual faces an external source of control but has little discretion about whether to respond to some oversight function. Like professional accountability relationships, political accountability relationships rely on discretion being exercised; but the behavior expectation involves responsiveness to a key external reference group, which may or may not be consistent with adherence to accepted professional practice.

The contrast between political and professional accountability relationships is evident in the different behavioral expectations brought to bear on a traffic safety engineer facing a request from a neighborhood group for a stop sign at an unregulated intersection. The engineer's professional reference point is the

National Highway Traffic Safety Standards, which articulate the accepted norms of professional practice. Deference to professional norms will result in fewer stop signs than neighborhood groups typically like because highway safety standards require certain minimum threshold levels of traffic to warrant stop signs, traffic lights, and so on. That same engineer, when trying to be responsive to a neighborhood group troubled by perceptions of unsafe traffic on their streets, may recommend placing a stop sign even if the stop sign is not warranted under professional standards. In this instance, the neighborhood group would applaud the engineer's recommendation for its responsiveness even though professional standards were given lower priority. To neighborhood groups, responsiveness is often more important than expertise, especially when expert judgments conflict with group interests.

Although these accountability relationships are based on different behavioral expectations, they are not necessarily in conflict. An engineer who tries to accommodate both professional and political accountability relationships will seek to devise a traffic solution that complies with professional norms and is also responsive to neighborhood concerns regarding safer traffic patterns. An example of this same dynamic is the personnel officer who finds ways to promote diversity in the work force (thereby being responsive to the priorities of important external stakeholders) without compromising the operation of the merit system and thereby obeying directives of one's hierarchical superiors. Human resource directors sometimes face similar cross-pressures based on differing behavioral expectations when they undertake job and/or pay reclassifications. Reclassification judgments that are based on one's expert judgment sometimes are unresponsive to key organizational interests, and vice versa.

Dynamics of Accountability

The various types of accountability relationships are used to hold individuals and agencies answerable for their performance. In theory, any one individual or agency can be answerable for his or her or its performance under four different accountability relationships simultaneously. Most often one or two types of accountability relationships are primary, with the other types in place but invoked less frequently—but certainly in times of crisis or scandal (Romzek and Dubnick, 1987; Dubnick and Romzek, 1991).

Sometimes sources of control (individuals and agencies in a position to hold someone answerable for performance) can shift from invoking one kind of accountability relationship to another. In other words, the same actors can be involved in different accountability relationships at different times. For example, sometimes a boss will issue organizational directives and signal that the employee is expected to answer for his or her performance under a hierarchical account-ability relationship. At other times that same boss will delegate sufficient discretion to his or her subordinates that the subordinates will be held to answer for their performance under professional accountability relationships, wherein they are expected to exercise their best judgment rather than follow rules and directives. In this latter instance, the employees' performance will be judged on whether their decisions were responsible and consistent with accepted practices.

Police work provides an example of all four types of relationships being relevant for the same individual. The para-military nature of most police departments lends itself to hierarchical accountability relationships. Police officers typically work under tight chains of command and detailed organizational rules relating to shift assignments, uniforms, use of force, and so on. In this aspect, organizational superiors control a great deal of the work rules of police department staff. But once on patrol, police officers operate with substantial discretion under professional accountability relationships. They have to exercise their best judgment about whom to arrest and how much force to use. The expectation is that they will behave responsibly and make decisions consistent with their peers. We have already noted the legal accountability relationships under which police officers work vis-a-vis suspects' rights. Police operate under court-ordered requirements that they deliver Miranda warnings to everyone they arrest. Political accountability relationships, wherein the emphasis is on responsiveness to external clientele, show up in police work, too. The most recent manifestation of this is the latest wave of community-based policing reforms. Under community-based policing the role of the officer is to reach out to the neighborhood with an emphasis on close collaboration and problem solving (Wilson, 1994).

Similarly, when a centralized personnel office establishes rules for managers' hiring decisions, it is creating hierarchical accountability relationships that will be the basis for scrutiny. When that same central personnel office is monitoring supervisors' recruitment procedures for compliance with affirmative action goals, it is in an audit or oversight capacity and is invoking a legal accountability relationship. When the centralized personnel office grants discretion to public managers to determine how many staffers they need and what kind of skills mix they need, then they are establishing a professional accountability mode. When that centralized personnel office tells managers to adopt a customer service orientation, it is suggesting the behavioral expectation is responsiveness to some external clientele, which is the basis for political accountability relationships.

In summary, the accountability context for public employees is complex. They must accommodate expectations from several different legitimate sources and be answerable for their behavior under whichever accountability relationships are relevant. And they must be able to shift the accountability standard under which they answer for their behavior, as needed. Like actors in repertoire theater, public employees must be able to work within a repertoire of accountability relationships: obey directives, comply with external mandates, exercise discretion responsibly, and be responsive to external stakeholders. Successful public employees stand ready to answer for their behavior under any of the different standards.

An important yet often overlooked aspect of these accountability relationships is the fact that the public administrators subject to the accountability relationships are not passive partners in them. Instead, administrators can influence the expectations they face and the accountability relationships under which they answer for their behavior. Public employees can adopt different levels of activism as they try to manage their accountability relationships. They can assume reactive, adaptive, and strategic postures vis-a-vis their work, depending upon which aspect of their work they focus their energies on: consequences, situations, or the task environment (Romzek, 1996).

ACCOUNTABILITY IMPLICATIONS OF REFORM

At the present time there is enormous interest in government reform at all levels. Some reforms are already in place, others are in demonstration and experimentation stages, and yet other ideas are still in the proposal phase. As a result, the public management arena is currently very fluid. The public service has been downsized under the National Performance Review (Kettl, 1994), decentralized and deregulated in terms of its personnel functions (Horner, 1994), and is currently the subject of numerous efforts at reinvention and reengineering (Gore, 1993, 1995; Moe, 1994; Kettl, 1995). These changes are going forward, often without much thought about the accountability implications (Garvey, 1995; Moe, 1994).

One cannot discuss the accountability implications of reform without first discussing the issue of the fit between organizational activities and accountability relationships in use. The decision as to which accountability relationships are primary is a function of the organization's institutional environment, managerial strategy, and agency or individual tasks (Romzek and Dubnick, 1987). The institutional environment affects the nature of the assignments agencies and individuals are given and the expectations they face. The American public service's recent institutional environment has been a turbulent one. In addition to the changes noted above, the American public service has been subject to a steady stream of severe criticism from elected officials, popularly known as "bureaucrat bashing" (Garvey, 1995). Managerial strategies that underlie the different reforms vary in their emphases. Some focus on inputs and processes; others emphasize outcomes; others outputs. Agency tasks are also shifting under these reforms as governments seek to downsize, deregulate, shift responsibilities, and contract out many of their former functions (Milward, 1994).

Exploring the accountability implications of the various reforms requires systematic thinking about how the various kinds of accountability relationships fit with the current environment, managerial strategies, and tasks. Although the conditions of public administration are rarely ideal, it is possible to discuss "ideal" accountability configurations in the same sense that Max Weber (Gerth and Mills, 1973) afforded us a profile of "ideal" bureaucracy. Romzek and Dubnick (1994) provide a baseline framework that illustrates how managerial strategy and core tasks can be aligned in terms of accountability relationships. Figure 3.2 represents an adaptation of that framework to the issue of reform. This figure will help place various governmental deregulation and reform efforts in an accountability context.

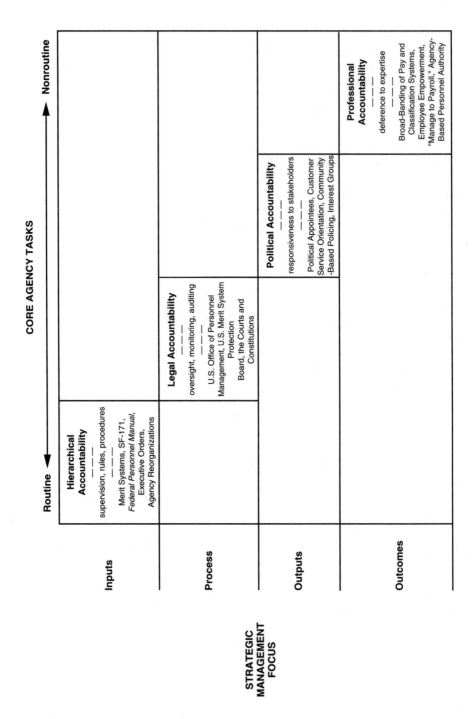

FIGURE 3.2 Accountability and personnel management: An "ideal" alignment—type of accountability, basis of control, and examples.

Public service tasks that are relatively routine and emphasize inputs lend themselves to hierarchical accountability relationships. Traditional "merit"-based civil service systems that are organized around a position classification schema are the most common example of this. The abolition of the *Federal Personnel Manual* and the elimination of the standardized federal personnel application form, SF-171, represent efforts to break away from an overreliance on hierarchical accountability relationships. Proposals to reform the position classification system from the 15-level General Schedule to a smaller number of broad bands represent other efforts to break away from rule-bound, inputs-oriented hierarchical accountability relationships and encourage professional accountability relationships emphasizing outcomes. Such reform of the position classification system was the subject of experimentation at the China Lake Naval Weapons Center (Cayer, 1992; Merit Systems Protection Board, December 1992; National Academy for Public Administration, 1991; Wilson, 1994).

Agency reorganizations typically change hierarchical reporting relationships. Such was the case with the "OMB 2000" reorganization of the Office of Management and Budget (OMB). This reorganization merged the budget and management sides of OMB and sought broader, more results-oriented perspectives on the part of OMB analysts and federal agencies in the budget review process (Kettl, 1995). As such, the reorganized OMB should rely more heavily on professional accountability relationships in its agency budget review process. At this point it is not clear whether the intended effects of OMB's approach to budget and agency review, which are admittedly ambitious, will be realized.

When an agency's managerial focus is on processes and its tasks are still relatively routine, legal accountability systems are a good alignment. Investigations by the Merit Systems Protection Board and the Equal Employment Opportunity Commission are examples of this kind of oversight and monitoring function. The Office of Management and Budget's role in setting personnel ceilings and the Office of Personnel Management's (OPM) role as regulatory agency, when it oversees and monitors for compliance with federal government merit system processes (Merit Systems Protection Board, November 1992), are examples of agencies operating as external auditors through oversight. Proposals to change the role of OPM from regulatory agency to consulting firm (Kettl, 1995: 29–31) represent an effort to diminish the emphasis on process and to create political and professional accountability relationships that emphasize responsiveness and deference to expertise.

Circumstances wherein agency tasks are less routine and managerial strategies focus on outputs lend themselves to political accountability relationships, where the emphasis is on responsiveness to some external stakeholders. The long-standing system of political appointees is intended to ensure responsiveness to elected officials. In the jargon of reinventing government, all public employees—not just top appointees—should be focused on responsiveness; the key external constituency is the citizen-as-customer (Osborne and Gaebler, 1992). Of course, the challenge for public agencies is to identify all their "customers" and to ascertain the difference between citizens and customers (Frederickson, 1992).

President Clinton's Executive Order 12862, which mandated aggressive pursuit of customer service plans for federal agencies, is an example of one kind of accountability relationship (hierarchical) being used to promote the use of another kind (political). When an executive order is issued, the president utilizes his position as chief executive to issue a directive to subordinate agencies. Executive Order 12862 puts far more discretion into the hands of front-line managers and emphasizes responsiveness to external clientele. It requires agencies to define customer service standards, identify who agency customers are or should be, survey them about satisfaction, post service standards and measure results against them, establish best-in-business benchmarks, survey front-line employees, and make information services and complaint systems easily accessible (Kettl, 1995: 54). Presumably agencies that fail to obey this directive will face sanctions from their supervisor, the chief executive.

In circumstances wherein the task is very specialized and the managerial strategy is focused on outcomes, professional accountability relationships represent the best alignment. This allows for the exercise of discretion in the application of expertise. Decentralizing the personnel procurement system into agency-based authority is an example of professional accountability relationships at the agency level. Agencies are granted autonomy to make their own decisions regarding hiring.

The China Lake demonstration project allowed managers greater flexibility and autonomy in assigning, promoting, and rewarding subordinates at the defense lab by establishing five broad career paths (professional, technical, specialist, administrative, clerical) and correspondingly broad pay bands (ranging from four to six, depending on career path) (Merit Systems Protection Board, December 1992; Wilson, 1994). To date, Congress has extended this broad-banding authority to other defense laboratories. In a demonstration project within the U.S. Department of Agriculture, the Forestry Service and the Agriculture Research Service have experimented with a broad three-category grouping system (quality, eligible, ineligible) for hires rather than hierarchical rankings of scores and a "rule of three." Like the China Lake experiment, managers were granted much more discretion to make hiring decisions. The emphasis is on outcomes, "hires," not on rules and process about how to hire (Feller et al., 1995; Merit Systems Protection Board, December 1992).

CONCLUSION

Since the passage of the Pendleton Act of 1883, the American public service has been structured with an eye toward eliminating favoritism and constraining managerial choices. The result has been a large accumulation of administrative rules and regulations concerning acquisition, allocation, development, and sanctions in the personnel arena. Implicitly, those rules and regulations have condoned a trade-off between administrative accountability and administrative efficiency. Diminished efficiency has been the price for accountability. Pressures for government reform have forced a reexamination of this trade-off.

Personnel systems had become too slow and cumbersome (Ingraham and Rosenbloom, 1992).

Calls for reform emphasize downsizing, decentralization, deregulation, and reengineering to yield smaller, more responsive, more entrepreneurial, and more effective public management systems. In essence, these reforms call for more discretion on the part of managers, more flexibility in administrative operations, and greater emphases on outcomes and outputs. The reforms under way and under consideration at the close of the twentieth century represent a swinging of the accountability pendulum away from rigidity and tight monitoring and toward greater discretion and flexibility. The main goal of these reforms is to enable government to tackle its new challenges better than the old procedure and rule-based approaches allowed.

These reforms will result in increasing the reliance on some kinds of accountability relationships and deemphasizing others. Accountability issues are central to the work of human resource managers. They must concern themselves with the accountability of everyone within their domain as well as themselves. For human resource managers the challenge is how to pursue their various personnel functions within the context of shifting emphases *away from* a focus on inputs and processes and *toward* outcomes and outputs.

Human resource managers need to be cognizant of the web of accountability relationships that are legitimate within the American context and how each can be used to hold employees answerable for their performance. Recognizing the various types of accountability relationships and the values and dynamics associated with each will help managers discern which accountability relationships are relevant to their own circumstances. This, in turn, can help managers deal with situations wherein cross-pressures or misalignments exist and help them identify which other accountability relationships might be more appropriate in light of the particular managerial strategy and core tasks.

Of course, managers in the public sector rarely have ideal alignments. Rather, some alignments are well suited to the unit's political environment, managerial strategy, and core tasks; others may be less than ideal. The pattern of multiple, overlapping accountability relationships indicates that the likelihood of facing at least one less-than-ideal alignment is the norm rather than the exception. Recognition of this pattern and anticipation of the need to answer for one's performance under several kinds of accountability relationships are necessary conditions for success in American public service. This multi-method approach to accountability, wherein several accountability relationships exist simultaneously, is not a problem in itself; it has been the pattern throughout most of the history of American government. In fact, given the presence of multiple expectations, a multi-method approach to accountability may be most appropriate, even if the situation occasionally presents human resource managers with cross-pressures.

Deregulatory reforms reflect a changing view among the American public of what government should do and how public employees should go about doing their jobs. Reformers now ask public employees to shift from a risk-averse approach to their jobs (which emphasizes obedience and compliance) to an entrepreneurial approach (which requires making administrative changes toward increased flexibility and discretion) (Gore, 1993, 1995; Kettl, 1995; Light, 1994). Because accountability relationships organized around outcomes and outputs require greater exercise of discretion, public employees find themselves with fewer detailed directives; hence they face much less certainty about the accountability consequences of their actions. Some personnel managers may be more comfortable than others with increased discretion and flexibility (Ban, 1995).

These reforms present opportunities and uncertainties for human resource managers. First, managers need to recognize that there are accountability implications of various management reforms. Cutting red tape and speeding up procedures that ensure due process represent efforts to lessen the constraints from hierarchical and legal types of accountability relationships. Reforms that seek worker empowerment and increased flexibility represent professional accountability relationships insofar as they rely on increased employee discretion. Emphases on customer satisfaction (whether internal or external customers), as a measure of employees' responsiveness to key clientele, reflect political accountability relationships. If reforms seek new managerial strategies and reconfigured tasks, then accountability relationships need to be reconfigured, too. The worst situation of all is to have changes in administrative approaches without appropriate shifts in the emphases on accountability relationships. Even if policy makers have not thought through the accountability dynamics that follow logically from reforms, personnel managers need to be cognizant of them and make appropriate adjustments.

The challenge of designing performance appraisal systems that measure performance against outcomes and outputs is substantial. It requires agreement on outcomes and outputs as well as deference to standards of acceptable practice and responsiveness to customers. Such adjustments also encompass deemphasis on obedience to organizational directives and compliance with external mandates. The latter two standards of accountability are never completely abandoned, but the success of the current wave of reforms necessitates shifting emphases. Reforms that are implemented without suitable adjustments in accountability relationships will have dimmer prospects of taking firm hold within the organizational context. If managers do not hold employees answerable for their performance under accountability relationships that are appropriate to the newer strategies and tasks, then administrative reforms are not likely to become deeply rooted in organizational practices (Schein, 1992).

There are always questions about the future of any government reform effort due to the inevitable ebb and flow of political and administrative support for such changes. There are questions for this wave of deregulation as well. It is unclear whether the American populace, its political institutions, and its managerial culture are ready to afford public agencies and their employees the discretion and flexibility that such reforms entail. The institutional context within which public management operates in the United States has never been very trusting of government and its administrators. And there is no sign that trust is on the upswing; rather, it is declining (Ruscio, 1995). Currently public managers in the United States have strong disincentives for taking bureaucratic risks. And the American political culture has demonstrated an increasing intolerance for any missteps in government; a single error can be fatal to one's standing or career. Until the political culture can forgive "honest mistakes committed in an effort to improve the way things are done," the incentive system for entrepreneurial management will be inadequate (National Academy for Public Administration, 1994: 23). These reforms may be deemphasizing old, familiar accountability relationships *before* the American polity is comfortable with the heavy reliance on accountability relationships that are appropriate for the new reforms. If history is a good predictor of the future, then at the first sign of problem or scandal under these reformed management systems, a reactivation of hierarchical and legal accountability mechanisms is likely. The pattern is all too common: an early search for someone to blame, identification of individuals at fault or scapegoats, and generation of new rules and regulations to ensure such mistakes do not reoccur.

In summary, the accountability dynamics in the American public service are complex. Deemphasizing inputs and processes and emphasizing outcomes and outputs do not necessarily mean more or less accountability from government administrators. Rather, they mean different kinds of accountability relationships should be emphasized, ones that encourage entrepreneurial management, increased discretion and worker empowerment in daily operations, and greater responsiveness to key stakeholders and customers. "The key is not to avoid all risk . . . but to develop bureaucrats' judgments about which risks are prudent and to improve the system's ability to reduce the level of risk in general" (Kettl, 1995: 71).

The challenge facing reformers is how to change the administrative culture of risk aversion toward entrepreneurial management. The challenge facing public managers will be the age-old one: how to manage the conflicting expectations they face in an institutional environment that relies on multiple mechanisms of accountability. Reforms in government operations often have accountability implications that represent a shift in emphases rather than discarding one or another type of accountability relationship altogether. Administrators who are cognizant of this complexity will be better able to manage their accountability relationships and those of their subordinates. Human resource managers who develop and sustain repertoires of accountability relationships that can be invoked quickly—as warranted by changes in the relevant political context, managerial strategies, and core tasks—will find themselves better able to manage accountability for themselves and the employees who work within their domain.

NOTE

1. For scholars who are familiar with the earlier work of Romzek and Dubnick (1987), the category labeled "hierarchical" in this discussion corresponds to the same category labeled "bureaucratic" in earlier writings. The new label better signals the foundation of this accountability relationship; it is based on obedience.

REFERENCES

Ban, Carolyn. 1995. *How Do Public Managers Manage? Bureaucratic Constraints, Organizational Culture, and the Potential for Reform.* San Francisco: Jossey-Bass.

Behn, Robert. 1995. "The Big Questions of Public Management." *Public Administration Review* 55, no. 4: 313-324.

Burke, John. 1986. *Bureaucratic Responsibility.* Baltimore, Md.: Johns Hopkins Press.

Cayer, N. Joseph. 1992. "Classification in the Federal Service: New Looks at Alternative Approaches." *Public Administration Review* 52, no. 2: 217-220.

DiIulio, John J., Jr., ed. 1994. *Deregulating the Public Service: Can Government Be Improved?* Washington, D.C.: Brookings Institution.

Dubnick, Melvin J., and Barbara S. Romzek. 1991. *American Public Administration: Politics and the Management of Expectations.* New York: Macmillan.

————. 1993. "Accountability and the Centrality of Expectations," in James Perry, ed., Research in Public Administration, vol. 2. Greenwich, CT: JAI Press.

Feller, Irwin, Melvin Mark, Jack Stevens, Lance Shotland, Haleh Rastegary, Scott Button, Joe Vasey, and Laurie Hyers. 1995. "Decentralization and Deregulation of the Federal Hiring Process." Paper presented at the Trinity Symposium in conjunction with the meeting of the American Society for Public Administration, San Antonio.

Finer, Herman. 1941. "Administrative Responsibility and Democratic Government." *Public Administration Review* 1 (Summer): 335-350.

Frederickson, H. George. 1992. "Painting Bull's Eyes around Bullet Holes." *Governing* 6 (December): 13.

Friedrich, Carl J. 1940. "Public Policy and the Nature of Administrative Responsibility," in Carl J. Friedrich and Edwards S. Mason, eds., *Public Policy.* Cambridge, Mass.: Harvard University Press.

Garvey, Gerald. 1995. "False Promises: The NPR in Historical Perspective," in Donald F. Kettl and John DiIulio Jr., eds., *Inside the Reinvention Machine: Appraising Government Reform.* Washington, D.C.: Brookings Institution.

Garvey, Gerald, and John J. DiIulio Jr. 1994. "Sources of Public Service Overregulation," in John J. DiIulio, ed., *Deregulating the Public Service: Can Government Be Improved?* Washington, D.C.: Brookings Institution.

Gerth, Hans H., and C. Wright Mills, eds. 1973. *From Max Weber: Essays in Sociology.* New York: Oxford University Press.

Gore, Alfred. 1993. *From Red Tape to Results: Creating a Government That Works Better and Costs Less.* Report of the National Performance Review. Washington, D.C.: U.S. Government Printing Office.

————. 1995. *Common Sense Government: Works Better and Costs Less.* Third Report of the National Performance Review. Washington, D.C.: U.S. Government Printing Office.

Gruber, Judith. 1987. *Controlling Bureaucracies.* Berkeley: University of California Press.

Horner, Constance. 1994. "Deregulating the Federal Service: Is the Time Right?" in John J. DiIulio Jr., ed., *Deregulating the Public Service: Can Government Be Improved?* Washington, D.C.: Brookings Institution.

Ingraham, Patricia W., and Barbara S. Romzek, eds. 1994. *New Paradigms for Government.* San Francisco: Jossey-Bass.

Ingraham, Patricia W., and David Rosenbloom, eds. 1992. *The Promise and Paradox of Civil Service Reform.* Pittsburgh: University of Pittsburgh Press.

Kaufman, Herbert. 1977. *Red Tape: Its Origins, Uses and Abuses.* Washington, D.C.: Brookings Institution.

Kearns, Kevin P. 1994. "The Strategic Management of Accountability in Nonprofit Organizations: An Analytical Framework." *Public Administration Review* 54, no. 2: 185–192.

Kettl, Donald. 1994. *Reinventing Government: Appraising the National Performance Review.* A Report of the Center for Public Management. Washington, D.C.: Brookings Institution.

———. 1995. "Building Lasting Reform: Enduring Questions, Missing Answers," in Donald Kettl and John DiIulio Jr., eds., *Inside the Reinvention Machine: Appraising Government Reform.* Washington, D.C.: Brookings Institution.

Kettl, Donald, and John DiIulio Jr., eds. 1995. *Inside the Reinvention Machine: Appraising Government Reform.* Washington, D.C.: Brookings Institution.

Klingner, Donald, and John Nalbandian. 1993. *Public Personnel Management: Contexts and Strategies,* 3rd ed. Englewood Cliffs, N.J.: Prentice-Hall.

Light, Paul. 1994. "Creating Government That Encourages Innovation," in Patricia W. Ingraham and Barbara S. Romzek, eds., *New Paradigms for Government: Issues for the Changing Public Service.* San Francisco: Jossey-Bass.

Lipsky, Michael. 1980. *Street Level Bureaucracy.* New York: Russell Sage.

Merit Systems Protection Board. November 1992. "Civil Service Evaluation: The Role of the U.S. Office of Personnel Management." A Report to the President and the Congress by the U.S. Merit Systems Protection Board. Washington, D.C.: U.S. Government Printing Office.

———. December 1992. "Federal Personnel Research Programs and Demonstration Projects: Catalysts for Change." A Report to the President and the Congress by the U.S. Merit Systems Protection Board. Washington, D.C.: U.S. Government Printing Office.

Milward, H. Brinton. 1994. "Implications of Contracting Out: New Roles for the Hollow State," in Patricia W. Ingraham and Barbara S. Romzek, eds., *New Paradigms for Government: Issues for the Changing Public Service.* San Francisco: Jossey-Bass.

Moe, Ronald C. 1994. "The 'Reinventing Government' Exercise: Misinterpreting the Problem, Misjudging the Consequences." *Public Administration Review* 54 (March/April): 111–122.

Mosher, Frederick C. 1982. *Democracy and the Public Service,* 2nd ed. New York: Oxford University Press.

National Academy for Public Administration. 1991. *Modernizing Federal Classification: An Opportunity for Excellence.* Washington, D.C.: National Academy for Public Administration.

———. 1994. "Helping Government Change: An Appraisal of the National Performance Review." Draft. Washington, D.C.: National Academy for Public Administration.

Osborne, David, and Ted Gaebler. 1992. *Reinventing Government: How the Entrepreneurial Spirit Is Transforming the Public Sector.* Reading, Mass.: Addison-Wesley.

Radin, Beryl, Robert Agranoff, Ann Bowman, C. Gregory Buntz, J. Steven Ott, Barbara S. Romzek, and Robert H. Wilson. 1996. *New Governance for Rural America: Intergovernmental Partnerships and Rural Development.* Lawrence: University Press of Kansas.

Romzek, Barbara S. 1996. "Enhancing Accountability," in James Perry, ed., *Handbook of Public Administration,* 2nd ed. San Francisco: Jossey-Bass.

Romzek, Barbara S., and Melvin J. Dubnick. 1987. "Accountability and the Public Service: Lessons from the *Challenger* Tragedy." *Public Administration Review* 47 (May/June): 227–238.

———— . 1994. "Issues of Accountability in Flexible Personnel Systems," in Patricia W. Ingraham and Barbara S. Romzek, eds., *New Paradigms for Government: Issues for the Changing Public Service.* San Francisco: Jossey-Bass.

———— . 1997. "Accountability," in Jay M. Shafritz, ed., *International Encyclopedia of Public Policy and Administration.* New York: Henry Holt and Company.

Ruscio, Kenneth P. 1995. "Trust, Democracy, and Public Management: A Theoretical Argument." Paper presented at the Trinity Symposium in conjunction with the annual meeting of the American Society for Public Administration.

Sanders, Ronald P. 1994. "Reinventing the Senior Executive Service," in Patricia W. Ingraham and Barbara S. Romzek, eds., *New Paradigms for Government: Issues for the Changing Public Service.* San Francisco: Jossey-Bass.

Schein, Edgar. 1992. *Organizational Culture and Leadership,* 2nd ed. San Francisco: Jossey-Bass.

Volcker Commission. 1989. *Leadership for America: Rebuilding the Public Service.* Task Force Reports to the National Commission on the Public Service. Lexington, MA: D.C. Heath and Co.

Wilson, James Q. 1994. "Can the Bureaucracy Be Deregulated: Lessons from Government Agencies," in John J. DiIulio Jr., ed., *Deregulating the Public Service: Can Government Be Improved?* Washington, D.C.: Brookings Institution.

Winter Commission. 1993. *Hard Truths/Tough Choices: An Agenda for State and Local Reform.* The First Report of the National Commission on the State and Local Public Service. Albany, N.Y.: Rockefeller Institute.

section ▐▐

Challenges of Inclusion

Public personnel administration is an evolving field. As the nature and character of public work continue to change, the field expands and evolves to accommodate changes in the government workplace. One area of public personnel in which this evolving state is particularly striking is the new and changing work force. The makeup of the government work force is remarkably different today as compared with ten years ago, and concomitantly the needs and interests of the new government worker have become more diverse. Women, people of color, members of various ethnic groups, gay men and lesbians, and persons with AIDS are all part of this new work force; and they bring different strengths, abilities, and demands that will require distinctive forms of organizational attention. Public personnel administrators and human resources managers will largely be the caretakers of the changing workplace, responsible for developing, implementing, and overseeing programs and policies that support the inclusion of the new public worker. A number of challenges are evident.

For example, as Norma Riccucci points out in "Will Affirmative Action Survive into the Twenty-First Century?" public personnel administrators will be challenged by the changing laws and regulations around, as well as the diminishing popular support for, affirmative action. As Riccucci indicates, this creates conflicting messages in that on the one hand, affirmative action programs are being eviscerated, yet on the other, public and private sector employers are being encouraged to develop diversity programs to prepare for the changing demographics of the labor force.

Tamu Chambers and Norma Riccucci continue with this theme in "Models of Excellence in Workplace Diversity," where they profile three public sector employers and highlight two private firms that have made a serious commitment to promoting and managing diversity in their work forces. This chapter illustrates

55

the various diversity strategies embraced by the employers and points to the commonalities among all of them.

Katherine Naff, in "Colliding with a Glass Ceiling," discusses the barriers that women and people of color face in their efforts to ascend organizational hierarchies and also offers descriptions of the strategies employed and needed to dismantle these barriers. One of the barriers that women continue to face on the job is sexual harassment. Robert Lee and Paul Greenlaw, in "A Legal Perspective on Sexual Harassment," illustrate the legal ramifications of sexual harassment for organizations and discuss the programs and policies employers have developed to prevent it from occurring in their workplaces.

Charles Gossett, in "Lesbians and Gay Men in the Public Sector Work Force," addresses issues surrounding the inclusion of gay men and lesbians in government work forces. He examines the current status of legal protections for gay men and lesbians in the workplace and also examines the various personnel functions (e.g., recruitment, selection, training) that are affected when legal protections are in place for lesbians and gay men.

The latter part of the twentieth century has been devastated by the deadly disease called AIDS. In "AIDS and Disability Policy," James Slack examines the legal rights of job applicants and employees with HIV or AIDS. Particular attention is given to the legal requirements mandated by the 1990 Americans with Disabilities ACT (ADA). Slack discusses the strategies employers can utilize to provide a supportive organizational climate for persons with HIV or AIDS and, at the same time, maintain worker morale and high levels of productivity.

chapter **4**

Will Affirmative Action Survive into the Twenty-First Century?

Norma M. Riccucci

Almost since its inception, affirmative action has been pummeled by attacks from the citizenry, scholars, and even individual lawmakers and jurists. Efforts to curb discrimination (e.g., in the form of equal employment opportunity—EEO—programs) have also been subject to the whims of hiring authorities and policy makers. Yet despite this resistance, one or more of the three branches of the federal government, at least until recently, could be relied on to support the use of affirmative action. The courts in particular, until 1989, provided the necessary legal support for the continued use of affirmative action. Today, however, this is no longer the case. We are seeing a slow erosion of support for affirmative action on the part of government. Moreover, the American people have become more vocal and aggressive in their opposition to affirmative action.

By the mid-1990s, for example, throughout the country there were grass-roots efforts aimed at dismantling all types of affirmative action programs. In a well-publicized instance in California, a citizens group pushed for an amendment to the state constitution that would end the use of affirmative action in employment, college admissions, and the awarding of contracts. As of this writing, the citizens of California have not yet voted on the initiative.[1] But responding to this popular movement, California governor Pete Wilson, in May 1995, ordered an end to all state affirmative action programs not required by law or court order; and two months later the University of California's Board of Regents voted to end the use of affirmative action in college admissions, hiring, and contracting.

In addition, and also in response to popular movements, the Republican-controlled Congress[2] and even the president have been unwilling to provide the necessary support for affirmative action. Indeed, key members of Congress such as Senators Bob Dole (R-Kansas) and Phil Gramm (R-Texas), who were candidates for the 1996 presidential race, placed on their campaign platforms a promise to halt the use of racial and gender preferences in federal programs. Even President Clinton, who has vowed not to end affirmative action, has ordered the first major revision of affirmative action programs[3] since President Reagan in the 1980s. And the U.S. Supreme Court, now with a majority of Reagan and Bush appointees, has been readily scrapping affirmative action and has also greatly curtailed the reaches of EEO or employment discrimination law.

At the same time, however, mixed messages are being sent by public and private sector employers, who have been pursuing diversity programs in various shapes and forms. If we juxtapose the proactive diversity efforts of public and private employers against the aggressive legal, political, and citizen-based crusades to dismantle affirmative action, confusion arises over the future of programs aimed at promoting diversity in any form or fashion.[4]

What does this portend for affirmative action? This chapter seeks to provide some answers by examining the legal and political challenges that affirmative action as well as EEO have faced since their inception. In particular, the chapter considers how the three branches of government, over time, have shifted their support for affirmative action and EEO, and the implications of having done so.

DEFINITION OF THE CONCEPTS AND PROBLEM

EEO is largely viewed as a means to prevent discrimination in the workplace. Title VII of the Civil Rights Act of 1964, for example, as amended, is intended to prevent discrimination on the basis of race, color, religion, gender, and national origin in public and private sector work forces. Affirmative action, on the other hand, which also emerged during the 1960s in response to pervasive employment discrimination, refers to proactive efforts to diversify the workplace in terms of race, ethnicity, gender, and even physical abilities.[5] Its emphasis on proaction has led to a good deal of controversy and public debate over its use as an employment tool or social policy (Rosenbloom, 1977; Riccucci, 1991; Cornwell and Kellough, 1994; Kellough, 1997; Nalbandian and Klingner, 1987). Indeed, we have never gotten past the seminal backlash that evolved out of the *Regents v. Bakke* (1978) case, which not only upheld the principle of affirmative action for the first time but also popularized the concepts of "reverse discrimination" and "quotas."[6]

Notwithstanding the harsh resistance from a variety of sources, affirmative action prevailed in large part because—at least until Ronald Reagan became president—there was bipartisan political consensus around affirmative action from the executive, legislative, and judicial branches of government. Democrats and Republicans alike in the White House and in Congress worked to maintain affirmative action.[7] The U.S. Supreme Court also supported its continued use by upholding its legality.

But, since Reagan took office in 1981, we have seen a classic separation of powers jockeying for control over affirmative action as well as EEO. In particular, the battle between Congress and the Supreme Court has been prominent. The executive branch, by comparison, under Presidents Reagan and Bush, has had a more limited impact on EEO and affirmative action. As we will see shortly, to the extent that Reagan and Bush have had a strong impact it has been indirect, through the courts.[8]

Let's take a closer look by examining, first, how the executive branch under Presidents Reagan and Bush has altered the use of EEO and affirmative action. Then we will consider the Supreme Court's role in shaping affirmative action with particular emphasis on its 1989 rulings, which virtually eviscerated not only affirmative action but EEO as well. Next we'll examine the role of the legislative branch, particularly the efforts of Congress to put EEO and affirmative action back on track with passage of various civil rights laws. Finally we'll look at recent legal and political developments and then make some assessments regarding the future outlook for affirmative action and EEO.

THE ROLE OF THE EXECUTIVE BRANCH

As noted, prior to the Reagan presidency the executive branch of the U.S. government had strongly supported the use of affirmative action and EEO. President Kennedy issued Executive Order 10925 in 1961, which represents the first time the term *affirmative action* was used, albeit in a nondiscrimination or EEO capacity. President Johnson signed into law the Civil Rights Act of 1964 and also issued Executive Order 11246, the very first affirmative action mandate. This executive order, issued in 1965 and amended in 1967, requires federal contractors not only to refrain from discrimination on the basis of race, color, religion, gender, or national origin but also to take affirmative steps to recruit, hire, and promote workers on the basis of these characteristics. The Nixon and Ford administrations carried forward the EEO and affirmative programs established by Kennedy and Johnson and, in some respect, strengthened them. For example, President Nixon in 1969 issued an executive order requiring federal government agency heads to establish and maintain an "affirmative program" of EEO. In addition, he instituted changes to the federal EEO program that were designed to increase the population of Latinos in the federal work force. He also signed into law the Equal Employment Opportunity Act of 1972, which expanded and strengthened the Civil Rights Act of 1964.

When Reagan took office in 1981, however, we saw for the first time a president who was willing to dismantle affirmative action altogether and restrict the use of EEO. Even Reagan's Republican predecessors had supported EEO and affirmative action. While in office, Reagan did everything possible to undermine affirmative action as well as civil rights policies in general. And although he was not able to fully eradicate affirmative action during his two terms in office, he was successful in disrupting its use. For example, he not only weakened the enforcement of Executive Order 11246 but also made a strong (but futile) attempt to rewrite it so that it would require affirmative action *solely* in recruitment—not in hiring or making promotions. This would have effectively killed the executive order. No president before him had made any effort to tamper with this critical affirmative action mandate.

In addition, President Reagan's appointments to such bodies as the Equal Employment Opportunity Commission (Clarence Thomas was appointed chair in 1982) and the U.S. Commission on Civil Rights (Clarence Pendleton was appointed chair in 1982) proved to be detrimental to EEO and affirmative action. One example can be seen in the EEOC's decision in 1986 to abandon the use of numerical hiring goals and timetables to settle discrimination cases against private employers. Clarence Thomas, by executive fiat, changed the way in which the EEOC had remedied discrimination complaints almost since the agency's inception ("Equal Employment Panel Drops Numerical Goals as Bias Remedy," 1986).

Also, President Reagan's Justice Department, under the leadership of Attorney General Edwin Meese III, issued, in response to a very narrow Supreme Court ruling rendered in 1984 (*Memphis v. Stotts*), a directive to cities, counties, school districts, and state agencies to ignore their affirmative action plans. The *Stotts* ruling struck down the use of affirmative action *only* in the area of layoffs, not in other realms of employment decisions. Many jurisdictions abandoned their entire affirmative action programs in response to Meese's request. In addition, President Reagan, during his eight years in office, attempted to push the Supreme Court into striking down the use of affirmative action, and he stacked the federal courts with conservative judges whom he expected to do the same. (Ironically, as we will see shortly, it was only after Reagan left office that he achieved major Supreme Court victories in terms of affirmative action.)

President Bush, although less aggressive in his efforts to decimate affirmative action, was responsible for maintaining Reagan's regressive policies and also for a good deal of foot dragging around affirmative action and EEO. And Bush, like Reagan, also attempted to gut Executive Order 11246.

Perhaps the greatest impact of both Presidents Reagan and Bush has been felt in their appointments to the Supreme Court. Reagan's appointments of Sandra Day O'Connor[9] in 1981 and Antonin Scalia in 1986 have contributed to the Court's regressive rulings in terms of EEO and affirmative action. But Reagan's appointment of Anthony Kennedy in 1988, replacing Justice Lewis Powell (who was a crucial swing vote in a number of areas, including affirmative action), may have been the coup de grace.[10] Bush's appointment of Clarence Thomas in 1991 took the Court further to the right on EEO and affirmative action. (Bush's appointment of the moderate David Souter may have actually been a benefit for affirmative action, but one that will not be realized because, even with Clinton's appointments of Ruth Bader Ginsburg in 1993 and Stephen Breyer in 1994, there is no longer a majority or plurality of progressive justices who will cast favorable votes for EEO and affirmative action.) In the final analysis, given their appointments to the High Court as well as to the lower federal courts, Reagan and Bush were successful in eviscerating affirmative action and EEO. In short, since 1989 we have no longer been able to rely on the Court to provide legal justification for affirmative action or for the broad use of EEO.

THE ROLE OF THE COURT

One of the reasons affirmative action prevailed at least through 1989 is that Court majorities upheld its legality and constitutionality when certain criteria had been met.[11] Table 4.1 presents a snapshot of the rulings issued by the Supreme Court in terms of affirmative action from 1979 to 1987. As we can see, it is only in the area of layoffs that the Court has not permitted the use of affirmative action.

The 1987 *U.S. v. Paradise* decision, which upheld the use of affirmative action in the promotions of Alabama state troopers, represents virtually the last in a series of favorable Supreme Court rulings.[12] By 1989, when the next series of decisions was issued, the High Court not only abruptly shifted its position on affirmative action programs but also altered the contours of employment discrimination law in unfathomable ways.[13] Given the widespread ramifications of the Supreme Court's 1989 rulings, it would be useful to take a closer look at them.

TABLE 4.1. U.S. Supreme Court decisions on affirmative action, 1979–1987.

Case	Legality/Constitutionality of Affirmative Action in:		
	Hiring	*Promotions*	*Layoffs*
United Steelworkers v. Weber (1979) (Title VII)	YES*		
Memphis v. Stotts (1984) (Title VII)			NO
Wygant v. Jackson Bd. of Ed. (1986) (Fourteenth Amendment)			NO
Sheet Metal Workers' International Association v. EEOC (1986) (Title VII and Fifth Amendment)	YES**		
Int'l Assoc. of Firefighters v. City of Cleveland (1986) (Title VII)	YES	YES	
Johnson v. Transportation Agency, Santa Clara County (1987) (Title VII)		YES	
U.S. v. Paradise (1987) (Fourteenth Amendment)		YES	

*Involved selection of trainees for in-plant program.
**Involved recruitment, selection, training, and admission to union.

The U.S. Supreme Court's 1989 Decisions

The most perplexing decision issued by the Supreme Court was *Wards Cove v. Atonio,* which undercut the long-standing *Griggs v. Duke Power Co.* (1971) ruling. It may be recalled that out of the *Griggs* ruling came the concept of adverse impact, a statistical means for alleged victims of discrimination to establish a prima facie case of discrimination. Once adverse impact is established, the burden of proof shifts to the employer to demonstrate "business necessity" (i.e., that the employment tools resulting in statistical disparities or adverse impact are being used for legitimate business reasons). The *Griggs* decision not only made it less complicated for the alleged victims to show that their employer may have discriminated against them, but also encouraged employers to develop affirmative action programs in an effort to avoid costly EEO litigation. The *Wards Cove* decision abrogated the standards of law created by *Griggs.*

In *Wards Cove,* the Court ruled that statistical disparity or adverse impact was not sufficient to establish a prima facie case of employment discrimination. Instead, opined the *Wards Cove* Court, alleged victims of discrimination must show that the employment practices resulting in the disparities were being used, not out of business necessity but for illegal purposes. It was a sophisticated way of saying that the alleged victims would now need to show that the employer *intentionally* discriminated against them. This decision would not only create a chilling effect for employment discrimination suits but it would also encourage employers to weaken or gut their affirmative action efforts, since it would be extraordinarily difficult for alleged victims of discrimination to submit the necessary evidence to shift the burden of proof to their employers.

Other rulings were similarly mystifying. For example, in *Patterson v. McLean Credit Union* the Court majority ruled that a Reconstruction-era civil rights statute could be used to protect racial minorities from hiring discrimination but not from other forms of bias on the job (e.g., harassment). In so doing, the Court narrowed—some have said overturned—its *Runyon v. McCrary* (1976) decision, which held that Section 1981 of the Civil Rights Act of 1866 prohibits racial discrimination in the making and enforcement of private contracts.

In another 1989 ruling, *Martin v. Wilks,* the Court threatened the continued existence of affirmative action programs. In *Wilks* the Court held that white firefighters faced no time limitations in challenging affirmative action consent decrees approved by lower courts. In effect, this left open the possibility of an endless series of lawsuits challenging long-standing, court-approved affirmative action programs.

Interestingly enough, while the *Wilks* Court ruled there were no time limitations for white males in filing their lawsuits, the Court said in *Lorance v. AT&T* (a ruling issued the very same day as *Wilks*) that women challenging the legality of a seniority system must file suit within the first 300 days of the system's adoption. In *Lorance,* three women were promoted to the nontraditional job of "tester" at an AT&T plant. About a year after the first woman was promoted, the union and AT&T renegotiated the seniority provision for this particular job title. Seniority for testers would now be determined by time in the job title or position rather than by length of plantwide service. A few years later, an economic downturn forced the plant to make demotions. Because the women testers had the least amount of seniority based on the new time-in-position system, they were all demoted. (They would not have been demoted had the former plantwide seniority system been in place.) The women filed a lawsuit but were told by the Supreme Court that they didn't have a valid claim, because they hadn't filed their suit within 300 days of the new seniority system's adoption.

In short, by 1989 several Supreme Court rulings were issued which eviscerated affirmative action and EEO. One cogent explanation for this precipitous shift, as noted earlier, revolves around the changing composition of the Court. These 1989 decisions would comprise the current body of law around EEO and affirmative action had it not been for the Civil Rights Act of 1991.

THE ROLE OF THE LEGISLATIVE BRANCH

Like the other branches of government, Congress as a whole has been a long-time promoter of EEO and affirmative action.[14] Indeed, Congress could be relied on to maintain the policies' use when other branches of government began to retract their support and commitment. And the legislature's passage of the Civil Rights Act of 1991 was not the first instance in which Congress, in a separation of powers move, rebuffed the executive branch and slapped the Supreme Court's wrist for a negative ruling on affirmative action.

For example, in 1988 Congress enacted the Civil Rights Restoration Act, which overturned the Supreme Court's ruling in *Grove City College v. Terrel H. Bell* (1984). In this case, the Court ruled that the gender discrimination provisions of Title IX of the Education Amendments of 1972 applied *only* to the programs receiving federal financial assistance, and not to the entire educational institution. The 1988 Act restored the broad coverage of civil rights laws, making it clear that discrimination is prohibited throughout an entire organization or agency and not just in the program receiving federal assistance.

Enactment of this law also represented a defeat to the Reagan administration, which advanced arguments in *Grove City College* in favor of narrowing Title IX. Reagan also vetoed the four-year, bipartisan effort to enact the Restoration bill; instead, he proposed an alternative, watered-down bill. However, Congress voted by large margins to override the president's veto, thereby clearing the way for enactment of the Civil Rights Restoration Act.

The Court's 1989 rulings once again galvanized Congress into passing another civil rights act. After an earlier bill was vetoed by President Bush, the Civil Rights Act of 1991 was signed into law. Many members of Congress continued to oppose the law, however, arguing that its provision around goals was a subterfuge for "quotas" (Cayer, 1996). In fact, President Bush shared those views but signed the measure largely in response to concerns that a failure to

TABLE 4.2. The Civil Rights Act of 1991 overturns the U.S. Supreme Court's 1989 decisions.

Case	Supreme Court Ruling	Civil Rights Act of 1991
Wards Cove Packing Co. v. Atonio (Title VII)	Plaintiffs must show that adverse impact was intentional, i.e., that the employment practice resulting in disparities was used not out of business necessity, but for illegal reasons.	Plaintiffs required to demonstrate adverse impact. Employer must then "demonstrate that the challenged practice is job-related for the position in question and consistent with business necessity."
Patterson v. McLean Credit Union (42 USC Section 1981)	42 USC Section 1981 of the Civil Rights Act of 1866 is limited to hiring and some promotion decisions, but does not extend to harassment on the job, discriminatory firing, or other post-hiring conduct by the employer.	42 USC Section 1981 of the Civil Rights Act of 1866 covers all forms of racial bias in employment.
Martin v. Wilks (Title VII)	White male firefighters can challenge, without time limitations, affirmative action consent decrees settling employment discrimination dispute, even if they were not original parties to the consent decree.	The Act prohibits challenges to consent decrees by individuals who had reasonable opportunities to object to the decrees.
Lorance v. AT&T (Title VII)	Women challenging the legality of a collective bargaining seniority system must file suit within the first 300 days of the system's adoption.	Employees may challenge a seniority system when it affects them, as well as when the system is adopted.
Price Waterhouse v. Hopkins (Title VII)	In "mixed motive" cases (i.e., those where lawful and unlawful factors motivated the employment decision), the employer can avoid liability by demonstrating that the same action would have been taken without the discriminatory motive. The burden of proof rests with the employer.	*Any* intentional discrimination is unlawful, even if the same action would have been taken in the absence of the discriminatory motive.

SOURCE: Adapted from "Civil Rights Act of 1991: Text and Analysis." *Employment Guide,* Special Supplement 6, no. 23 (November 11, 1991): 5. Washington, D.C.: Bureau of National Affairs.

support it would hurt him in the 1992 presidential race. On November 21, 1991, the Civil Rights Act of 1991 went into effect.

As seen in Table 4.2, the Act overturned the 1989 Supreme Court decisions on EEO and affirmative action. There are several additional features of the Civil Rights Act, including the following:

- creates Glass Ceiling Commission to study the artificial barriers to the advancement of women and persons of color in the workplace;
- extends coverage of anti-discrimination laws (including the 1991 Act, the 1964 Civil Rights Act, the Age Discrimination in Employment Act of 1967, the Rehabilitation Act of 1973, and the Americans with Disabilities Act of 1990) to political employees in the executive branch and to employees of the Senate;
- allows compensatory and punitive damages to be recovered by victims of intentional discrimination based on gender, religion, or disability. (Previously, such damages were available only to racial and ethnic minorities.) Damages are capped—at $50,000 to $300,000, depending on the size of the employer—for cases of gender, religious, and disability discrimination only. This provision does not apply to government employers;
- extends protections of the Act and the Americans with Disabilities Act to U.S. citizens employed by U.S. companies abroad;[15]
- prohibits "race norming" of employment tests (i.e., score adjustments, use of different cutoff scores, or other alterations to the results of employment tests, on the basis of race, color, religion, gender, or national origin) ("Civil Rights Act of 1991," 1991).

In sum, the 1991 Civil Rights Act restored EEO and affirmative action to their pre-1989 legal status (see Table 4.1). However, the Supreme Court's actions in 1995—as well as the changing mood of Congress and the president, which mirror the shifting public debate over affirmative action—cast serious doubt on its future.

RECENT AFFIRMATIVE ACTION DEVELOPMENTS

A *Washington Post*-ABC News national poll conducted in March 1995 showed that Americans feel anger, ambivalence, and deep frustration around affirmative action. Of the 1,524 persons randomly selected to participate in the survey, three out of four said that they oppose affirmative action measures for persons of color, and about the same proportion said they oppose it for women as well. The survey found sharp schisms between African Americans and whites, and also within the races. For example, nearly half of all African Americans surveyed said they oppose affirmative action programs for people of color (Morin and Warden, 1995). The

American people, as seen by this survey as well as other indicators (e.g., the grass-roots movement in California discussed at the beginning of this chapter), are unwilling for a variety of reasons to support the continuation of affirmative action in employment, education, and the awarding of government contracts.

So, too, is the U.S. Supreme Court. In 1995 the Court issued a ruling that, once again, struck a blow to the use of affirmative action—this time in the form of set-asides, whereby the government requires or encourages a certain portion of federal contracting dollars to be earmarked or set aside for minority- or women-owned businesses. In *Adarand Constructors v. Peña, U.S. Secretary of Transportation,* a white contractor challenged the constitutionality of a federal program when he lost his bid to a Latino-owned company for a subcontract to build guardrails on a federal highway in Colorado. The program provided primary contractors with bonuses if they subcontracted some of the work to minority-owned businesses. The white contractor, whose bid was lower than that of the Latino-owned firm, claimed that the program amounted to "reverse discrimination."

The Court majority in *Adarand* issued a ruling that did not directly find the program to be unconstitutional but, rather, now subjects all federal affirmative action programs to very strict judicial inquiry. In the past, and in accordance with two previous Supreme Court decisions—*Fullilove v. Klutznick* (1980) and *Metro Broadcasting v. Federal Communications Commission* (1990)—the federal government was granted broad authority to develop affirmative action programs, particularly in the area of contracting or set-asides, and the programs were not subjected to the same "strict scrutiny" analysis that state and local governments have been held to in order to justify their affirmative action programs (e.g., see *Richmond v. Croson* 1989).[16] Strict scrutiny is a two-pronged test that asks: (1) whether there is a compelling governmental interest for the program (e.g., to redress past discrimination), and (2) whether the program is sufficiently narrowly tailored to meet its specified goals (e.g., whether there are alternative programs that could be employed that do not classify people by, for instance, race). The *Adarand* decision effectively overturns the *Fullilove* and *Metro Broadcasting* rulings.

Although the decision fell short of a finding that affirmative action in the form of set-asides can never be constitutionally justified,[17] the ruling may have the same effect in that it creates extraordinarily tough standards that even state and local governments have been hard-pressed to meet. The fate of the Colorado program, which will have resounding implications for all affirmative programs, now rests with the U.S. Court of Appeals for the Tenth Circuit, to which the case has been remanded. But notwithstanding the appellate court ruling, the Supreme Court's *Adarand* ruling, some have said, marks "the end of an era in affirmative action—or at least the beginning of the end" (Lewin, 1995: D25).

There were two additional legal developments in 1995 that represent a major legal setback for affirmative action. The Supreme Court let stand, without comment, two federal appeals decisions that struck down affirmative action programs. In one case, *In re Birmingham Reverse Discrimination Employment Litigation (BRDEL,* 1994), the U.S. Court of Appeals for the Eleventh Circuit invalidated a promotion plan aimed at promoting African-American firefighters to the position of lieutenant. In another case, *Claus v. Duquesne Light Company* (1994), the Third Circuit Court of Appeals awarded a white engineer for a utility company $425,000 in damages because, according to the court, he was "passed over" in favor of an African American for promotion to a managerial job (also see Greenhouse, 1995; Savage, 1995). Although the Court's refusal to accept an appeal does not constitute a judgment on the merits of a case, it certainly indicates that the Court is willing to rubber-stamp the ruling of appellate courts.

The Supreme Court's decision in *Adarand* and its refusal to grant certiorari to *BRDEL* and *Claus* do not completely abrogate the legal status of affirmative action as presented in Table 4.1. But these actions certainly do send a signal to the lower courts that affirmative action can be dismantled.

OUTLOOK FOR THE FUTURE

The American people's contentious attitudes toward EEO and affirmative action programs in recent years have left many personnelists and human resources specialists to wonder about the fate of their affirmative action programs. Likewise, the legacy of the Reagan and Bush years, the Supreme Court's 1989 and 1995 decisions on affirmative action and EEO, and now the conservative legislatures at the national and state levels of government suggest that some of the progress made around affirmative action—however large or small—will come to a screeching halt.

As discussed earlier in this chapter, since Reagan was elected president there has been a classic "separation of powers" treatment of affirmative action, with the end result generally being a favorable reaction by Congress. However, we have now arrived at a point in time where the political tides have turned against affirmative action in large part because it has become politically risky for Republicans as well as Democrats to support policies that American voters now vociferously oppose. Conservative Democrats, for example, have threatened to bolt from the party over the continued use of affirmative action because they believe it alienates a key voting bloc—the so-called "angry white male" (Yoachum and Freedberg, 1995). It is very unlikely, then, that Congress will counteract the Supreme Court's 1995 or even future decisions with amendments to the Civil Rights Act.

Likewise, a Democratic president has only cautiously and haltingly supported the continued use of affirmative action. He, too, risks the loss of conservative Democrats from his party. Although President Clinton's slogan for affirmative action came to be "mend it, but don't end it," he has taken a hard-line approach toward its continued use. For example, in 1996 he ordered the suspension of all federal set-aside programs for at least three years. In addition, after many months of studying affirmative action, his long-awaited affirmative action directive issued in 1995 to all federal departments and agencies merely called for additional studies. The directive may also ultimately lead to the elimination of programs that create "quotas" or "reverse discrimination," or that "continue after their purposes have been met" (Yoachum and Freedberg, 1995: A8). Clinton, it would seem, has also bought into the rhetoric of the "angry white male."

But even if the support from the executive branch were stronger, without backing from Congress or the High Court the continuation of affirmative action would still be precarious. The executive branch, on its own, may not have the necessary force to sustain affirmative action programs. This was evident during the Reagan administration, which had a difficult time getting its regressive policies past Congress or the Court.

It seems to be the case, as we move into the twenty-first century, that the system of law around affirmative action and EEO will continue to break down. Moreover, there is no longer a political consensus in support of affirmative action, which is the exact opposite of what the political environment was when affirmative action first emerged. In short, we will no longer see government-mandated affirmative action programs or the wide scope of employment discrimination law that existed in the past. Instead, we will see some public and private sector organizations developing diversity programs, which differ from affirmative action in scope, purpose, and stimulus (Klingner, 1997). As Dobrzynski (1995) points out, corporations are silently supporting diversity amidst a backlash toward affirmative action because they recognize the economic exigencies of doing so. Moreover, some government employers will voluntarily develop and also maintain diversity programs even in the wake of voter initiatives to end government-*mandated* affirmative action programs because of the changing demographics of the populations they serve (see Chapter 5 for a further discussion).

The quandary here, however, is that because the impetus for diversity programs hinges on social, demographic, and economic factors, commitment to diversity may be ephemeral. Specifically, without a legal catalyst, public and private sector organizations will have the power to promote diversity in their workplaces when it suits them, but completely disregard it when it doesn't. For example, those jurisdictions around the country that have experienced fewer demographic changes will have no incentive to promote diversity of any sort. In addition, there is no assurance that organizations will be concerned with diversity beyond the lower levels of the organization.

To be sure, the former affirmative action programs were never very successful in promoting women and people of color to the upper reaches of organizations (Guy, 1993; Rosenbloom, 1981), but they at least created some protections and opportunities for them to do so. With movements to downsize, rightsize, and flatten organizations, mid- and upper-level jobs are becoming more scarce. The question, then, remains: Will diversity efforts, in the absence of legal requirements, help move certain groups (e.g., women and people of color) out of the lower-level, low-paying jobs they have traditionally held? Or are the social and economic incentives enough to encourage employers to be more proactive around diversity? (Chapter 5 provides some answers to these questions.)

Finally, we cannot shift the debate away from affirmative action to diversity and expect workers and society in general to now be supportive. Despite efforts to portray diversity in broader terms, it is still largely seen in racial, ethnic, and gender terms; thus many persons and groups (e.g., unions, white men, and even white women) will continue to set up roadblocks, whether the efforts are labeled as diversity or affirmative action. Obviously, employers can work with their employees to help avoid such resistance and to help them understand the differences between the two concepts, but in the end some employees will view the "muscle" behind diversity efforts no differently from how it was viewed for affirmative action efforts.

In sum, the legal status of EEO and affirmative action will continue to erode as we move into the twenty-first century. Moreover, Congress and the president, because of the attitudes and beliefs of a large segment of the American populace, can no longer offer unconditional support for affirmative action. In light of these phenomena, personnelists, human resource specialists, and researchers are turning their attention toward workplace diversification endeavors, which seem to be the next stage in the evolutionary process of EEO (Klingner, 1997). As they do, careful attention should be paid to such issues as the purpose and scope of these programs, the manner in which they are implemented, whether they are effective in achieving their goals, and how they differ from previous affirmative action efforts. In this vein, the chapter that follows provides an exploratory assessment of the workings of a few diversity programs that have been developed by public and private sector organizations.

POSTSCRIPT

While this book was in press, the U.S. Supreme Court denied certiorari to an additional affirmative action case (see *State of Texas v. Hopwood,* 1996 WL 227009, July 1, 1996). In *Hopwood* the U.S. Court of Appeals for the Fifth Circuit struck down the constitutionality of an affirmative action program at the University of Texas Law School aimed at increasing the number of African-American and Mexican-American students (see appeals court ruling, 78 F.3d. 932, 5th Cir. 1996). The Supreme Court's refusal to hear the appeal lets the appellate court's ruling stand. The Court's action here is another indication of its lack of support for affirmative action.

NOTES

1. Initially, it appeared that insufficient signatures on petitions could have prevented the initiative from actually making it to the ballot. However, Governor Pete Wilson, the state Republican party, and the Republican national party took over the signature-gathering process to ensure that the petitions acquired the necessary number of signatures to make the November 1996 ballot. Also see Ayres (1995), who points out that some state legislatures, in response to pressures from civil rights and womens organizations, have been reluctant to eliminate affirmative action outright, but instead have taken an "amend it, don't end it" approach.

2. For example, Bob Dole and other Republican members of Congress have introduced bills to limit the use of affirmative action. Senator Dole and Representative Charles Canaday (R-Florida) have introduced the "Equal Opportunity Act of 1995," which would, among other things, prohibit preferential treatment on the basis of race, color, national origin, or gender in federal employment, contracts, and programs. Several other bills to limit the scope of affirmative action were introduced in Congress in 1995.

3. President Clinton's reforms are discussed later in the text.

4. It should be stressed that although they are conflated, affirmative action and diversity are not one and the same. Affirmative action may be *one* component in a diversity program and, as such, may be seen as a means to the end—diversity. But diversity differs from affirmative action in scope and purpose. See Klingner (1997) for further discussion of the differences.

5. The Rehabilitation Act of 1973 and the Americans with Disabilities Act of 1990 both define disability in terms of physical as well as mental impairments. See Chapter 9 in this volume for further discussion.

6. For a discussion of the *Bakke* decision, see Shafritz, Riccucci, Rosenbloom, and Hyde (1992).

7. This is not to say, of course, that all Democrats and all Republicans supported affirmative action.

8. However, see discussion later in text for examples of how the Reagan administration was able to weaken affirmative action.

9. Justice O'Connor's voting pattern on affirmative action cases has been completely inconsistent and, thus, unpredictable. For example, she supported affirmative action in the 1987 *Johnson v. Santa Clara County* decision but wrote the dissenting opinion in *U.S. v. Paradise* (see Table 4.1). In the 1986 *Sheet Metal Workers* case, Justice O'Connor concurred in part with the majority's support for affirmative action but also dissented in part. In 1989 she joined the majority in several regressive rulings, including *Wards Cove, Patterson v. McLean Credit Union,* and *Martin v. Wilks.*

10. In every one of the 1989 affirmative action or EEO cases, which are addressed later in the text, Justice Kennedy joined the conservative majority to strike down affirmative action or constrict employment discrimination law in favor of the employer.

11. An exception, as discussed later in the text, is the Court's 1984 *Grove City College v. Bell* decision. It should further be noted that most affirmative action decisions came from a divided Court.

12. It should be noted, however, that the Supreme Court, in its 1990 decision *Metro Broadcasting v. Federal Communications Commission,* upheld a "set-aside" program established by the federal government that sought to increase the number of broadcast licenses awarded to people of color. In 1995 this ruling was overturned by *Adarand Constructors v. Peña,* which is discussed later in the text.

13. The lower federal courts, to which Reagan had made many appointments (see Sullivan, 1989), may have also contributed to the backsliding of law around affirmative action and EEO. This chapter, however, solely addresses the impact of the Supreme Court.

14. This can be seen, for example, in the various laws enacted to protect or promote the employment of women, persons of color, and disabled persons.

15. This provision stems from the 1991 Supreme Court decision in *EEOC v. Aramco,* wherein the Court ruled that Title VII of the Civil Rights Act of 1964 did not apply outside the territorial jurisdiction of the United States. The 1991 Act overturned this

ruling by extending Title VII as well as Americans with Disabilities Act coverage to U.S. citizens employed by American companies abroad.

16. One might argue, however, that even though the strict scrutiny test was not explicitly applied in *Fullilove* and *Metro Broadcasting,* the Court nonetheless invoked the two criteria and applied a less rigorous test—which the Court later called *intermediate scrutiny.* See, for example, *Fullilove* (1980) at 451, and *Metro Broadcasting* (1990) at 548-549.

17. However, two members of the Court majority in *Adarand,* Justices Scalia and Thomas, wrote in separate opinions that affirmative action can never be justified.

REFERENCES

Adarand Constructors v. Peña, U.S. Secretary of Transportation, 1995 WL 347345 (1995).

Ayres, B. Drummond, Jr. 1995. "Efforts to End Job Preferences Are Faltering." *New York Times,* November 20: A1/B10.

Cayer, N. Joseph. 1996. *Public Personnel Administration in the United States,* 3rd ed. New York: St. Martin's Press.

"Civil Rights Act of 1991: Text and Analysis." *Employment Guide,* Special Supplement 6, no. 23 (November 11, 1991). Washington, D.C.: Bureau of National Affairs.

Claus v. Duquesne Light Company, 46 F. 3d 1115 (3rd Cir. 1994).

Cornwell, Christopher, and J. Edward Kellough. 1994. "Women and Minorities in Federal Government Agencies: Examining New Evidence from Panel Data." *Public Administration Review* 54, no. 3: 265-270.

Dobrzynski, Judith H. 1995. "Corporations Silently Support Affirmative Action amid a Backlash." *Albany Times Union,* April 20: C15.

"Equal Employment Panel Drops Numerical Goals as Bias Remedy." 1986. *New York Times,* February 12: A24.

Fullilove v. Klutznick, 448 U.S. 448 (1980).

Greenhouse, Linda. 1995. "Court Lets Stand Ruling That Found Plan on Bias Unfair." *New York Times,* April 18: A14.

Griggs v. Duke Power Co., 401 U.S. 424 (1971).

Grove City College v. Terrel H. Bell, 465 U.S. 555 (1984).

Guy, Mary E. 1993. "Three Steps Forward, Two Steps Backward: The Status of Women's Integration into Public Management." *Public Administration Review* 53, no. 4: 285-292.

In re Birmingham Reverse Discrimination Employment Litigation, 20 F. 3d 1525 (11th Cir. 1994).

International Association of Firefighters v. City of Cleveland, 478 U.S. 501 (1986).

Johnson v. Transportation Agency, Santa Clara County, 480 U.S. 616 (1987).

Kellough, J. Edward. 1997. "Affirmative Action," in Jay M. Shafritz, ed., *International Encyclopedia for Public Policy and Administration.* New York: Henry Holt.

Klingner, Donald E. 1997. "Work Force Diversity," in Jay M. Shafritz, ed., *International Encyclopedia for Public Policy and Administration.* New York: Henry Holt.

Lewin, Tamar. 1995. "5-4 Decision Buoys Some; For Others, It's a Setback." *New York Times,* June 13: D25.

Lorance v. AT&T, 490 U.S. 900 (1989).

Martin v. Wilks, 490 U.S. 755 (1989).

Memphis (& Firefighters of Local Union #1784) v. Stotts, 467 U.S. 561 (1984).

Metro Broadcasting v. Federal Communications Commission, 497 U.S. 547 (1990).

Morin, Richard, and Sharon Warden. 1995. "Affirmative Action Loses Popular Support, Survey Shows." *Albany Times Union,* March 24: A11.

Nalbandian, John, and Donald E. Klingner. 1987. "Conflict and Values in Public Personnel Administration." *Public Administration Quarterly* 11, no. 1: 17-33.

Patterson v. McLean Credit Union, 491 U.S. 164 (1989).

Price Waterhouse v. Hopkins, 490 U.S. 228 (1989).

Regents v. Bakke, 438 U.S. 265 (1978).

Riccucci, Norma M. 1991. "Affirmative Action in the Twenty-First Century: New Approaches and Developments," in Carolyn Ban and Norma M. Riccucci, eds., *Public Personnel Management: Current Concerns—Future Challenges,* pp. 89-99. White Plains, N.Y.: Longman.

Richmond v. Croson, 488 U.S. 469 (1989).

Rosenbloom, David H. 1977. *Federal Equal Employment Opportunity.* New York: Praeger Publishers.

———. 1981. "Federal Equal Employment Opportunity: Is Polarization Worth the Preference?" Southern Review of Public Administration 5, no. 1: 63-72.

Runyon v. McCrary, 427 U.S. 160 (1976).

Savage, David G. 1995. "High Court Actions Stir Controversy over Quotas." *Albany Times Union,* April 18: A6.

Shafritz, Jay M., Norma M. Riccucci, David H. Rosenbloom, and Albert C. Hyde. 1992. *Personnel Management in Government,* 4th ed. New York: Marcel Dekker.

Sheet Metal Workers' International Association v. EEOC, 478 U.S. 421 (1986).

Sullivan, Teresa. 1989. "Reagan Appointed 47% of the Federal Judiciary." *Chicago Daily Law Bulletin,* July 11: 1ff.

U.S. v. Paradise, 480 U.S. 149 (1987).

United Steelworkers of America v. Weber, 443 U.S. 193 (1979).

Wards Cove Packing Co. v. Atonio, 490 U.S. 642 (1989).

Wygant v. Jackson Board of Education, 476 U.S. 267 (1986).

Yoachum, Susan, and Louis Freedberg. 1995. "Clinton's Affirmative Action Risk." *San Francisco Chronicle,* July 19: A1/8.

chapter **5**

Models of Excellence
in Workplace Diversity

Tamu Chambers and Norma M. Riccucci

America's labor force is undergoing major demographic change. As a result of these shifts, public and private firms have launched a variety of diversity programs to prepare for "work force 2000" (Klingner, 1997; Golembiewski, 1995). For many private sector organizations, the incentives to embrace diversity measures also revolve around their desire to compete successfully in global markets and to attract customers beyond the suburbs.

Yet many of these diversity programs have been superficial or simply not funded at adequate levels (SHRM/CCH, 1993; Gard, 1994; Riccucci, 1997). For example, a survey of public and private sector human resources specialists, conducted by the Society for Human Resources Management and the Commerce Clearing House, revealed that over 70 percent of the diversity training programs offered by the survey participants' employers are one day or less in length. The survey concluded that this strategy results in the failure of diversity programs. In addition, some employers, including the federal government, have merely replaced the term *affirmative action* with *diversity,* without making significant substantive changes to their old affirmative action programs (Gard, 1994; USMSPB, 1993). These programs, too, are bound for failure.

On the other hand, however, there are some public and private sector employers that have made a serious commitment to workplace diversification. This chapter takes a closer look at three public sector employers that have taken a very proactive approach toward diversity. Given the notable gains made by some private sector organizations, the chapter also looks briefly at the efforts of two private firms that have also done so. We begin with a short discussion of the concept of diversity.

WHAT IS WORK-FORCE DIVERSITY?

As Klingner (1997) points out, the term *work-force diversity* refers to "the range of employee characteristics that are increasingly present in the contemporary work force of the United States and other developed countries." Diversity or diversification strategies, then, refer to those efforts to change the mission, culture, policies, and programs of an organization so that diversity is genuinely valued and embraced. The purpose ultimately is to enhance organizational effectiveness and productivity (Klingner, 1997). As noted, America's labor force has become increasingly diverse given the shifts in the nation's demography. This, in turn, has encouraged many public and private sector employers to develop workplace diversity strategies.

THE CHANGING DEMOGRAPHICS OF AMERICA'S LABOR FORCE

In 1987 the Hudson Institute published a report, *Workforce 2000* (Johnston and Packer, 1987), that predicted radical shifts in the demographic makeup of the American labor force. Although the initial estimates offered in this report may have been overstated (Victor, 1991), Tables 5.1, 5.2, and 5.3 show that the nation's labor force is becoming increasingly diverse.

As Table 5.1 indicates, America's work force is aging. The percentage of workers between age 16 and 34 continues to decrease steadily, whereas workers between age 35 and 54 increase their ranks in the work force. In addition, as seen in Table 5.2, America's work force is becoming more racially diverse. There will be a steady increase in persons of color through 2005 if the projections are correct, whereas the percentage of white males will continue to decline. In addition, immigrants will increase their share of jobs as we move into the twenty-first century. Although it is not shown in the tables here, Workforce 2000 projections indicate that immigrant men will represent 13 percent of the

TABLE 5.1   The aging work force, 1985, 1990, 1992, and projections for 2000 and 2005 (in percentages).

Age Group	1985	1990	1992	2000	2005
16–34	48.3	45.8	43.7	38.2	36.9
35–54	38.5	41.9	44.1	49.3	49.0
55+	13.2	12.3	12.2	12.5	14.1

SOURCE: Compiled from *Labor Force Statistics Derived from the Current Population Survey, 1948–1987* (Washington, D.C.: U.S. Department of Labor, Bureau of Labor Statistics, August 1988); *Outlook 1990–2005* (Washington, D.C.: U.S. Department of Labor, Bureau of Labor Statistics, May 1992); and *The American Work Force: 1992–2005* (Washington, D.C.: U.S. Department of Labor, Bureau of Labor Statistics, April 1994).

TABLE 5.2 Work force by race and ethnicity, 1985, 1990, 1992, and projections for 2000 and 2005 (in percentages).

Group	1985	1990	1992	2000	2005
African American	9.8	10.8	10.9	11.3	11.6
Latino	6.2*	7.7*	8.0	10.1	11.0
Asian and Other	2.8**	3.2	3.5	4.9	5.5
White	87.5	85.9	77.8	74.6	72.9

*Based on the Bureau of Labor Statistics calculations for this year, Latinos may be of any race; thus there is overlap with other racial/ethnic categories, and percentage totals will not equal 100.
**1986 calculation.
SOURCE: Compiled from *Labor Force Statistics Derived from the Current Population Survey, 1948–1987* (Washington, D.C.: U.S. Department of Labor, Bureau of Labor Statistics, August 1988); *Outlook 1990–2005* (Washington, D.C.: U.S. Department of Labor, Bureau of Labor Statistics, May 1992); and *The American Work Force: 1992–2005* (Washington, D.C.: U.S. Department of Labor, Bureau of Labor Statistics, April 1994).

TABLE 5.3 Women in the work force, 1980, 1986, 1990, 1992, and projections for 2000 and 2005.

	Women in Work Force (1,000)	Female Labor Force Participation Rate (%)	Female Share of Work Force (%)
1980	45,487	51.5	42.5
1986	52,414	55.3	44.4
1990	56,554	57.5	45.3
1992	57,798	57.8	45.5
2000	66,555	61.6	47.0
2005	71,798	63.2	47.7

SOURCE: Compiled from *Projections 2000* (Washington, D.C.: U.S. Department of Labor, Bureau of Labor Statistics, March 1988); *Outlook 1990–2005* (Washington, D.C.: U.S. Department of Labor, Bureau of Labor Statistics, May 1992); and *The American Work Force: 1992–2005* (Washington, D.C.: U.S. Department of Labor, Bureau of Labor Statistics, April 1994).

net new workers between 1985 to 2000, and immigrant women will represent 9 percent (Johnston and Packer, 1987). Finally, women's participation in the labor force continues to grow. Table 5.3 indicates that by 2005, women's share of the work force will be close to 50 percent. The demographic shifts vary by geographic location, so the changes may be more dramatic in some jurisdictions than others.

The shifts in America's labor force have encouraged some employers to seriously embrace diversity. What exactly do their programs look like? The following section takes a closer look at the operations of a handful of these programs.

FIVE SUCCESS STORIES IN PREPARING FOR DIVERSITY

We were interested in profiling employers that have gone beyond merely offering a "one-shot" diversity training program, or that have developed policies to curtail practices that are already outlawed by federal mandates (e.g., sexual harassment). Although such efforts are indeed important, we were looking for sustained, *institutionalized* efforts that seek to create positive change for the climate and culture of the organization, so that diversity is not just a program sponsored by the personnel department but a way of life for the entire organization.

We located the public sector employers through a variety of means, including a review of the literature and contacts with representatives from such organizations as the National League of Cities (NLC), the International City Management Association (ICMA), the International Personnel Management Association (IPMA), and the Society for Human Resources Management (SHRM). In addition, we surveyed diversity consultants nationwide to ascertain those public employers that could serve as "models" of excellence. Our search produced a short list—a total of eight local government employers.[1] In fact, we were told by many of the diversity consultants that comprehensive, large-scale diversity initiatives are more popular in the private sector primarily because private companies can afford the costs of such efforts. Even though some public sector employers may be committed to broad diversity efforts, dwindling budgets and taxpayers' never-ending demands for less government—but more services—often prevent government employers from expending large sums of money on diversity efforts. Of course, some governments may simply not be willing to invest in diversity efforts, even if they had the financial capability. In any event, we profile three of the government employers identified by our search that can be held up as models of excellence. For the sake of comparison, we also look at the diversity experiences of two private sector firms.[2] As we will see, there are many similarities in the five diversity programs.

City of Santa Ana, California

The City of Santa Ana is one of the most diverse communities in California. Close to 75 percent of its total population, which hovers around 300,000, is comprised of people of color. Almost 62 percent of the population is Latino, 9.1 percent is Asian, 2.2 percent is African American, 0.3 percent is Native American, and 23.1 percent is white. Also, the city's immigrant or foreign-born population, which is included in these statistics, is very high. The Latino population in Santa Ana, for example, is mostly foreign born. In the city's efforts to better serve this diverse community, it has developed a work force that reflects the social composition of the city.

It was around 1989 that Santa Ana embarked on a TQM initiative—called Total Quality Service—to improve the quality of services to its residents. Given its very heterogeneous population, the city (in particular the city manager, David

Ream), believed that the best way to accomplish this was to create a demographically diverse work force. So, shortly afterwards, under the leadership of Ream, it launched the Employment Outreach Program (EOP) aimed at promoting and valuing diversity throughout the city's entire work force. As explained by Kermit Francis (1995), the city's executive director of personnel, the primary goal of the program is to "develop a work force that is reflective and representative of the community." To be sure, a diverse work force does not necessarily ensure that the city's diverse population will be better served. But city officials maintain that it does increase its probability (Ream, 1992). In fact, as Francis notes, the city believes that the EOP has improved the delivery of quality services to its community, in large part because it has fostered *cultural sensitivity* inside and outside of the workplace (also see Ream, 1992).[3]

The centerpiece of the EOP rests in the bona fide occupational qualification, or BFOQ, theory. Because a vast majority of the city's residents are bilingual, a BFOQ for many jobs throughout all departments is the ability to speak Spanish or an Asian language such as Vietnamese. Setting bilingual capability as a BFOQ has greatly helped the city in reaching its diversity goals.

The program works as follows. Each department in the city is required to develop outreach plans. These plans are created by a team of employees within each department and with the assistance of Francis and his staff in the personnel department. This team determines the outreach priority for various departmental jobs by comparing the existing diversity within job categories throughout every level of the department with the diversity levels of the city at large (Ream, 1992). When a job opening occurs, the department is prepared to target specific ethnic or gender groups. Strong efforts are made to target young persons and encourage them to seek careers in city government service. This entails, for example, the use of internships as well as partnerships with schools, both of which seek to improve the image of government service (Farr, 1992; Ream, 1992). Through very aggressive recruitment, the city is able to create a pool of applicants for the job opening. It is important to note that because the recruitment efforts target persons who will meet designated entry requirements and are sure to be competitive in passing an oral or a written exam, the city has been successful in hiring persons of color without facing fallacious claims that "standards have been lowered" or that "reverse discrimination" is occurring.

Also key to the program's success is its emphasis on accountability. In a manner similar to an MBO system, the program requires department heads to sit down with the city manager on an annual basis and develop a written contract, based on the outreach plans, that outlines the departments' goals for achieving diversity.[4] At the end of the year the department heads' performance is evaluated on a number of criteria, one being whether the diversity goals of the department were met. Department heads evaluate their supervisory staff along the same lines. Ultimately, raises are linked to whether the diversity goals have been met (Farr, 1992).

Another critical feature of the program is ongoing training for managers, supervisors, and rank-and-file employees to help them understand, accept, and value diversity. The culture of the government work force is one in which diversity is a priority of the city. As Francis (1995) notes, "developing and maintaining a culturally diverse work force continues to be one of the highest priorities of the city . . . and our commitment to it has never been diminished by other important goals of the city." Thus training is offered to make clear to city employees that diversity is not just a fad but an important *way of life* in the workplace. Mr. Francis further notes that the training has minimized city employees' resistance to diversity efforts.

Francis points out that the EOP has led to improved services to the city's residents, who, as noted earlier, are largely minority or immigrant. He notes that the positive feedback from citizens and the accompanying press are indicators that interactions with the citizenry, including the delivery of services, have improved. The efforts have been successful citywide, but particularly in police work, firefighting, recreation, community development and services, library services, code enforcement, and economic development (Ream, 1992). The city manager points out that:

> We value Hispanic police officers, for example, because of their insight and ability to communicate effectively with the Hispanic residents and business community. Another special need caused by diversity . . . is people with bilingual abilities. Whether the city is investigating a crime or helping a patron use the library, city employees with bilingual skills are essential in providing quality services. (Ream, 1992: 19)

Figure 5.1 shows that persons of color have increased their share of new city jobs since the EOP was instituted in 1990. In 1993, for example, 82 percent of the new hires were people of color. In addition, as Table 5.4 (p. 80) shows, people of color (in particular Latinos) have increased their ranks at all levels. These gains comport with the city's efforts to establish a work force that is representative of its population, which is comprised largely of Latinos.

It should also be noted that whites continue to overwhelmingly dominate the highest job category of official/administrator. Because of low turnover in these positions, it has been difficult for the city to move people of color upward into the higher ranks. However, because the city's diversity efforts have brought in predominantly young persons, there will be considerable opportunities for them to move upward in the organization over the next five to ten years (Mouet, 1995). In addition, the city has made a special effort to retain people of color during periods of layoffs.[5] In particular, the BFOQ strategy has enabled the city to retain persons with bilingual skills.

Finally, it is worth noting that improved service is not the only benefit resulting from the city's diversity efforts. Another has been the promotion of racial and ethnic harmony in the city. As the city manager notes, "An ethnically diverse local government workforce helps residents to feel that their unique needs are understood and served in a professional manner" (Ream, 1992: 19).

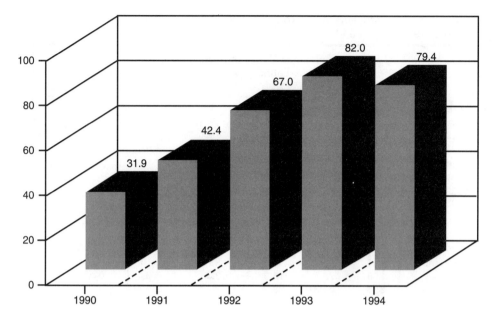

FIGURE 5.1   City of Santa Ana, new hires based on race and ethnicity, 1990–1994.

SOURCE: City of Santa Ana, Personnel Department.

City of San Diego, California

In 1990 the City of San Diego began moving away from traditional affirmative action programs and launched "Diversity Commitment," a series of ongoing efforts aimed at bringing about institutional changes that would foster diversity in the city's work force. The program was largely the brainchild of then assistant city manager Jack McGrory, who developed Diversity Commitment in response to the demographic shifts that were under way in San Diego (Ossolinski, 1992). McGrory, who is currently the city manager, continues to be the driving force behind Diversity Commitment and, in fact, has placed it at the top of the city's agenda for the past five years.[6]

As Danelle Scarborough (1995), one of the overseers and managers of Diversity Commitment, has said, the overall purpose of the program is to

> create an environment where differences are valued and at the same time, all city employees are part of a high performance team delivering quality services to the community. . . . Diversity Commitment is driven by business interests in the sense that the city could be more effective in delivering services to a diverse population if the city's work force were representative of that population.

TABLE 5.4 City of Santa Ana, work force diversity by total work force and by job category, 1989 and 1994.*

	TOTAL	White (%)	Latino (%)	African American (%)	Asian (%)	American Indian (%)	Women (%)
TOTAL, Citywide							
1989	1527	62.4	28.0	4.2	5.0	0.4	30.2
1994	1530	56.9	34.0	4.2	4.6	0.3	30.1
Officials/ Administrators							
1989	63	76.1	10.4	6.0	7.5	0	26.9
1994	64	71.9	10.9	6.3	10.9	0	31.3
Professionals							
1989	168	70.5	12.9	5.5	11.0	0.1	39.3
1994	165	66.7	15.8	4.2	13.3	0	41.2
Technicians							
1989	338	72.5	18.9	3.3	5.3	0	16.9
1994	356	64.3	29.2	3.7	2.8	0	24.2
Protective Services							
1989	389	66.4	28.9	2.8	1.8	0.1	5.1
1994	436	61.9	33.0	2.8	1.8	0.5	3.7
Paraprofessionals							
1989	111	54.9	32.4	7.2	5.4	0.1	60.4
1994	73	38.4	46.6	6.8	8.2	0	72.6
Administrative Support							
1989	267	57.9	31.1	4.5	6.4	0.1	87.6
1994	252	52.0	37.7	5.2	4.8	0.4	85.3
Skilled Craft							
1989	71	47.6	44.8	4.5	3.0	0.1	0
1994	65	38.5	52.3	4.6	1.5	1.5	0
Service/ Maintenance							
1989	120	31.5	59.7	5.6	3.2	0	2.4
1994	119	26.1	63.9	5.9	4.2	0	2.5

*A breakdown of the city's work force by immigrant or foreign-born status is not available.
SOURCE: City of Santa Ana, Personnel Department.

Diversity Commitment is an organizational development (OD) approach to bringing about systemic change to the culture of the city's work force. That is to say, planned, careful intervention into the city's institutional framework through strategic planning, policy change, and the training and education of employees has been the method for advancing diversity in the city. But more than this, the OD approach, as Scarborough notes, has made diversity a way of life in the city, in every department, at every level, from the top of the organization to the bottom, at the front line and beyond. Moreover, because Diversity Commitment is decentralized, department and division heads are ultimately accountable to the city manager for the attainment of the city's goals.

San Diego's diversity program encompasses a commitment to recruitment, hiring, and promotion. For example, the city continues to use entrance exams, but by recruiting diverse applicant pools and then "coaching" applicants, the city has been successful in promoting diversity in its hiring decisions. In addition, the city has instituted policy changes that have ensured upward mobility for women and people of color. For example, the city requires promotion panels to themselves be comprised of a broad array of employees. Second, recognizing that candidates for promotion can sometimes "choke" during an interview, the promotion decision is no longer based solely on the oral interview but also considers such indicators as past performance and potential for future performance at a higher-level job.

The city also seeks to maintain diversity during economic downturns, which invariably force some layoffs. Scarborough points out that the city has strong employee unions that will not budge on the issue of seniority; but she further notes that because the work force has become so diverse over time, some layoffs have not negatively affected the overall representation of diverse groups in the city's work force.

Scarborough adds that the attitudes of unions reflect those of white male workers, who have demonstrated a good deal of resistance to the city's diversity efforts. But the city, through ongoing training, education, and development, has been able to avert the effects of this resistance. She said that "the city promotes a policy of inclusion, where *all* voices are heard, and so an effective way to deal with resistance has been to create ongoing dialogues where employees and trained experts come together to process concerns and fears."

Scarborough also notes that the Latino, African-American, and gay and lesbian advocacy groups that were formed as the city's work force became more diverse have been an important voice in the conduct of city affairs and serve to demonstrate to white employees as well as to unions that diversity is the way of life in San Diego; it is a reality of working for the city.

How effective has Diversity Commitment been? One indication of its success can be seen in Table 5.5. Women and people of color have experienced some gains in several job categories over the past few years, particularly in the traditionally white male job category of police manager.

It should be stressed, however, that although the city recognizes the importance of such employment statistics, it maintains that placing too much emphasis on "the numbers" results in all the trappings and problems encountered with old affirmative action programs. So, as Scarborough points out, the city relies on other measures as well. For example, another way in which the city has measured the effectiveness of the program is to track grievances and lawsuits based on such factors as race, gender, ability, and so forth. The city found that since Diversity Commitment was instituted, the number of lawsuits filed against the city has decreased substantially. And, it is interesting to note,

TABLE 5.5 City of San Diego, work-force diversity by total work force and selected job category, 1992 and 1994 (in percentages).*

	White	Latino	African American	Asian	Filipino	American Indian	Women
TOTAL, Citywide							
1992	61.3	15.7	15.6	3.4	3.1	0.9	32.7
1994	59.9	16.1	15.3	3.7	3.4	0.9	33.1
Managers/ Administrators							
1992	78.5	10.2	9.7	1.1	0.5	0	29.6
1994	76.7	7.9	12.4	2.0	0.5	0	31.7
Professional/ Technical							
1992	65.4	12.5	12.5	5.2	3.5	0.9	42.0
1994	63.6	13.2	11.4	5.7	4.2	0.8	42.6
Clerical							
1992	55.0	15.1	18.4	4.4	6.0	1.1	80.2
1994	53.2	15.4	19.0	3.9	6.3	1.2	79.3
Crafts							
1992	66.0	15.1	12.6	2.3	3.2	0.8	5.0
1994	62.5	15.6	13.4	2.1	3.6	0.8	5.9
Fire Managers							
1992	80.0	8.6	11.4	0	0	0	5.7
1994	75.0	15.6	9.4	0	0	0	6.3
Fire Fighters							
1992	66.7	14.8	9.5	4.9	2.5	1.6	13.9
1994	66.3	14.6	9.8	5.0	2.6	1.7	13.6
Police Managers							
1992	84.8	3.8	3.8	3.8	0	3.8	15.4
1994	71.4	9.5	9.5	4.8	0	4.8	23.8
Police Officers							
1992	74.3	12.4	8.0	2.7	1.8	0.8	13.9
1994	72.1	13.7	8.2	3.2	1.9	0.8	14.3
Service Workers							
1992	11.0	43.0	38.8	1.2	4.8	1.2	27.9
1994	11.2	42.4	38.4	0.8	5.6	1.6	28.0

*Breakdown by race and ethnicity is not available before 1992. Percentages are available for "total minority" only.
SOURCE: Compiled from data provided by the City of San Diego.

internal grievances have increased, which the city takes as an indicator that the training and educational efforts around diversity are working—that is, that the efforts have heightened employees' expectations to be treated fairly and with dignity.

Finally, Scarborough states that San Diego would maintain Diversity Commitment even if the California voter initiative to end the use of affirmative action passes (see Chapter 4 in this volume). She says that the initiative would simply eliminate government-mandated affirmative action programs but would not prevent local governments from voluntarily developing new, or maintaining existing, diversity programs.

City of Seattle, Washington

The city of Seattle has had a long-standing commitment to diversity. In fact, since the early 1980s, when Seattle was undergoing significant demographic shifts, the city has attempted to create a work force that would be representative of the city at large. But it was at the beginning of the 1990s, just after Norman Rice, an African American, was elected mayor, that diversity efforts went well beyond traditional affirmative action programs and were linked to cultural and institutional changes in the city. The city's diversity coordinator, Joanne Anton (1995), notes that

> diversity efforts would not only be long-term, sustainable ones but they would be part of the city's corporate culture . . . they would be integrated into the "psyche" of the city and its work force. . . . Diversity efforts must be given priority status and actively reinforced by top-level officials to be successful and to be credible in the eyes of employees.

Anton added that the success of Seattle's programs is largely due to the mayor's strong commitment to diversity as a cornerstone of his administration and his insistence that department heads actively support diversity initiatives.

The diversity efforts of Seattle are multifold. First, the city designed a comprehensive two-day diversity training program that was mandatory for all supervisory and management staff. Second, each city department was required to develop a diversity plan drafted by human resource managers, EEO officers, and departmental diversity committees.[7] Like the Santa Ana and San Diego programs, the key here was to decentralize the operations as much as possible so that the diversity efforts would not be mandated from the mayor's office. This, according to city officials, would give departments more flexibility and control over diversity initiatives and, as such, lead to less resistance.

Seattle, like Santa Ana and San Diego, has encountered resistance from white employees but has avoided serious problems because of its strong emphasis on diversity training, whereby employees learn how to work in a heterogeneous environment. Anton points out that diversity is not warmed over affirmative action, it's a *business* issue . . . not a racial or gender issue with a business concern on the side, but a *business* issue that deals with inclusion of *all* people. Diversity is a necessary, prudent response to the city's demographic changes.

Indeed, Anton notes, the city has worked hard with its employees via training and other means not only to instill a value in terms of diversity but also to clarify the distinctions between EEO, affirmative action, and managing diversity. Whereas diversity is separate and distinct from EEO and affirmative action, the city stresses the importance of understanding the common ground and connections they share. Table 5.6 highlights how the city distinguishes among EEO, affirmative action, and managing diversity.

As Table 5.6 shows, there are some similarities between and among the concepts; but an important distinction to the city is that diversity is voluntary and proactive, and is viewed as the next logical step in successfully *managing* an integrated work force.

It is also important to note that the city's diversity efforts go beyond recruitment and hiring to include training, mentoring, promotion, and retention. And the city has been successful in all categories for a variety of reasons. For example, other than the uniformed services, the city has abolished the use of civil service exams for hiring. Moreover, once a person is hired, the city diligently attempts to avert a sink-or-swim situation by providing the training and mentoring

TABLE 5.6 Differences between EEO, affirmative action, and managing diversity.

EEO	Affirmative Action	Managing Diversity
• A business issue	• A business issue	• A business issue
• Mandated by federal legislation & city policy	• Mandated by executive order and city policy	• Voluntary, proactive tool to benefit all employees
• Ensures EEO for all employees and potential employees	• Requires long-range planning, recruiting, goal setting, staff development	• Recognizes and utilizes individual differences in working and learning styles
• Compliance with law	• Voluntarily develop goals to comply with law	• Not mandated by law; proactive
• Necessitated by a past history of discrimination	• Necessitated by a past history of discrimination	• Organization views differences as an asset
Outcome:	*Outcome:*	*Outcome:*
To provide a workplace free of discrimination and to guarantee the right of equal opportunity for all	To remedy past practices of discrimination	To contribute to productivity and quality work; support workplace equity; improve customer service; contribute to organizational success

SOURCE: City of Seattle.

that new hires need to perform well on the job. Diversity training for employees further ensures a supportive work environment for everyone. In addition, as Anton notes, "upward mobility is a citywide imperative." Department heads are accountable to the mayor for ensuring that diversity exists throughout the department, not simply at the bottom of the organizational structure.

Also, unions have in general supported diversity initiatives. Anton notes that unions have been cooperative because they, too, recognize the realities of a changing work force.

The city has also developed an internal program, "project hire," which helps those city employees targeted for layoffs to retool for jobs in other city departments. In this sense, the city is constantly tracking all its employees and looking out for their best interests. Anton notes that out-placement services to help employees find employment other than with the city would be ideal but are cost prohibitive.

The city has not yet developed formal measures to evaluate the success of its diversity efforts. City officials, like those in San Diego, have said that measurement presents a conundrum of sorts. As Anton observes, "How do we measure the sense of worth and well-being that employees now feel as a result of the program? Some of the outcomes of our diversity programs are simply not quantifiable." With the implementation of a new Human Resource Information System currently in development, the city will seek to identify means of meaningful measurement.

In the meantime, the city has looked for other creative ways to evaluate the effectiveness of its diversity programs. For example, in early 1994 the city established an awards ceremony to honor employees for distinctive accomplishments around diversity. In one case, two police captains received awards; they were nominated by one of the female lieutenants in the police department for creating a safe, non-hostile environment for women police officers. In fact these two police captains, who are white males, created the opportunities for women to advance upward in the police department. In another case, park employees who are responsible for cleaning parks were honored for their efforts to assist homeless families and individuals. Instead of turning their backs on the homeless, a group of these park employees reached out to them. The employees were successful in developing linkages with social services agencies to provide these persons and families with food and shelter.

Of course, as the city recognizes, another way to look at the potential effectiveness of the diversity programs is to examine whether the city's work force has become diverse as a result of *both* successful affirmative action efforts and diversity initiatives. Recognizing that other factors may impinge on changes in work-force demographics, Table 5.7 illustrates, for example, that people of color increased their ranks in virtually all job categories from 1989 to 1995. African Americans and Asians, as well as women, made important gains in the highest job category, manager/administrator, and also the job categories of protective services and skilled craft, which have traditionally been dominated by white males. In sum, the "numbers" are viewed as a partial indicator that Seattle's diversity program, in tandem with affirmative action, is working.

TABLE 5.7 City of Seattle, work-force diversity by total work force and selected job category, 1989 and 1995 (in percentages).

	White	Latino	African American	Asian	American Indian	Persons with Disabilities	Women
TOTAL, Citywide							
1989	72.0	3.5	11.5	10.9	2.2	3.6	40.3
1995	67.9	3.9	13.0	13.0	2.2	3.8	39.2
Managers/ Administrators							
1989	81.4	1.2	8.7	8.7	0	1.2	27.9
1995	70.9	1.3	15.8	10.8	1.3	1.3	37.3
Professionals							
1989	73.8	2.8	9.3	12.9	1.3	3.4	49.9
1995	70.3	3.4	10.1	15.0	1.2	4.1	48.3
Technicians							
1989	80.0	2.7	7.2	8.4	1.8	3.3	21.6
1995	74.7	2.7	8.6	11.7	2.2	3.6	25.0
Protective Services							
1989	80.1	2.4	9.9	5.8	1.7	0.7	9.1
1995	76.1	3.8	11.1	7.2	1.7	0.3	11.7
Para- professionals							
1989	65.4	5.2	17.1	10.0	2.2	3.0	62.5
1995	62.7	6.7	18.3	9.5	2.8	3.6	63.9
Office and Clerical							
1989	60.5	4.5	16.2	15.9	3.0	4.5	80.4
1995	54.3	4.7	19.3	19.1	2.5	5.1	79.6
Skilled Craft							
1989	78.9	3.3	7.0	8.3	2.5	4.6	11.7
1995	73.9	4.2	9.1	10.0	2.7	4.6	12.6
Service and Maintenance							
1989	65.6	5.1	15.9	9.8	3.7	5.8	30.6
1995	61.9	4.7	17.4	12.6	3.4	5.8	29.0

SOURCE: City of Seattle, Personnel Department.

Private Sector Experiences with Diversity

We looked at two private sector firms that have been identified as having a strong commitment to diversity. They are *Owens-Corning*—headquartered in Toledo, Ohio, and the world's leader in the production of advanced glass and composites materials; and *Niagara Mohawk Power Corporation* (NiMo)— headquartered in Syracuse, New York, supplying gas and electricity to a large area of upstate New York and parts of southern Ontario. Although we initially expected to find notable differences between the public and private sector diversity programs (e.g., because of differences in the availability of resources), we discovered in fact that the programs were very similar.

For example, both Owens-Corning and NiMo are interested in diversity measures to better serve their diverse clienteles. Similar to the city governments we profiled, they view diversity as a "bottom-line" business issue, one where gaining a competitive advantage is key. As Owens-Corning's chief executive officer (CEO) and chair, Glen Hiner, says, "We want to be a company that attracts and retains the very best people. If we don't have a culture that embraces diversity, then it is impossible for us to attract and retain the very best. It is just that simple."

In addition, both Owens-Corning and NiMo have a top-down management philosophy with respect to diversity, whereby commitment and leadership start at the top. Managers are then responsible for translating the broad policy objectives into workable measures and attainable goals. Also, both firms have MBO-type evaluation systems that hold managers accountable for reaching the established diversity goals.

Also, ongoing training programs are a key component of Owens-Corning's and NiMo's diversity efforts; and all employees, including senior managers, are required to participate. Both firms also have Diversity Councils, which oversee the training programs and other features of the firms' overall diversity strategies.

Both companies track the social representation of their work forces as one indicator of whether their diversity programs are working. However, neither company was able to provide substantial statistical data on social representation. For example, a NiMo representative was only able to state that its current work force consists of approximately 8,800 full-time employees, of which 18 percent are women and 7.5 percent are people of color. Similarly, Owens-Corning was able to furnish data on its salaried employees and vice presidents for 1995 only. (See Table 5.8 for the breakdown.)

In sum, the diversity programs embraced by the private sector companies we studied are very similar to the programs of the public sector employers.

TABLE 5.8 Owens-Corning (North America), diversity by salaried employees and vice-presidents, 1995.

	TOTAL	White Males (%)	White Females (%)	Men of Color (%)	Women of Color (%)
Salaried Employees	3,989	66.3	25.9	4.9	2.9
Vice-Presidents	50	94.0	6.0	0	0

SOURCE: Interview with representative from Owens-Corning.

SUMMARY AND CONCLUSIONS: WHAT ARE SOME OF THE INGREDIENTS TO SUCCESSFUL DIVERSITY PROGRAMS?

As we see from the descriptions of the five programs presented above, there are some commonalities to the development of effective diversity programs. First, all the programs were ongoing, long-term, institutionalized efforts to bring about change in the culture, mission, and structure of the organizations. One common feature was ongoing training and educational programs. Such programs are viewed as critical because, unlike legislative and judicial mandates, they are aimed at changing not only behaviors around diversity but *attitudes* as well. This is key if programs aimed at promoting and managing diversity are to be successful.

Second, all programs benefited from strong leadership. In the case of the public employers, city managers (San Diego and Santa Ana) or the mayor (Seattle) provided the leadership and vision to ensure success. For the private sector firms, it was the CEOs. And interestingly enough, these leaders in almost every case were not persons of color. The mayor of Seattle is African American, but the city managers in both San Diego and Santa Ana are white males. The CEOs for Owens-Corning and Niagara Mohawk are both white males. It must be stressed, however, that the *teams* running all the programs profiled here are diverse.

Another factor contributing to the success of the diversity programs is resource commitment. In every one of the five cases presented above, the organizations ensured that resources were available to run the programs, even during times of fiscal stress.

Also, all the employers recognize the business necessities of a diverse work force—remaining competitive, developing the ability to hire quality workers, and improving the effectiveness of service delivery. It is a "bottom-line" issue for most, driven by economics. For example, as we saw in the case of every employer, a primary motivating force for the diversity program was better serving a diverse population, be it through a TQM, OD, or other approach. For the public employers, the goal is a "representative bureaucracy," organization-wide or at the upper levels (see Krislov and Rosenbloom, 1981; Mosher, 1982; Meier, 1993). For the private sector employers a representative work force, reflecting the diversity in the business or customer community, is viewed as the sine qua non to achieving a competitive advantage in the marketplace.

In addition, the public and private sector officials view diversity differently from affirmative action. Diversity is seen as a way of life, not just a method for increasing the representation of women and people of color. Scarborough (1995) from San Diego sums it up in this fashion: "We are concerned with institutionalizing a set of core norms or values that fosters an environment where all people are respected and treated with dignity."

Yet, interestingly enough, some of the programs bear a resemblance to previous affirmative action efforts (e.g., in the case of Santa Ana). What sets the new diversity programs apart in every case, however, is (1) striving to change the culture of the organization so that diversity is a "way of life"; (2) holding managers accountable for the attainment of diversity goals; (3) ongoing multicultural training to instill a value around diversity; (4) serious efforts to target persons of color who will meet entry requirements; (5) coaching; and (6) a commitment to keep the programs on the front burner when other important concerns emerge.

It should further be noted that despite the tendency of the public and private sector officials to downplay "the numbers," organizations continue to look at the demographic makeup of their work forces as one indicator of successful diversity strategies. Similarly, researchers and other "outside" analysts will continue to have an interest in whether diversity programs, in conjunction with affirmative action, are indeed resulting in greater diversity. One reason for monitoring the numbers is that for now, they provide a hard measure of success. Of course, a notable flaw in the way in which the numbers are monitored is that they tend to focus almost exclusively on the old affirmative action categories of race, gender, and sometimes disability rather than the broader categories embraced by diversity initiatives (e.g., parental and marital status, sexual orientation, age, religion, nationality, and so forth).[8]

Although we can't generalize from the small set of programs profiled here, we can state that some public and private sector employers, including those presented in this chapter, have genuinely embraced diversity measures. In the wake of calls to dismantle affirmative action programs at every level of government, as discussed in Chapter 4, the importance of diversity efforts becomes amplified.

NOTES

1. Readers should bear in mind that our study is exploratory in nature and that our search for employers may not have been completely exhaustive. As such, there may be many other government employers that could serve as models of excellence around diversity.
2. Publicity around private firms' experiences with diversity helped in our identification and selection of the two private sector employers.
3. This statement is based on the observations of city officials. Neither the city nor this study attempts to examine the theory of active representativeness (see Mosher, 1982; Krislov and Rosenbloom, 1981).
4. Santa Ana has a council-manager form of government, so the city manager as compared to the mayor assumes great responsibility over all city programs. The mayor of the city, Miguel Pulido, is very supportive of the city's diversity program but has little control over its operation.
5. No data could be provided on racial, ethnic, or gender makeup of layoffs (Mouet, 1995).
6. It is worth noting that San Diego has a council-manager form of government, so the city manager as opposed to the mayor has the authority needed to institute, along with the city council, such programs as Diversity Commitment, and can do so without resistance from the mayor. This is critical because Susan Golding, the current mayor of San Diego, who is Republican, has offered only tacit support for the program (i.e., in the form of budget allocations to fund Diversity Commitment).

7. In large and mid-sized departments, these committees, comprised of employees from all levels of responsibility within the department, were established to address diversity issues and develop recommendations for initiatives unique to the department.
8. Of course, part of the reason for focusing on race, gender, and ethnicity is that this type of demographic information is more readily available or provided by employees. Information on sexual orientation, religion, and other factors may be more difficult to collect.

REFERENCES

Anton, Joanne. 1995. Diversity Coordinator, City of Seattle, Washington. Personal Interview (May 19).

Farr, Cheryl. 1992. "Building and Supporting a Multicultural Workforce." *Public Management* (February): 20-26.

Francis, Kermit. 1995. Executive Director of Personnel, City of Santa Ana, California. Personal Interview (May 4).

Gard, Karen K. 1994. "MSPB Reevaluates Workforce 2000 for the 1990s." *Public Administration Times,* February 1: 1 and 13.

Golembiewski, Robert T. 1995. *Managing Diversity in Organizations.* Tuscaloosa: University of Alabama Press.

Johnston, William B., and Arnold H. Packer. 1987. *Workforce 2000.* Indianapolis, Ind.: Hudson Institute.

Klingner, Donald E. 1997. "Work Force Diversity," in Jay M. Shafritz, ed., *International Encyclopedia of Public Policy and Administration.* New York: Henry Holt.

Krislov, Samuel, and David H. Rosenbloom. 1981. *Representative Bureaucracy and the American Political System.* New York: Praeger Publishers.

Littlejohn, Melanie. 1995. Diversity Manager of Diversity Management and Compliance, Niagara Mohawk Power Company, Syracuse, N.Y. Personal Interview/Questionnaire (June 22).

Meier, Kenneth J. 1993. "Representative Bureaucracy: A Theoretical and Empirical Exposition," in *Research in Public Administration,* pp. 1-35. Greenwich, Conn.: JAI Press.

Mosher, Frederick C. 1982. *Democracy and the Public Service,* 2nd ed. New York: Oxford University Press.

Mouet, Gerardo. 1995. Outreach Coordinator for City of Santa Ana. Personal Interview (May 17).

Ossolinski, Rita Soler. 1992. "Celebrating Workplace Diversity." *Public Management* (April): 18-21.

Ream, David. 1992. "Employment Outreach: A Quality Approach to Workforce Diversity." *Public Management* (June): 18-20.

Riccucci, Norma M. 1997. "Cultural Diversity Programs to Prepare for Work Force 2000: What's Gone Wrong?" *Public Personnel Management* 26, no. 1.

Scarborough, Danelle. 1995. Project Manager, City of San Diego. Personal Interview (May 23).

SHRM/CCH (Society for Human Resources Management/Commerce Clearing House) Survey. 1993. Commerce Clearing House, Inc., May 26: 1-12.

Tedhams, Gale L. 1995. Human Resources, Owens-Corning, Toledo, Ohio. Personal Interview/Questionnaire (July 17).

USMSPB (U.S. Merit Systems Protection Board). 1993. *Evolving Workforce Demographics: Federal Agency Action and Reaction.* Washington, D.C.: USMSPB, November.

Victor, Kirk, 1991. "Work Force Warfare." *National Journal,* September 28: 2354-2356.

chapter **6**

Colliding with a Glass Ceiling: Barriers to the Advancement of Women and Minorities

Katherine C. Naff

The *glass ceiling* is a term used to describe subtle, almost invisible barriers that inhibit the advancement of women and minorities into senior-level positions in public and private sector organizations. The origin of the term is credited to an article that appeared in the *Wall Street Journal* in 1986 describing barriers that confront women who try to advance to the top of the corporate hierarchy (Hymowitz and Schellhardt, 1986). Later the concept was broadened to explain the scarcity of minorities in top corporate positions as well as barriers to the advancement of women and minorities in the public sector. This chapter will explain the origin of the term, describe the nature of these subtle barriers, and discuss how employers are and should be responding to them. It will close with projections for the future prospects of women and minorities in the public sector.

CHANGING DEMOGRAPHICS
CREATE A NEW PROBLEM

In the past few decades minorities and, particularly, women have made impressive gains in moving into the labor force. The percentage of women participating in the civilian labor force, for example, grew from 37.7 percent in 1960 to nearly 60 percent in 1993 (see Figure 6.1) (U.S. Bureau of the Census, 1994: 396). Yet women and minorities remain severely underrepresented in mid and senior levels of management. In a 1991 report the U.S. Department of Labor noted that its review of a random sample of Fortune 1000 companies revealed that only 6.6 percent of executives were women, and only 2.6 percent were minorities (U.S. Department of Labor, 1991a: 6).

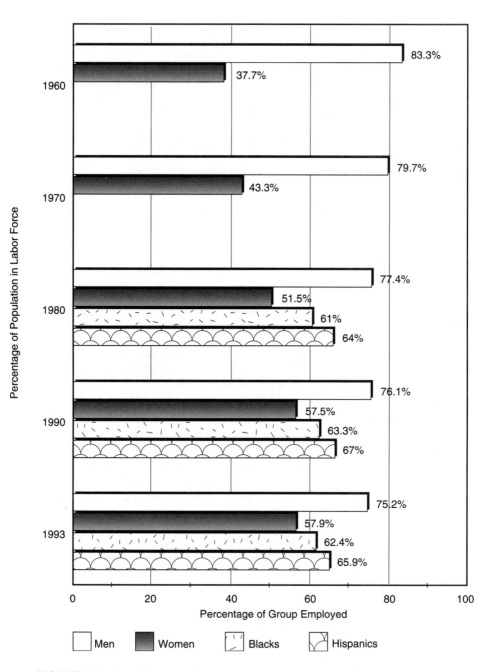

FIGURE 6.1 Employment of men, women, blacks, and Hispanics, 1960–1993.

SOURCE: U.S. Bureau of the Census, *Statistical Abstract of the United States*, 114th ed. (Washington, D.C.: U.S. Department of Commerce, 1994): 396.

NOTE: Data not available for blacks or Hispanics for 1960, 1970.

The glass ceiling metaphor suggests that the absence of women and minorities in management positions does not result from their lack of qualifications, aspirations to hold these positions, or even overt discrimination. Rather, there are barriers to the advancement of women and minorities that are so subtle as to be nearly invisible. Hence, women and minorities can see their way to the top of the organizational career ladder, but when they attempt to climb it they bump their head against these invisible barriers—or the glass ceiling.

Discrimination on the basis of race, national origin, and sex has been unlawful since the passage of the Civil Rights act of 1964. That act established the Equal Employment Opportunity Commission (EEOC) to oversee the elimination of discrimination in employment, primarily through investigating charges of discrimination filed by employees against their employers.[1]

However, the barriers that comprise the glass ceiling are often so subtle that they do not constitute the kind of overt discrimination that the EEOC was set up to monitor or investigate. As will become clear later in this chapter, the glass ceiling consists largely of expectations about what managers look like and do that run headlong into stereotypes of women and minorities. Since these expectations often appear to be neutral with regard to employees' race, national origin, and gender, they do not constitute unlawful discrimination and thus cannot easily be addressed through litigation. The elimination of a glass ceiling cannot simply be left to an oversight agency like the EEOC, but rather requires the changing of societal attitudes as well as organizational expectations that work against the advancement of women and minorities.

THE DEVELOPMENT OF THE GLASS CEILING AS A NATIONAL POLICY ISSUE

Despite the intangibility of glass ceiling barriers, it has become an important public policy issue. More than one federal agency has conducted extensive research to identify barriers that constitute the glass ceiling.

Efforts to systematically understand the nature of the glass ceiling in private sector companies began in the late 1980s in the Department of Labor's Office of Contract Compliance Programs (OFCCP). Created by Executive Order 11246 in 1965, OFCCP conducts several thousand compliance reviews of companies each year, and it requires those of a certain size to actively recruit, and make training and advancement opportunities available to, every segment of the work force[2] (U.S. Department of Labor, 1991b). In 1988, satisfied that women and minorities were entering the professional work force in increasing numbers, then director of OFCCP Cari Dominguez proposed to labor secretary Elizabeth Dole that the department undertake a pilot study to identify the reasons that so few women and minorities were to be found in the senior levels of corporations. The report of this much-publicized "glass ceiling initiative" was released in August 1991 (U.S. Department of Labor, 1991a). It found that in the nine corporations it reviewed, women and minorities faced attitudinal and organizational barriers including restricted access to the networks and credential-building experiences required for advancement. In addition to focusing considerable attention on the glass ceiling issue, OFCCP ultimately institutionalized evaluation of the glass ceiling as part of its regular compliance reviews.

Moreover, and perhaps understandably given his wife's interest in the issue, Senator Robert Dole introduced legislation to create a Federal Glass Ceiling Commission charged with "examining the reasons behind the existence of the glass ceiling and making recommendations with respect to policies which would eliminate any impediments to the advancement of women and minorities" (*Congressional Record,* U.S. Senate, February 21, 1991). This legislation was ultimately included as Title II of the Civil Rights Act of 1991 (Pub.L. 102-166, 105 Stat. 1071), signed into law in November 1991. The initial "fact-finding" report of the 21-member Commission, released in March 1995, confirmed that "Despite the growing number of corporate leaders who consider diversity at the managerial and decisionmaking levels to be an important issue impacting their bottom line, significant barriers continue to exist at various levels within organizations . . . [which] impede the advancement of qualified minorities and women" (Federal Glass Ceiling Commission, 1995a: 9). Included among the recommendations issued in its final report the following November, the Commission called on government to lead by example in making equal opportunity a reality for women and minorities (Federal Glass Ceiling Commission, 1995b).

With respect to federal sector employment, the glass ceiling has received attention within both Congress and the executive branch. In May and October 1991, Senator John Glenn, then chair of the Senate Committee on Governmental Affairs, held hearings to address "the 'Glass Ceiling' in Federal Agencies." Confronted with the poor representation of women and minorities in senior federal positions, the EEOC admitted that it was partly responsible for the glass ceiling in that it had not fully enforced affirmative employment requirements in the government, which, according to its own regulations, require agencies to submit a plan for removing barriers to the advancement of women and minorities (Newlin, 1991). In response to requests from Senator Glenn and others, the General Accounting Office (GAO), the legislative branch agency responsible for oversight of executive agencies, conducted a number of analyses of the underrepresentation of women and minorities in executive branch agencies (see, for example, U.S. General Accounting Office, 1991a, 1991b, 1991c, 1993).

Meanwhile, and also in part due to the attention being given the glass ceiling in the private sector by the labor department, the U.S. Merit Systems Protection Board (MSPB) undertook a study of the glass ceiling. The MSPB, whose responsibilities include oversight of the federal civil service, undertook a comprehensive study of the glass ceiling as it affected women in federal employment in 1992; its report stated that there are barriers that result in women being promoted fewer times over the course of their careers than men with comparable experience and education (U.S. Merit Systems Protection Board, 1992). The MSPB has also undertaken a separate study to address disparities in the treatment of minorities, which it expects to release in 1996. Following on the heels of the

Department of Labor, GAO, and MSPB, the U.S. Office of Personnel Management (OPM) developed an interagency glass ceiling planning group that met initially in October 1992 but disbanded shortly after the new OPM director took over the agency in 1993.

Attention was brought to the issue of a glass ceiling facing women in state and local government by the Center for Women in Government at the State University of New York, Albany, in its Winter 1991/92 bulletin (Center for Women in Government, 1991/92).

In summary, the possible existence of the glass ceiling has clearly become a national policy issue. Although this issue is clearly linked with other "challenges of inclusion" described in this book, it is important to keep in mind that the glass ceiling has been the focus of much national attention.

It is the central argument of this chapter that barriers to the advancement of women and minorities should be of concern to any employer. After all, anything that impedes the full utilization of employees' talents and abilities means that some of the potential contributions of those employees to the organization are left untapped. But in the public sector, there is an additional reason for understanding the nature of disparate treatment of women and minorities. As the nation's largest employer and enforcer of its laws with respect to equal employment opportunity (EEO), the government has a special responsibility to ensure that all its employees have the opportunity to advance into senior, policy-making positions. In addition to the symbolic role this serves, it ensures that a diverse array of talents and skills will be included in the policy-making process (Krislov, 1967).

THE DISTRIBUTION OF MEN, WOMEN, MINORITIES, AND NONMINORITIES IN THE PUBLIC SECTOR WORK FORCE

Although for decades discriminatory practices against women and minorities meant that they were denied equal access to public sector employment, by the 1970s it became clear that the problem was less one of entry into employment than of distribution within the organizational hierarchy (Rosenbloom, 1977). For example, whereas in 1993 women made up nearly half of the state and local work force, they held only one-quarter of the top-paying jobs (see Table 6.1). White men, on the other hand, held 61 percent of the top-paying jobs but only 35 percent of the lower paying jobs. In other words, whereas the distribution of women and minorities represents a pyramid wherein the proportion of lower level positions they hold is greater than the proportion of higher level positions, the pattern for white men is reversed. White men hold a greater proportion of top-level jobs than lower level jobs—an inverted pyramid.

This pattern can also be seen with respect to the distribution by grade level in the federal sector (see Table 6.1). In 1994, white men held one-third of lower level positions and more than three-quarters of senior executive jobs. White

TABLE 6.1 Percentage of top-level and other positions held by sex and race/ national origin.

	State and Local Employees Annual Salary (1993)			Federal Employees Grade Level (1994)		
	$43,000 Plus	*$33,000- 42,900*	*Below $33,000*	*Senior Execs*	*Midlevel (GS 13-15)*	*Other (GS 1-12)*
Men						
White	61.3%	52.1%	34.6%	76.5%	67.1%	33.5%
Black	6.2	9.0	9.6	4.0	4.0	5.3
Hispanic	4.6	4.6	3.5	1.7	2.4	2.9
Asian/PI	3.0	1.7	0.6	1.1	2.7	1.7
Am Ind/AN	0.4	0.4	0.3	0.3	0.6	0.7
Women						
White	17.4	22.6	34.3	13.8	18.0	35.7
Black	3.8	6.1	12.3	1.7	3.5	13.9
Hispanic	1.4	1.9	3.5	0.5	0.7	3.1
Asian/PI	1.9	1.5	0.9	0.3	0.9	1.8
Am Ind/AN	0.1	0.2	0.3	0.1	0.2	1.3

NOTE: "Asian/PI" includes Asian Americans and Pacific Islanders. "Am Ind/AN" includes American Indians and Alaskan Natives. Figures may not add up to 100 percent due to rounding.
SOURCES: Data for federal employees are from U.S. Merit Systems Protection Board, 1994. "Working for America: An Update." Data for state/local employees are from EEOC, *Job Patterns for Minorities and Women in State and Local Government,* 1993.

women held a slightly greater percentage of the lower level jobs (36 percent) but only 14 percent of senior executive positions.

Thus it is clear that although they constitute a significant portion of the public sector work force, women and minorities remain underrepresented in senior level positions. What the numbers in Table 6.1 don't tell us is why. Is it because there are fewer qualified women and minorities in the public sector work force, or are there other obstacles to their advancement?

FACTORS AFFECTING ADVANCEMENT

A variety of factors affect the likelihood that individuals will advance in organizations. In Figure 6.2, these factors are grouped into three categories—human capital, subjective factors, and a third category that, for reasons that will become clear later, are depicted at the intersection of human capital and subjective factors. Each of these categories will be discussed in turn.

Human Capital

Human capital is a term that is used to describe the attributes that "improve an individual's societal standing, employment position, or career opportunities" (Dugan et al., 1993: 30). Such factors represent investments individuals make in themselves that yield a return in terms of opportunities for advancement.

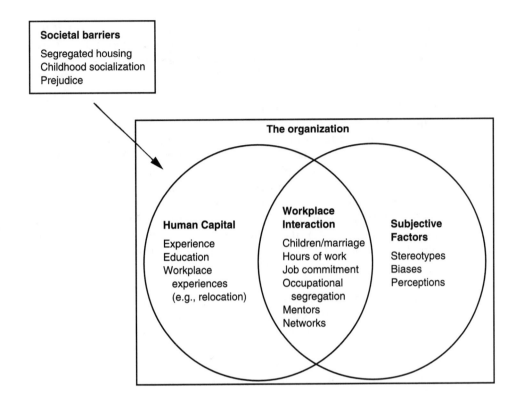

FIGURE 6.2 Factors affecting advancement in organizations.

Most professional jobs, for example, require a certain level of educational attainment; in order to advance beyond entry levels, professionals are expected to have a certain amount of experience as well. In the federal civil service, senior executives have, on average, 22 years of federal service and two-thirds of them have an advanced degree beyond the bachelor's level (U.S. Office of Personnel Management, 1990). In many organizations, advancement is also tied to certain labor market experiences, such as relocating geographically (particularly in the federal sector) or having experience working in more than one agency (particularly at the local level). From the perspective of many employers, these kinds of experiences demonstrate a breadth of experience and level of commitment to one's career (Markham et al., 1983).

The human capital that individuals bring to the job depends, in turn, on the choices they make and the opportunities they have to gain experience and education. These factors are depicted in the box in Figure 6.2. People who choose to invest in their education or to gain the kinds of experiences that make them competitive will have an advantage in competing for promotions. However, it must also be recognized that a variety of factors, ranging from segregated housing to childhood socialization, have an impact on the choices people make as well as the opportunities available to them. Women and minorities often find they do not have as many opportunities to gain human capital before entering the work force as nonminority men. These factors are largely outside of the control of the organizations in which people work, so they are depicted separately in Figure 6.2.

It is sometimes suggested that it is not a "glass ceiling" that accounts for the dearth of women and minorities in senior-level jobs; rather, it will take time for them to have achieved the same level of human capital as their nonminority male peers. Despite the fact that human capital theory ignores limitations in opportunities to acquire human capital, there is some validity to the theory from organizations' standpoint. Only 9 percent of Native Americans and 10 percent of Latinos in the work force hold college degrees (Federal Glass Ceiling Commission, 1995a). Although women have largely closed the educational gap with men (Tomaskovic-Devey, 1994), they have less experience than men, and are less likely to have relocated (Markham et al., 1983; Bullard and Wright, 1993; U.S. Merit Systems Protection Board, 1992).

Nevertheless, these human capital factors do not entirely account for the poor representation of women and minorities in senior-level positions; research has shown that even controlling for differences in human capital, women and minorities have not advanced as far as nonminority men (Stroh, Brett, and Reilly, 1992; U.S. Merit Systems Protection Board, 1992, 1995a; Newman, 1993; Tomaskovik-Devey, 1994). The lack of greater progress by women and minorities into senior level positions can be partly explained—but *only* partly—by human capital factors.

Subjective Factors

On the other end of the spectrum are factors that most people would agree clearly should have no role in promotion decisions, particularly in a civil service system that purports to base such decisions purely on merit. In Figure 6.2 these are categorized as "subjective factors" and refer to stereotypes and biases that people often hold about minorities and women. Some researchers have posited that such attitudes are one of the major causes of inequities in employment (see Morrison, White, and Van Velsor, 1987; Dugan et al., 1993; Federal Glass Ceiling Commission, 1995b).

Such biases and stereotypes are often subconscious and therefore difficult to identify. However, considerable research over the past five decades has systematically documented that stereotypes of women affect how women are treated in the workplace (American Psychological Association, 1988). In addition, there is a body of research showing that minorities, and particularly minority women, are also disadvantaged by such cognitive processes (Dugan et al., 1993; Bass, 1990).

Stereotypes are a normal process by which people categorize information about the world around them; as such, stereotypes are not necessarily inaccurate or harmful. The problem is that stereotypes often overgeneralize about people. Assumptions are made about the group to which an individual belongs that are inaccurate or simply don't apply to the individual in question. For example, women are often assumed to be incompetent, weak, passive, and uncompetitive—just the opposite of what it is believed is necessary to be an effective manager (Heilman, 1983). Minorities also face stereotypes; for example, Native Americans are sometimes believed to be irresponsible and lazy, and Asian Americans are thought of as passive and more equipped for technical than people-oriented work (Federal Glass Ceiling Commission, 1995b).

Research conducted under experimental conditions has shown that such stereotypes can have a very powerful effect on the behavior of both the person holding the stereotype and the individual being stereotyped (see, for example, Heilman, 1983; Pettigrew and Martin, 1987). Stereotypes tend to be self-fulfilling in that people who are presumed to be unsuitable for a job based on a stereotype tend to doubt their own competence and so do not perform up to their potential.

Stereotypes are also self-reinforcing in that people tend to ignore information that challenges a stereotype and remember information that confirms it. Thus if a woman is successful as a manager, her accomplishments are likely to be attributed to luck and are discounted, whereas her mistakes confirm the pre-conceived notion of her incompetence. At the same time, since nonminority men fit the stereotype of a successful manager, their accomplishments are more often attributed to their skill, and their mistakes are more easily forgotten. Women and minorities are also much more likely to be stereotyped when they are very few in number in a particular job or organization, or what Rosabeth Moss Kanter (1977) called "tokens." In that case their mistakes are much more visible, and differences among women and among minorities are not readily observable (Kanter, 1977).

Thus biases, stereotypes, and other subjective factors have an impact on the likelihood of people to advance in an organization. They can provide an advantage to nonminority men who fit the stereotype of a successful manager just as they can create a self-perpetuating barrier to the advancement of women and minorities. As long as women and minorities are few in number in senior level positions, they are liable to be stereotyped. The stereotypes, in turn, make it more likely that they will fail and that their failures will be remembered, reinforcing the stereotype and making it more difficult for other women and minorities to compete successfully for a similar position.

Workplace Interactions: When Human Capital Meets Subjectivity

As noted above, most people would agree that stereotyping and biases are invidious and have no place in a civil service system devoted to promotion based on merit. Rather, advancement opportunities should be granted to those who demonstrate through their qualifications and work products that they are the most likely to make the greatest contribution to the organization once promoted into higher level jobs. The problem is that expectations about what characterizes an employee with promotion potential are based on a model that is out of date and that conflicts with assumptions and stereotypes about women and minorities. These are the factors that are listed in the middle column of Figure 6.2, under the heading "Workplace Interaction."

One only need watch reruns of "Ozzie and Harriet" and "Leave It to Beaver" to realize that the traditional model portraying the two-parent household with a husband who dedicates himself to his career while his wife stays at home to take care of the children and household chores is hopelessly out-of-date; the percentage of such traditional families declined from nearly 70 percent in 1940 to 20 percent in 1990 (U.S. Merit Systems Protection Board, 1991). Yet that image continues to pervade the underlying culture and expectations of many organizations. Permeating workplaces on a very subtle level are images of women as more devoted to their families than their careers, and expectations that those who can most easily rise to the top are men who can work long hours, relocate, and otherwise dedicate themselves wholly to their careers because they have a wife at home to manage the family and household.

One indication of the persistence of this image is that married women and women with children are less likely to advance than single and childless women, whereas the presence of children has either no impact or a positive impact on the careers of men (U.S. Merit Systems Protection Board, 1992; Kelly et al., 1991; Johnson and Duerst-Lahti, 1992; Guy, 1993). One of the reasons for this is that senior public administrators are expected to work long hours (U.S. Merit Systems Protection Board, 1992; Bullard and Wright, 1993); indeed, the amount of time one spends in the office, or what has been called "face time," is often seen as an indication of job commitment and thus adds to employees' promotability in the eyes of many employers. However, the expectation that employees on their way to the top are those who work long hours works against women in two ways.

First, women continue to bear primary responsibility for childrearing and so are often not able to work long hours. Second, even if they *are* able to stay at work late, it is often *assumed* that they will be unable to; so women are passed over for promotion or career-enhancing assignments. Even when organizations offer flexible work arrangements, employees report that making use of such arrangements will render them ineligible for promotions (Schwartz, 1994). The image of the best employee as the one who demonstrates his or her commitment to the job by working long hours remains in force in many organizations. Yet there is no hard evidence that there is any direct correlation between working long hours, the quality and quantity of an employee's work, and commitment to career.

Interestingly, this same phenomenon provides an advantage to men who are married and have children. Several studies have shown that men who have wives at home caring for their children—again, conforming to the traditional model—earn more than men whose wives work (Lewin, 1994).

Also included under the heading of workplace interactions in Figure 6.2 is occupational segregation. This refers to the notion that there are certain occupations that are more valued than others and are more likely to be in the pipeline to management. At the same time, women and minorities are less likely to be found in these occupations. Some argue that this is a human capital issue in that women and minorities, for whatever reasons, are simply not choosing to enter occupations that yield the greatest return. However, there is also considerable evidence that occupational segregation occurs because of stereotypes and expectations. This is partly because when a job is thought of as "women's work" or a "minority position," it is devalued (Tomaskovic-Devey, 1994; Dugan et al., 1993). Moreover, women and minorities are more often steered into work (such as human resources or administration) that makes them less competitive for promotion to more powerful positions (U.S. Department of Labor, 1991a).

The effects of occupational segregation are further reinforced by patterns through which networks and mentors are established. Informal networks in organizations and mentors facilitate career advancement in a variety of ways, including providing feedback and generating contacts, recognition, and access to information and key assignments (Morrison, White, and Van Velsor, 1987; Brass, 1985; Moore, 1992; Dreher and Ash, 1990; Newman, 1993; Vertz, 1985). The reality is that people tend to network with and mentor other employees who resemble themselves, further reinforcing the segregation of women and minorities within the workplace (Fernandez, 1981; Dugan et al., 1993; Cox, 1993; Catalyst, 1992).

Summary: Barriers to the Advancement of Women and Minorities

Thus there are a variety of factors that affect women and minorities' prospects for advancement. Women and minorities, in general, bring lower levels of human capital to organizations, although their ability to develop human capital is often dampened by societal barriers. Moreover, the gap between most minority groups, women, and nonminority men is closing and becoming less of an explanation for their poor representation in senior-level positions. Even when they have similar levels of human capital, minorities and women face stereotypes, often reinforced by their "token" status in most organizations, that tend to be self-reinforcing and self-fulfilling.

Finally, there is the set of barriers that lie at the intersection of expectations about human capital on one hand and stereotypes on the other. The notion that those who should be promoted are the employees who have demonstrated their commitment to their career by working long hours and forgoing marriage and children (if they are women) puts women in particular at a distinct disadvantage even when such practices have no relationship to their contribution to their organizations. Moreover, the devaluing of "women's work" and "minority positions" and a tendency to shuttle women and minorities into less prestigious jobs further reduces their prospects for promotion into management (Braddock and McPartland, 1987).

Women and minorities have made progress in moving into the work force and in moving up the career ladder. Yet the prospects for their obtaining management jobs in proportion to their numbers in the work force seem dim in light of the pervasiveness and subtlety of barriers collectively known as the glass ceiling. The final section of this chapter will address prospects for dismantling the glass ceiling.

DISMANTLING THE GLASS CEILING: PROSPECTS FOR THE FUTURE

Most efforts to shatter the glass ceiling with respect to women have focused on the introduction of "family friendly" policies, whereas efforts to enhance career prospects for minorities have emphasized training in "diversity awareness." It is clear that given the complex nature of the glass ceiling, these efforts, albeit important, do not go far enough. The progress that women and minorities have made in moving into the work force and in increasing their numbers in upper level positions will continue but will also remain discouragingly slow unless conscious efforts are made to recognize and remove barriers at all levels. Given the complex and subtle nature of the barriers contributing to the glass ceiling in organizations, it is clear that strategies must be focused at three levels—the individual, the organization, and societywide (see Table 6.2).

Societal Strategies

Human capital and subjective barriers have their roots in attitudes and practices that begin long before individuals approach the workplace. As long as segregation continues in neighborhoods and schools, access by minorities to the educational and occupational opportunities they need to develop their "human capital" will remain restricted (Braddock and McPartland, 1987). Similarly, women who are socialized to believe that certain kinds of jobs or achievements are "unfeminine" remain at a disadvantage. Societal strategies must be aimed at recognizing and eliminating the effects of past discrimination, including attitudes and bias that weaken the likelihood that women and minorities will pursue or receive

TABLE 6.2 Examples of strategies for breaking the glass ceiling.

Societal	Organizational	Individual
• Dismantle segregated neighborhoods/schools • Change socialization practices • Increase opportunities to gain human capital	• Institute flexible work policies combined with end to focus on traditional criteria for evaluation • Provide diversity awareness training and programs • Employ affirmative action procedures	• Examine assumptions and stereotypes • Take advantage of opportunities to demonstrate competence

the kind of education and experiences they need to make them competitive in the workplace.

Organizational Strategies

As noted above, many organizations are now implementing "family friendly" policies such as leave time for family care responsibilities,[3] flexible schedules, and the ability to work at home on a regular schedule. Many of these arrangements were designed in recognition of the tremendous stress faced by women who must both earn a living and care for their families, and from the fact that declines in productivity that may result from this stress hurt the employer as well as the employee. However, despite the effectiveness of these policies in reducing stress and increasing job satisfaction (Schwartz, 1994), they are not enough to break the glass ceiling if women (and men) who take advantage of them are then presumed to be less career-oriented and so are funneled into a non-career enhancing career track.

The term *mommy track* was coined to define such a career track in response to an article by Felice Schwartz (1989) in the *Harvard Business Review.* Schwartz suggested that companies should distinguish between "career-primary" women and "career-and-family" women, most of whom would be "willing to trade some career growth and compensation for freedom from the constant pressure to work long hours and weekends" (Schwartz, 1989: 70). Unfortunately, this notion of a mommy track accepts the premise that women who have children are less worthy of promotion without examining whether the willingness or ability to work long hours really does define a better manager. Rather, an organization that is truly committed to dismantling the glass ceiling as it affects women should not only provide flexible work arrangements where possible, but also consciously eliminate these traditional criteria for advancement that have no link to the quality of an employee's work. In fact, an article in the *Wall Street Journal* a few years ago suggested that some private sector companies are doing just that. They are urging managers to replace "corporate rituals" such as time spent in the office and numbers of transfers with results as a way to evaluate employees' potential ("Averting Career Damage," 1992).

Another strategy adopted by many organizations as a way to increase the advancement prospects of minorities as well as women is in providing "diversity training." In a survey of 33 federal agencies, 20 responded that one of the ways in which they are addressing diversity issues is through providing diversity training or "valuing diversity" programs (U.S. Merit Systems Protection Board, 1993). Such training generally focuses on teaching employees (and especially supervisors) to be sensitive to differences among people of different cultural backgrounds and to see these differences in a positive light rather than as factors that limit employees' contributions to their organizations. However, there has been little effort to evaluate the effectiveness of such initiatives. A recent article in *Government Executive* magazine noted rather cynically that despite increased diversity training, the number of EEO complaints based on race and sex discrimination filed by federal employees is on the rise, growing from about 10,500 in 1989 to over 13,200 in 1992 (Kaufman, 1994: 16). Another possible interpretation is that this training has succeeded in making employees more aware of their rights and the process for filing a complaint. It has also been alleged, however, that some "diversity" training does more harm than good by alienating workers, creating a backlash from some white males who see diversity as discrimination against them (Rivenbark, 1994) and even producing a lawsuit at the Federal Aviation Administration (Harris, 1995). These problems may stem from the way in which diversity programs are developed and implemented (see Chapter 5 for further discussion).

A third strategy to address the career advancement of women and minorities is affirmative action programs. As discussed in more detail elsewhere in this book, affirmative action programs are a means for increasing the proportion of women and minorities in organizations and at higher grade levels by taking racial, ethnic, or gender underrepresentation into account when making selection decisions. Some researchers argue that since stereotypes and subtle forms of discrimination are exacerbated in situations in which minorities and women are severely underrepresented, a critical mass of minorities and women are needed to overcome such stereotypes (see, for example, Pettigrew and Martin, 1987; Braddock and McPartland, 1987). Affirmative action programs are clearly a means for achieving such a critical mass, yet they continue to meet with resistance, particularly on the part of nonminorities. In a survey of federal employees, only about one-third of nonminority employees agreed that affirmative action considerations should be taken into account when choosing among highly qualified candidates (U.S. Merit Systems Protection Board, 1994). The very existence of affirmative action programs can result in people assuming that women and minorities have been placed in positions for which they are not well qualified, thereby reinforcing stereotypes. Although outcome-based measures like affirmative action can be an important means for reversing the tremendous inertia against minority and female advancement caused by stereotypes, they must be implemented carefully and in combination with other efforts to ensure that women and minorities are also given every opportunity to prove their competence.

Individual-Level Strategies

Although the burden must remain on society and on organizations to eliminate practices and attitudes that serve as a barrier to the advancement of women and minorities, individuals can also play a role in eliminating prejudice and increasing their own competitiveness.

First, individuals, particularly supervisors who make assignment and pro-motion decisions, must consciously recognize assumptions they may be making in evaluating employees. Are they assuming a woman is not interested in advancing her career just because she has a family? Are they assuming an African-American colleague earned his position based on an affirmative action pro-gram rather than his own qualifications? Are they assuming that the employee who works until late in the evening is making a greater contribution to the organization than the one who leaves at 5:00 PM, without any demonstrated nexus between the time employees put in at work and the quality and quantity of their work? Although unconscious biases and stereotypes are not easily dismissed, they can be eliminated through a conscious effort on the part of individuals.

Second, women and minorities should be aware that, as unfair as they are, stereotypes and biases do exist. Even though the primary burden to address such stereotypes rests with the organization, individuals can also help overcome them by taking advantage of opportunities to demonstrate their competence. Studies of the effect of sex stereotyping have shown that women's potential is often judged more harshly than their actual accomplishments. In one experiment, for example, when subjects were told that paintings were art contest *entries,* those done by men were judged more favorably than those done by women. But when subjects were told the paintings were *prize winners,* this did not occur, presumably because an evaluation had already been made that the paintings were good; they had won a prize (Heilman, 1983).

Thus women and minorities who can take advantage of opportunities to demonstrate their capabilities through volunteering for particularly difficult assignments or temporary details may help to dissolve stereotypes that women and minorities are not suited for such challenges. (Of course, it should also be recognized that given the visibility of mistakes made by "tokens" in organizations, such a strategy does involve considerable risk as well.) Nevertheless, when federal employees were asked about the effect of various items on their career advancement, 42 percent of women (and only 26 percent of men) said developmental assignments had "helped a lot," and 44 percent of women (as opposed to 30 percent of men) said the opportunity to act in a position(s) prior to appointment had helped a lot (U.S. Merit Systems Protection Board, 1992).

These are just some examples of strategies that can and should be taken at the individual, organizational, and societal level if advancement opportunities are to be made equal among men, women, minorities, and nonminorities. Although this is only a partial list, it demonstrates the range of issues that must be addressed and the complexity of barriers that constitute the glass ceiling.

CONCLUSION

Women and minorities have made—and no doubt will continue to make—progress in moving into senior level positions in public sector organizations. But until the combination of factors working against their advancement, known as the glass ceiling, is recognized and consciously addressed, their opportunity to engage fully in the policy-making process that takes place at these levels will be limited. It will be limited by stereotypes that cast doubt on their competence, by traditional criteria for evaluating their potential that underrate their commitment and abilities, and by the perpetuation of occupational segregation that restricts their opportunities. It is probably not surprising that none of the entities addressing the glass ceiling at the national level have come up with a simple or straightforward solution to it. The Federal Glass Ceiling Commission provided a series of recommendations directed toward business and government before it was dismantled in late 1995, but it also acknowledged that "Glass ceilings in the business world are not an isolated feature of corporate architecture; rather they are held in place by the attitudes of society at large" (Federal Glass Ceiling Commission, 1995b; 46). The GAO and Senate reviews, discussed earlier in this chapter, only called for improved measurement and enforcement by the EEOC, rather than making any specific recommendations for dismantling the glass ceiling. The Merit Systems Protection Board's recommendations were more comprehensive, addressing many of the factors listed under Organizational and Individual solutions in Table 6.2; but given its mission, it was not in a position to recommend strategies at the societal level. As should be clear by now, only a range of strategies at the societal, organizational, and individual level can break this cycle that leaves the potential of millions of public servants untapped.

More recently, the glass ceiling metaphor has spawned other metaphors to describe barriers to the advancement of women and minorities, including *glass walls* (Lopez, 1992), referring to the concentration of women and minorities in occupations that aren't in the pipeline to the top, and *sticky floors* (Center for Women in Government, 1992), referring to the concentration of women and minorities in the lowest paying jobs. Regardless of the metaphor used, the point is that in indirect and often inadvertent ways, complete equality of opportunity to advance into policy-making positions continues to elude most women and minorities. Because of the attention the glass ceiling has received at the national level, the glass ceiling is becoming more opaque, if not more brittle.

NOTES

1. The Civil Rights Act was extended to cover public sector employees in 1972, at which time the EEOC was also given enforcement authority. The EEOC assumed jurisdiction for federal employees from the Civil Service Commission in 1979.
2. The Executive Order applies to all contractors and subcontractors holding any federal or federally assisted contract worth more than $10,000 annually. Affirmative employment requirements apply to contractors and subcontractors with a federal contract of $50,000 or more who have 50 or more employees (U.S. Department of Labor, 1991a).
3. Under the provision of the Family and Medical Leave Act (Public Law 103-3, 29 U.S.C. §2601 et seq.), enacted on February 5, 1993, employers are now required to grant employees 12 weeks of leave to care for family members.

REFERENCES

American Psychological Association. 1988. "Brief for *Amicus Curiae* in support of Respondent in the case of *Price Waterhouse v. Ann B. Hopkins.* U.S. Supreme Court, October Term 1987 (June 18).
"Averting Career Damage from Family Policies." 1992. *Wall Street Journal,* June 24.
Bass, Alison. 1990. "The Bias below the Surface." *Washington Post,* March 20.
Braddock, Jomills H., and James M. McPartland. 1987. "How Minorities Continue to Be

Excluded from Equal Employment Opportunities: Research on Labor Market and Institutional Barriers." *Journal of Social Issues* 43: 5-39.

Brass, Daniel J. 1985. "Men's and Women's Networks: A Study of Interaction Patterns and Influence in an Organization." *Academy of Management Journal* 28: 327-343.

Bullard, Angela M., and Deil S. Wright. 1993. "Circumventing the Glass Ceiling: Women Executives in American State Governments." *Public Administration Review* 53: 189-202.

Catalyst. 1992. *On the Line: Women's Career Advancement.* New York: Catalyst.

Center for Women in Government. 1991/92. "Women Face Barriers in Top Management." *Women in the Public Service* 2 (Winter).

————. 1992. "Women Still Stuck in Low-Level Jobs." *Women in the Public Service* 3 (Fall).

Cox, Taylor. 1993. *Cultural Diversity in Organizations.* San Francisco: Berrett-Koehler Publishers.

Dreher, George F., and Ronald A. Ash. 1990. "A Comparative Study of Mentoring among Men and Women in Managerial, Professional, and Technical Positions." *Journal of Applied Psychology* 75: 539-546.

Dugan, Beverly A., et al. 1993. *The Glass Ceiling: Potential Causes and Possible Solutions.* Alexandria, Va.: Human Resources Research Organization.

Federal Glass Ceiling Commission. 1995a. *Good for Business: Making Full Use of the Nation's Human Capital.* Washington, D.C.: Glass Ceiling Commission.

————. 1995b. *A Solid Investment: Making Full Use of the Nation's Human Capital.* Washington, D.C. Glass Ceiling Commission.

Fernandez, John. 1981. *Racism and Sexism in Corporate Life.* Lexington, Mass.: Lexington Books.

Guy, Mary E. 1993. "Three Steps Forward, Two Steps Backward: The Status of Women's Integration into Public Management." *Public Administration Review* 53: 285-292.

Harris, Christy. 1995. "Culture Shock: Is Diversity Training Really Curbing Bias?" *Federal Times,* January 23.

Heilman, Madeline E. 1983. "Sex Bias in Work Settings: The Lack of a Fit Model," in L.L. Cummings and Barry M. Staw, eds., *Research in Organizational Behavior,* vol. 5, pp. 269-298. Greenwich, Conn.: JAI Press.

Hymowitz, Carol, and Timothy D. Schellhardt. 1986. "The Glass Ceiling." *Wall Street Journal,* March 24: 1D, 4D-5D.

Johnson, Cathy Marie, and Georgia Duerst-Lahti. 1992. "Public Work, Private Lives," in Mary E. Guy, ed., *Women and Men of the States.* Armonk, N.Y.: M.E. Sharpe.

Kanter, Rosabeth Moss. 1977. *Men and Women of the Corporation.* New York: Basic Books.

Kaufman, Leslie. 1994. "Painfully Aware." *Government Executive* 26: 16-22.

Kelly, Rita Mae, et al. 1991. "Public Managers in the States: A Comparison of Career Advancement by Sex." *Public Administration Review* 51: 402-412.

Krislov, Samuel. 1967. *The Negro in Federal Employment.* Minneapolis: University of Minnesota Press.

Lewin, Tamar. 1994. "Men Whose Wives Work Earn Less, Studies Show." *New York Times,* October 12.

Lopez, J.A. 1992. "Study Says Women Face Glass Walls as Well as Ceilings." *Wall Street Journal,* March 3: B1-2.

Markham, William T., et al. 1983. "A Note on Sex, Geographic Mobility, and Career Advancement." *Social Forces* 61: 1138-1146.

Moore, Gwen. 1992. "Gender and Informal Networks in State Government." *Social Science Quarterly* 73: 46-61.

Morrison, A.M., Randall P. White, and Ellen Van Velsor. 1987. *Breaking the Glass Ceiling.* Reading, Mass.: Addison-Wesley.

Newlin, Eliza. 1991. "Doing What Feds Say, Not What Feds Do." *National Journal* 25 (June 22): 1570-1572.

Newman, Meredith Ann. 1993. "Career Advancement: Does Gender Make a Difference?" *American Review of Public Administration* 23: 361-364.

Pettigrew, Thomas F., and Joanne Martin. 1987. "Shaping the Organizational Context for Black American Inclusion." *Journal of Social Issues* 43: 41-48.

Rivenbark, Leigh. 1994. "Resistance by White Men Slows Diversity Progress." *Federal Times,* October 3.

Rosenbloom, David H. 1977. *Federal Equal Employment Opportunity.* New York: Praeger.

Schwartz, Debra B. 1994. "An Examination of the Impact of Family-Friendly Policies on the Glass Ceiling." Paper prepared for the Glass Ceiling Commission, U.S. Department of Labor.

Schwartz, Felice N. 1989. "Management, Women, and the New Facts of Life." *Harvard Business Review* 67: 65-76.

Stroh, Linda K., Jeanne M. Brett, and Anne H. Reilly. 1992. "All the Right Stuff: A Comparison of Female and Male Managers' Career Progression." *Journal of Applied Psychology* 77: 251-260.

Tomaskovic-Devey, Donald. 1994. "Race, Ethnic, and Gender Earnings Inequality: The Sources and Consequences of Employment Segregation." Paper prepared for the Glass Ceiling Commission, U.S. Department of Labor.

U.S. Bureau of the Census. 1994. *Statistical abstract of the United States,* 114th ed. Washington, D.C.: U.S. Department of Commerce.

U.S. Department of Labor. 1991a. *Report on the Glass Ceiling Initiative.* Washington, D.C.: U.S. Department of Labor.

——— . 1991b. *Director's Report Fiscal Year 1991.* Washington, D.C.: Office of Contract Compliance Programs, U.S. Department of Labor.

U.S. General Accounting Office. 1991a. "Federal Affirmative Employment: Better EEOC Guidance and Agency Analysis of Underrepresentation Needed." GAO/GGD-91-86 (May 10).

——— . 1991b. "Federal Affirmative Employment: Status of Women and Minority Representation in the Federal Workforce." GAO/T-GGD-92-2 (October 23).

——— . 1991c. "Federal Workforce: Continuing Need for Federal Affirmative Employment." GAO/GGD-92-27BR (November 21).

——— . 1993. "Affirmative Employment: Assessing Progress of EEO Groups in Key Federal Jobs Can Be Improved." GAO/GGD-93-65 (March 8).

U.S. Merit Systems Protection Board. 1991. "Balancing Work Responsibilities and Family Needs: The Federal Civil Service Response." Washington, D.C.: U.S. Merit Systems Protection Board (November).

——— . 1992. "A Question of Equity: Women and the Glass Ceiling in Federal Employment." Washington, D.C.: U.S. Merit Systems Protection Board (October).

——— . 1993. "Evolving Workforce Demographics: Federal Agency Action and Reaction." Washington, D.C.: Merit Systems Protection Board (November).

——— . 1994. "Working for America: An Update." Washington, D.C.: U.S. Merit Systems Protection Board (July).

U.S. Office of Personnel Management. 1990. "The Status of the Senior Executive Service 1990." Washington, D.C.: U.S. Office of Personnel Management.

Vertz, Laura L. 1985. "Women, Occupational Advancement, and Mentoring: An Analysis of One Public Organization." *Public Administration Review* 45: 415-423.

chapter 7

A Legal Perspective on Sexual Harassment

Robert D. Lee Jr. and Paul S. Greenlaw

For more than 30 years, sex discrimination in employment has been banned in the United States. Title VII of the Civil Rights Act of 1964 prohibits sex discrimination regarding the terms, conditions, and privileges of employment. Through administrative and judicial interpretation, sexual harassment has been deemed to be a form of sex discrimination and has been outlawed in federal, state, local, nonprofit, and for-profit employment.

This chapter, which takes a legalistic approach to the topic of sexual harassment, begins with a brief discussion of the significance of sexual harassment and an overview of the law. Next, the two main types of sexual harassment are reviewed. The processes used in sexual harassment cases are discussed, including the remedies that may be available to those who are successful in bringing harassment suits. The responsibilities of employers are considered. The chapter concludes with a discussion of two selected topics, namely the rights of gay and lesbian employees and the possible development of a backlash by men.

THE SIGNIFICANCE OF SEXUAL HARASSMENT

Sexual harassment, although illegal, is prevalent in the workplace and most often involves women as the victims. A majority of working women are likely to be sexually harassed sometime during their careers (National Council for Research on Women, 1991; also see Kelly and Stambaugh, 1992). Nearly half the women responding in a survey of federal workers reported having been sexually harassed during just a two-year period (U.S. MSPB, 1988: 2). In 1992–1993, 8 percent of all cases filed before the Equal Employment Opportunity Commission and human rights commissions involved sexual harassment charges. These cases are to be distinguished from other forms of sex discrimination, such as being denied a promotion or denied equal pay because of one's gender (unpublished data from EEOC; also see Greenlaw and Lee, 1993; U.S. MSPB, 1988; 1994). Thousands of additional instances of sexual harassment go unreported every year. People who are harassed often feel intimidated and fear reprisals if they report abuses. A 1994 Harris poll found that nearly two-thirds of workers who were harassed took no action to remedy their plights ("Survey Finds 31 Percent of Women Report Having Been Sexually Harassed at Work," 1994).

Sexual harassment is expensive both psychologically and financially. The psychological toll it takes on its victims includes lowered self-esteem, reduced career ambitions, and health problems. Sexual harassment results in increased absenteeism and employee turnover, which translate into increased employer costs.

THE CIVIL RIGHTS ACT OF 1964

Title VII of the Civil Rights Act of 1964 prohibits employment discrimination based on "race, color, religion, sex, or national origin" (42 U.S.C. §2000e-2). In the language of the law, discrimination is outlawed "with respect to . . . compensation, terms, conditions, or privileges of employment."

Over time, lower courts came to recognize sexual harassment as one form of sex discrimination, and the Equal Employment Opportunity Commission took this position in its important 1980 Guidelines on Discrimination Because of Sex (29 C.F.R. §1604). Not until 1986, however, was a sexual harassment case brought before the Supreme Court. In *Meritor Savings Bank, FSB v. Vinson,* a unanimous Court held, "Without question, when a supervisor sexually harasses a subordinate because of the subordinate's sex, that supervisor 'discriminate[s]' on the basis of sex" (1986: 64). The decision, handed down more than two decades after passage of the Civil Rights Act, made official the concept that sexual harassment is one form of sex discrimination.

The law applies to private and public employers in virtually all aspects of work. One exception is that military personnel may not use Title VII, although civilians in the Defense Department may use the law. Also, labor unions may be charged with contributing to sexual harassment. The Congressional Accountability Act of 1995 gave congressional workers the right to sue when sexually harassed.

QUID PRO QUO SEXUAL HARASSMENT

Harassment Defined

There are two forms of sexual harassment, with the first involving a quid pro quo set of conditions. "Here the plaintiff attempts to prove that the harasser has denied job benefits, such as a promotion, [or] salary increase . . . because sexual favors were not granted; or the harasser has taken away job benefits (e.g., discharge or demotion) because sexual favors on the part of the employee were not forthcoming" (Greenlaw and Kohl, 1992: 164-165). This is a form of sexual extortion in which someone in power, typically a man, attempts to use his power for sexual advantage. The EEOC's guidelines state:

> Unwelcome sexual advances, requests for sexual favors, and other verbal or physical conduct of a sexual nature constitute harassment when (1) submission to such conduct is made either explicitly or implicitly a term or condition of an individual's employment [and] (2) submission to or rejection of such conduct by an individual is used as the basis for employment decisions affecting such individual. (29 C.F.R. §1604.11; also see U.S. EEOC 1990)

Legal Standards Involved in Quid Pro Quo Harassment

Courts hold plaintiffs to a rigorous set of standards in proving quid pro quo sexual harassment (see Chan, 1994; *Giordano v. William Paterson College of New Jersey,* 1992). The employee must show that she experienced unwelcome sexual advances or requests for sexual favors, that these favors constituted conditions for obtaining job benefits or avoiding harm, and that the employer is responsible under the law. A woman must show that she told the harasser to stop and that he refused. She must indicate examples of threats of what would happen to her if she refused to comply with demands for sexual favors.

In some situations, both quid pro quo and the other form of sexual harassment (hostile environment, to be discussed below) may be alleged. The plaintiff may be unsuccessful in proving one type but successful in proving the other.

Reprisals stemming from a worker rebuffing sexual advances sometimes are difficult to prove. Was a worker fired because of her failure to comply with demands for sex, or was she fired for being incompetent? Was a worker passed over for promotion because someone else was better qualified, or because she ignored warnings that she would be denied the promotion unless she had sex with her supervisor? The plaintiff has the burden of proving by a "preponderance of the evidence" that the rationale for the action taken was only a pretext to cover up the real reason, namely discrimination.

HOSTILE ENVIRONMENT SEXUAL HARASSMENT

The second form of sexual harassment involves a hostile environment (see Lee and Greenlaw, 1995). The EEOC's guidelines refer to "an intimidating, hostile, or offensive work environment" (29 C.F.R. §1604.11; also see U.S. EEOC 1990). In some situations, supervisors or peers may not necessarily pressure women to engage in sex but may create an intimidating atmosphere that hampers the ability of women to excel in their jobs.

Types of Harassers

Quid pro quo cases only involve supervisors as harassers, since only they have authority that can be used to force an employee's compliance; but hostile environment harassment can result from actions of supervisors, co-workers, and non-employees such as customers (*Janopoulos v. Harvey L. Walner & Associates, Ltd.*, 1993; Shearer, 1994). In governmental settings, customers can sexually harass women employees in such places as libraries, hospitals, unemployment offices, Social Security offices, and the like. Delivery personnel, such as express-mail delivers, can be sources of harassment. Co-workers can collaborate with clients, as in the case of male guards condoning prisoners' harassment of women prison personnel.

Gender-Based Harassment

Verbal comments of workers create a hostile environment even though they have minimal or no sexual connotations. A male supervisor engages in sexual harassment when calling a woman subordinate "honey," "dear," "baby," "sugar," and similar names. Comments, such as "women belong barefoot and pregnant," negatively stereotype women and, when expressed by a supervisor, set in motion the evaluation of women based on the stereotype rather than their individual job performances.

The *Meritor Savings* Case

Two major sexual harassment cases have been heard by the Supreme Court, and both have dealt with hostile environment harassment, indicating that this form of harassment is more difficult to identify and rule upon than quid pro quo harassment. In the first of the cases, *Meritor Savings Bank, FSB v. Vinson* (1986), the Court ruled with lower courts that Title VII encompassed a prohibition against a "hostile or abusive work environment." The Court quoted approvingly from a case from the Eleventh Circuit: "Surely, a requirement that a man or woman run a gauntlet of sexual abuse in return for the privilege of being allowed to work and make a living can be as demeaning and disconcerting as the harshest of racial epithets" (*Henson v. City of Dundee*, 1982). The *Meritor Savings* case involved a bank employee who was forced to have sex with her superior on perhaps 40 or 50 occasions and who was fondled by him in front of other employees. The Court noted that an economic effect on her employment did not have to be shown; the environment by itself would be sufficient to constitute harassment prohibited by Title VII. Further, the Court ruled that she was not required to prove she participated in these activities on an involuntary basis but *only* prove that they were unwelcome.

The *Meritor Savings* decision and a host of lower-level court decisions have yielded a set of standards for showing the existence of a hostile environment. The employee needs to show she was subjected to intentional discrimination based on sex, that it was not merely occasional, and that the discrimination detrimentally affected her. The person bringing the suit—usually a woman—must make a prima facie case alleging discrimination, after which the defendant has an opportunity to rebut. The defendant employer might claim not to be subject to the law, that the woman was overly sensitive to comments, or that she had only been subjected to one or two inappropriate comments rather than any pervasive and severe situation.

The *Harris* Case

The Supreme Court in the second sexual harassment case, *Harris v. Forklift Systems, Inc.* (1993), further discussed the standards to be used in determining the existence of prohibited conditions. "Whether an environment is 'hostile' or 'abusive' can be determined only by looking at all the circumstances. These may include the frequency of the discriminatory conduct; its severity; whether it is physically threatening or humiliating, or a mere offensive utterance; and whether it unreasonably interferes with an employee's work performance" (1993: 371). The Court, however, left unresolved when the severity and pervasiveness thresholds have been reached (Robinson, Fink, and Allen, 1994).

The 1993 *Harris* decision is important in that it held that psychological harm need not be demonstrated by a woman alleging hostile environment harassment. "Title VII comes into play before the harassing conduct leads to a nervous breakdown" (*Harris*, 1993: 370). The hostile environment, although not harming one's psychological well-being, could have negative effects on job performance, limit one's ability to qualify for and seek promotions, and discourage one from staying with the employer.

The Reasonable Woman Standard

A plaintiff must show not only that she was offended by a situation but that any other reasonable person in the same situation also would find the environment hostile (*Currie v. Kowalewski*, 1994). In the *Harris* case, the Supreme Court seemed to edge toward applying what is known as the reasonable woman standard—what is reasonable to the average man may be unreasonable to the average woman (Robinson, Reithel, and Franklin, 1995–1996; Thacker and Gohmann, 1993).

Ellison v. Brady, a 1991 circuit court case, illustrates the reasonable woman concept. At an office of the U.S. Treasury Department, a male worker passed handwritten notes to a female co-worker. Rather than being lascivious, the correspondence mainly expressed strong affection for the woman. "I know that you are worth knowing with or without sex. . . . Leaving aside the hassles and disasters of recent weeks [sic]. I have enjoyed you so much over these past few months. Watching you. Experiencing you from O so far away. Admiring your style and elan . . ." (1991: 874). The woman's reaction to the notes was that the man was "crazy," and the court agreed that a reasonable woman would be frightened of such behavior. The dissenting judge in the case held that the reasonable man standard should be used when defined as the "average adult person."

The Supreme Court's *Harris* opinion seems to support the reasonable woman concept. Although the Court did not explicitly approve this concept, the Court noted its use by the lower courts and did not use this case as an opportunity to reverse those courts. The Court instead quoted approvingly from a district court opinion that held that behavior considered inoffensive by men could easily be regarded as offensive by women. The woman who brought the suit testified that on numerous occasions her superior had said, "You're a woman, what do you know?" He called her a "dumb ass woman" and said they should go to a motel to negotiate her pay increase.

The reasonable woman standard, if it continues to be used by the courts, may well cut in two directions. In some situations, men will be found to have created a hostile environment, which to them may not have seemed hostile at the time. In other situations, women who file complaints may be unsuccessful as they are found to be overly sensitive, that what they regarded as creating a hostile environment would not be considered such by the average woman (*Sudtelgte v. Reno*, 1994).

Employer Liability

The law is somewhat ambiguous as to employers' responsibilities for the harassing behavior of their supervisors, co-workers, and customers, clients, and other non-employees. Much of that ambiguity originates from the Supreme Court's 1986 decision in *Meritor Savings:*

> Congress' decision to define "employer" to include any "agent" of an employer . . . surely evinces an intent to place some limits on the acts of employees for which employers under Title VII are to be held responsible. For this reason, . . . employers are [not] always automatically liable for sexual harassment by their supervisors. . . . For the same reason, absence of notice to an employer does not necessarily insulate that employer from liability. (72)

Employers are not absolved of liability through an "ostrich defense" in which they claim ignorance that harassment was occurring. On the other hand, employers may be free of liability in situations where the harassed employee withstood quid pro quo and/or hostile environment harassment and never reported it, providing the employer can show no knowledge of the harassing conditions. (See Chapter 15 for a more general discussion of employer and employee liability.)

Courts have fashioned a compromise position between the EEOC's guidelines that hold employers strictly accountable and *Meritor Savings*, which may provide an escape from liability. Case law generally "seems to hold that employers are liable for failing to remedy or prevent a hostile or offensive work environment of which management level employees knew, or in the exercise of reasonable care should have known" (*U.S. EEOC v. Hacienda Hotel*, 1989: 1515-1516). If harassment was pervasive or openly in evidence, then an employer would be expected to know of its existence and remedy the situation.

PROCESSES FOR HANDLING
SEXUAL HARASSMENT CASES

Informal resolution of sexual harassment problems is preferable to judicial resolution. The informal process should be more speedy, thereby avoiding a protracted period when both the person bringing the complaint and the accused remain in doubt about their futures.

Employers are expected to have in place procedures for handling complaints. Generally in government employment, a worker can contact the equal employment office (EEO) in her agency and present her side of the story. The EEO representative may informally investigate the charge. If the problem is still unresolved, the next step is to file a formal charge. Federal employees may file with the Equal Employment Opportunity Commission or the Merit Systems Protection Board. State and local employees may file with EEOC and/or a state or local fair employment practices (FEP) agency. If the FEP agency is unsuccessful in handling the complaint, the EEOC may take charge.

After investigating a case, the EEOC has a number of choices. It may work toward achieving a negotiated settlement between the parties. It may dismiss the charges as unfounded. The commission may make a "reasonable cause determination," namely that evidence indicates an unlawful practice probably occurred. The commission may then bring formal charges against an employer or, in the case of a government agency, refer the matter to the Justice Department. If the EEOC decides against further action, the complainant must then obtain a "right to sue" letter in order to file suit in a U.S. district court. Important deadlines are involved with these procedures, and a plaintiff who fails to comply with the deadlines can be blocked from legal redress (U.S. EEOC, 1977).

Remedies

The purpose of any trial is to remedy harm that has occurred. In sexual harassment cases, the remedies concentrate upon overcoming problems in the worksite by eliminating harassment and putting in place procedures that will discourage its recurrence. Remedies additionally are intended to make whole or to restore the person who has been victimized.

An injunction is one of the most common remedies used by courts. These can be both positive and negative. On the negative side, a judge may issue an injunction instructing an employer to remove offensive pictures of nude women and the like and never to allow these again in the workplace. Positive forms of injunctions are also used in which employers are instructed to take specific steps in establishing procedures that will prevent future instances of sexual harassment.

With regard to restoring the worker to a whole person, a court can award employment-related remedies. If the court finds that a worker was forced to resign because of intolerable conditions, the court can order her reinstatement. If harassment has caused her emotional distress that resulted in excessive absenteeism, a court can order an employer to erase all absenteeism notices in the employee's personnel file. The employee may be able to win a promotion as a remedy.

Besides these types of orders, a victim of sexual harassment can receive financial compensation. A prevailing plaintiff normally will be entitled to back pay from the date when she was forced to resign her job. Interest on that income is compounded. Judges also may award front pay, which is the amount a worker would earn in the future. Front pay is awarded when a work situation is so hostile that it would be foolhardy for a worker to return to her former position.

Several other financial remedies are possible. Victims can be compensated for the costs of litigating their cases. The Civil Rights Act of 1964 as amended by the Civil Rights Act of 1991 permits compensation for attorneys' fees and expert witness fees. Another form of remedy is compensatory damages for emotional distress. The Civil Rights Act of 1991 covers "emotional pain, suffering, inconvenience, mental anguish, [and] loss of enjoyment of life" as nonpecuniary losses (see *U.S. v. Burke,* 1992). This law allows for punitive damages against private employers but specifically excludes public employers.

EMPLOYERS' RESPONSIBILITIES

Employers are responsible for establishing policies and procedures that prohibit sexual harassment, prevent its occurrence, and enforce these policies on transgressors (Lindenberg and Reese, 1995). With this affirmative responsibility, an employer typically is unable to claim ignorance of harassment having occurred and using that as justification for why it was allowed to continue; the test applied is whether the employer should have known about the harassing situation. As noted earlier, the ostrich defense is ineffective in court. A grievance process must be in place so that employees have an office that will objectively listen to their complaints. If an employer has a grievance procedure in name only and as a consequence employees are fearful of using it, then in effect a grievance procedure does not exist (see *Meritor Savings*).

Training

Several specific training techniques may be useful in preventing sexual harassment. These include lecture or lecture/discussion sessions, case studies, films and videos, and role playing/role reversal.

The lecture is probably the most common method for training individuals. It can provide factual information to large numbers of workers at relatively low cost. Group discussions that encourage a more active role for trainees may be somewhat more effective than the more passive lecture method. With specific respect to sexual harassment, the lecture/discussion materials may vary from the legal (e.g., an analysis of *Harris*) to the psychological (e.g., an analysis of the psychological damage incurred by a harassed woman).

Case studies provide written descriptions of organizational problems and then expect trainees to consider alternative methods of resolving the problems. For example, in one course taught by the authors, students analyze the case of a young woman manager who is asked by her supervisor to go out with a client and "do whatever is necessary to get his business." The case ends with her responding angrily to this suggestion. Students then must evaluate the situation and make recommendations; later the students are provided with additional factors that require a reevaluation of the initial recommendations that were presented. Through this iterative process students have an opportunity to develop their decision-making skills and come to appreciate more fully the problems associated with sexual harassment.

Films and videos, like lectures, can be used to convey factual information. They also can be used for presenting case situations. Several films and videos are available from commercial vendors (BNA, 1994).

Role playing entails having trainees perform roles and experience situations in a controlled environment (Moreno, 1945; Wohlking and Weiner, 1971). A common practice is to reverse roles to help trainees gain insights into the problems, feelings, and attitudes of others. With respect to sexual harassment, since it is mostly women who are harassed, men may be harassed in training groups so that they learn how it feels to be harassed. Caution must be exercised to ensure that such training does not become too vulgar and that all propriety is not lost (*New York Times,* 1994).

Assessing the effectiveness of training is difficult, and sexual harassment training is no exception. Although training may be particularly helpful in informing employees as to what constitutes sexual harassment and in sensitizing workers to how harassment "feels," training may be of limited utility in changing the mind-set of men who hold women in low esteem and who are unable to perceive harassment as morally wrong. These individuals may only respond to strict enforcement of anti-harassment policy, especially the application of disciplinary actions against harassers.

Discipline Policies and Procedures

How management deals with known harassers is an important ingredient of sexual harassment policy. Many policies in place use a progressive discipline approach that may begin with a reprimand and, if harassing activity is repeated, provide for counseling, suspension without pay, reassignment, demotion, and eventually discharge (*Swentek v. USAIR, Inc.,* 1987). Penalties may be specified in the policy so that would-be harassers know in advance the consequences of their actions. Other policies may provide for immediate discharge, as in single incidents of harassment that are particularly egregious.

Although there are alternative views of how to discipline employees who engage in sexual harassment, the courts have taken a firm stance that discipline must be sufficient and prompt in order to deter future harassment. A slap on the wrist for having engaged in sexual harassment will be considered no discipline at all. Courts frown upon employers providing their harassing employees only with training when disciplinary action seems warranted. Ineffective disciplining may encourage harassers to engage in further and more intense acts. On the other hand, prompt investigation of a reported problem and decisive disciplinary action may resolve a problem and may relieve the employer of liability.

Retaliation

A substantial amount of time can pass between when an individual seeks help from an EEO counselor and when the matter is resolved, especially if the case is brought to trial. During this period, claimants may be exposed to retaliation by superiors and co-workers, a practice that is clearly contrary to law. Plaintiffs can then amend their claims to include retaliation.

Retaliation practices can include outright demotions or disguised demotions such as relieving an employee of many of her responsibilities. Heavy work standards that cannot be met can be imposed, and when a woman fails to meet the standards, she receives negative performance evaluations. A retaliatory tactic sometimes used against women in supervisory positions is to deny them the staff they need to accomplish their assigned duties, and then evaluate them unfavorably. Being ostracized is another form of retaliation. Further, outright dismissal based on "trumped up" charges may be attempted. Third parties may feel the sting of retaliation; namely, other employees who have come forward to corroborate harassment charges can have retaliatory actions taken against them.

SPECIAL TOPICS

Bisexuals, Transsexuals, Gay Men, and Lesbians

Special problems arise in situations where either the supervisor or a subordinate is bisexual, transsexual, gay, or lesbian. If a supervisor is bisexual and demands sexual favors of both male and female subordinates in return for favorable treatment on the job, does quid pro quo sexual harassment exist? The answer is usually yes, in that gender has played a part in the employment status of the workers. However, not all courts agree.

What is the status of a transsexual, that is, someone who is undergoing hormone injections in preparation for surgery to change from being male to female? Such an individual who experiences harsh treatment on the job might well claim that his sex was the subject of discrimination in violation of Title VII (*Dobre v. Amtrak,* 1993).

Quid pro quo harassment can be alleged by people of the same sex, as in the instance of a male supervisor making sexual advances toward a male subordinate. The Equal Employment Opportunity Commission has held that harassment by lesbians and gay men is proscribed by Title VII, and courts generally have agreed (*Polly v. Houston Lighting and Power Company,* 1993).

Backlash by Men?

Throughout this discussion reference has been made continually to men being the harassers and women the victims, but are the men who are accused always harassers? In any given year, about one-third of all sexual harassment cases are dismissed. Some of those dismissals are probably due to workers making patently false claims against others, whereas other dismissals are due to a lack of sufficient evidence to proceed in a case or due to the complaints being filed in the wrong manner, under the wrong legal provision, or after the filing deadline. But the truth remains that some cases simply are unwarranted.

To some extent a backlash may be developing in which those charged with harassment—usually men—counter-sue their accusers for defamation of character. Showing malice on the part of the accuser is necessary, a matter that is often difficult to prove. These counter-suits are seen as an effort by a person to clear his own name and receive some financial compensation for the damage to his reputation. When a harassment suit becomes known, there may be a tendency to presume the accused is guilty; and even when charges are dropped, a person may be considered by some people to be a sexual harasser who simply escaped punishment. Financial settlements, then, are considered compensation for past and future injury (Murray, 1994; *Garraghty v. Williams,* 1995).

The old adage that "the best defense is a strong offense" may apply here. Some would suggest that counter-suits are being used to intimidate plaintiffs. A woman who has been subjected to sexual harassment may have been reluctant to file suit, but when it is filed and she is counter-sued, she may decide to drop the matter altogether. Not only might she lose her case, but she could be forced to pay her harasser for defaming him.

CONCLUSION

Sexual harassment is one of the most prominent issues of the 1990s. Title VII is of primary concern in prohibiting sexual harassment in federal, state, and local public employment and in nonprofit and for-profit employment. Quid pro quo and hostile environment are the two main forms of sexual harassment. Proving each of these requires following a set of rigorous standards.

Complaints of harassment are handled administratively and then may be pursued in court either by a government agency or by the alleged victim after having received a right to sue letter. A wide variety of remedies exists, such as injunctions, back pay and front pay, compensatory damages for emotional suffering, attorneys' and expert witness fees, and in some situations, punitive damages. Employers are responsible for establishing complaint processes that result in timely investigation and sufficiently severe disciplining of harassers.

Although considerable progress has been made in framing the law pertaining to sexual harassment, important legal issues remain. Uncertainties exist about a potential backlash by men and the legal status of bisexuals, transsexuals, gay men, and lesbians. On the first item, there is the potential for an increase in counter-suits by men who are accused of harassment, and this could have a chilling effect on women pursuing their legal rights. Whether such a trend emerges is to be determined. On the other item, sexual preference, the courts are not fully in agreement with each other as to whether such harassment falls within the purview of sexual harassment.

Although these issues that have been noted are important, clearly the most compelling problem is developing a workable definition of "hostile environment." The fact that the Supreme Court has dealt with two hostile environment cases is indicative of the problem. In the more recent case, *Harris v. Forklift Systems, Inc.* (1993), the Court provided some clarification by indicating that all aspects of a situation need to be considered in determining whether harassment exists and by ruling that psychological harm need not be shown by a plaintiff.

However, the Court has held that the ambiguous term *reasonableness* is to be applied and perhaps in conjunction with what is reasonable to women as distinguished from men, when women are the alleged victims of harassment. The Court in its *Harris* decision stopped just short of endorsing the reasonable woman standard.

A related area of ambiguity pertains to gender harassment in which overt sexual references need not be present but only that one gender is treated in a demeaning fashion. Lower courts generally regard such behavior as a form of sexual harassment, but the Supreme Court has yet to rule on the matter. In 1993 the EEOC issued draft regulations that would have provided greater clarity in defining gender harassment, but for some reason the commission decided against issuing final regulations, thereby continuing the uncertainty over the status of this form of harassment (U.S. EEOC, 1993).

Employer responsibilities remain ambiguous under the law. The Supreme Court's ruling in *Meritor Savings Bank, FSB v. Vinson* (1986) seemingly provided an escape hatch for employers in being held responsible for harassment, namely that they were not liable if they did not know of the harassment and reasonably could not be expected to know of it. The proposed EEOC guidelines of 1993 would have provided some clarification, but they were never adopted.

The field of sexual harassment has evolved considerably since 1964 when the Civil Rights Act was passed, but legal questions remain to be resolved either by Congress amending the law, the EEOC issuing clarifying guidelines, or the Supreme Court ruling definitively.

REFERENCES

BNA. 1994. *Sexual Harassment Plain and Simple.* Two-part video program. Rockville, Md.: BNA Communications.

Chan, A. A. 1994. *Women and Sexual Harassment.* New York: Harrington Park Press.

Civil Rights Act. 1964. P.L. 88-352, 78 Stat. 241, Title VII, 42 U.S.C. §2000e 2(a).

———. 1991. P.L. 102-166, 105 Stat. 1071, 42 U.S.C. §1981.

Congressional Accountability Act. 1995. P.L. 104-1, 109 Stat. 3.

Currie v. Kowalewski. 1994. U.S. Dist. LEXIS 909 (N.O.N.Y.).

Dobre v. Amtrak. 1993. 63 FEP Cases 923 (E.D.Pa).

Ellison v. Brady. 1991. 924 F.2d 872 (9th Cir.).

Garraghty v. Williams. 1995. 33 GERR 373 (Va.).

Giordano v. William Paterson College of New Jersey. 1992. 804 F. Supp. 637 (D.N.J.).

Greenlaw, P.S., and J.P. Kohl. 1992. "Proving Title VII Sexual Harassment." *Labor Law Journal* 43: 164-171.

Greenlaw, P.S., and R.D. Lee Jr. 1993. "Three Decades of Experience with the Equal Pay Act." *Review of Public Personnel Administration* 13 (Fall): 43-57.

Harris v. Forklift Systems, Inc. 1993. 114 S. Ct. 367.

Henson v. City of Dundee. 1982. 682 F.2d 897 (11th Cir.).

Janopoulos v. Harvey L. Walner & Associates, Ltd. 1993. 835 F. Supp. 459 (N.D.Ill.); 1994. U.S. Dist. LEXIS 11869 (N.D.Ill.).

Kelly, R.M., and P.M. Stambaugh. 1992. "Sexual Harassment in the States," in M.E. Guy, ed., *Women and Men of the States.* Armonk, N.Y.: M.E. Sharpe.

Lee, R.D., Jr., and P.S. Greenlaw. 1995. "The Legal Evolution of Sexual Harassment." *Public Administration Review* 55: 357-364.

Lindenberg, K.E., and L.A. Reese. 1995. "Sexual Harassment Policy Implementation Issues." *Review of Public Personnel Administration* 15 (Winter): 84-97.

Meritor Savings Bank, FSB v. Vinson. 1986. 477 U.S. 57.

Moreno, J.L. 1945. *Psychodramatic Treatment of Marriage Problems.* New York: Beacon House.

Murray, K. 1994. "A Backlash on Harassment Cases." *New York Times* 143 (September 18): B23.

National Council for Research on Women. 1991. *Sexual Harassment: Research and Resources.* New York: National Council for Research on Women.

New York Times. 1994. "Male Employees Accuse F.A.A. of Sex Harassment at Workshops." 143 (September 8): A22.

Polly v. Houston Lighting and Power Company. 1993. 825 F. Supp. 135 (S.D.Tex.).

Robinson, R.K., R.L. Fink, and B.M. Allen. 1994. "Unresolved Issues in Hostile Environment Claims of Sexual Harassment." *Labor Law Journal* 45 (February): 110-114.

Robinson, R.K., B.J. Reithel, and G.M. Franklin. 1995-1996. "An Exploratory Study of the *Reasonable Woman* Standard: Gender-Bias in Interpreting Actionable Sexual Harassment." *Journal of Individual Employment Rights* 4: 1-14.

Shearer, R.A. 1994. "Sexual Harassment by Nonemployees: Employer Liability for Conduct of Third Parties." *Journal of Individual Employment Rights* 3: 75-84.

Sudtelgte v. Reno. 1994. U.S. Dist. LEXIS 82 (W.D.Mo.).

"Survey Finds 31 Percent of Women Report Having Been Sexually Harassed at Work." 1994. 32 *Government Employee Relations Report* 459.

Swentek v. USAIR, Inc. 1987. 830 F.2d 552 (4th Cir.).

Thacker, R.A., and S.F. Gohmann. 1993. "Male/Female Differences in Perceptions and Effects of Hostile Environment Sexual Harassment: 'Reasonable' Assumptions?" *Public Personnel Management* 22: 461–472.

U.S. v. Burke. 1992. 112 S.Ct. 1867.

U.S. EEOC v. Hacienda Hotel. 1989. 881 F.2d 1504 (9th Cir.).

U.S. Equal Employment Opportunity Commission (EEOC). 1977 as amended. "Procedural Regulations." 29 CFR §1601.

——— . 1980. "Guidelines on Discrimination Because of Sex." 29 C.F.R. §1604.11.

——— . 1990. "Policy Guidance on Current Issues of Sexual Harassment." N-915-050.

——— . 1993. "Guidelines on Harassment Based on Race, Color, Religion, Gender, National Origin, Age or Disability." 58 Fed. Reg. 51,266.

U.S. Merit Systems Protection Board. 1988. *Sexual Harassment in the Federal Government: An Update.* Washington, D.C.: U.S. Government Printing Office.

——— . 1994. *Working for America: An Update.* Washington, D.C.: U.S. Government Printing Office.

Wohlking, W., and H. Weiner. 1971. "Structured and Spontaneous Role Playing: Contrast and Comparison." *Training and Development Journal* 25 (January): 8–14.

chapter **8**

Lesbians and Gay Men in the Public Sector Work Force

Charles W. Gossett

Most public sector organizations already have a diverse work force with respect to the sexual orientation of their employees. However, they are unaware of this fact or unwilling to acknowledge it. Ironically, while government agencies struggle to increase the representation of historically underrepresented racial and ethnic groups and women, many have until very recently actively sought to prevent lesbian, gay male, and bisexual job applicants from being hired or to remove such employees from their jobs. This contradictory situation—success in recruiting and promoting personnel that the organization, in many instances, would prefer not to have—makes the issue of lesbians, gay men, and bisexuals in the public workplace substantially different from the problems faced by historically underrepresented groups. At the same time, however, the struggle between advocates and opponents of laws that would provide legal protection against discrimination on the basis of sexual orientation makes remarkably similar use of the strategies and rhetoric of the supporters and enemies of the civil rights movement of African Americans and the women's movement. Thus personnel administrators, who will inevitably face questions concerning sexual orientation and employment, need familiarity with the historical experience of lesbians and gay males employed in the public sector, the current status of legal protections (or lack thereof) for lesbian and gay male employees, and some of the ways that traditional aspects of personnel administration are affected by the increasingly open presence of lesbians and gay men in the work force.

HISTORICAL OVERVIEW

Although the written record of sexual relations between persons of the same sex indicates that such practices are hardly a new phenomenon, the concept of such persons as a "class" different from persons who have sexual relations with persons of the opposite sex is usually traced to the latter half of the nineteenth century. At that time, homosexual behavior moved from being a "sinful" act to being viewed as an "illness," more specifically a psychiatric abnormality (Katz, 1995). Despite the characterization of homosexuality as a disease, however, it retained an identity as a sin as evidenced by the fact that, in the United States, all states had laws that criminalized sexual relations between persons of the same sex for most of this century (Nice, 1994), although between 1960 and 1995, 30 states and the District of Columbia decriminalized such behaviors (Chibbaro, 1993). Only in 1973 did the American Psychiatric Association vote to remove homosexuality from its list of psychological disorders. Most recently, scientific investigations into a biological origin for homosexuality have become prominent in discussions of whether or not sexual orientation is a personal characteristic more appropriately compared to race, ethnicity, or gender or whether comparison to some voluntary behaviors like religious choice is more suitable. The very fact that the term *sexual orientation* has replaced *sexual preference* in the discussion of this topic suggests that the arguments in favor of at least a partial biological explanation have gained fairly wide acceptance (Burr, 1993). This brief discussion of how homosexuality has been conceptualized is important because, as in all policy matters, how the "problem" is stated has great influence on how "solutions" are developed.

In the United States, there is evidence that from its founding, persons engaging in sexual activity with persons of the same sex have been dismissed from public service (Shilts, 1993). For the most part, such dismissals were focused on the acts allegedly committed and not because the accused was a particular "type" of person. With the development of the concepts and terms of *homosexual* and *heterosexual* in the late 1800s and early 1900s, shorthand labels that purported to predict everything from sexual desires to fitness for particular types of employment became available to society. Public employers now had available scientifically defined "groups" that could be favored (heterosexuals) or discriminated against (homosexuals) (Katz, 1995).

The Military

Perhaps the best known efforts at using the criterion of homosexuality to make employment decisions are in the military. Shilts (1993) recounts the long history of "gays in the military," but his story clearly demonstrates that the use of this classification as a tool of personnel management really accelerated during World War II. Until 1993, the question as to whether or not a person was a homosexual appeared on military application forms; it was dropped only as part of a compromise between the president and Congress over the issue of officially allowing lesbians and gay men to serve in the armed forces (Aspin, 1993). This "Don't Ask, Don't Tell" compromise policy implies that homosexual conduct—including the mere statement that one is a gay male, lesbian, or bisexual—is still grounds for discharge from military service, regardless of performance. The rationale offered in defense of this policy, given that several studies have demonstrated no perceptible differences in ability or performance between homosexual and heterosexual military personnel (e.g., Dyer, 1990), is that military readiness is compromised by the fact that many military personnel are made uncomfortable by the knowledge that homosexuals are serving with them. This argument is strikingly similar to the arguments raised when President Truman ordered the integration of armed forces units rather than continuing to segregate different races in separate units (Keen, 1992). In the current case, however, gay male and lesbian soldiers are already integrated into all units, which makes it not surprising that some opponents of homosexuals serving openly in the military proposed segregation of homosexuals and heterosexuals as a compromise solution. Currently, several cases are working their way to the Supreme Court for a decision on the constitutionality of the policy prohibiting continued military service by persons known to be homosexuals.

Federal Civilian Employment

In the post–World War II period, especially during the early years of the cold war, civilian government employees who were lesbians and gay men were also targeted for removal from public employment. Although the early 1950s are better known for the McCarthy hearings that sought to identify and remove alleged Communist Party members and sympathizers from government positions, homosexuals were also a major target of congressional investigating committees (Lewis, 1993; Katz, 1992: 91-105). Despite a variety of epithets and accusations of moral weakness, the "official" reason given as to why homosexuals were unfit for public service was that they posed a "security risk" to the nation. The logic behind this claim was that lesbian and gay male employees, being members of socially despised groups and, almost by definition, engaging in criminal acts every time they had sexual relations, would not want their employer or family members to know of their homosexuality. Thus homosexual employees were highly susceptible to blackmail by foreign agents who would either threaten exposure or simply prey on the fact that they were morally weak. That there was no evidence of any homosexual American government employee having engaged in espionage or betrayal of government secrets was irrelevant. Nor did the circularity of the argument—homosexuals must be dismissed from employment because they could be blackmailed because they would lose their jobs if it was known that they were homosexuals—have any effect on the policy. Not surprisingly, given the nature of the "security risk" argument, most of the dismissals of homosexual employees occurred in the State Department and among civilian employees in defense agencies (Lewis, 1993). It wasn't until August 1995 that President Clinton issued an Executive Order prohibiting government agencies from denying security clearances simply because the person is a lesbian or gay man (Chibbaro, 1995).

Although specific numbers are hard to come by, it appears that during the late 1950s and throughout the 1960s the number of dismissals of lesbian and gay male employees declined from the heights reached during the McCarthy era. In addition to the security risk argument, Lewis (1993) identifies three other reasons used to justify the dismissal of homosexual employees from civilian federal service: (1) homosexuality is an example of the "criminal, infamous, dishonest, immoral, or notoriously disgraceful conduct" that always justifies a refusal to hire or a dismissal; (2) the presence of homosexuals impairs "the efficiency of the service" because some employees would be so upset working with known homosexuals that they could not perform their own jobs; and (3) employing homosexuals would "embarrass" the agency and impair its standing in the public's eyes. Over the years, the courts struck down each of these reasons for dismissing or refusing to hire openly lesbian and gay male personnel, although never completely closing the door to the possibility that in some circumstances a dismissal or refusal to hire on the basis of sexual orientation might be legitimate. Relying on the "nexus" arguments developed during the 1960s and 1970s, absent a clear connection between a person's sexual orientation and the ability to perform a particular job, discrimination against lesbians and gay men is not permissible. Of course, whether or not there is a connection is left to the judge reviewing the discriminatory claim.

As the social climate changed—particularly in the period following the historic Stonewall rebellion, which is often cited as the beginning of the current press for equal rights for lesbians and gay men (Duberman, 1993)—the now defunct Civil Service Commission (CSC) began to modify its official policies in response to both court decisions and political pressure. In the mid-1970s the CSC advised agencies that "merely" because a person is a homosexual, absent a showing that conduct affects ability to perform the job, there was insufficient grounds for a finding of "unsuitability." In 1980 the first director of the Office of Personnel Management, Alan Campbell, reemphasizing the importance of a nexus between off-duty behavior and job performance, issued a memorandum stating that "applicants and employees are to be protected against inquiries into, or actions based upon, non-job-related conduct, such as religious, community or social affiliations, or sexual orientation" (Lewis, 1993). Despite a change in administration, this policy remained in effect throughout the 1980s.

During the 1992 election campaign, the question of lifting the ban on "gays in the military" was a clear policy difference between the Democratic and Republican candidates. And even though the victory of Bill Clinton did not lead to a repeal of this particular prohibition, there was hope that a presidential order prohibiting employment discrimination on the basis of sexual orientation in the civilian branches of government would be issued. However, a different strategy emerged based on concerns that the anti-gay frenzy that had been whipped up over the military debate would lead to congressional action overturning an Executive Order covering civilians. Instead of a single order, the White House encouraged each Cabinet department and independent agency to issue its own nondiscrimination policy. By mid-1995, 13 of 14 cabinet departments and more than 15 agencies had issued such statements.

Current Federal Activity

In 1995, a bill known as the Employment Non-Discrimination Act (ENDA) was introduced into the U.S. Congress. Similar bills had been previously introduced in Congress since 1974 (Rutledge, 1992), although in 1995 the bill had a record 138 sponsors on the day of its introduction. This bill would prohibit employment discrimination in the public and private sectors on the basis of sexual orientation in a manner similar to, but more restricted than, the way such discrimination is prohibited by the Civil Rights Acts of 1964 and 1991 for the categories of race, color, national origin, religion, and sex. In addition to exemptions for small employers and religious organizations that can be found in other civil rights laws, ENDA includes some unique features designed to disarm potential critics, but of great importance to personnel managers who would be responsible for seeing that the law is followed in their organizations. First, the act does not apply to the provision of employee benefits to an individual for the benefit of his or her partner, an issue discussed in greater detail below. Other sections of the proposed law forbid both the use of statistics to establish disparate impact as prima facie evidence of discrimination and establishment of quotas or preferential treatment for lesbians or gay men. Also, the law makes clear that the nondiscrimination requirement does not apply to the armed forces, nor will it "repeal or modify any Federal, State, territorial, or local law creating special rights or preferences for veterans." The latter statement recognizes that the issue of veterans' preference, a policy employed by many government jurisdictions, becomes problematic if the military is allowed to arbitrarily exclude lesbians and gay men. In *Personnel Administrator v. Feeney* (1979), the Court found that providing veterans' preference in employment decisions did not constitute illegal sex discrimination because women could join the military. Lesbians and gay men prohibited from serving in the armed forces will be unable to earn veterans' preference. Without this specific protection guaranteeing "special rights and preferences for veterans," a decision quite different from *Feeney* would be likely should the bill become law.

State and Local Government

Although no legal protections against discrimination based on sexual orientation have been enacted at the federal level, 9 states and more than 140 local governments had passed such laws by 1995 (Riccucci and Gossett, 1996). The forms and types of discrimination against lesbian and gay male public employees historically practiced by the federal government were often repeated at the state levels as well. Even the congressional hearings of the 1950s attempting to root out homosexuals from federal service had their counterparts in state legislatures, the best known being the Johns Committee hearings in Florida in the 1960s (*Government versus Homosexuals,* 1975). However, because one consequence of American federalism is that the national and state levels of government have somewhat different responsibilities, the concerns of state and local governments about homosexuality were not exactly the same as the concerns of political leaders in Washington, D.C. Rather than using "national security" as the core element of an anti-homosexual campaign, state and local leaders focused on the issue of education and an alleged danger to children from lesbian and gay male teachers. As was true with fear of the national security risk, fears of teachers molesting or "recruiting" students were based less on evidence than on emotion. The articulation of specific fears about homosexual teachers is a development of the post–World War II era when courts began demanding that public employers show a "nexus" between an employee's behavior off duty and job performance. Courts were somewhat lenient in accepting evidence of a nexus when cases involved school board decisions to dismiss lesbian and gay male teachers, largely because of the traditional "role model" responsibilities of teachers and acceptance of the unsupported claim that homosexual teachers pose a danger to children (Harbeck, 1992). Although teachers were the primary focus of anti-gay discrimination at the state and local levels, the generally negative climate affected employees in other types of jobs as well.

As indicated earlier, however, some state and local governments have decided to treat sexual orientation as a category similar to race, sex, and religion in laws prohibiting employment discrimination. Unlike the federal government, however, most jurisdictions have not set about writing special legislation in the style of ENDA. Instead, where such laws have been adopted, the term *sexual orientation, sexual preference,* or *affectional preference*[1] was simply added to the list of all protected categories. The city first credited with adopting such a law was East Lansing, Michigan, in 1972; the first territory was the District of Columbia in 1973; the first county was Santa Cruz, California, in 1975; and the first state was Wisconsin in 1983 (Singer and Deschamps, 1994). Although there is great variety in the extensiveness of coverage of such laws, where they exist, public employment, at a minimum, is covered. However, due to the nature of multiple types of governments found in American states, laws passed by one jurisdictional unit do not always apply to other overlapping jurisdictions. For example, although a city council may have passed a sexual orientation nondiscrimination ordinance, such a law may not apply to the employees of that town's school system, which is under the authority of a separately elected school board. Obviously, in order to effectively perform their jobs, personnelists must be aware of whether or not the jurisdiction in which they work provides such protections.

IMPLICATIONS OF NONDISCRIMINATION LAWS FOR PERSONNEL FUNCTIONS

If a jurisdiction adopts a law that prohibits discrimination on the basis of sexual orientation—especially if that protection is achieved by adding the term *sexual orientation* to the list of other criteria rather than developed as a separate law similar to ENDA with a series of exceptions to the traditional interpretations of such laws—there are a number of corollary issues that must be faced by personnel administrators. These include issues involving recruitment, selection, and affirmative action; discrimination complaints; terminations; sexual harassment; diversity training; compensation and employee benefits; and miscellaneous related tasks.

Recruitment, Selection, and Affirmative Action

For many people, two of the most important contributions to personnel management coming out of the movements for civil rights for African Americans and women have been the focus on (1) expanding the number and variety of sources from which job applicants are recruited, and (2) improving personnel selection methods by insisting that jobs be carefully defined and that the methods for selecting people be validly related to identifying the necessary skills for each job. Expanded outreach helps organizations attract previously underutilized or overlooked talent, and better selection tools are supposed to weed out "irrelevant" considerations such as race or sex or religion in determining whether or not a person is qualified for a particular job. In jurisdictions that prohibit sexual orientation discrimination, that characteristic is also to be treated as irrelevant.

As noted earlier, because the sexual orientation of a job applicant or an employee is not usually apparent, it is probable that most lesbians and gay men do not face the blatant discrimination faced historically and currently by persons of color and women. This is particularly true with respect to recruitment and access to job information, since sexual orientation is a characteristic that overlays other demographic (and legally protected) characteristics such as race, ethnicity, sex, and religion. To the extent that information and recruitment activities are targeted toward one of those groups, many lesbian and gay men will receive the information as well. However, organizations that have historically discriminated against lesbians and gay men may find (just as agencies that discriminated against African Americans or women have found) that positive, specifically targeted, and sustained recruitment efforts are necessary to overcome the resistance to working for previously hostile organizations. Thus police departments in some cities have set up recruitment booths at lesbian and gay male festival sites or have established community liaisons to overcome negative perceptions earned after years of anti-gay harassment.

There are two specific situations in which discrimination against homosexuals may occur at the selection stage also. One occurs because popular stereotypes often associate certain physical and behavioral characteristics with homosexuality—for example, men who exhibit mannerisms society views as feminine and women who exhibit mannerisms considered masculine. Such a person may or may not be a homosexual but is much more likely to face discrimination based on perceived sexual orientation than is a lesbian or gay man who exhibits socially defined gender-appropriate behaviors. The second exception is for lesbians, gay men, and bisexuals who make known their sexual orientation to potential employers. For a variety of reasons, more and more lesbians and gay men and bisexuals are choosing to publicly identify their sexual orientation and do so in a variety of ways. Application forms provide a number of opportunities for people to reveal their sexual orientation. Perhaps the most obvious is when application forms ask about organizational memberships. In fact, required listings of organizational memberships have been used by public employers to screen out certain job applicants (*Shelton v. Tucker,* 1960). Failure to list a particular organizational membership has become grounds for dismissal on the basis of having submitted a fraudulent application. This Catch 22 scenario has been replicated with respect to the hiring of lesbians and gay men (*Acanfora v. Board of Education of Montgomery County,* 1974), although in the absence of a nondiscrimination law this method of identifying and discriminating against people may still be used.

A second feature of the application form that is relevant here is the marital status box. Many jurisdictions prohibit discrimination on the basis of marital status, but some do not, including several that prohibit discrimination on the basis of sexual orientation. Marriage is both a legal and a religious ceremony; and although currently no American jurisdictions legally recognize marriages between two people of the same sex, some religious denominations do perform such unions (Sherman, 1992). In any event, a person who considers him- or herself married to someone of the same sex, may very well choose to indicate that by checking the "Married" box on an application form as the most honest representation of his or her relationship status (*Shahar v. Bowers,* 1993). In a similar manner, lesbian and gay male employees may reveal their sexual orientation informally, though not inadvertently, during the course of an interview.

The issue of affirmative action in the context of sexual orientation is somewhat more complex than it is in the case of race or gender. First, there is no reliable statistical way to determine whether or not lesbians and gay men are proportionally represented, overrepresented, or underrepresented in a particular type or level of a government job. This is not surprising given that there continues to be a dispute over what proportions of the total population should be classified as homosexual, bisexual, and heterosexual (Singer and Deschamps, 1994). And although there have been very few people calling for affirmative action programs similar to those in place for historically under-represented groups, there have been regular calls for the appointment of "openly gay" officials at the highest levels of each political jurisdiction.

Discrimination Complaints

For most employees, bringing a complaint of discrimination to the attention of the appropriate authorities is not easy. Such a complaint formalizes a conflict by bringing in a third party, often from the personnel department in the form of an employee relations specialist or an equal employment opportunity officer.

Employees who believe they are being treated in a discriminatory manner because of their race, gender, age, or disability must reach a point at which the personal psychic and physical costs of the discriminatory behavior outweigh the costs of the tension in the work environment that are likely to result from filing a formal complaint. But for many lesbian and gay male employees, particularly those who have not discussed their sexual orientation in the workplace but who experience discriminatory treatment based on people's perceptions that they are gay, the decision also involves making a public record of their sexual orientation. This is an additional cost not usually borne by people for whom the discriminatory treatment is based on a visible characteristic such as skin color or gender or on a less visible but socially more acceptable characteristic, such as certain disabilities or religion. As a consequence, it is not surprising that even when jurisdictions adopt nondiscrimination laws that include sexual orientation, the use of such protective provisions is relatively low (Riccucci and Gossett, 1996). Although several explanations are possible for the low number of complaints, the stigma still given to homosexuality in American society remains the most likely factor leading to reluctance to file a complaint.

Terminations

In the past few decades, the courts have been forcing public employers to demonstrate how any particular off-duty behavior has an impact on the job performance of an individual employee before using that off-duty behavior as justification for a termination of employment. At the federal level, *Norton v. Macy* (1969) was the first case involving homosexual activity to apply this standard in a way that overturned the agency's decision to terminate. Although this standard is now fairly well entrenched, application of the standard does not automatically lead to a finding of no relationship between sexual orientation (or a related aspect, such as a declaration of sexual orientation) and the requirements of a particular job. Several cases (e.g., *Singer v. United States Civil Service Commission,* 1976, and *Shahar v. Bowers,* 1993) have found that an individual could be denied a job because of some factor closely related to his or her sexual orientation.

The key element in much of the discussion about sexual orientation and the suitability for particular jobs is related to the fact that in 20 states "sodomy" is a criminal offense. Although the definition of "sodomy" or "unnatural acts" varies among the states that have such laws, all include sexual contact between people of the same sex as a criminal activity. Despite the fine legal distinctions between "sexual orientation" and "sexual activities" being made in the course of the "gays-in-the-military" court proceedings, most public employees in states with sodomy laws who say that they are gay or bisexual are "confessing" to a criminal offense. Some jurisdictions, including the state of Rhode Island (Keen, 1995), find themselves in the position of both guaranteeing nondiscrimination based on sexual orientation and enforcing sodomy laws.

Sexual Harassment

The distinction that courts make between quid pro quo sexual harassment and harassment created by a hostile environment is proving to be particularly important to lesbians and gay men as the federal courts develop case law in this area. To date, most federal courts have found that the Civil Rights Act of 1964 prohibits same-sex quid pro quo sexual harassment but that it does not provide protection for lesbians or gay men who are subject to ridicule or made to feel uncomfortable in the workplace because of their sexual orientation. (See Chapter 7 in this volume.) However, state and local governments that prohibit discrimination in employment based on sexual orientation are likely to find state courts making different decisions, because if sexual orientation discrimination is prohibited and if creation of a hostile environment is a form of discrimination, then an anti-gay hostile environment would not be defensible.

Compensation and Employee Benefits

Government entities, like private businesses, are governed by the Equal Pay Act of 1963. Lesbians, gay men, and bisexuals are not paid different wages or salaries based specifically on their sexual orientation. But the concept of "compensation" has in recent years been broadened beyond the idea of base pay and take-home pay to an idea called "total compensation" (McCaffery, 1992). Total compensation attempts to recognize that the value an employee receives from his or her employer in exchange for work includes not only wages and salary, but a variety of monetary and nonmonetary benefits as well. Whereas 30 or 40 years ago such benefits made up a relatively small proportion of total payroll expenses, by the 1980s such benefits constituted up to 40 percent of payroll costs (Gossett, 1994). Unlike actual wages and salaries, however, many employers distribute benefits of different value to different types of employees. The most common distinction made that results in differential benefit treatment is between married and unmarried employees. Although technically this is a distinction between single and married employees, the fact that gay male and lesbian employees are prohibited from marrying a same-sex partner (whom they see as the equivalent of a legal spouse) makes this an issue of particular concern to them. Differences in treatment can be seen in a wide variety of benefits including sick leave, bereavement leave, life insurance, health insurance, disability compensation, and retirement benefits.

Leave benefits are important because they usually include allowances for an employee to take leave to care for an ill family member or to attend the funeral of a deceased family member. "Family member," however, is usually defined as a blood relative or someone related by marriage. Even when lesbian and gay male employees are willing to make known to their employers that they are in a relationship with someone of the same sex, a person who is their family, existing rules generally do not enable an employee to take leave to care for or grieve for such partners (or the children of such partners). Employee life insurance programs many times permit employees to purchase additional group coverage on the lives of their spouses and children, a benefit denied to unmarried employees. Disability (or workers') compensation in some jurisdictions provides different levels of benefits for employees with a spouse and/or dependent children than it provides for "single" employees. And pension programs, particularly defined benefit programs, usually include an option for an employee to elect a reduced annuity in order to provide a survivor's annuity for his or her spouse or minor children, another benefit denied to unmarried employees except in unusual circumstances (District of Columbia, 1990).[2]

For gay male and lesbian activists, the issue of unequal access to health benefits for the same-sex partners of homosexual employees is highest on the agenda for change once legal protection against employment discrimination has been obtained. In the United States, access to health insurance is, for all practical purposes, tied to employment. Most government employers offer their permanent employees the opportunity to purchase subsidized health insurance for themselves and for certain members of their family, namely their legal spouse and their own minor children and any minor children of their spouse. Given that employers may subsidize family health benefit plans at a higher dollar value (even if it is at the same percentage rate) than the subsidy given to single employees, an argument can be made that single and married employees are receiving unequal pay for equal work. More common, however, are complaints that the partners of heterosexual employees are being treated differently from the partners of homosexual employees. Technically, however, courts and human relations commissions that receive such complaints in a formal manner usually argue that the distinction made is not on the basis of sexual orientation but on the basis of marital status, and that marital status is not always covered by nondiscrimination laws or is covered in such a way that this specific issue is exempted to allow for different treatment in the field of employee benefits (Riccucci and Gossett, 1996).

In addition to seeking redress through the legal system, lesbians and gay men have used the political process to secure such benefits. In nearly 30 local governments (municipalities, counties, school boards, special districts), laws have been passed, collective bargaining agreements negotiated, or executive orders issued that provide for access to health benefits and various leave benefits by employees with same-sex partners on the same or similar terms available to employees who have opposite-sex partners. These programs are usually referred to as "domestic partnership" benefit programs. Opposition to such programs often turns on the fear of significant increases in costs to the employer, although in practice cost increases have been very limited (Hostetler and Pynes, 1995). Although most of the jurisdictions adopting the domestic partnership benefit programs treat unmarried opposite-sex partnerships in the same way they treat same-sex partnerships, a few have proposed limiting access to benefits only to same-sex partners on the theory that opposite-sex partners have the option of marriage whereas same-sex partners do not. Private corporations that offer domestic partnership benefits to their employees usually limit such benefits to same-sex couples (Reckard, 1993). Although there is some logic in this latter position, a public entity that adopts it is open to criticism as discriminating against heterosexuals and creating "special rights" for homosexuals alone. Of course, this argument can be countered by saying that the different treatment is only offered because civil marriage is a "special right" only available to opposite-sex partners.

Diversity Training

In recognition of the changing composition of the American work force, a number of employers, public as well as private, have begun to focus on ways of utilizing work-force diversity to facilitate achievement of the organization's goals. "Diversity training" is one approach that employers take to teach workers and supervisors to deal with cultural and value differences among their co-workers and subordinates. Such training attempts to eliminate dysfunctional friction at the worksite and to train supervisors to recognize, avoid, or properly handle discriminatory treatment so as to minimize legal actions against the employer. Sexual orientation, however, is a topic ignored in many discussions of diversity (Cox, 1993; Caudron, 1995).

In organizations governed by laws or policies that prohibit discrimination on the basis of sexual orientation, inclusion of this issue in diversity training courses flows naturally from the official policy. This does not mean, however, that sexual orientation will be a particularly comfortable or easy topic to address in such training. When there is no protection against discrimination, handling the issue of sexual orientation can be quite explosive and even threatening given that self-revelation by lesbians and gay men may lead to dismissal or harassment. On the other hand, avoiding the topic may defeat the purpose of much diversity training that is aimed at making people tolerant and understanding of important differences among co-workers, which in turn builds trust and facilitates the work of the organization (McNaught, 1993).

Other Issues

Personnel offices are frequently assigned responsibility for addressing a variety of other workplace-related issues in addition to the core personnel functions. Many of these tasks can be grouped under the very broad heading "Quality of Work Life" (QWL). The presence of lesbian, gay male, and bisexual employees in the work force is not often addressed in the existing QWL literature, but personnel officials who wish to ensure inclusive work environments need to be aware of how certain actions affect nonheterosexual employees.

Lesbians and gay men are often accused of "flaunting" their sexuality whenever it becomes known to other workers; they have violated the pre-sumption of heterosexuality that pervades most organizations. Whether the employee simply made a statement about his or her sexual orientation, discussed his or her social activities over the weekend with a person of the same sex, displayed a picture of his or her family on the desk, or appeared at an office function with the person he or she lives with or is dating, many employees are scandalized and find such behavior inappropriate in a work setting. Yet if any of these situations had involved a heterosexual employee, no notice would have been taken. If the organization is committed to equal treatment regardless of sexual orientation, managers and their advisors in the personnel office must be able to distinguish *unacceptable* behavior from *unexpected* behavior. Standards concerning appropriate levels of discussion or knowledge about an individual's life outside the office need to be consistent, although, of course, every employee is entitled to determine the amount of personal information shared for him- or herself.

"Celebrating diversity" is a somewhat recent addition to the responsibilities of the personnel office and is considered part of maintaining organizational morale. In the public sector, events such as Black History Month may be even more important than in the private sector because they also reinforce the idea that the government is there to serve all the people. Activists are working to establish a "Gay, Lesbian, and Bisexual History Month" in October (Jennings, 1994). For the past several years, October 11 has been celebrated as "Coming Out Day" when lesbians, gay men, and bisexual people are encouraged to identify themselves in some way to their families, friends, and co-workers. Late June is traditionally the time for Gay Pride celebrations. Again, to the extent that personnel offices are responsible for making all employees feel that the organization respects and values the contributions any group makes, they must be knowledgeable about events and times of the year that have special meaning to each particular group.

Employee recognition is often an important part of an organization's traditions. Annual award dinners, employee appreciation picnics and parties, holiday parties, and other similar activities frequently fall to the personnel office to organize. Many times these events are designed to include family members in appreciation of the important role that family life plays in support of the productivity of each worker. Invitations to "husbands" and "wives" are likely viewed as limited to only legally married partners of employees; more inclusive invitations to "your guest" or "your partner" will indicate that the partners and family members of lesbian and gay male employees are welcome.

Occupational safety and health is another responsibility often assigned to the personnel office. Although there are no occupational injuries or diseases that are unique to lesbian and gay male employees, the high incidence of Acquired Immunodeficiency Syndrome (AIDS) among gay men has created a volatile workplace issue that must be addressed by personnel officers. (See Chapter 9 in this volume.) Effective education about how AIDS is and is not transmitted has become one of the most important occupational safety issues of the last ten years.

Many organizations have anti-nepotism provisions in their personnel policies, and the question of how these policies apply to lesbian and gay male partners who work for the same organization presents a quandary. In organizations that provide for the registration of domestic partners and treat such partnerships in a manner similar to the way marital partnerships are treated with respect to employee benefits, for example, application of anti-nepotism rules to homosexual partners would seem to be appropriate. But if the organization does not recognize such partnerships in any other way, "legitimizing" the relationship through the application of anti-nepotism rules would undercut the rationale for not recognizing the partners for other purposes.

CONCLUSION

Public sector organizations in the 1990s have three options for addressing issues pertaining to lesbians, gay men, and bisexual people who currently, or may potentially, work for them. Historically, government agencies actively sought to identify and remove such employees; to some extent, this is still the policy of the U.S. military. A second option is to simply ignore the fact that the organization has nonheterosexual employees and omit the issue of sexual orientation from personnel policies or practices. This probably describes the current situation in most public sector organizations. Finally, governments can choose to recognize, appreciate, and attempt to find advantages in the diversity of sexual orientations to be found in its work force. A minuscule, but increasing, proportion of the 83,000 government units found in the United States have chosen this strategy. Although only a few cities and counties have adopted this approach, those that have include some of the country's largest municipal jurisdictions; so, in practical effect, many public employees work in places that officially forbid discrimination on the basis of sexual orientation.

Regardless of which strategy any particular organization currently applies to the issue of sexual orientation and the workplace, the pressures for a policy change will confront every public sector organization within the next few years. Whether it is simply to remove a policy of automatic exclusion of homosexuals as in the military, or to provide the protection of a nondiscrimination law, or to treat domestic partnerships in the same way that marriages are treated for employee benefits, the demands for change are unlikely to subside. Even in those jurisdictions that have done the most to develop "gay-friendly" personnel policies, there will be new challenges. Currently several localities have, or are considering, extending protection to transgendered employees[3] and job applicants by adding the category of "gender identity" to the list of categories under which discrimination is prohibited. The implications of such a policy change for personnel administration are only beginning to be understood.

NOTES

1. In recent years, the term *sexual orientation* has become more common. Older laws still use the term "preference." The change is due largely to both scientific findings and political pressures that argue that to whom one is sexually attracted is less a matter of choice than of biological predisposition (Burr, 1993).

2. The federal Civil Service Retirement System, for example, allows an unmarried employee to show that a third party is financially dependent on the retiree and provision for a survivor annuity can be made for that person. However, if the employee died before actually retiring, such a dependent third party, unlike a spouse and/or minor children, would not be eligible for an annuity. There is no requirement that spouses or children actually be financially dependent on the retiree in order to receive a survivor's annuity.

3. "Transgendered" is a term used to describe persons whose psychological gender identity does not correspond with their biological sex characteristics. Some transgendered individuals undergo surgical and hormonal treatments to bring their physical traits into line with their psychological identity, others merely dress in the clothing usually worn by persons of their opposite gender. The term "transsexual" is often applied to the former and "transvestite" is sometimes applied to the latter group, although the specific terminology used for such categories is still evolving (Bornstein, 1994).

REFERENCES

Acanfora v. Board of Education of Montgomery County, 491 F.2d 498 (1974).

Aspin, Les. 1993. Memorandum to Secretaries of the Army, Navy, Air Force and Chairman of the Joint Chiefs of Staff, July 19.

Bornstein, Kate. 1994. *Gender Outlaw: On Men, Women, and the Rest of Us.* New York: Vintage Books.

Burr, Chandler. 1993. "Homosexuality and Biology." *Atlantic Monthly* (March): 47–65.

Caudron, Shari. 1995. "Open the Corporate Closet to Sexual Orientation Issues." *Personnel Journal* 74 (August): 42–55.

Chibbaro, Lou, Jr. 1993. "Sodomy Law Repealed." *Washington Blade* [Washington, D.C.], September 17: 1ff.

———. 1995. "Clinton: Being Gay Is 'Not a Security Risk.'" *Washington Blade* [Washington, D.C.], August 4: 1ff.

Cox, Taylor, Jr. 1993. *Cultural Diversity in Organizations: Theory, Research and Practice.* San Francisco: Barrett-Koehler.

District of Columbia. 1990. *Final Report and Recommendations.* Washington, D.C.: Commission on Domestic Partnership Benefits for D.C. Employees, vol. 1, July.

Duberman, Martin. 1993. *Stonewall.* New York: Dutton.

Dyer, Kate, ed. 1990. *Gays in Uniform: The Pentagon's Secret Reports.* Boston: Alyson Publications.

Gossett, Charles W. 1994. "Domestic Partnership Benefits: Public Sector Patterns." *Review of Public Personnel Administration* 14 (Winter): 64–84.

Government versus Homosexuals. 1975. New York: Arno Press.

Harbeck, Karen M. 1992. "Gay and Lesbian Educators: Past History/Future Prospects," in Karen M. Harbeck, ed., *Coming Out of the Classroom Closet,* pp. 121–140. New York: Harrington Park Press.

Hostetler, Dennis, and Joan E. Pynes. 1995. "Domestic Partnership Benefits: Dispelling the Myths." *Review of Public Personnel Administration* 15 (Winter): 41–59.

Jennings, Kevin. 1994. "Why We Need a Lesbian and Gay History Month." *TWN* [Miami, Fla.], October 19: p. 6.

Katz, Jonathon Ned. 1992. *Gay American History: Lesbians and Gay Men in the U.S.A.,* rev. ed. New York: Meridian.

———. 1995. *The Invention of Heterosexuality.* New York: Dutton.

Keen, Lisa. 1992. "Military History: Blueprint for Bias." *Washington Blade* [Washington, D.C.], December 11: 1ff.

———. 1995. "Despite Setbacks, Sodomy Law Challenges 'on a Roll.'" *Washington Blade* [Washington, D.C.], June 30: 1ff.

Lewis, Gregory B. 1993. "Lifting the Ban on Gays in the Civil Service: Federal Policy toward Gay and Lesbian Employees, 1950–1993." Paper presented at the American Political Science Association meeting, Washington, D.C.

McCaffery, Robert M. 1992. *Employee Benefit Programs: A Total Compensation Perspective,* 2nd ed. Boston: PWS-Kent Publishing.

McNaught, Brian. 1993. *Gay Issues in the Workplace.* New York: St. Martin's Press.

Nice, David C. 1994. *Policy Innovation in State Government.* Ames: Iowa State University Press.

Norton v. Macy, 417 F.2d 1161 (D.C. Cir. 1969).

Personnel Administrator v. Feeney, 422 U.S. 256 (1979).

Reckard, E. Scott. 1993. "Hollywood Moving Forward on Recognizing Needs of Gay Employees." *Bay Windows* [Boston], July 8: 5–6.

Riccucci, Norma M., and Charles W. Gossett. 1996. "Employment Discrimination in State and Local Government: The Lesbian and Gay Male Experience." *American Review of Public Administration,* vol. 26, no. 2: 175–200.

Rutledge, Leigh W. 1992. *The Gay Decades: From Stonewall to the Present.* New York: Plume Books.

Shahar v. Bowers, 836 F. Supp. 869 (1993).

Shelton v. Tucker, 364 U.S. 479 (1960).

Sherman, Suzanne, ed. 1992. *Lesbian and Gay Marriage.* Philadelphia: Temple University Press.

Shilts, Randy. 1993. *Conduct Unbecoming: Lesbians and Gays in the U.S. Military: Vietnam to the Persian Gulf.* New York: St. Martin's Press.

Singer v. United States Civil Service Commission, 530 F.2d 247 (1976); vacated, 429 U.S. 1034 (1977).

Singer, Bennett L., and David Deschamps, eds. 1994. *Gay and Lesbian Stats: A Pocket Guide to Facts and Figures.* New York: New Press.

chapter **9**

AIDS and Disability Policy: How Can the Public Sector Prepare Itself?

James D. Slack

With more than 50 million people enduring some kind of impairment that can affect their capacity to work, disabled Americans make up the second largest protected class of people in the nation. Within the protected class of disabled Americans are people with the Human Immunodeficiency Virus (HIV), the retrovirus that causes Acquired Immunodeficiency Syndrome (AIDS). This chapter examines the rights of job applicants and employees within the HIV spectrum, as well as the workplace ramifications of this disease.[1] It also addresses ways in which management might develop a more supportive organizational environment that can help postpone and minimize workplace costs associated with the disease, as well as sustain the highest possible levels of workplace productivity and work-force morale. Gaining skills to manage the workplace ramifications of this disease will give managers greater insight into the handling of issues pertinent to other groups within the American work force.

DISABLED AMERICANS AND THE NEED FOR PROTECTION

Disabled Americans can be found in all segments of society; they are rich and poor, Anglo and non-Anglo, men and women. The one common denominator is that each has at least one physical or mental impairment that tends to be chronic in nature. Some individuals have disabilities, such as blindness or facial disfigurements or mental retardation, that are very apparent to everyone. Other people suffer disabilities, such as hearing loss, epilepsy, or manic depression, that may not be so immediately apparent to other people. Still others have disabilities, such as heart disease or cancer or an anatomical loss, that may not be evident at all. Whether or not one can actually see the infliction, people with chronic physical or mental impairments are considered to be disabled.

Disabled individuals need protection because society makes them vulnerable in at least three ways. First, historically we have neglected the needs of disabled people. It was not until the early 1970s that the first piece of legislation was enacted in the United States that actually dealt with the issue of providing disabled people with access to fundamental social and community activities, such as entering public buildings or using the bathrooms in those buildings. By ignoring their needs for nearly 200 years, we also denied them meaningful participation in society. Second, various disabilities are often misunderstood, and as a result the capabilities of disabled individuals are frequently underestimated. Our initial tendency is to assist the paraplegic person in the wheelchair, or to refrain from directing too many questions to the person with a speech impairment. By wanting to help them in this fashion, we often make the assumption that disabled people cannot participate meaningfully in our society. Third, disabilities can make us feel uncomfortable, and therefore we tend not to want disabled individuals around us. The history of cancer certainly reflects this feeling. Uncomfortableness is always pronounced when it comes to being around people with contagious diseases. Our own fears about disabilities can also block opportunities for meaningful participation on the part of the disabled person.

PEOPLE WITH HIV/AIDS

How many people have HIV? We simply do not know the answer to this question. Estimates range from 1 million to over 5 million people in the United States.[2] We cannot know the exact count unless everyone agrees to take a HIV antibody blood test. Even then, we would still not know with certainty because the internal validity of the test is threatened in cases where the retrovirus has been introduced only recently into the person's body.[3]

Although we can only guess the number of people with HIV, we do know a lot about people with AIDS. Approximately 500,000 Americans have contracted it, half of whom are dead and all of whom are destined to die. The number of Americans with AIDS increases by about 25 percent each year. Of great importance to us here is that most people with AIDS are between the working ages of 20 and 65 (U.S. Department of Health and Human Services, 1995). The vast majority of Americans with HIV/AIDS were employed, or at least had jobs and careers, at the point when they discovered their seroconversion.

WORKPLACE RIGHTS OF PEOPLE WITH HIV/AIDS

Two pieces of federal legislation protect the workplace rights of all disabled employees, including those in the HIV spectrum.[4] The 1973 Rehabilitation (Rehab) Act protects those who are employed by federal, state, and local governments, as well as those employed by nonprofit organizations and companies that receive funding directly or indirectly from the federal government. The 1990 Americans with Disabilities Act (ADA) protects disabled individuals who work in state and local governments, as well as those in most private organizations that employ at least 15 people on a full-time basis for at least 20 weeks annually.[5] Rehab and the ADA require management to be "disability-blind." Management is prohibited from taking into consideration physical or mental disabilities in the hiring, promotion, and compensation processes if the person is otherwise qualified to perform the essential functions of the job. At the same time, Rehab requires management to be "disability-conscious." Theoretically management must take affirmative action in hiring and promoting workers who have HIV/AIDS or other disabilities. Both laws also require management to devise reasonable accommodations for disabled workers to assist them in performing the essential functions of the job.

Determination of Disability

Rehab and the ADA are identical in providing a three-pronged definition of "disability." A person can claim to be disabled if he or she:[6]

1. has a physical or mental impairment that substantially limits one or more of the major life activities; or
2. has a record of such an impairment; or
3. is regarded as having such an impairment.

The second and third prongs of the definition are intended to prevent speculation on the part of the employer as to what employee-related costs the future might bring to the organization. The second prong protects a person from either being denied employment or terminated from employment as a result of fear that additional costs might be borne at the end of the impairment's remission. The third prong protects those individuals with impairments that might never manifest yet present the possibility of someday adding to the organization's healthcare and workplace expenses. Both (2) and (3) are, therefore, more important than the first (1) prong in combating subtle and clever disability-based discrimination in the workplace.

Substantially Limiting Major Life Activities. Rehab and the ADA take a broad view of what constitutes "major life activities": walking, seeing, hearing, speaking, breathing, learning, participating in group or community activities, performing manual tasks, or caring for oneself. All or a combination of these activities are central to performing anyone's job. In order to be deemed "substantially limiting," both laws require the disability to be severe in nature, long-term in duration, and permanent in terms of impact on major life activities. The courts have long recognized that HIV/AIDS is a terminal disease that substantially limits many of the major life activities.

The three-pronged definition of disabilities permits employees with either HIV or full-blown AIDS to claim protection against workplace discrimination (Slack, 1995; Strama, 1993). A person with at least one opportunistic infection, or an AIDS-related cancer, is covered under the first prong of the definition—having a physical or mental impairment. If all opportunistic infections recede temporarily, or if an AIDS-related cancer enters an ephemeral stage of remission, the employee can still enjoy protection under the second prong of the definition—that of possessing a record of having a physical or mental impairment. People who are asymptomatic are covered under the third prong of the definition of disability because they are regarded as having a physical or mental impairment (DeSario and Slack, 1995; Duffy, 1994a, 1994b).

Notification and Documentation Requirement

The ADA and Rehab are similar to other pieces of civil rights legislation in that the burden of proving membership within the protected class belongs solely to the individual member. Hence it is the responsibility of the person with HIV/AIDS to provide management with clear notification and accurate documentation of having either the retrovirus or one of its resultant opportunistic diseases and infections.

Given the stigma that still surrounds HIV/AIDS, providing documentation is a risky task for many people infected with the retrovirus. The person must present *official* documentation that directly links the retrovirus to him- or herself. Hence the presentation of an anonymous HIV antibody blood test result is simply insufficient. The person must either present a test result that has his or her name on it[7] or have a physician write a letter to the employer outlining the details of the infection. In either case, management reserves the right to conduct its own verification of the disability. Whichever route is taken in documenting the presence of HIV/AIDS, the employee is forced to trust that the employer will comply with the tenets of either piece of legislation. Without proper notification and documentation, management bears no responsibility in protecting the workplace rights of people with HIV/AIDS.[8]

WORKPLACE RAMIFICATIONS OF HIV/AIDS

Since the outbreak of the epidemic in the late 1970s, most nonmedical AIDS research has been directed toward public health issues (Koehler, 1994; LeBlang, 1994), international considerations (Closen and Isaacman, 1992; Slack, 1992), and public policy debates over HIV testing (Adams, 1994; Sternlight, 1994). Scholarly attention to workplace issues is growing, particularly pertaining to the legal (Strama, 1993; Marx and Goldberger, 1991; Jones and Johnson, 1989a) and exogenous factors (Closen, 1994; Slack and Luna, 1992; Jones and Johnson, 1989b) of the AIDS epidemic. The many side effects of the disease certainly make HIV/AIDS a very interesting workplace issue.

Impact on Employees and Job Applicants with HIV/AIDS

The ability to deal with both the life-taking crisis of HIV/AIDS and the bigotry that often accompanies the epidemic, coupled with the varying strength of each person's immune system and the syndrome of opportunistic infections, diseases, and cancers that have the potential to manifest sequentially or in combination—all make living with and dying from HIV/AIDS a unique experience. So much has been written on the social stigma of having HIV/AIDS (Montoya, 1994; Muir, 1991; Shilts, 1988) that this section will focus more on what each individual with HIV/AIDS experiences and how these experiences become part of the fabric of the workplace.

Consequences of HIV/AIDS at the Workplace.   Management must remember that a good employee is a good employee, and a bad one is a bad one. HIV/AIDS does not affect that equation. The trauma and experiences of those with HIV/AIDS will certainly find its way into the job setting. Therefore, we should expect alterations in the performance of an employee with HIV/AIDS, which will require a heightened understanding on the part of management if it seeks to keep good employees.

HIV/AIDS-Related Stress.   Upon learning of the seroconversion, the person often falls into an extended state of shock lasting perhaps as long as six months to a year. As a result, the person may not be able to think clearly and may even appear to be suffering from an attention deficiency disorder. An employee's work will ultimately suffer. For example, he or she may not be able to give concise instructions to subordinates or to understand instructions from supervisors. The employee may also "daydream" more than usual.

The first few months of knowing that one has HIV/AIDS is also the period when the emotion of anger is most pronounced. Anger typically manifests itself in the workplace in fairly predictable ways. The person becomes unusually "short" with co-workers or irritable with subordinates. The person may even display antisocial behavior, distancing himself or herself from the dynamics of the organization. He or she may also simply "take it out" on someone at the workplace.

Given the great levels of emotional stress weathered by the employee with HIV/AIDS, anger might also manifest itself in taking advantage prematurely of "disabilities retirement" plans rather than working with the employee assistance program (EAP) to find ways to help reduce stress. Some workers even take this route to "get even" with the organization. Unfortunately there are also job applicants with HIV/AIDS who wish to "get even" by seeking employment with organizations just so they can claim disability retirement within the shortest amount of time.

As workers with HIV/AIDS become more accustomed to living with the retrovirus, job performance can be expected to begin to return to normal.

However, the nature of the disease means that extraordinary levels of stress will return periodically. For instance, one day each month the employee typically visits an AIDS clinic, sits next to people who have deteriorating immune systems, receives a new T-cell count that is probably lower than the prior month's result, and has to think of ways to inform the spouse or significant other of the disappointing test results. He or she must then return to work and act as if "nothing's wrong." He or she must find ways of coping with the resultant stress in order to help limit further reductions to the effectiveness and health of the immune system. The search for ways to cope with stress continues until the next month's visit. The process then begins all over again.

Fear of Bigotry and Discrimination.   Employees and job applicants with HIV/ AIDS face peculiar cultural challenges in the workplace as they do elsewhere. Because of this, they are perhaps the most vulnerable members of a protected group in terms of becoming victims of flagrant and subtle violations of work-place rights (Slack, 1995). Whereas employees in the HIV spectrum may feel some sense of security as a result of workplace policies and union contracts, job applicants with this retrovirus enjoy no such "in-house" protections. Consequently, the plight of job applicants with HIV/AIDS is exponentially more severe (Slack, 1996).

Fears about bigotry stem from the primary mode of transmission of the retrovirus, sexual intercourse. For the heterosexual employee with HIV/AIDS, fear centers on the perception of co-workers and supervisors that he or she might be gay in a society that simply is uncomfortable with homosexuality. Many gay men continue to feel the need to hide their homosexuality at the workplace. For these employees, having HIV/AIDS affirms in the minds of co-workers and supervisors a lifestyle that remains unacceptable. For gay men who are "out" at the workplace, having HIV/AIDS often adds one additional and often unexpected source of prejudice: other gay men, "out" or in hiding, who fear for their own positions within the organization.

The cultural stigma attached to HIV/AIDS increases the level of emotional stress felt by the employee. One consequence is that the person feels he must hide his seropositive condition and not seek protection and assistance from management. Precluding the possibility of early intervention at the workplace, however, ultimately contributes to the immune system's decreasing ability to respond to the retrovirus.

Impact on Management

HIV/AIDS also presents tremendous challenges to workplace and personnel managers. Some of the more critical issues include (1) redefining job descriptions, (2) determining the agency's capacity to provide reasonable accommodations, (3) developing strategies to maintain confidentiality, and (4) controlling costs throughout the work life of the employee with HIV/AIDS.

Job Descriptions.   Although required in neither Rehab nor the ADA, it is wise to re-analyze each job description within the organization so that tasks deemed to be "essential" in nature can be distinguished from tasks that are "marginal." Doing so permits management to determine—and document in court, if necessary—whether a job applicant or employee with HIV/AIDS, or any disability, is otherwise qualified to perform the essential functions of a job. It is especially important to modify job descriptions prior to beginning the hiring process, since they are the basis for most job announcements.

Reasonable Accommodation.   Rehab and the ADA require management to provide reasonable accommodations to otherwise qualified employees and job applicants with disabilities if such accommodations are needed in performing the essential functions of the job. Both laws also require management to do so only in response to requests by the employees for such accommodations. Although management cannot impose reasonable accommodations on employees or job applicants, it should be prepared to enter into a discussion about specific workplace accommodations.

What Is Reasonable Accommodation?   Because the intent of both pieces of legislation suggests that reasonable accommodation is very much in the eye of the beholder, management must recognize that each worksite—indeed, each set of essential functions, type of disability, stage and level of disability, and individual capability—constitutes a unique situation and, thereby, calls for unique accommodations. Hence what is needed for one disabled American to perform the essential functions of a particular job in a specific workplace will not be identical to what is needed for another disabled American in either the same or different place of employment. A case-by-case approach is required.

In many ways, devising reasonable accommodations for a job applicant or employee with full-blown AIDS is more straightforward than it is at the earlier stages of the retrovirus. Typically their needs are similar to those required by other individuals who are extremely ill. Because of the outward appearance of good health, finding effective reasonable accommodations for asymptomatic persons is a much more difficult task. From management's point of view, however, it is important to do so for two reasons. First, early intervention through reasonable accommodation keeps employees healthier and, therefore, more productive for a longer period of time. Second, adoption of reasonable accommodation strategies for asymptomatic employees can be submitted in court as further evidence that the organization is attempting to comply with both the letter and the spirit of the law.

The following are examples of possible reasonable accommodations for individuals who are in the early stages of HIV. They are relatively inexpensive but effective strategies in minimizing the daily stress that results from constant internal reminders that one is going to die of AIDS.

The first strategy involves providing the opportunity for "time-outs" through-out the work day. Here management allows the employee to take, at his or her own discretion, short breaks to regain composure needed to perform the essential functions of the job. If an employee lounge is unavailable, a manager might permit the use of her private office or she might know of a hide-away area—a storage room or unused office—where the employee would not be disturbed. Where appropriate, time-outs might also be offered in the form of having the opportunity to take short walks outside in the fresh air.[9] However applied, short time-outs can help reduce stress. They are also an inexpensive alternative to sick day utilization, which occurs prematurely in settings that do not permit this kind of accommodation.

Second, management might consider the use of flexitime for employees with HIV/AIDS. This can help reduce the stress of missed productivity as a result of time-outs. It can also help reduce the anxiety of having to ask for time off for a variety of activities: going to AIDS clinics for the monthly T-count, participating in support groups, or attending funerals. The use of flexitime can also minimize the cost of sick day utilization by allowing the employee to make up missed time.

Third, management should make every effort to encourage the employee with HIV/AIDS to participate in its employee assistance program (EAP). Given the manifestations of denial and anger after finding out one is seropositive, EAP activities in drug and alcohol abuse can be particularly beneficial to sustaining the employee's physical and mental health. EAP programs that deal with stress management, or those that address issues pertaining to relations with the spouse or significant other, are also quite useful for people who find out they have HIV.

Fourth, management should consider the benefits of allowing employees with HIV/AIDS to have access to food throughout the day. This is especially helpful for workers who are in the bargaining stage of dying, and who are now trying everything possible to stay alive. Gaining weight is important physio-logically and mentally, since one of the first symptoms of AIDS can be wasting syndrome, or a rapid and often permanent loss in weight. Hence permitting employees with HIV/AIDS to eat snacks throughout the day at their own work space can be an inexpensive accommodation that helps keep them healthy and performing the essential functions of the job for as long as possible.

Fifth, having the right kinds of food at the workplace can be an important accommodation for people trying to survive HIV/AIDS. These people tend to avoid junk foods—high saturated fat and cholesterol content—and eat primarily fresh, healthy foods with high caloric value. Management might, therefore, ensure that employees have adequate options of healthy foods in both the cafeteria and snack machines.

Finally, management might ensure that its restrooms have plenty of hot water. One of the basic fears of employees with HIV/AIDS is catching illnesses, typically the flu or the common cold, from co-workers. The bargaining and acceptance stages of dying make them particularly aware that proper hygiene can sustain the immune system. They become keenly aware that washing hands in hot water helps to curtail the spread of germs, viruses, and many types of fungi. Hence knowing that the restrooms have an adequate supply of hot water for washing hands helps to minimize the anxiety level, especially during the flu season.

Confidentiality. The nature of confidentiality changes when Rehab and the ADA are applied to workplace situations. Although both laws protect the disabled employee's right to confidentiality, neither indicate how this should be accomplished. The traditional view of confidentiality suggests that no one outside of the personnel and legal offices should have a need to know that the person has HIV/AIDS.[10] Furthermore, management is ultimately responsible for controlling rumors and gossip; failure to do so can lead to additional litigation and costs.

However, both laws place management in a quandary over maintaining confidentiality. This is especially true when it provides reasonable accommodations because that process requires the involvement of many units within the organization: (1) the personnel office, for purposes of notification and documentation, (2) the legal office, for guidance on applying Rehab and the ADA, (3) the medical staff, for purposes of verifying the infection (if the organization wishes to do so) and for preparing for case-specific emergencies stemming from medication, (4) the insurance office, for purposes of benefit consultation and processing pharmaceutical claims,[11] (5) EAP personnel, for counseling, intervention, and crisis management, (6) the immediate supervisor, in order to devise specific reasonable accommodations, (7) co-workers, in case rearrangement of marginal job functions is needed, (8) other supervisors, in case a transfer is used as a reasonable accommodation, and (9) the union representative, if modifications in job assignments or job transfers require such notification.

One byproduct of Rehab and the ADA, therefore, is the need to develop new strategies toward, and perhaps a new definition of, the concept of confidentiality. If this is not done, then conflict will escalate between the requisites of confidentiality and the prerequisites of notifying all pertinent groups. Similar to reasonable accommodation, however, this new strategy will certainly have to be hammered out on a case-by-case basis. Although management will still bear responsibility for controlling rumors, the level of required confidentiality might well become as unique as each individual and each workplace.

Workplace Costs. HIV/AIDS is an expensive disease, but how much will it cost an organization? The answer will vary according to factors that management can control, especially in terms of the nature of its workplace environment and reasonable accommodations it provides, as well as those factors that are simply beyond its control.[12] A fairly conservative[13] estimate is that each person with HIV/AIDS will cost a self-insured workplace approximately $270,000 over a period of about 12 years (DeSario et al., 1994: 33–36). If the workplace has a group insurance plan, however, the cost will drop to about $135,000 over the same 12-year period (Slack, 1997).

Reasonable Accommodation Costs. Despite fears to the contrary, providing reasonable accommodations proves to be one of the least expensive activities (Job Analysis Network, 1995). There is no added cost for allowing snacks at the work unit or ensuring that food machines include an assortment of healthy items. When reasonable accommodations are provided at the earliest stage, moreover, costs can be minimized substantially. Using "time-outs" is a case in point. Assuming an employee earns $30,000 annually, an extra 10-minute time-out four times a day will cost an organization $9.60 a day.[14] If the person uses a sick day in lieu of time-outs, then the cost to the organization is $150.07.[15] A careful consideration of all accommodations can sometimes reduce the workplace cost by a factor of more than fifteen.

Healthcare Costs. Although HIV/AIDS is an expensive illness, its costs over the length of the disease are no greater that those that are typically associated with heart disease or kidney failure. A person might easily spend $20,000 annually on pharmaceuticals in the fight against this disease. There are also non-pharmaceutical costs, as much as $10,000 annually for the person who is asymptomatic. The annual cost for nonpharmaceutical care will reach approximately $40,000 when the person develops AIDS.

Undue Hardship. Using identical language, Rehab and the ADA allow management to claim that specific accommodations present undue hardship for the organization. As with reasonable accommodations, undue hardship is interpreted from the eye of the beholder and is determined on a case-by-case basis. Typically larger organizations will be required to provide more accommodations than their smaller counterparts prior to claiming undue hardship. In all cases, however, four factors are taken into consideration:[16]

1. the nature and cost of the accommodation needed;
2. the specific work unit or department's human and financial resources;
3. the entire organization's human and financial resources;
4. type of operation of the organization, that is, construction or temporary work sites.

Cost of Litigation. The amount of ADA-related workplace litigation is growing rapidly. Between 1992, the year the ADA was enacted, and October 1994, there were over 34,000 workplace cases (Duncan, 1994). Although only 2 percent of these cases involved either employees with HIV/AIDS or clients with HIV/AIDS doing business with public organizations, by far the largest workplace cost stemming from this epidemic will soon center on activities that take place within the courtroom rather than in the workroom. Future litigation will focus increasingly on (1) controlling rumors and maintaining new definitions of confidentiality (Sarch, 1994), (2) establishing insurance caps (Scheffey, 1994), (3) HIV antibody blood testing at the workplace (Bobinski and LeMaistre, 1993; Slack,

1991), and (4) issues pertaining to the balance between reasonable accommodation and undue hardship (Cooper, 1991).

A POSITIVE WORKPLACE ENVIRONMENT

People with HIV/AIDS work, and apply for positions, in every sector of the economy. Chances are, you either work with someone who has HIV/AIDS or will work with someone infected before the turn of the century. Unfortunately, that person probably is not yet aware of his or her seropositivity or is not prepared to tell anyone about it for reasons discussed above: stress, fear of bigotry, the possibility of discrimination. More likely than not, your organization is also unprepared to address the workplace ramifications of HIV/AIDS (Slack, 1997, 1996, and 1991).

One thing is abundantly clear about the workplace: healthy people are less expensive and more productive than sick people are. Since Rehab and the ADA prohibit the exclusion of people with HIV/AIDS from the workplace, management must do whatever it can to keep them healthy and productive for as long as possible. Whether it is a result of humanitarian feelings of compassion for the employee or businesslike concerns about profit and productivity, it is in management's best interest to develop a workplace environment that supports the needs of employees within the HIV spectrum.

How does management build a supportive, positive workplace environment in the age of AIDS? Because it too is only found in the eye of the beholder, the quality of any workplace environment must be built solely on a case-by-case basis. Certainly implementing the strategies of reasonable accommodation, discussed above, is a starting point. In doing so, management should consider three basic ideas: preparing first-level supervisors to deal with the "front line" workplace ramifications of HIV/AIDS, providing workplace-specific training on the subject to both managers and employees, and preparing a workplace-specific HIV/AIDS plan.

Being Prepared

Being prepared to deal with an issue requires the initial ability to talk about it. This is difficult in the case of HIV/AIDS. Because sexual practices and illegal use of drugs represent the most common modes of transmission, HIV is an incredibly personal illness.[17] Even if people do not place a social stigma on those who have HIV/AIDS, the fact that someone they know has contracted the retrovirus typically shifts thought and private speculation into areas that are the most intimate in the human experience. Perhaps this accounts for why so many people feel uncomfortable talking about HIV/AIDS, especially with someone infected with the disease.

The awkwardness of the subject matter is exacerbated in the case of workplace managers. The fact that the common modes of transmission are so far removed from the activities of most workplaces only reinforces the tendency to avoid entering into discussions about HIV/AIDS. Nevertheless, first-line supervisors must be prepared to discuss the issue and to do so in a professional and confidential manner. If management is successful in building a supportive environment, the supervisor should encourage and expect the discussion to be frank and, at times, very graphic. First-line supervisors must be prepared to show neither shock nor judgment about the contents of such conversations, as well as to be able to provide needed information and reassurance to the employee. Perhaps of greatest importance for developing a supportive workplace environment, employees must be made aware that management is prepared to participate wholeheartedly in that initial conversation.

Training

Training is essential in preparing the work force to deal with the workplace ramifications of HIV/AIDS. In order for management to send an unambiguous message to both supervisors and employees that it is serious about creating the environment, training must be mandatory, workplace-specific, and periodic. It should include such topics as (1) understanding HIV/AIDS, (2) managing workplace issues, and (3) dealing effectively with noninfected co-workers as well as seropositive employees (DeSario et al., 1994: 110–112; Slack and Luna, 1992). In addition to formal training, routine staff meetings should include relevant topics, such as updates on pertinent court rulings and reports from the U.S. Centers for Disease Control and Prevention, case-study reviews of how effectively supervisors (within the organization and in other agencies) managed particular HIV/AIDS-related situations, and an annual reassessment of job descriptions with an eye toward updating and further clarifying essential functions.

HIV/AIDS Plan

From the perspective of developing a positive and supportive workplace environment, having a plan of action in place to deal with the workplace ramifications of HIV/AIDS is as important as being trained in how to handle specific situations (DeSario et al., 1994; Slack and Luna, 1992; Slack, 1991). Although the plan must be workplace-specific, it should include four components: (1) a statement reaffirming the organization's intent to comply with Rehab and the ADA, (2) a set of procedures that management will follow when an employee seeks to provide notification and documentation, or when that employee chooses to enter into that initial conversation with her first-line supervisor, (3) a set of services provided by the organization, including concrete but preliminary sketches of possible reasonable accommodations, and (4) an outline of the content and scheduling of training sessions. The HIV/AIDS plan should be disseminated to all employees and incorporated into the employee handbook.

CONCLUSION

This chapter has outlined some of the HIV/AIDS-related issues that face workplace and personnel managers. Rehab and the ADA, as well as laws in some states, protect job applicants and employees within the HIV spectrum from discrimination at work. As with other disabled Americans, individuals with HIV/AIDS can seek reasonable accommodations if they are otherwise qualified to perform the essential functions of their jobs.

Workplace ramifications of this epidemic are multiple and, if left unattended, will lead to unexpected costs to the organization. These ramifications stem from the fact that employees in the HIV spectrum suffer from a uniquely horrific and painful process of dying. In order to deal with the consequences of this retrovirus, managers must know more than the intricacies of the law. They must also have a firm grasp on the stages of the retrovirus, the many symptoms of the resultant diseases and infections, the specific job in question, and both the human strengths and weaknesses as well as the workplace needs of the individual holding that position.

If management learns to address effectively the complexities surrounding HIV/AIDS, it will be able to handle more proactively issues pertaining to employees with other kinds of disabilities. A workplace environment that facilitates positive, supportive, and proactive approaches to finding solutions acceptable to both management and its employees with disabilities will also prove equally useful in facilitating a better understanding of the problems and concerns of everyone in the work force. Such skills will become increasingly important to the success of the organization as the members of its work force become increasingly diverse.

NOTES

1. Much of the analysis in this chapter is the result of personal interviews with employees with HIV/AIDS that took place throughout California in 1995. Funding for the project was provided by the University Research Council and the School of Business and Public Administration, California State University at Bakersfield.
2. The Centers for Disease Control and Prevention (CDC) of the U.S. Public Health Service, Department of Health and Human Services, estimates that approximately 1 million Americans are infected with HIV. The CDC suggests that for every person with AIDS, there are between 50 and 100 people who are HIV-positive. The CDC also believes that the number of AIDS cases might be underreported by as much as 20 percent. Leadership within the group known as "AIDS Coalition to Unleash Power" (ACTUP) suggests that as many as 5 million Americans are infected. Experienced counselors at Gay Men's Health Crises offer figures around 2-3 million people.
3. The period in which seroconversion occurs limits current testing procedures to assess the HIV status of a person to no less than three months prior to the time

the test is administered. If a person takes an HIV antibody blood test on April 1, the results only report the "well-being" of the person as of January 1.

4. Many states also protect a large portion of people with HIV/AIDS—homosexuals—through civil rights laws.
5. Several types of organizations are exempt from both pieces of legislation: the federal government, Native American tribes, private clubs, and in certain situations, religious organizations.
6. See 42 USC 12102-12211.
7. In most states, the consequences of non-anonymous testing is that the person's name is forwarded to the state public health department and is accessible by insurance companies.
8. 56 Fed.Reg. 35,748, July 26, 1991.
9. These walks can sometimes be incorporated into the work assignment.
10. The medical office can verify seropositivity through confidential testing at the public health department. The HIV antibody test results of "employee X" are reported to the medical office as well as to "employee X."
11. For employees trying to keep information about the seroconversion from the organization, filing claims for AZT is a common "red flag" in the insurance office. Even using the generic term *retrovir* will sometimes trigger suspicion.
12. For instance, warmer climates reduce the chance of catching colds and flu, and stronger economies generally are beneficial to feelings of well-being. In addition, management really has little control over an employee's decisions to stay as healthy as possible.
13. It assumes a relatively low salary ($25,000) and assumes that the employee will be responsible for 25 percent of healthcare costs. It does not take into consideration the cost of temporarily replacing an individual who is hospitalized, nor does it factor in the cost of replacement when the individual dies or is too sick to work any longer.
14. This is based on $30,000 ÷ 2,080 hours in a work year, or $14.43 per hour. The $14.43 is divided by 60 minutes, or $0.24 cents per minute. Hence a 10-minute time-out costs $2.40, and four per day cost $9.60.
15. This is based on $30,000 ÷ 2,080 (hours in the working year), or $14.43 per hour. The $14.43 is multiplied by 8 hours in the day, or $115.44. This figure is multiplied by 30 percent to account for fringe benefits, or $34.63. Both figures are added together to total $150.07.
16. See Section 101(10) (B) of the ADA.
17. This is not typically the case with other diseases. For instance, few people would wonder, "How on earth did she get cancer?" There is little shame accompanying the way someone might have developed heart disease.

REFERENCES

Adams, William. 1994. "The Dilemma for Minors Seeking HIV-Testing and Treatment." *John Marshall Law Review* 27, no. 2 (Winter): 493-512.

Bobinski, Mary Anne, and William S. LeMaistre. 1993. "HIV Testing and Confidentiality," in Brenda T. Strama, ed., *AIDS and Governmental Liability*. Chicago: American Bar Association: 7-44.

Closen, Michael L. 1994. "Introduction: HIV-AIDS in the 1990s." *John Marshall Law Review* 27, no. 2 (Winter): 239-250.

Closen, Michael L., and Scott H. Isaacman. 1992. "HIV-AIDS and Governmental Control of Information: International Denial of Human Rights." *St. Thomas Law Review* 4 (Spring): 107-123.

Cooper, Jeffrey O. 1991. "Overcoming Barriers to Employment: The Meaning of Reasonable Accommodation and Undue Hardship in the Americans with Disabilities Act." *University of Pennsylvania Law Review* 139, no. 5 (May): 1423-1468.

DeSario, Jack P., and James D. Slack. 1994. "The Americans with Disabilities Act and Refusals to Provide Medical Care to Persons with HIV/AIDS." *John Marshall Law Review* 27, no. 2 (Winter): 347-362.

DeSario, Jack P., Sue R. Faerman, and James D. Slack. 1994. *Local Government Information and Training Needs in the 21st Century.* Westport, Conn.: Quorum Books.

Duffy, Shannon P. 1994a. "Doe Case Presented to Judge; Oral Arguments Are Given." *Legal Intelligencer,* July 12: 1.

——— . 1994b. "Doe Suit Goes forward as Judge Rules HIV, without Visible Symptoms, Is Disability." *Pennsylvania Law Weekly,* August 8: 12.

Duncan, Laura. 1994. "Illinois Ranks 4th in ADA Complaints, EEOC Says." *Chicago Daily Law Bulletin,* October 27: 24.

Job Analysis Network. 1995. 809 Allen Hall, P.O. Box 6122, Morgantown, West Virginia 26507-9984. Phone (800) 526-7234. Conversation.

Jones, Walter J., and James A. Johnson. 1989a. "AIDS in the Workplace: Legal and Policy Considerations for Personnel Managers." R*eview of Public Personnel Administration* 9 (Summer 1989): 40-61.

——— . 1989b. "AIDS: The Urban Policymaking Challenge." *Journal of Urban Affairs* 11, no. 1: 16-35.

Koehler, Richard J. 1994. "HIV Infection, TB, and the Health Crisis in Corrections." *Public Administration Review* (January/February): 31-35.

LeBlang, Theodore R. 1994. "Obligations of HIV-Infected Health Professionals." *John Marshall Law Review* 27, no. 2 (Winter): 317-330.

Marx, Gary S., and Gary G. Goldberger. 1991. *Disability Law Compliance Manual.* Boston: Warren, Gorham & Lamont.

Montoya, Mauro A., Jr. 1994. "If I Tell You, Will You Treat Me?" *John Marshall Law Review* 27, no. 2 (Winter): 363-372.

Muir, Marie A. 1991. *The Environmental Context of AIDS.* New York: Praeger.

Sarch, Anne Covey. 1994. "Solutions to an Employment Nightmare." *New Jersey Law Journal* (December 19): 26.

Scheffey, Thomas. 1994. "Uncapping AIDS Health Benefits," *Connecticut Law Tribune* (March 21): 1.

Shilts, Randy. 1988. *And The Band Played On.* New York: Viking Penguin.

Slack, James D. 1991. *AIDS and the Public Work Force: Local Government Preparedness in Managing the Epidemic.* Tuscaloosa: University of Alabama Press.

——— . 1992. "Responding to the Global Epidemic of AIDS: Cultural and Political Challenges Facing Governments." *Policy Studies Journal* 20 (Winter): 124-134.

——— . 1995. "The Americans with Disabilities Act and the Workplace: Management's Responsibilities in AIDS-Related Situations." *Public Administration Review* 55, no. 4 (July/August): 365-370.

——— . 1996. "Workplace Preparedness and the Americans with Disabilities Act: Lessons from Municipal Government's Management of HIV/AIDS." *Public Administration Review* 56, no. 2 (March/April): 159-167.

————. 1997. *HIV/AIDS and the Public Workplace Revisited: Local Government Preparedness in the 1990s,* 2nd ed. Tuscaloosa: University of Alabama Press.

Slack, James D., and Anelia Luna. 1992. "AIDS-Related Documents from 96 American Cities and Counties." *Public Administration Review* 52, no. 3 (May-June): 305-309.

Sternlight, Jean R. 1994. "Mandatory Non-Anonymous Testing of Newborns for HIV." *John Marshall Law Review* 27, no. 2 (Winter): 373-392.

Strama, Brenda T., ed. 1993. *AIDS and Governmental Liability: State and Local Government Guide to Legislation, Legal Issues, and Liability.* Chicago: American Bar Association.

U.S. Department of Health and Human Services. 1995. *AIDS Surveillance Report.* Atlanta: Public Health Service, Centers for Disease Control and Prevention, Center for Infectious Diseases, Division of HIV/AIDS.

section III

The Outlook for Labor-Management Relations

The outlook for public sector labor relations is precarious at best. With movements to reinvent, reengineer, and downsize government, public sector labor unions fight to stave off layoffs, which invariably decimate membership rolls. The challenges facing public sector unions, like their private sector counterparts, are immense given the political, social, and economic climates that no longer support labor union activities. Their greatest task is to evolve in accordance with the demographic, political, and technological revolutions occurring in the workplace. They will also need to develop, in turn, appropriate strategies for increasing their membership rolls and for maximizing their ability to participate in decisions that affect the economic status of, and overall quality of life for, their constituents.

As George Sulzner sets forth in "New Roles, New Strategies," public sector unions must develop ways to reinvent themselves in order to remain viable as we move into the next century. As he suggests, micro-initiatives in the workplace include efforts to better serve the diverse constituencies of labor unions and, when appropriate, a greater willingness on the part of unions to accept participative management strategies, as they are an important trend of the future. Macro-initiatives include improving the public image of government employee unions and being more politically active. The reinvention of unions, as Sulzner stresses, is imperative if survival is a goal.

T. Zane Reeves, in "Labor-Management Partnerships in the Public Sector," examines the LMP initiative propounded by the National Performance Review. He explores the overall significance of partnership and the extent to which unions are truly brought in as partners. For example, the government's motive for building a partnership may be to get labor on board for massive downsizing

155

of the federal bureaucracy. Perhaps labor comes on board for the cuts; but with labor's involvement, those expunged from the bureaucracy are mid-level managers, personnelists, and other professionals not currently represented by labor unions.

chapter **10**

New Roles, New Strategies: Reinventing the Public Union

George T. Sulzner

$\mathbf{A}$n appropriate starting point for consideration of the task facing labor unions in the United States is the following observation by John Hoerr:

> Unions must reinvent themselves much as some companies are trying to do. The United States industrial relations system cannot be reinvigorated unless unions carve out a new role for themselves. They must develop a vision of how workers should help shape the technological and social revolution that is transforming the workplace. They must identify new "leverage points" for union influence. Finally, they must improve their own human resources to help put labor's new vision into practice. (1991: 31)

This is certainly a difficult assignment, especially in the private sector, but its validity holds as well for public sector unions.

The distinctions between private and public sector unionism are gradually eroding. The boundaries between them are blurring. As cases in point, the early development of public labor relations systems was modeled on private sector practices. Increasingly, dispute resolution procedures developed for the special problems of government unions have spilled over into the private sphere. The list of "mixed" public sector-private sector unions is growing. The arrival of competition in the communication, service, and transportation sectors of the private economy is becoming a more prominent feature of the government landscape. For example, Massachusetts has contracted out nearly all its human service delivery to private contractors. A number of large cities have done this as well with respect to their public education systems, and it probably is the norm in most government jurisdictions now for maintenance services to be provided by private contractors. With more and more governments trying to reinvent themselves, *downsizing, rightsizing,* and *reengineering* have become buzzwords in the public sector along with consequent reductions in the public work force. Further, the dramatic decline in the number of unionized workers in the private sector and their corresponding loss of political influence in Washington and the state capitols has recently had a negative impact, as well, on public sector unions. Solidarity, with fewer private sector brethren in alliance, has been weakened. The anti-union sentiment of the populace has washed across the public terrain also. In short, although the climate for public sector unionism is not likely to contain as many storm warnings as forecast for the private sector, it behooves its movers and shakers to think about reinventing the public union. The task ahead will not be accomplished without difficulties and risks for public unions. They can, however, build upon current trends, accentuate present strengths, and correct evident deficiencies. Public unions need to accept the reality that efforts to reinvent themselves cannot be postponed; they must begin now.

MICRO-INITIATIVES AT THE TABLE AND AT THE WORKPLACE

The first matter on the agenda is to relate positively to what Hoerr has characterized as the technological and social revolution that is transforming the workplace. The record of public sector unionism is already substantial on this front. They have compiled a list of accomplishments with regard to pay equity for women. They have brought large numbers of women and visible minorities into the leadership ranks of public unions. They have initiated numerous innovations with regard to work schedules and employee services that have benefited their diverse constituencies.[1] Representing large numbers of professional employees, public unions have also been leaders in the accommodation of new technologies into the workplace (Klingner, 1993; Sulzner, 1985). However, much still needs to be accomplished. Unions should be more aggressive in publicizing the findings of a significant amount of research showing that productivity gains are greater in unionized workplaces than in nonunion workplaces. The common explanation relates to the higher motivation and skill of union workers and the greater stability of the work environment. Because of favorable wages and benefits, worker morale is higher, turnover and absenteeism is lower, job security and process continuity is greater, and management practices are more professional (Freeman and Medoff, 1984; Kelly and Harrison, 1992; Roberts and Bittle, 1981; and Sulzner, 1983). This experience provides a solid footing for further union initiatives in the area of increasing worksite efficiencies.

Participative Decision-Making Scenarios

Vehicles for collaborative problem solving are being advocated nearly universally by analysts of the modern workplace. Additionally, a recent national survey in the United States reveals that a majority of workers surveyed, including those in a unionized setting, desire a greater voice in deciding what happens at work (Freeman and Rogers, 1995). These various forms of participative decision making (the most common types being quality circles, process improvement teams, and labor-management committees) have been functioning at all levels of government for more than a decade. Contributions to productivity, job satisfaction, and employee commitment to the enterprise seem to be associated more with on-line work reorganization experiments than with off-line participatory forms such as labor-management committees (Batt and Appelbaum, 1995). Many of the new schemes for employee participation have been introduced by management as substitutes for marginalized union influence as in the United States and France, but also in situations where unionism is firmly embedded in statute or institutional structures such as Germany or Australia. Unions in the United States and elsewhere have reluctantly accepted these collaborative mechanisms, recognizing, perhaps, as Berndt K. Keller (1995: 35) observes, "Unions will definitely not be able to reverse these dominating trends; careful acceptance of the new models of more direct employee involvement, not straightforward opposition, is the only viable alternative."

An approach that seems to have worked well in Australia is for unions to accept these participatory approaches as an extension of a union's traditional role of representation at the workplace. Apparently there, some unions have developed close cooperation with progressive management in the processes of change. They have done so in order to promote their members' interest with respect to present and future training needs and the development of new and additional skills (McLean, 1995). Following this tack might also enable public unions to make a difference with regard to the effects of the development of a dual labor market. Government employers increasingly differentiate between "asset" employees in a primary labor market consisting of skilled managerial, professional, and technical positions that carry high pay and benefits, status, and job security; and "cost" employees in a secondary market consisting of less skilled laborer and service positions filled on a temporary or part-time basis with low pay and no benefits, no status, and no job security (Johnston and Packer, 1987; O'Rand, 1986). Interestingly, we are seeing this differentiation emerging even within the professional and managerial ranks where key personnel—whether they be professors, managers, or social workers—are working with growing numbers of temporaries who are disconnected from the ongoing life of the institution and workplace. Forestalling the creep of the secondary market and opening up primary market opportunities for their members is likely to be one of the important future agendas of public sector unions.

Arguing that public unions should not ignore the opportunity to utilize cooperative mechanisms to their advantage does not preclude taking into account the risks involved for the unions. First, these participatory vehicles have been initiated primarily by employers in a unilateral fashion on a more or less voluntary basis motivated for the most part by purely economic objectives and a desire to introduce "union-free" processes of representation. This is not an encouraging context for unions. Most of the research evaluating collaborative decision making has focused on the impact of new forms of representation on different economic outcomes such as firm or organizational performance, cost reduction/productivity, efficiency, and product or service quality. Much less attention has been directed toward employee-related outcomes such as material rewards, improvements in working conditions, the humanization of work, and organizational democracy (Keller, 1995). Unions, in brief, prior to entering into cooperative arrangements, must ask whether the results will matter for employees as well as for their employers and under what specific conditions will they occur.

Second, the union representatives must be cognizant of and make clear to all that a broad and general consensus on participation by both sides does not necessarily imply that there are no more differences of interest. What are the exact subjects to be probed within these cooperative forums? Are different forms merely consultative, or can they become substantive/delegative? Do they or could they possibly challenge the well-established scope of managerial prerogatives? For example, Kelly and Harrison report that successful collaboration requires the possibility that employees may "achieve outcomes that also empower them" (Kelly and Harrison, 1992: 277). Reviewing the literature leads one to highlight the fact that there seems to be a large difference between a comparatively far-reaching delegation of autonomy in personnel/operational task-related matters and much less participation in strategic decisions. Participation on whose terms is the key question. The answer will determine whether it is symbolic or real.

Third, unions need to think ahead with regard to the nature of the future relationship between collective bargaining as a form of interest representation and the different new forms of employee participation and consequent interest representation. Can they co-exist? Certainly this seems to be the case in certain situations. Will they (participative forms) further erode the legitimacy of unions and assist in their withering away? Evidence indicates that this result also occurs in particular situations (Keller, 1995; Kelley and Harrison, 1992). Strategic thinking is obviously a necessity for public unions as well as for public agencies.

Fourth, unions need to be aware of the fact that worker participation has the potential for widening rather than reducing the gap between the primary and secondary labor market. There may be a tendency toward further segmentation or even dualization between winners and losers, between key groups and marginalized workers in these participation schemes. After all, logic would dictate that in the overwhelming majority of organizations, not all employees would be given the opportunity to participate because the returns on investment in human capital are likely to differ significantly and the costs would ultimately outweigh the benefits. Moreover, it is also reasonable to assume that at least some of the participative forms were launched as potential instruments of workplace rationalization designed to lower labor costs.

The above commentary illustrates that endorsing the new forms of participation holds out the risk that the union might be coopted by management. The external environment of law and politics also contains hazards for public unions who are engaged in participatory decision-making formats. Here, the risk is that even with mutual goodwill existing on the part of labor and management, outcomes will be blunted by the lack of flexibility and receptivity in the political system. Currently there are a number of legal and procedural impediments to the successful implementation of participative schemes. Management rights are too entrenched in statute or in contract, and thus the scope of bargaining is too narrowly defined, for collaborative negotiations to occur on substantive matters. Position classification schemes are too rigid and performance appraisal systems are too individualistic to reward group enterprise and facilitate team building in the workplace. Moreover, labor relations boards' or commissions' interpretations of public collective bargaining statutes have tended to favor centralized decision processes that are far removed from the point of service delivery, the zone of action that seems most amenable to joint endeavors. The Supreme Court's decision in *National Labor Relations Board v. Yeshiva University* (1980) was also thought to have a chilling effect on efforts to encourage participative decision making. Perhaps the most difficult obstacle to overcome, however, as Kearney and Hays (1994) note, is the short-term focus of public actions. Sustained commitment of time and effort to implement participative decision making is a necessary element for accomplishment. As they state, "Truncated time horizons are serious enough in the private sector, but tend to be even more common and confounding in the public sector, where elected officials and their political appointees enter and depart government with startling rapidity and where budget shortfalls can disrupt even the most peaceful labor relations setting" (p. 48). Why should public unions move toward endorsing cooperative problem solving when the probability of failure is perhaps greater than the likelihood of success? Because, when the ship of state is sinking, the only way it can continue afloat is for all the passengers (labor and management) to accept their common plight and work together to bail out the excess water and plug the leaks.

Representing the Voice of the Members at the Workplace

The voice function of unions has received a lot of attention since Freeman and Medoff published their book *What Do Unions Do?* in 1984. Freeman and Medoff (1984: 8) refer to voice as "the use of direct communication to bring actual and desired conditions closer together." They further observe that in industrialized economies and large enterprises, "A trade union is the vehicle for collective voice—that is, for providing workers as a group with a means of communicating with management" (p. 8). The notion of communicating the collective voice of the workers as an essential element of unionism is an old one. Beatrice and Sidney Webb highlighted the importance of voice for industrial unions in their classic study, *Industrial Democracy,* published in 1902. They held that it was a requirement that unions as institutions provide mechanisms to hear the voices of their members and use those mechanisms to ascertain and advance the will of their constituents. Moreover, Senator Robert Wagner, the principal author of the National Labor Relations Act passed in 1935, claimed that "the [workers'] struggle for a voice in industry through the process of collective bargaining is at the heart of the struggle for the preservation of political as well as economic democracy in America" (Gross, 1985: 10). Greenfield and Pleasure (1993), in their comprehensive study of workers' voice, spotlight a troubling tendency in the empirical examinations of the voice function following the work of Freeman and Medoff. They write, "In the burgeoning literature on employee voice, however, a significant, consistent and troubling underlying assumption appears: that voice is desirable primarily or solely insofar as it creates or contributes to the efficiency of the firm" (Greenfield and Pleasure, 1993: 170). We have already commented about a similar flaw in the research on participative decision making, obviously an activity associated closely with the exercise of voice. Greenfield and Pleasure assert this is a misplaced emphasis. "In a particular time, place, union, or industry," they observe, "voice may be directed to the improvement of production; in another context it may be the establishment of a particular system of industrial justice. Goals may vary over time and issue and multiple objectives may exist" (1993: 172). The key point is that the legitimacy of voice does not derive from its object but from its source, the voices of the workers themselves.

Public unions, as previously noted, have incorporated the voices of an increasingly diverse work force in their contractual, judicial, and legislative initiatives. They have, in this sense, been "out in front" of their private sector colleagues. More should be done, however, and this may be an activity that public unions can practice and in so doing regain some political leverage. Donald Klingner (1993: 23) argues that "what public unions must do, if they can, is to rebuild their political constituency by championing broad public interests." He thinks that current social and economic conditions present public unions with some potent issues for their function of voice (i.e., supportive career opportunities for a diverse work force; organizational democracy in the allocation of benefits, training, and participation; organizational justice with regard to the continuity and solvency of retirement and health care plans). Public unions, he claims, need to step up and articulate how they, as the chosen representatives of workers, can address these matters constructively.

The impact of unions in communicating that effective voice is demonstrated by Weil's (1992, 1995) research on the role of unions in enforcement of the Occupational Safety and Health Act (OSHA). He found that unionized workplaces are more likely to be inspected by OSHA, that inspectors give greater scrutiny to inspections of unionized workplaces, and that union workplaces pay higher penalties for health and safety violations. Weil's studies highlight the fact that unions are credible agencies for the voice of workers. Unions have the ability to listen, articulate, and implement the interests of an increasingly diverse work force in public organizations. Their success in shaping the social revolution at the worksite will depend on their willingness to engage this challenge.

Improving the Instruments of Industrial Justice: The Grievance Arbitration Process

The grievance process, culminating if necessary in contract arbitration, is also an aspect of employee voice in that it provides a well-established mechanism for workers to give reasoned expression to their complaints. Lewin and Mitchell

(Lewin and Mitchell, 1992) observe that similar to studies of other agencies of voice, recent research on grievance procedures has evaluated their utility in terms of their contribution to the productivity of the firm. Again, as Greenfield and Pleasure have emphasized, this focus is slanted toward an imposed value. The grievance/arbitration process was not originally designed or incorporated to enhance the efficiency of an organization. That end may be a byproduct, but the grievance/arbitration system was implemented at worksites as a form of industrial justice to guarantee due process for handling employee discipline and other operational problems. Many questions are being raised currently with respect to the practice of the grievance/arbitration process and its continuing effectiveness in handling complaints dealing with the administration of collective bargaining agreements.

The primary role of local unions in the labor-management system in the United States is to protect the integrity of the contract through the grievance/arbitration procedure. The day-to-day problems of employees that in numerous other countries would be dealt with by works councils, labor courts, or job actions are the responsibility of locally elected union officers in the United States. Inadequate resolution of these work-related problems can erode the agreement, undermine the authority of the local union representatives, and, in the minds of members, raise questions about the utility of having a union represent them.

Among contemporary unionists there are a number of dissatisfactions with the operation of the grievance/arbitration procedure (Roberts, 1994). Generally speaking, complaints relate to the process becoming too time-consuming, unpredictable, and costly. Concern has arisen about the delays in the process. From start to finish (filing a grievance to an arbitrator's decision) can easily take 12 to 18 months. This obviates one of the major intended attributes of the grievance/arbitration process: to bring closure to problems at work before they fester and grow from molehills into mountains. Part of the difficulty is the reluctance of the parties to accept relatively inexperienced arbitrators. Relying on busy, experienced arbitrators adds to scheduling difficulties and concurrent delays. The time for resolution is also stretched out by the apparent growing reluctance on the part of management to settle disputes at the earlier stages of the grievance process. Increasingly, it seems, management is prepared to "just say no" at every step short of arbitration, forcing the union to either arbitrate or accept management's position on the grievance.

The impact and value of precedent with regard to compliance with decisions throughout the process has also declined. Virtually all collective bargaining contracts have, at the end of the section outlining the grievance procedure, the declaration that the arbitrator's decision is "final and binding." In the past this statement, with the exception of a small fraction of cases, was honored by the parties. No more. Traditionally, rarely did either party go to court to adjudicate an arbitrator's decision. Rather, they were committed to the system as the vehicle for resolving conflicts at work. They also knew the courts were reluctant to overturn arbitrators' decisions, generally deferring to the private law of the workplace. Now, management is more disposed to sue and the courts are more disposed to intervene with decisions based on a judge's view of the contract.

Of course, litigation can add years of delay to final decisions. Further, the past practice of accepting the finality of an arbitrator's decision as binding on a particular matter until the next set of contract negotiations is fading away. Management practice currently is more likely to force the union to grieve and arbitrate the same or similar issues each time they arise if the original arbitration has not gone management's way. Needless to state, this pattern adds to the frustration of the unions with the process and lowers the morale of workers.

Finally, the process of arbitration has become rather costly. Insistence on briefs, official transcriptions, and representation by attorneys—all formalizations of the hearing format—have raised the cost of arbitration. Typically, arbitration costs each side between $1,200 and $2,000 per case. For most organizations this is a negligible expense, simply another cost of operations even if they appeal the decision to the courts. Unions fund the costs from membership dues. If the dues collected decrease, so does the union's ability to exercise its option to arbitrate and adjudicate. In this context, unions increasingly accept management's solution to workplace problems. Looking at the contemporary situation, unionists are fully aware that access to financial resources can bias the grievance/arbitration process. Companies and governments, for the most part, have much deeper pockets than unions do, and by exercising their financial leverage they have tilted the outcomes of the grievance/arbitration process in their direction.

From the public unions' point of view, what can be done? They can advocate in the literature, in the legislature, and at the table for incremental changes in the process that would level the playing field (e.g., expedited arbitration, establishment of a panel of arbitrators assigned to their occupational domain, or experimentation with mediation to resolve grievances). All and each of these measures would reduce costs and lessen the delays in reaching decisions on grievances. Unions can highlight the negative effect upon the morale of employees of the current attempts by management to manipulate the grievance/arbitration system to its advantage. After all, even hard-ball strategies under some circumstances may have diminishing returns. The U.S. Postal Service is an example. True, homicides at the worksite are extreme examples but they reflect an environment at work in which problems festered for too long without resolution. Recently the Service has been engaging in various experimental practices with arbitration to expedite the backlog of grievance cases, and they have been significantly reduced.

Public unions might also decide to engage in job actions, such as work-to-rule, to get management's attention relative to their dissatisfaction with the present operation of grievance/arbitration procedures. After all, the grievance/arbitration system was introduced during World War II as an alternative to job actions and work stoppages by labor as expressions of their dissatisfaction with management practices. Perhaps what is needed to restore its integrity is a new version of union militancy at the workplace.

Public unions should also push hard at the table for the expansion of the scope of the grievance process. Public unions are prohibited from negotiating many important aspects of employment such as position classifications, job restructuring, work assignments, and agency organization. Although they can often negotiate or demand consultation about the impact of these decisions, by then it is often too late to effectively represent the members' views on these matters. Yet, as has been often pointed out (Kearney, 1995), if government is to be reinvented, unions will have to be part of the decision process (see Chapter 11 in this volume). John Sturdivant, president of the American Federation of Government Employees, bluntly declared, "There will be no reinventing government . . . only bureaucratic tinkering around the margins—without fundamental changes in the union's role in the workplace" (Sturdivant, quoted in Walters, 1993: 28). It remains to be seen whether the unions will have enough political leverage or member militancy to expand the general scope of negotiable matters. Regardless, a first step might be to expand the scope of the grievance process to include position classifications and job assignments. These can be grieved in the private sector, and some unionized public employees in Canada (Chodos and Sulzner, 1995) have the right to grieve position classifications. Expanding the scope of the grievance process along these lines at public worksites would increase the relevancy of unions for their members as public employees adjust to new management initiatives with regard to the rationalization of work processes.

Finally, though, it must be recognized that all of these potential reactions by public unions to the dilution and erosion of the legitimacy of the grievance/arbitration process, albeit important, are marginal. What is truly needed is a return to an attitude by management that a willingness to make the procedures work is in their interest as well as that of the unions. After World War II, Roberts (1994: 396) relates, management in the United States followed a "kind of implied policy of accommodation" relative to industrial unions. Thinking that unions were here to stay, management agreed to a mutually beneficial trade-off; companies would not try to oust unions and unions would not try to push bilateralism into vital areas of corporate decision making. The key to holding the policy together was the growing membership of unions and their corresponding gains in economic and political power. Today, with unionism practically disappearing off the map in the private sector and just holding its own in the public realm, management has been freed up to reject accommodation with unions. They believe that unions are not here to stay and that management's long-term interest lies in getting rid of established unions and resisting the attempts of unions to organize nonunion work facilities. Moving from the present hostile environment into a more cooperative context in the future seems to be dependent on unions regaining a significant independent power base. Given current trends in the United States, this will take some doing on the part of both public and private sector unions.

MACRO-INITIATIVES IN THE PUBLIC ARENA

The most significant challenge for public unions has been the difficult adjustment to an era of fiscal restraint. Since most public services are highly labor intensive, the response to budget shortfalls has been to cut personnel, freeze hiring, eliminate some agencies and services, and privatize a number of services traditionally performed by regular government employees. In fact, as Kearney (1995: 180) observes, the "principal victim of government retrenchment has been public employees." These steps have been taken by elected chief executives of both major parties, proving once again that regardless of party ideology, political regimes in their role as employer act in similar fashion. Beyond the damage to the economic well-being of individual government workers, the labor-management system as a whole has suffered. In many instances, pay freezes and furloughs of employees have been established by executive order or through legislation. In other instances, political executives have made it clear they are not able to put any additional monetary items on the table. Often, they are only prepared to talk about reductions in the existing wage and benefit package. When pay is finally negotiated a year or two later, increasingly there is no retroactivity. All these actions, in effect, leave the essence of the collective bargaining process in limbo, in a form of suspended animation. When this happens, the legitimacy of the process is eroded and the negative effect spills over into all the other dimensions of the labor-management relationship. Amelioration of the situation is inherently limited, however, if the only resort is to the bargaining table. Unions must enter the public arena if they wish to redress the opposing forces that confront them currently.

A possible approach is to litigate. American Federation of State, County, and Municipal Employees (AFSCME) has won watershed court decisions dealing with pay equity for women (Cook, 1991). Recently AFSCME, along with the Massachusetts Teachers Association, successfully challenged a priori actions by Governor Weld of Massachusetts in furloughing state employees and increasing their individual contributions to health plans without an opportunity for negotiation. The National Treasury Employees Union has been noteworthy for its success in litigating disputed matters at the federal level of labor-management relations. It is likely that we will witness even more litigation on the part of public unions as they attempt to restore rights or benefits that are the object of take-away actions by public executives and/or legislatures. Litigation, though, is basically a defensive action on the part of unions to restore elements of the status quo. To turn around present conditions, unions need to explore, as Hoerr claims, new "leverage points" for union influence in the public arena.

One new source of leverage might be the marketing of public unionism. More and more government agencies are engaging in systematic public relations, adding staff to assist in putting their best foot forward. Unions are late arrivals to this activity, but they urgently need to market their mission—persuading the public that government service is a must, at least in the areas of health, education, welfare, transportation, and the protective services, and that public unionized employees deliver it efficiently and effectively. Messages along these lines reflect the underlying motivations of public employees. For the most part they sought public employment originally because they wanted to promote the common good rather than private greed. Unions need to demonstrate that they do not exist solely to enhance the private interests of their members. Citizens have a residue of goodwill for the individual acts of service performed daily by public employees. That feeling can be turned to good advantage by public unions. AFSCME has sponsored a series of informational television bites throughout the Northeast to good effect. Other unions should follow their example. The current explosion in the number of cable channels offers abundant opportunities for public unions to get the message across to the citizenry. At a minimum, community public access television should be utilized more than it is presently. Unions could organize programming that features, in part, local government innovation in the provision of service and in approaches to problem solving that capitalize on the expertise of their members. Public unions seem uniquely situated to engage the prevailing political culture that is so opposed to collective action by governments and unions. Public service is a noble calling, and public unions have a responsibility to get the message out to the taxpayers who fund them.

Public unions also have to adapt better than they have to the era of government by referendum. It is no longer enough to lobby the executive and legislative branches and turn out the members to campaign for particular elected officials. Today, the boundaries of the domain of governments are being set by referenda, and in this medium the anti-union constituencies so far seem to have the upper hand. Decades after Proposition 13 in California, governments are still trying to live within the restrictive confines of referendum revenue limitations set by the voters. Recently unions, both public and private, formed an alliance with other human service organizations to defeat an additional revenue limitation by referendum in Massachusetts. These kinds of associations should be retained and promoted for future ballot initiatives in the public interest as defined by progressive rather than regressive coalitions. The 13 ballot questions approved by the attorney general of Massachusetts for the 1996 general election, however, are not products of any progressive coalition (*Boston Globe,* September 7, 1995: 30). One problem, of course, is that a variety of needs have to be met by a given and shrinking pool of public funds. As the largess from the federal government continues to decrease, state and local governments face additional burdens in meeting the perceived crises in health care, corrections, and public education. All these concerns leave less money for public employee wages, benefits, and jobs (Kearney, 1995). It is hard to build solidarity among diverse interests under these circumstances; but public unions, because they represent employees in all these service areas, could be the instrument for unified collective action at the polls. Further, even though the battle seems uphill—business interests spent, for example, five times as much on the nine referendum ballot questions as spent by labor and nonprofit interests in Massachusetts in 1994 (*Boston Globe,* May 24, 1995: 32)—there are some positive signs. Polls have indicated that citizens support designated tax increases, especially in the areas of health, education, and corrections. Unions should explore sponsoring referenda that set aside tax increases for specific purposes. The effect would be to reduce the present cut-throat competition for shares of the general fund of revenues where supporting one worthy cause means opposing another.

Along these same lines, public unions must, even in these difficult financial times, put more resources into research. They need to enter the policy fray more positively—not just opposing change, but presenting their own reasonable alternatives to deal with pressing matters on the government agenda. The economic expertise of unions must be increased so they can go head-to-head with the policy recommendations of government budget and finance agencies. They also should rely more on the expertise of their members relative to the line operations of government. Managers, as we know, are listening more to their staff with regard to ways in which service can be improved in both content and delivery. Unions could do much more than they have done to utilize this advice in developing counterproposals that address problems but do not exclusively rely on personnel reductions as the most favored solution.

PROSPECTS

A crucial question that should be asked is the following one. Even if unions decide to try and reinvent themselves, are they capable of doing it? Public unions are labor-intensive organizations. They are very dependent on the human resources of their members and staff for accomplishment. Ninety percent of union officials are part-time voluntary representatives, and 90 percent of them are located in union locals throughout the United States (Roberts, 1994). Nearly all are elected and serve at the pleasure of the members. This grass-roots structure ensures that the union will be in touch with the voice of the workers it represents. The structure also works against the leadership becoming entrenched in office and isolated from its constituents. Further, it typically means that changes in the way unions operate at the workplace cannot be implemented without the support of the membership. If leaders want to redirect scarce union resources, they must spend the time and energy to persuade and educate the members regarding the merits of the proposals. The flip side of this situation is that "as the local goes, so goes the union." If the local unit is not up to the job, the union as a whole suffers. Unfortunately, too often the performance of locals is inadequate.

Virtually all union constitutions and bylaws mandate an array of officers and committees to perform the separate tasks of the organization. Usually there are four or five principal officers, an executive board made up of regular members to oversee the officers, and two or three committees charged with particular assignments. Typically none of the individuals serving in these capacities have received any training for the union positions. Their respective talents are those they bring from their primary occupations. Under these circumstances it is rather important that locals sustain a critical mass of members from which they can draw leaders and activists. Union business is generally conducted after working hours or, in part, during regular hours of work. If union officers leave their regular duties to engage in union business, either lost wages are paid from union dues or, more commonly in the public sector, contracts contain clauses that permit union officials a "reasonable amount" of paid agency time to deal with work-related problems. Presently, though, given the pressures for efficiency in government operations, there has been a consistent narrowing of management's view of "reasonable." The net effect often is "catch as catch can" with respect to fulfilling union responsibilities at the job site.

Few locals have any pool of expertise that they can resort to with respect to research or advice in the areas of law, economics, education, or politics. For that kind of assistance they must rely on their respective state or national organizations. This dependency is also present, although perhaps to a lesser degree, when collective bargaining agreements are negotiated or arbitrated. What level of support can local unions expect from their regional, state, and national organizations? The amount and quality of assistance obviously varies from union to union, but one constant exists—unions are only as strong as their membership and consequent financial and political resources permit.

The contemporary situation for public sector unions is a mixed bag. The traditionally weak federal unions are even weaker today as the Clinton administration moves forward toward its goal of reducing the number of employees by 272,000 persons. Union membership has always been low (around 25 percent of those eligible) and obviously will decline further, greatly reducing the ability of federal unions to provide services to their members. Indeed, federal unions appear to be an "endangered species." The picture is brighter at the state and local levels. Although only one state, New Mexico in 1992, has enacted a collective bargaining law since Ohio and Illinois in 1984, the number of public employees covered by collective bargaining agreements has been growing. For example, in 1992, fully 90,000 employees were added to the ranks of those represented by unions, which was nearly double the number of new state and local government positions created in 1992. As might be expected, gains did not occur in uniform fashion around the country. New Jersey and Pennsylvania had a high degree of organizing, whereas California, Massachusetts, and Michigan had very little (Bronfenbrenner and Juravich, 1994). Regardless of the level of organizing, it is a fact that public employee rolls have declined in the Northeast and the Midwest, those areas where public unionization took root. Although the overall numbers show a slight increase in unionization at the state and local areas of government, many states in the above-mentioned regions show a decline. For most states where public unionization is embedded in statute and in the personnel systems, the present situation regarding membership is stagnant, with marginal increases in some years offset by marginal declines in other years. Political and financial resources have not grown, and it is likely in many circumstances that union revenues have barely kept even with the rate of inflation. In a number of instances they have probably fallen below the rate of inflation. Generally, public unions, if they wish to launch new initiatives or add to their quotient of expertise, are looking at reallocations of existing resources. Public unions, like other public organizations, have turned to their payrolls to reduce costs. Whether the reductions in staff are applied at headquarters or in the field, the net result to union locals is a cutback in service from the regional, state, or national organization and a corresponding obligation to be more self-reliant. The problem is that relying on the indigenous talents of the local organization will not enable public unions to reinvent themselves.

What can be done to free up resources for the future viability of public unions? Perhaps it is time to reduce competition and a go-it-alone approach. More joint organizing efforts are called for, as well as consolidation of unions in the public sector. Why should the American Federation of Teachers and the National Teachers Association remain independent of each other or, for that matter, the various fraternal orders of police officers? With the same goals for their organizations, consolidation would cut organizing costs and reduce administrative overhead, releasing funds for more strategic purposes. Perhaps these groups should follow the lead of the International Brotherhood of Machinists, the United Auto Workers, and the United States Steel Workers, who are currently exploring the possibility of a major consolidation. All the public unions, moreover, might seek affiliation with the AFL-CIO. Some public unions now play a major role in its councils, and bringing more into the fold would give them an even greater voice. Further, affiliation with the AFL-CIO would provide access for many public unions to the institution-building facilities already operating within the confines of the AFL-CIO. These would include the Organizing Institute, a new training program to centralize and upgrade the organizing efforts of its affiliates; the Labor Institute for Public Affairs, charged with improving labor's overall public image; the George Meany Center for Labor Studies, charged with educating union personnel broadly in terms of organized labor's current concerns as well as specific programs dealing with human resource utilization; and the Union Privilege Benefit Program, which is tied to the associate membership recruiting program of the AFL-CIO. This is not to say that public unions do not have similar programs, but none are as comprehensive or as well funded. Public unions would not just be drawing benefits from this association, they would also be bringing expertise to the AFL-CIO regarding their experience in servicing a work force that is representative of the kind that will inhabit future job sites. Given the limitations on resources that all unions face, pulling together in common avoids costly redundancies and increases the critical mass of talent that public unions need to counter the prevailing civic culture and government policies.

It must be observed that a linking of previously unaffiliated public unions with the AFL-CIO would be a controversial move for both entities. For many public unions, their history of independence during a time of growth in the 1960s and 1970s was tied, in part, to a cultivated image of being different from the blue-collar industrial unionism of the private sector. Blue-collar industrial unionism is, however, a vestige of the past. The singularity of the issues that confront both public and private sector unions should overcome any leftover antagonisms. Secretary of Labor Robert Reich, on the eve of Labor Day 1995, described the common plight of American labor as that of "frayed-collar workers in gold-plated times" (*USA Today,* September 1, 1995: 5a). More extensive assimilation of public and private unions, as suggested above, will not be easy to accomplish. We will have to see whether, with their backs to the wall, recognition of the harsh realities of the present will solidify the union movement beyond what has happened in the past. "Going it alone" or "doing your own thing," it seems pretty evident, are not prescriptions that will provide an adequate sense of direction for handling the multiple tasks that lie ahead for public unions.

NOTE

1. Not all public unions have welcomed women and visible minorities into their ranks. Public safety unions (police, fire, and corrections) in particular have responded in many instances only after intervention by the courts. See Riccucci, 1990.

REFERENCES

Batt, Rosemary, and Eileen Appelbaum. 1995. "Worker Participation in Diverse Settings: Does the Form Affect the Outcome, and If So, Who Benefits?" Paper presented at the 10th World Congress of the International Industrial Relations Association, Washington, D.C., May 31–June 4.

Boston Globe. May 24, 1995: 32, and September 7, 1995: 30.

Bronfenbrenner, Kate, and Tom Juravich. 1994. *The Current State of Organizing in the Public Sector: Final Report.* Amherst, Mass.: Labor Relations and Research Center.

Chodos, Philip, and George T. Sulzner. 1995. "The Public Service Reform Act of Canada and Federal Labor Relations." *Journal of Collective Negotiations in the Public Sector* 24, no. 2: 97–110.

Cook, Alice H. 1991. "Pay Equity: Theory and Implementation," in Carolyn Ban and Norma M. Riccucci, eds., *Public Personnel Management: Current Concerns—Future Challenges.* New York: Longman.

Freeman, Richard B., and James L. Medoff. 1984. *What Do Unions Do?* New York: Basic Books.

Freeman, Richard B., and Joel Rogers. 1995. "Worker Representation and Participation Survey: First Report of Findings." *Proceedings of the Forty-Seventh Annual Meeting of the Industrial Relations Research Association, January 6–8,* Washington, D.C., 336–345.

Greenfield, Patricia A., and Robert J. Pleasure. 1993. "Representatives of Their Own Choosing: Finding Workers' Voice in the Legitimacy and Power of Their Unions," in Bruce E. Kaufman and Morris M. Kleiner, eds., *Employee Representation: Alternatives and Future Directions.* Madison, Wisc.: Industrial Relations Research Association.

Gross, James A. 1985. "Conflicting Statutory Purposes: Another Look at Fifty Years of NLRB Law Making." *Industrial and Labor Relations Review* 39, no. 1: 7–18.

Hoerr, John. 1991. "What Should Unions Do?" *Harvard Business Review* 69, no. 3: 30–40.

Johnston, William B., and Arnold H. Packer. 1987. *Workforce 2000: Work and Workers for the 21st Century.* Indianapolis: Hudson Institute.

Kearney, Richard C. 1995. "Unions in Government: Where Do They Go From Here?" in Steven W. Hays and Richard C. Kearney, eds., *Public Personnel Administration: Problems and Prospects,* 3rd ed. Englewood Cliffs, N.J.: Prentice-Hall.

Kearney, Richard C., and Steven W. Hays. 1994. "Labor-Management Relations and Participative Decision Making: Toward a New Paradigm." *Public Administration Review* 54, no. 1: 44–51.

Keller, Berndt K. 1995. "Emerging Models of Worker Participation and Representation." *Proceedings of the 10th World Congress of International Industrial Relations Association,* Washington, D.C., May 31–June 4, pp. 32–38.

Kelly, Mary Ellen R., and Bennett Harrison. 1992. "Unions, Technology, and Labor-Management Cooperation," in Lawrence Mishel and Paula B. Voos, eds., *Unions and Economic Competitiveness.* New York: M.E. Sharpe.

Klingner, Donald E. 1993. "Public Sector Collective Bargaining: Is the Glass Half-Full, Half-Empty, or Broke?" *Review of Public Personnel Administration* 13, no. 3: 19–28.

Lewin, David, and Daniel J.B. Mitchell. 1992. "Systems of Employee Voice: Theoretical and Empirical Perspectives." Paper presented at the 45th Annual Meeting of the Industrial Relations Research Association, New Orleans, La., January 3–5.

McLean, Greg. 1995. "Reform—Unions' Future." Paper presented at the 10th World Congress of the International Industrial Relations Association, Washington, D.C., May 31–June 4.

National Labor Relations Board v. Yeshiva University, 444 U.S. 672 (1980).

O'Rand, A. 1986. "The Hidden Payroll: Employee Benefits and the Structure of Workplace Inequality." *Sociological Forum* 1: 657–683.

Riccucci, Norma M. 1990. *Women, Minorities and Unions in the Public Sector.* Westport, Conn.: Greenwood Press.

Roberts, Higdon C., Jr. 1994. "Contemporary Perspectives and the Future of American Unions," in Jack Rabin, Thomas Vocino, W. Bartley Hildreth, and Gerald J. Miller, eds., *Handbook of Public Sector Labor Relations.* New York: Marcel Dekker.

Roberts, M., and W.E. Bittle. 1981. "The Union Contract: A Solid Investment." *Federationist* 88, no. 5: 8–10.

Sulzner, George T. 1983. "Productivity and Job Security: The Issues of the 1980s in United States Public Sector Labor Relations." *Journal of Collective Negotiations in the Public Sector* 12, no. 2: 79–86.

———. 1985. "Public Sector Labor Relations: Agent of Change in American Industrial Relations?" *Review of Public Personnel Administration* 5, no. 2: 70–77.

USA Today. 1995. September 1: 5a.

Walters, Jonathan. 1993. "The Chastening of Public Employees." *Governing* 6, no. 4: 26–30.

Webb, Sidney, and Beatrice Webb. 1902. *Industrial Democracy.* London: Longmans, Green.

Weil, David. 1991. "Enforcing OSHA: The Role of Labor Unions." *Industrial Relations* 30, no. 1: 20–36.

———. 1992. "Building Safety: The Role of Construction Unions in the Enforcement of OSHA." *Journal of Labor Research* 13, no. 1: 121–132.

———. 1995. "Mandating Safety and Health Committees: Lessons from the States." *Proceedings of the Forty-Seventh Annual Meeting of the Industrial Relations Research Association, January 6–8,* Washington, D.C., 273–281.

chapter **11**

Labor-Management Partnerships in the Public Sector

T. Zane Reeves

$\mathbf{T}$his chapter examines the effectiveness of labor-management partnerships in public sector organizations in the United States as they emerged during the 1990s and their future in the 2000s. Under a labor-management partnership (LMP), both parties to a collective bargaining agreement commit to equally share decision-making responsibilities in the workplace. An LMP is a far more comprehensive commitment than formerly occurred with labor-management cooperation in the past. The LMP should not be confused with techniques to increase individual employee participation in problem solving (i.e., total quality management, continuous quality improvement, daily decision making, reinvention, and others). Only two partners have thus far been designated as partners, the union and top level agency managers, to the exclusion of all other interested parties.

In order to appreciate the challenges faced by LMPs it is important to understand the traditional nature of industrial relations as well as why LMPs represent a possible final stage in the evolution of labor-management cooperation.

INDUSTRIAL RELATIONS IN AMERICA

The history of private sector industrial relations in the United States, as in other industrial nations, was fraught with economic warfare, and, often violence between workers and employers. Nineteenth-century America in particular witnessed deadly strikes, union busting, and beatings by both sides. Whether it was the Homestead, Pennsylvania, steel strike where the Monongahela River "ran red" with the blood of strikers and Pinkerton agents were hired to quell the disturbance, or the Colorado minefields, no one ever considered that industrial relations could be anything less than adversarial. By the late twentieth century, industrial relations had evolved to a less confrontational stage and even occasionally became cooperative in nature.

The evolution of industrial relations in the United States to a more cooperative phase was primarily due to a decline in union membership in the private sector, brought about by a variety of socioeconomic factors including active government intervention to control the worst health and safety abuses in the workplace. Although industrial relations became less confrontational, the adversarial assumptions of labor-management relations remained largely unchanged in both the public and private sectors with the exception of occasional experiments with cooperative endeavors.

LABOR-MANAGEMENT ADVERSARIES

Public employee unions, although without generally experiencing the violent history of their private sector counterparts, also have played roles as adversaries to government managers and as advocates for employee rights. Public sector unions grew most rapidly during the 1960s and 1970s by perfecting their adversarial roles. Many union activists still urge their brothers and sisters in solidarity to steadfastly hold to an adversarial stance and not be deceived by employers who now speak of teamwork, cooperation, and partnership. Bill Burris, vice-president of the American Postal Workers Union, contends, "There is absolutely no evidence in history that cooperating with the employer does unions any good. . . . There are just conflicting interests. Once you dissipate the militancy and cohesiveness of working people, you destroy the primary strength of labor unions. . . . Our strength comes from our members" (1994: 8). Amy Newell, secretary-treasurer of the United Electrical Workers, unequivocally states what she believes to be the most basic fact of unionism:

> We, the labor movement, are virtually the only mass organization in the United States today that are [sic] organized along class lines—uniting men and women, black, white and brown, skilled and unskilled—on the basis of our economic interest as workers and in opposition to the economic self-interest of our corporate employers. (1989: 8)

Regarding the potential for labor-management cooperation, John Patterson, a local executive board member with the United Auto Workers union, contends:

> I believe there will never be an equal partnership between workers and their managers, only between some misguided union leaders and their partners in management. The solidarity of workers is the only partnership that will protect us from the abuse that the corporations and managers of the new world order heap upon the people who do the work. (1995: 2)

Thus the labor movement in the United States was predicated upon the gospel that an adversarial stance was necessary to counterbalance management's one-sided, arbitrary, and capricious treatment of workers. As indicated, the public sector model of labor-management relations that evolved during the decades from 1960 to 1990 was based on an adversarial approach by both sides, much akin to industrial relations in the private sector. States, municipalities, counties, and school districts followed the lead of federal labor-management relations as it developed from a simple "meet and confer" relationship in the early 1960s, usually reinforced by executive orders, to a formal labor-management program enforced by federal and state law or local ordinance. The federal system would ultimately be monitored by an independent administrative agency, the Federal Labor Relations Authority (FLRA), whereas among most states and many local jurisdictions Public Employee Relations Boards (PERBs) and local labor relations boards or arbitrators adjudicated disputes between unions and employers.

Consequently the public sector labor-management model that had emerged by the 1990s was based on mistrust, noncooperation, and a formal dispute resolution process between two warring adversaries. A General Accounting Office report regarding the federal labor-management relations program concluded that it was not working well, in part because "the program is too adversarial and often bogged down by litigation over procedural matters and minutiae" (U.S. GAO, 1991: 2). Not only were unions and employers adversarial at the bargaining table; they were often enemies in disciplinary grievance hearings, arbitration proceedings, and hearings to resolve alleged "unfair labor practices." Thus along with a formalized adversarial *structure* of labor-management interaction, there developed an adversarial *culture* as well—an "us" versus "them" mentality whose low productivity and increased costs have never been fully documented (Marzotto, 1994).

The assumption that labor and management would always be adversaries was not only accepted as inevitable, it was imbedded into labor law as it emerged following passage of the National Labor Relations Act (NLRA) in 1935. The NLRA legitimized the private sector employees' right to join unions, bargain collectively, and strike. Decades later, the NLRA became the model for statutes and ordinances that recognized the right of public employees to organize and bargain collectively for conditions of employment. Even the Civil Service Reform Act (CSRA) of 1978, which legislatively guaranteed collective bargaining rights for federal employees, continued the adversarial structure. For example, the CSRA precludes an agency's employees from working with management on a number of issues of importance to the quality of federal worklife, such as negotiation over wages, benefits, and contracting out.

Despite the ingrained adversarial pattern of collective bargaining in the public sector, labor-management cooperation in specific areas flourished during the 1970s and 1980s. Labor-management cooperative experiments demonstrated that the adversarial mold could be broken and cooperation was possible. At issue is whether it is feasible to move beyond labor-management cooperation to full-fledged partnership.

LABOR-MANAGEMENT COOPERATION

Labor-management committees (LMCs) were intended to foster cooperation between union and management in areas not resolved by the collective bargaining agreement. An LMC was typically comprised of representatives from labor and management, usually in equal numbers, who met at regular intervals or as needed to examine, discuss, and solve mutual problems. By 1978 the U.S. National Center for Productivity and Quality of Working Life could identify 215 labor-management committees in the public sector (1978).

Basically, LMCs performed either of two possible functions: (1) to resolve bargaining impasses without resorting to strikes or arbitration, or (2) to address noncontractual issues that developed during day-to-day operations. For instance, effective impasse resolution committees functioned in jurisdictions such as the Commonwealth of Massachusetts; Toledo, Ohio; Milwaukee, Wisconsin; Decatur, Illinois; Troy, Michigan; and others (Indiana University, 1979). An even greater number of LMCs were created during this era to expand cooperation to issues that arose once collective bargaining was concluded. Examples of operational and problem-solving committees included the following public sector organizations: Columbus, Ohio; Wichita, Kansas; Milwaukee; Troy; the District of Columbia; New York City; Memphis, Tennessee; Washington State; and Denver, Colorado.

According to surveys conducted by LMC participants, immediate improvements in labor-management relations were cited (Indiana University, 1979). Specifically, they recognized improved clarity in communication whereby confrontational issues tended to become more frequently substantive rather than personal: "both labor and management have come to recognize that there are other issues of mutual interest that can be reserved for a cooperative approach" (30).

Similarly, several experiments with labor-management cooperation in the federal sector during the 1980s were seemingly quite successful and probably lent credibility to the partnership movement in the 1990s. The Internal Revenue Service (IRS) entered into cooperative initiatives with the National Treasury Employees Union (NTEU) "because its adversarial relationship had gotten out of hand" (U.S. Department of Labor, 1987: 6). A successful cooperative relationship at Keesler Air Force Base with the National Federation of Federal Employees (NFFE) was also preceded by a combative and hostile labor-management environment (U.S. Department of Labor, 1987). The NASA Research Center in Cleveland and the American Federation of Government Employees (AFGE), Local 2182, developed a cooperative arrangement that utilized joint teams to resolve problems. Finally, the U.S. Postal Service and the American Postal Workers' Union (APWU) concluded an agreement in 1993 for labor-management cooperation in certain areas, which proclaimed that "The amicable resolution of our differences . . . marks a milestone in the relationship between the Postal Service and the APWU" (American Postal Workers' Union, 1994: 12). Perhaps not coincidentally, these successful LMC ventures involved the three federal unions that subsequently entered into partnership with their federal employers in 1993.

LABOR-MANAGEMENT PARTNERSHIPS

The purpose of labor-management partnerships was proclaimed in the National Performance Review chaired by Vice-President Al Gore: "We can only transform government if we transform the adversarial relationship that dominates federal union-management interaction into partnership for reinvention and change" (Gore, 1993: 15). Thus the National Performance Review (NPR) envisions labor-management relations as a partnership of equals, rather than an unrelenting struggle between adversaries.

To reach this goal, President Clinton appointed a National Partnership Council (NPC) that, in addition to management representatives, included the presidents of three federal employee unions (AFGE, NTEU, and NFFE) and a representative of the Public Employee Department of the AFL-CIO. The National Partnership Council's mandate was to "propose the statutory changes needed to make the labor-management partnership a reality" (Gore, 1993: 15). President Clinton's Executive Order #12871 (October 1, 1993) promised a new era of labor management relations:

> Only by changing the nature of Federal labor-management relations so that managers, employees, and employees' elected union representatives serve as partners will it be possible to design and implement comprehensive changes necessary to reform government.

Certainly, federal employee unions might be quite willing partners in the Clinton administration's plan to reform procurement procedures or reduce rigid personnel policies and procedures, but plans to cut 272,000 federal jobs by 1998 would not likely have similar appeal.

Partnership in Cutback

Quite surprisingly, union participation as partners in the process of decreasing the number of federal employees is precisely what has occurred, as 75,000 federal jobs were eliminated during the first year of the labor-management partnership (Carroll, 1995). Specifically, two of the initial federal unions and agencies that entered into partnership agreements are as follows:

- *The National Treasury Employees Union (NTEU) and the Customs Service* agreed to a partnership that NTEU president Robert Tobias commented was essential because "agency reorganizations or reinventions cannot be implemented without the cooperation and involvement of the union. Union and management need each other in order to succeed" (1994). The agreement seeks organizational "transformation . . . participation as an equal partner in meetings . . . appointment to all task forces and groups for the purposes of changing work processes," and "treating each other with dignity and respect, sharing ideas, proposals, information and concerns with each other" (Hyde, 1994).

- *The American Federation of Government Employees (AFGE) and the Office of Personnel Management (OPM)* reached a partnership agreement that survived a massive reduction in force (RIF) in the agency's administration group. AFGE president John Sturdivant cited Local 2302 in Kentucky as an example of "successful experiences in partnership" where, evidently, the local's payroll was reduced by 16 percent in 14 months—4 percent more than was required over five years in the NPR (Parker and Slaughter, 1994). Remarkably, OPM laid off almost 20 percent of its employees in 1994 (Causey, 1994).

Partnership in Labor Law Reform

The president's Executive Order directed the National Partnership Council (NPC) to reform the adversarial state of federal labor law. Accordingly, the NPC moved to broaden the scope of collective bargaining by directing agencies to negotiate over issues (e.g., agency shop and performance appraisals) that were previously nonmandatory. Finally, the NPC directed federal agency heads to develop labor-management partnerships at appropriate levels throughout their respective agencies. However, these proposed agency agreements have yet to be approved by the president.

LIMITATIONS AND OPPORTUNITIES FOR "PARTNERING"

Participation by unions as equals in labor-management partnerships is deemed essential for "reinvention and change" (Gore, 1993: 15); otherwise the adversarial climate will remain unchanged. Of course, terminology describing new decision-making processes becomes confusing at times, depending on whether one is referring to Quality of Work Life programs in the 1970s, Employment Involvement/ Employee Participation during the early 1980s, or the Team Concept of the late 1980s.

Along with the aforementioned concepts are two other terms: *reengineering* and *reinventing* the organization. Reengineering's advocates claim it is not about "cutting fat or automating existing processes; it is about taking something that is irrelevant and starting over." They advocate, for example, breaking down job classifications, building the organization around generalists who handle a task from beginning to end, and contracting out for work (Hammer and Champy, 1995). Reengineering can be accomplished without labor-management cooperation or partnership as a management right. For instance, Congress could abolish or merge departments as a part of reengineering, but reinvention is a different matter. Reinvention requires union participation to succeed.

Reinvention of the organization (unlike reengineering, which is planned from the top down without employee input) involves corporate transformation necessitated by "new values and economic necessity" (Naisbitt and Aburdene, 1985). Employee participation is critical to reinventing the "new" organization wherein the employee is coequal with management in a team effort. Reinvention is intended to be a process in partnership.

However, reinvention in the corporate arena is quite different from reinventing government organizations—unions must be included as a partner in the government process. Reinventing corporate America apparently doesn't involve a union role; "Because unions don't understand the need to reinvent themselves to fit the informational society, their decline and eventual demise seem certain" (Naisbitt and Aburdene, 1985: 83). Several private sector models of reinvention that feature labor-management partnerships have been widely touted as successful models, most notably at AT&T/CWA (Baugh, 1995), General Motors (GM) UAW at the Saturn plant (Pennington, 1989), and the joint GM and Toyota venture with the UAW in Fremont, California. However, other observers contend that these LMPs are not the equal partnerships that were first envisioned (Lund, 1994; Parker and Slaughter, 1995).

By contrast, reinventing organizations in the federal sector is structured as a labor-management partnership in which unions are full partners. Why? The answer apparently is twofold: the comparatively large percentage of federal employees who are represented by unions, and the continued growth (albeit much more slowly than in past years) of public employee unions, especially at state and local levels. First, consider that about 1.3 million federal employees, or 57 percent of the total nonpostal federal work force, are represented by unions (U.S. Office of Personnel Management, 1992). Although the relative percentages are slightly lower in most other levels of government, public employee unions simply can't be ignored as partners in reinvention.

Whereas the number of employees represented by unions in the private sector continued to decline through 1992, public sector membership is actually increasing or maintaining its percentage at all levels of government (Judis, 1994). Although for the first year since 1948 union representation in the private sector actually increased in 1993, still only a small percentage of private sector employees are represented by unions (Judis, 1994).

Inducements to Union Participation in Reinvention

Quite simply, public employee unions were persuaded to become labor-management partners in the federal effort to reinvent government, even in the decision-making process to cut federal employee jobs by 272,000 in five years. In order to entice union participation in a partnership venture, the following promises were made by the Clinton administration (Ban, 1995):

- that many cuts in jobs would accrue through attrition and buyouts;
- that many of the jobs eliminated would be held by middle management, labor specialists, classification positions, and personnelists (positions not included within collective bargaining agreements);

- that partnership participation with the union would extend throughout civilian federal agencies, from top to bottom;
- that legislation would be sought to require management to negotiate certain issues that were not previously permissible items for bargaining (i.e., agency shop and fair share representation fees, classification, and performance evaluation).

None of the aforementioned promises have been honored; without obtaining agency shop provisions, federal employee unions simply lack the capability and finances to serve as strong federal partners. Union weakness is underscored by the fact that even though almost two-thirds of federal employees are within bargaining units, less than one-third voluntarily join a union (Masters and Atkin, 1995). By July 1995 the proposed legislative changes were still languishing. Furthermore, there was growing criticism from labor observers that the highly touted partnership was merely a facade: "it is being driven from the top down by the White House along the rigid vertical structure of each agency" (Anglin, 1994: 10). Others characterized the downsizing as a subterfuge for "putting the AFGE label on your pink slip" (Parker and Slaughter, 1994: 10). Finally, the 1994 elections, in which Republicans regained control of Congress, caused union leaders to feel "estranged" because the Clinton administration dropped proposed labor law reforms from the draft civil service reform bill (Ban, 1995).

BARRIERS TO UNION PARTNERSHIP

Although the federal labor-management partnership for reinventing government is ongoing, a number of conclusions can be drawn for public jurisdictions and their unions who might consider this arrangement. As one of its union critics surmised, "Partnership is a concept that has tremendous potential, but I have serious concerns about how it is implemented" (Anglin, 1994: 10).

First, obstacles to partnership must be recognized. It would be naive to pretend that very serious obstacles to labor-management partnerships did not exist or to ignore them. Primarily, the barriers to implementation are twofold: the existing adversarial culture, and the role dissonance created by partnership for managers, union representatives, and employees.

BARRIERS TO MANAGERS AS PARTNERS

Relinquishing adversarial roles for both unions and management is not easily accomplished. Toni Marzotto asks:

> If the union is to cooperate as a full partner with the management of the agency, who is to care for the union's traditional roles? Are grievances to be subservient to cooperation? Is the union so much a partner with management that it is management? Are all the union's former roles replaced by partnership? (1994: 10)

Marzotto and others (Causey, 1994; Ban, 1995) have described a "twin union" phenomenon that develops where, in some agencies, two types of stewards have been created—partnership stewards (responsible for talking with and negotiating with management) and grievance stewards. In another instance, at OPM, one group of AFGE's Local #32 cooperated wholeheartedly with a reduction in force while a separate group attempted to challenge the RIF through grievances and arbitration (Causey, 1994).

The unions are not alone in experiencing difficulty in deemphasizing the adversarial role and entering into a spirit of cooperation. Federal managers have proven reluctant to become equal partners with the union or to delegate authority to mid-management and supervisory levels in order to negotiate cooperative agreements at all levels of the agency. Initially almost all federal agencies with bargaining unit employees successfully negotiated partnership agreements at the "unit of recognition" level (the level where bargaining agreements are negotiated, i.e., regional or facility level). However, as Ban reports (1995), signing an agreement is merely the first step. Implementing partnership throughout an agency poses several technical and logistical problems, which remain largely unaddressed. Top agency managers are involved in national partnership agreements, but what about mid-level managers and supervisors on site? The NPC seemingly ignores these managers and does not provide for the formulation of partnership agreements at lower levels.

EMPLOYEE PARTICIPATION IN PARTNERSHIP

Employees also experience role dissonance within a partnership environment where they are asked to become self-directed work team members and empowered to make decisions in a client-directed effort. Again, Marzotto asks pertinent questions:

> If the employee is truly empowered and management does embrace the tenets of TQM, what is the role of the union for the employee? As a partner? The employee is part of the decision mechanisms. As an adversary? The employee does and is encouraged to speak and make recommendations. As a voice in the partnership? The employee is now encouraged to be part of management's roles. (1994: 11)

The federal partnership assumes that only two partners are party to the arrangement—unions and management. As indicated, partnership results in role dichotomy within both union and management ranks. However, LMP does not acknowledge the fact that a majority of federal employees within bargaining units are *not* dues-paying members of the union. Moreover, LMP ignores the fact that Total Quality Management (TQM), the most popular process for involving employees as participants in decision making, is viewed by many observers as a tool for weakening the union's fundamental responsibility as the *exclusive* employee representative. Thus a critical player in the partnership process is the nonunion member employee who participates in TQM activities.

Nonunion Employees in Partnering

It is widely noted that federal employee unions are relatively "weak" because only a minority of employees actually join the union (Ban, 1995; Masters and Atkin, 1995). Union effectiveness is thus seriously eroded because members of the bargaining unit cannot be compelled to pay union dues, although peer pressure may be effective in some instances. Although the NPC report posits that "union effectiveness requires strong, professional, financially secure unions that are able to operate as full partners with agencies," the same report fails to propose an agency shop or fair-share service fee alternative to the open shop status quo (Ban, 1995: 138).

Furthermore, the current Republican-controlled Congress would not be likely to approve such a proposal. Thus federal employees who for whatever reasons disdain to join the union are left with the union as their official representative in the partnering venture.

TQM and the Unions

As discussed in Chapter 18, Total Quality Management actually encompasses a variety of related techniques or processes to elicit "meaningful employee participation in organizational decision making . . . and employee views are given serious consideration" (Kearney and Hays, 1994: 45). TQM is the most recent innovation, deriving from the early Quality Circles movement whose goal was "to involve those who actually perform the tasks in decision making involving their work and/or production process" (Patton, 1994: 56).

Central to the TQM approach is the creation of self-directed work teams that are delegated authority to solve problems and make decisions in the workplace. Self-directed work teams function independently of the traditional demarcation between supervisor/manager and employee. These TQM "committees" include both employees and "clients" involved in the production of particular goods and services. Although not without its critics, TQM has been widely accepted in numerous organizations in the private and public sectors.

Of particular concern to many observers is whether TQM committees or other similarly comprised committees in the workplace could undermine an elected union's ability to represent members of the bargaining unit. Since 1935 it has been a fundamental policy of labor law, at least in the private sector, to encourage collective bargaining by protecting the right of workers to freely associate and select union representatives of their own choosing. A cornerstone of that policy was the prohibition contained in Article 8(a)(2) of the National Labor Relations Act, on employer domination of unions and employee representation plans. Prior to the act's passage, employer control of employee organizations was used widely and effectively to restrict workers from joining independent labor unions of their own choosing.

The fear that TQM committees might supplant or weaken the union as the exclusive employee representative was expressed in a 1992 ruling by the National Labor Relations Board, which found that "Actions Committees" sponsored at Automation, Inc., constituted labor organizations and were thus unlawful (*Electromation,* 1992).

With the advent of a Republican majority in Congress in 1994–95, efforts were made to amend the NLRA so that TQM committees could be protected from union interference. In February 1995 committees in both the House and Senate held hearings on the Teamwork for Employees and Management Act, known as the TEAM Act, which its supporters touted as a minor change in labor law that was simply intended to encourage cooperative labor-management relations. However, numerous scholars, researchers, and practitioners believe that the TEAM Act would negate the original purpose of Article 8(a)(2) because the proposed legislation contains no safeguards to guarantee that employer-created representation plans function democratically and independently of the employer. Quite simply, these observers are convinced that nothing in the TEAM Act would prevent employers from manipulating TQM-type committees in order to thwart genuine employee voice as expressed through elected union representatives (Wheeler, Katz, and Summers, 1995).

Whether one agrees with the TEAM Act's sponsors or its critics, the partnership concept is faced with what appears to be an insurmountable issue: to either create a partnership directly with employees through TQM committees and thereby bypass union representation, or to strengthen unions as the only employee representative. In all likelihood, partnership will be modified to simple labor-management cooperation on specific issues covered in collective bargaining agreements while employers move to eliminate official union representation on TQM committees.

PROSPECTS FOR PARTNERING

The prospects for partnering between the federal employer and its unions are more likely to be affected by the Republican-controlled Congress's "Contract with America" than by the implementation of the National Performance Review (Carroll, 1995). Nonetheless, several "realities" are apparent to those employers, unions, and employees who would contemplate a partnership agreement. They are as follows:

Unions must be employee champions. Even in a TQM work setting or self-directed work teams, some employees will file grievances with the union as the employee's representative. "Rights" grievances (i.e., employee disciplinary appeals, alleged unfair labor practices, contract interpretation, etc.) must be handled by union representatives if they cannot be resolved during the pre-grievance stage. At the same time, acceptance of the union's representational role does not preclude cooperation on issues of common interest. A union could certainly engage in cooperative decision making while guaranteeing its advocacy of employee rights in grievance hearings, arbitration, and negotiations. It may well be that formally negotiated collective bargaining agreements will disappear as outmoded relics of the past in lieu of continuously changing problem-solving committees equally comprised of labor and management representatives. But even if this scenario occurs, union stewards and representatives must necessarily perform representative functions.

Separation of roles must be maintained. Not every problem or issue should be brought before a TQM committee. Social contracts or partnerships cannot obfuscate the existence of legitimate differences of opinion regarding wages, benefits, and working conditions. Problem solving, workplace improvement, increasing work satisfaction, and decreasing bureaucratic procedures hold great promise for cooperative participation on TQM committees. However, other tasks requiring leadership and normally within the purview of "management rights" should not be shared. For example, downsizing where bargaining unit or professional employees are concerned is not a disinterested decision for unions to make, especially if job incumbents—even supervisors—are the targets of downsizing. Possibly for this reason, Osborne and Gaebler's analysis of rein-venting government at the local levels is predicated on first guaranteeing unions that downsizing will only occur following reassurances of "lifetime job security" for employees (1992). In other words, employees know there will be a job some-where if theirs is phased out and attrition of 10 percent average will cut government size eventually.

To reiterate, the federal partnership suggests that labor-management com-mittees can effectively make decisions regarding "doing more with less" or "working smarter, not harder." But partnerships have not proven to be a viable option for eliminating employee positions or coopting the union's adversarial role in the protection of federal employee rights.

Commitment and credibility are essential. As Ban concludes, implementation of partnership reforms requires management's commitment of resources to extensive training, "not just on the new culture and values but on the specific skills needed to do their jobs" (1995: 149). Commitment must be long-term and bipartisan rather than perceived as the political agenda of one party or the other. Credibility is built as both union and employers *behave* as partners rather than in preconceived adversarial roles. Union representatives, as well as managers, are expected to learn new styles of interaction.

Partnership encompasses all employees. The NPR assumed a partnership between only two parties: the union and agency managers. Middle managers were excluded, whether deliberately or unintentionally, as "sacrificial lambs" to the altar of workforce reduction. In addition, no mechanism was ever created whereby middle managers could provide feedback or enter into partnership arrangements at lower levels of the organization. Moreover, nonunion members of the bargaining unit must be made to feel as though they are partners as well. Probably the most realistic option is to permit collective bargaining in good faith regarding service fees for nonunion employees. However, it is politically unlikely that a Republican-controlled Congress will pass legislation that serves to increase the coffers of labor unions.

In conclusion, the prospects for continued labor-management cooperation appear optimistic when specific problems and issues in need of cooperative decision making can be identified. However, the proposition that unions and top managers in the federal sector can function as equal partners has already proven to be unrealistic for four reasons:

- Many members of the bargaining unit are not union members and do not recognize the union as their representative;
- Mid-level managers and supervisors are not perceived as partner participants;
- Cooperative committees too often undermine union roles;
- Unions cannot represent their membership fairly by helping managers decide who will lose their jobs.

Again, despite these limitations, labor-management cooperation can flourish and thereby reduce the traditionally adversarial environment of the workplace.

REFERENCES

American Postal Workers' Union. 1994. *CBR* 94-01 (February): 12–13.

Anglin, G. 1994. "Federal Sector Partnerships: Boon or Boondoggle?" *Labor Notes* (September): 10.

Ban, C. 1995. "Unions, Management and the NPR," in Donald F. Kettl and John DiIulio Jr., eds., *Inside the Reinvention Machine: Appraising Governmental Reform.* Washington, D.C.: Brookings Institution.

Baugh, R. 1995. *Changing Work: A Union Guide to Workplace Change.* Washington, D.C.: AFL-CIO Human Resources Development Institute.

Burris, B. 1994. "AFL-CIO Embraces Cooperation: Is John L. Turning in His Grave?" *Labor Notes* (April): 8.

Carroll, J.D. 1995. "The Rhetoric of Reform and Political Reality in the National Performance Review." *Public Administration Review* 55 (May–June): 302–312.

Causey, M. 1994. "The OPM Blues." *Washington Post,* July 7: B-2.

Electromation, Inc. and International Brotherhood of Teamsters, Local Union No. 1049, AFL-CIO, and "Action Committees," 309 NLRB No. 163, 1992.

Gore, Al. 1993. The Report of the National Performance Review: Executive Summary. *Creating a Government That Works Better and Costs Less.* Washington, D.C.: U.S. Government Printing Office.

Hammer, M., and J. Champy. 1995. *Reengineering the Corporation: A Manifesto for Business Revolution.* New York: HarperCollins.

Hyde, A.C. 1994. "Overcoming the Barriers: The Case of Customs and the NTEU." *PA Times* 17 (August 11): 6.

Indiana University. 1979. *Labor-Management Committees in the Public Sector: A Practitioners Guide.* Bloomington, IN.

Judis, J. 1994. "Can Labor Come Back?" *New Republic* (May): 25–32.

Kearney, R., and S. Hays. 1994. "Labor-Management Relations and Participative Decision Making toward a New Paradigm." *Public Administration Review* 54 (January–February): 44–51.

Larkin, J. 1994. "TQM Is Alive and Well in the Public Sector." *PA Times* 17 (September 1): 9.

Lund, C. 1994. "Union Beats 10-Hour Day at NUMMI." *Labor Notes* (September): 7.

Marzotto, T. 1994. "Employee Empowerment and Union-Management Partnership: A Dilemma for Reinventing Government?" Paper delivered to the 1994 annual meeting of the American Society for Public Administration, Kansas City, Mo., July 23–27.

Masters, M.F., and R.S. Atkin. 1995. "Bargaining, Financial, and Political Bases of Federal Sector Unions: Implications for Reinventing Government." *Review of Public Personnel Administration* 15 (Winter): 5–23.

Naisbitt, John, and Patricia Aburdene. 1985. *Reinventing the Corporation.* New York: Warner Books.

Newell, A. 1989. Quoted by K. Moody, "Viewpoint: Labor's Two Trends." *Labor Notes* (June): 8.

Osborne, D., and T. Gaebler. 1992. *Reinventing Government.* Reading, Mass.: Addison-Wesley.

Parker, M., and J. Slaughter. 1993. "AFL-CIO May Trade Away Law against Company Unions." *Labor Notes* (December): 7–11.

———. 1994. "From 'QWL' to Reengineering: Management Takes Off the Gloves." *Labor Notes* (April): 8–11.

———. 1995. "AFL's Manual Fosters the Win-Win Illusion of Workplace Reorganization." *Labor Notes* (March): 10–11.

Patterson, J. 1995. "Worker Solidarity: The Only Partnership That Protects Us." *Labor Notes* (January): 2.

Patton, D. 1994. "Teaching Labor Relations." *Review of Public Personnel Administration* (Fall): 52–64.

Pennington, R. 1989. "Collaborative Labor Relations: The First Line Is the Bottom Line." *Personnel* (March): 78–83.

Tobias, R.M. 1994. "Labor-Management Partnerships: The Union Perspective." *PA Times* 17 (August 1): 6.

U.S. Department of Labor, Bureau of Labor-Management Relations and Cooperative Programs. 1987. *U.S. Labor Law and the Future of Labor-Management Cooperation.* Washington, D.C.: U.S. GPO.

U.S. General Accounting Office. 1991. *Federal Labor Relations: A Program in Need of Reform.* Report to Congressional Committees. Washington, D.C.: U.S. GPO.

U.S. National Center for Productivity and Quality of Working Life. 1978. *Labor-Management Committees in the Public Sector: Experiences of Eight Committees.* Washington, D.C.: U.S. GPO.

U.S. Office of Personnel Management. 1992. *Union Recognition in the Federal Government.* Washington, D.C.: U.S. GPO.

Wheeler, H.N., H.C. Katz, and C.W. Summers. 1995. "To all members of congress: Dear colleague." Letters.

section IV

Traditional Personnel Issues in a Changing Environment

The wave of reform that is sweeping public management has affected all aspects of the personnel function, including the core functions of hiring, firing, and paying public employees. It has also affected the legal framework within which public managers manage. This section looks at the "traditional" personnel functions through distinctly nontraditional lenses, focusing on the rapid changes taking place in each.

The section begins with that most bedrock of personnel functions: hiring new employees. As Carolyn Ban shows in "Hiring in the Public Sector," the traditional system, with its reliance on civil service tests and lists, was slow, unwieldy, and unresponsive to the needs of managers and applicants alike. To cope with it, many managers turned to "expediency management" (i.e., to gaming the system). But reforms in the area of hiring are, in some places, leading to more streamlined, more flexible hiring methods, providing managers with more discretion and obviating the need to waste time and energy playing games to circumvent the system.

As Charles Fox and Kurt Shirkey demonstrate in "Employee Performance Appraisal," past reforms, particularly the Civil Service Reform Act, saw performance appraisal as the key to good management. But Fox and Shirkey maintain that performance appraisal is a "keystone made of clay." Their provocative discussion dissects the usual arguments in favor of individual performance appraisal and finds them wanting. In fact, current reform efforts reflect a decreased reliance on detailed individual performance appraisals and an increased focus on group accountability.

In the current environment of fiscal constraint, issues of pay and benefits for government employees become both important and increasingly politicized. On the one hand, delegation of authority to managers should increase their discretion over pay issues, enabling them to provide incentives that should improve organizational competitiveness and capability. On the other hand, all organizations are under pressure—sometimes severe—to keep costs in line. In "Issues in Compensation and Benefits," N. Joseph Cayer discusses the difficult trade-offs governments face in trying to cut costs without destroying employee morale.

David Rosenbloom, in "Public Employees' Liability for 'Constitutional Torts,'" addresses significant changes in the legal environment of public managers and personnel specialists, changes that bear directly on the accountability issues raised by Barbara Romzek in Chapter 3. Traditionally, public officials have been immune from personal liability for constitutional torts (i.e., from actions that violate individuals' constitutional rights). But recent court decisions have opened up the potential for those wronged to sue public officials (including personnel specialists) for redress.

Finally, in "Oppositional and Connectional Paradigms," Willa Marie Bruce addresses the difficult topic of employee discipline from a fresh perspective. Dealing with problem employees is one of the most difficult aspects of management. Bruce shows that new approaches focusing on what she terms the *connectional paradigm* may make this task somewhat less onerous by focusing not on punishment but on organizational and individual learning and cooperative problem solving.

As you read these chapters, you might consider to what extent the reforms discussed have been implemented. To what extent has the federal government adopted these new approaches? What about your own state and local governments? What, if any, roadblocks have been encountered by those attempting to introduce new approaches to the traditional functions of personnel?

chapter **12**

Hiring in the Public Sector: "Expediency Management" or Structural Reform?

Carolyn Ban

It may seem, in the current fiscal environment, that governments at all levels are more preoccupied with cutting back than with hiring. But even in tight times governments must continue to hire, and, as work forces shrink, maintaining a high quality work force is more important than ever. Traditional civil service systems for hiring new employees have come under increasing criticism for being too slow and rigid and thus making it harder for managers to get good people on the job quickly. Indeed, personnel offices have come in for broad criticism for being more focused on enforcing complex rules than on serving their "customers," the line managers (U.S. MSPB, 1993). As Chapter 18 makes clear, even though personnel offices are often involved in training other departments on Total Quality Management (TQM), they have been slow to espouse this approach themselves.

Managers, faced with the problem of how to get people hired, often find ways around the system (Ban, 1991, 1995). This kind of informal manipulation may solve their short-term problem, but it can have unintended longer-term consequences, both for the individual hired and for the legitimacy of the system as a whole. Over the past five years there has been increased recognition of the problems caused by an overregulated system (National Commission on the State and Local Public Service, 1993; National Performance Review, 1993) and attempts to address these problems at a systemic level, by improving and streamlining hiring methods. This chapter begins with a look at the traditional system and at individual-level strategies for coping with it. It then turns to an examination of some of the systemic changes that have recently been implemented, both by state governments and by the federal government. In so doing, it raises some questions about the most effective routes to reform.

THE TRADITIONAL MODEL OF THE MERIT SYSTEM

The traditional merit system was based on several key assumptions. First, it assumed that an individual's future job performance could be predicted by his or her score on a written test. Certainly the elaborate efforts at documenting the validity of written tests have shown that in some cases this was true, although with what precision is debatable. But recent critics have raised troubling questions about the validity of written tests. Even supporters have noted that written tests cannot test for such critical personal characteristics as motivation or ability to work with other people (Rudner, 1992). Further, there is disturbing evidence that some tests, both written tests and physical agility tests for some jobs, are not clearly job-related and have adverse impact on some protected classes (Riccucci, 1991).

The second assumption on which the traditional system is based is that managers should be kept at arms' length from the process until the very end, when they are presented with a short list of finalists (often only three) from which they are required to select. It was assumed (1) that professional personnelists were more qualified than managers to review the qualifications of applicants and to rank them, and (2) that keeping the managers out of the process until the very end would reduce the potential for abuse—that is, for hiring political cronies or personal friends.

Personnel psychologists continue to defend some aspects of this traditional system, particularly the use of written tests, but even they admit that the tests cannot make such fine distinctions that one can conclude that someone who received a 97 will perform better than an individual who received a 96. Yet the traditional approach of ranking candidates and requiring managers to choose from the top three names often assumes just this. And critics now challenge both the necessity and the appropriateness of keeping managers at arms' length from the process (Palguta, 1993).

"Expediency Management": How Managers Cope with the Traditional Hiring System

Line managers have long been critical of the traditional hiring systems. They see them as too slow and as often providing candidates who do well on tests but who may lack the specific skills needed for the position. Further, the hands-off nature of the system makes life much harder for aggressive managers who actively recruit candidates to ensure that they can then hire the people they recruit (Ban, 1995). In response to these problems, some managers have turned to what Ospina calls "expediency management." As she explains it:

> When excessively rigid procedures threaten effective management practices, it may be necessary to circumvent the rules in the name of legitimate organizational goals. This argument is at the basis of what may be viewed as creative management in public organizations.

According to the argument, under highly bureaucratic constraints, public managers may choose to emphasize administrative expediency, ignoring rules and regulations to expedite the decision-making process. (Ospina, 1992: 405)

Making Use of Existing Flexibilities

In fact, this image of excessive rigidity is, at least in part, a straw man. Particularly at the federal level, there are already a number of hiring methods that have introduced considerable flexibility and management discretion into the system. Three of the most important are case examining, the outstanding scholars program, and direct hire. In case examining, an agency advertises a specific position, determines the needed qualifications (with input from the manager), and rates and ranks the candidates, based either on scores on a test or, more typically, on an assessment of the individual's training and experience. If the manager has a preferred candidate, he or she can "name request," that is, can request that if that person is qualified, his or her name be placed on the final list. This process may still take two to three months to meet the requirements of advertising the position and to complete the ranking of candidates, but it provides 'the agency and the individual manager considerable control over the process.

Two other hiring techniques enable the manager to hire virtually on the spot, without requiring the candidate to take a test or to compete with other candidates. First, for entry-level positions, if a candidate had a 3.5 undergraduate grade-point average or was in the top 10 percent of his or her class, the candidate can be hired immediately under the outstanding scholars program. This program was originally designed to make it easier to hire minority candidates. Second, the direct hire authority allows agencies that have shortage categories (i.e., positions they are having difficulty filling) to hire candidates who meet specified qualifications, such as professional training or licenses, on the spot without a competitive process. Both these approaches speed up the process drastically and give managers great leeway in identifying and selecting candidates.

Managers' Coping Strategies: Functional or Dysfunctional?

Given the flexible methods described above, savvy managers in the federal government don't necessarily need to find a way around the system; rather, they need to understand the range of methods available and how to use them. Indeed, it is clear that they are increasingly choosing to use the more flexible methods as opposed to the traditional hiring method via a civil service test and certificate listing the top three names (U.S. MSPB, 1994).

However, many state and local governments don't permit use of the approaches described above—their systems still fit the model of the traditional system. And even in the federal government these methods were, until recently, not always available. So managers have developed a variety of ways to game the system—some legal, some borderline, and some clearly illegal.

Strategies to Save Time.   First, managers have tried to get around the long delay in hiring by finding ways to bring people on immediately. One technique that has been used for years is to hire an entry-level professional first into a secretarial position and then move him or her into a professional position. Although this is legal, bringing a new employee in as a temporary while waiting for a permanent position to open up is a borderline method—technically legal but beyond the intent of civil service law. Further, it's far from foolproof (Ban, 1995). Clearly over the line is getting a contractor working with the agency to hire the individual so that he or she can start work immediately while the manager is shepherding his or her application through the process. Indeed, some managers have faced sanctions because of this abuse of the process (Ban, 1995).

A different technique for speeding up the process, more common in state and local governments, involves hiring new employees as provisionals. Provisional employees can be hired noncompetitively, but they are supposed to occupy their positions only temporarily, usually until the time that the civil service department can conduct a formal test upon which a permanent appointment can be based. Of course, if the civil service department is overworked (as is often the case), it may be some time before the test is given. Managers in New York sometimes game the system further by reclassifying the position, creating a "unique" title, that is, a new job for which there is no existing test (Ban and Riccucci, 1994). They know that the overburdened civil service department will consider this a lower priority than testing for more common occupations, so their provisional employee may in fact stay in the job for years.

Many strategies for beating the system may be functional on a short-term basis but have unfortunate system-level consequences. One dysfunctional result of the strategy discussed above in New York is the proliferation of titles, many with only one or two occupants (Ban and Riccucci, 1994; Ban and Riccucci, 1993). Ospina (1992) documents effectively the use of expediency management in a municipal agency in New York City, where most analysts are hired as provisionals and stay in that status throughout their careers. Although hiring in this way has short-term benefits for managers and employees, since it permits faster hiring and gives managers more flexibility to negotiate terms of employment, there are significant long-term costs, in particular the lack of a clear career progression and a pervasive sense of inequity that lead eventually to lowered morale and higher turnover.

Strategies for Maximizing Managerial Discretion.   In addition to trying to speed up the process, managers use a variety of techniques to try to gain control of the process, so that they can hire the people they have recruited. Hiring employees provisionally may meet both goals. Similarly, moving a position from classified (i.e., competitive) to exempt is another, even more controversial, approach. Even when the position is competitive, managers can coach the desired applicant in how best to fill out the forms. More on the edge ethically is "tailoring," that is, fitting the job description for the opening to the specific skills of the individual the manager wants to hire. And clearly illegal is what is technically called "soliciting a declination," that is, talking people higher on the civil service list into withdrawing from consideration so as to reach a preferred candidate who is not among the top three candidates. They may be told that the position is undesirable, the work unpleasant, or the chances for promotion slim. Or they may be informed quite bluntly that if they say no to this position, they will be helped in the future.

Of course, not all managers use these techniques, even the legal ones. Some managers are quite content to take a relatively passive approach to the hiring process, simply turning in a request to the personnel office and waiting for a list of finalists to show up on their desk (U.S. MSPB, 1993; Ban, 1995). This passive approach is not a problem when applicants are plentiful, but some managers (and, in some agencies, most managers) have found that they need to play an active role in the recruitment process in order to attract high-caliber candidates. These are the managers most frustrated by the traditional system, since all too often the formal system makes it difficult or impossible to hire the promising candidates they have identified (Ban, 1995; U.S. MSPB, 1994). Thus these managers are more likely to try to find creative ways to circumvent the system in order to meet the laudable goals of hiring individuals they feel are most qualified in a reasonable period of time.

STRUCTURAL REFORM: EVOLUTIONARY OR REVOLUTIONARY?

Individual "gaming" of the system is, at best, a stop-gap solution to systemic problems. Increasingly there has been recognition of the need for system reform. In recent years, increased pressure to reform government personnel systems, including hiring, has come from a number of sources, starting with the 1983 report of the National Academy of Public Administration and including most prominently the National Commission on the Public Service (the Volcker Commission) and the National Commission on the State and Local Public Service (the Winter Commission). Although specific emphases varied, all raised concerns about the continued ability of government to attract top people, and all called for continued deregulation and decentralization of the recruiting and hiring process.

The approaches to reform have differed at the state and the federal levels. States have generally followed an incremental reform strategy, whereas the federal government has attempted to implement far-reaching, comprehensive changes flowing from the National Performance Review. The following section describes each process and discusses the pros and cons of these differing strategies.

State-Level Reforms: Evolutionary Change

State reforms have touched a number of areas in human resources management (see Chapter 1 in this volume for a broader discussion). Various states have introduced reforms in the hiring area, including the recruitment process, testing, and criteria for selection. Some themes that emerge from an examination of these changes are decentralization, opening up the process (including finding ways of bringing in different groups of people), streamlining the process, and increasing managerial discretion. Let us look at some examples of each.

Decentralization.   California is one state that has moved from a centralized to a far more decentralized system. It has decentralized to individual departments the entire hiring process (from recruitment through test development and administration, to certification of eligibles) although the central agency, the State Personnel Board, still administers exams for many generalist entry-level positions (Harmon, 1992; Jensen, 1992). Other states that have maintained a more centralized system have increased agency involvement in test development. In these cases the assumption is that the use of tests is valid, but that agencies will be better served if they can perform these functions themselves or at least play an active role in the process.

Opening Up the Process.   One of the biggest concerns of all levels of government is how to attract top-quality employees, given that salaries are often not competitive with those in the private sector and that they can no longer promise new employees job security. This has led to a variety of methods for opening up the process, both making access easier and actively recruiting from different groups than in the past. Efforts to open up the process include making access to civil service tests easier. For example, Illinois increased the number of testing sites around the state as well as the services available at those sites and also held job information workshops targeted at areas with minority populations. Illinois also established a Minority Management Training Program to attract potential management candidates and prepare them for administrative positions (Schnorf, 1994). Wisconsin took the bold step of moving to a walk-in testing process. Prospective employees are no longer required to sign up in advance (Wisconsin Department of Employee Relations, 1995; *PA Times,* 1995). Forms, like tests, can be daunting to applicants. Minnesota is exploring ways to make its application form more "user-friendly" (Minnesota Department of Employee Relations, 1994).

Changes in job requirements and testing procedures are also ways of opening up the process. California has abandoned a number of non–job-related requirements such as physical characteristics and educational levels. In addition, it has moved away from reliance on written tests and toward more alternative testing methods. One interesting effort in California was a demonstration project called the Limited Examination and Appointment Process (LEAP), designed to increase hiring of persons with disabilities through use of an alternative selection process that included a screening interview and an on-the-job trial period (Harmon, 1992).

Streamlining the Process.   Civil service systems have often been faulted for their slowness and rigidity. Many of the attempts to streamline the process make use of new technologies both to open up the process and to speed it up. Wisconsin has done both by putting vacancy announcements on-line, both within state government and, via the Internet, nationwide (Wisconsin Department of Employment Relations, 1995).

New technology can also be used to streamline and to strengthen the testing process. Even though machine scoring of tests is not a new idea, some new approaches to testing are quite creative. For example, New York adapted the test for corrections sergeants to make it more "real-life" by showing videos of typical prison situations and then asking how the individual would respond (Ban and Riccucci, 1994).

Similarly, many jurisdictions now maintain lists and generate hiring certificates (i.e., lists of top-ranked candidates) via computer. But some states have gone even further. Illinois, for example, is trying to make it easier for agencies to determine if applicants really are a good "fit" for the specific position by using "imaging" technology to permit the "hiring agent" to review the actual application forms on-screen (Schnorf, 1994).

Increasing Managerial Discretion.   As we saw above, the traditional civil service model intentionally limited managers' role in the hiring process to selecting from a small group of finalists, determined by the personnel staff. Often this was formalized into a "rule of three," that is, a requirement that selection be made from among the top three people on a civil service list. States have taken two different approaches in moving away from a rule of three. Some have simply increased the number—to a rule of five or ten (Ban and Riccucci, 1993). Minnesota adopted an interesting variant: a rule of 10 for internal hires and of 20 for external hires, but with what they call "expanded certification" as an affirmative action tool. If groups are underrepresented in that job category, they will go down the list to ensure the inclusion of at least two people from each underrepresented group who passed the test (Minnesota Department of Employee Relations, 1991).

A different option is zone scoring. Essentially, all those whose scores fall within a band (e.g., from 100 to 90) receive the same score and are referred as a group. Zone scoring is in increasingly widespread use (Ban and Riccucci, 1993). Even New York, which still adheres in most cases to the rule of three, has experimented with zone scoring but with mixed success. One of the tough issues in zone scoring is where to place the cut-offs, that is, how large the zones should be. In one case, the state was successfully sued by the unions for creating a top zone so large that almost everyone who passed fell into it (Ban and Riccucci, 1994). Zones that were more narrowly constructed were later upheld.

In sum, although many states have attempted to reform their hiring practices, most have taken a gradualist, evolutionary approach. Contrasting the relatively modest innovations in the states with the more drastic changes now being implemented in the federal government allows us to examine the pros and cons of evolutionary versus revolutionary approaches to reform.

Hiring in the Federal Government: Revolutionary Changes?

The National Performance Review (NPR), chaired by Vice-President Gore, called for sweeping reform of the federal personnel system. As Chapter 1 makes clear, the NPR recommendations stressed four values: cutting red tape, reengineering to cut waste, putting customers first, and empowering employees to get results. All four themes bear directly on the hiring process. The overall NPR report called for decentralizing the personnel process, delegating authority down to line managers "at the lowest level practical in each agency" (NPR, 1993a: 22), and cutting the size of personnel staffs.

These recommendations were expanded upon in the NPR report "Reinventing Human Resource Management." First on its list of priorities was the need to "create a flexible and responsive hiring system" (NPR, 1993b: 9). It faulted the system for being time consuming and unresponsive and singled out the requirement for Office of Personnel Management (OPM) testing as a serious problem:

> The issue is not merely convenience; more importantly, the public's perception of the federal government as a responsive employer suffers tremendously when agency managers are forced to send applicants to OPM for examination, with no guarantee that they will ever be within reach for positions at that agency on a centralized register. (NPR, 1993b: 11)

The NPR Human Resources report presented an image of an ideal system, which was decentralized, that empowered managers and held them "accountable for adherence to principles of merit and equal opportunity through a performance-based assessment of staffing outcomes" (NPR, 1993b: 12). The specific reforms called for by the NPR are discussed below.

Achieve Maximum Delegation of Examining.   Based on the Civil Service Reform Act of 1978 (CSRA), agencies could be delegated the authority to do their own examining only for positions that were unique to that agency. For positions common to several agencies, OPM conducted examinations centrally, often maintaining standing registers (i.e., ranked lists of qualified candidates) and sending the top scorers remaining on the list to agencies that wished to hire. The NPR report called for "authoriz[ing] agencies to establish their own recruitment and examining programs [and] abolish[ing] central registers and standard application forms." In other words, the NPR model is an "agency-based, market-driven hiring system" (NPR, 1993b: 13), much closer to a private sector model than to the traditional civil service model.

Simplify the System and Reduce Red Tape.   The traditional civil service system has long been faulted for its dependence on complex, rigid rules. The symbol of this system was the Federal Personnel Manual, which was literally thousands of pages long. In the hiring area, there were over 300 separate hiring authorities. The NPR recommended a drastic reduction—to only three competitive service appointment types: permanent, temporary indefinite, and temporary not to exceed (one-year limit). Recommendations for reducing red tape and empowering managers included giving agencies the authority to decide when they had a recruitment shortage (i.e., were having trouble filling specific positions) and could thus use streamlined hiring methods, called "direct hire" authority, without coming to OPM for prior approval.

The federal government has already begun implementing those recommendations of the NPR that do not require legislative approval. It has also sent to Congress a bill that would make more drastic changes (see Chapter 1). As we shall see below, the changes are quite dramatic in some areas, but there are other important issues that the NPR has avoided.

Decentralize.   The federal government had already made considerable strides in decentralizing the hiring process. Historically, there have been pendulum swings between decentralization and recentralization of federal hiring (Ban and Marzotto, 1984). Since the Civil Service Reform Act of 1978, the general trend (with the exception of the early Reagan years) has been toward decentralization, with responsibility for recruiting and testing for many positions being delegated to the agencies. That tendency was accelerated when the standardized test used for entry-level hiring for over 100 job titles was abolished as a result of a consent decree settling a lawsuit charging the test with having adverse impact (i.e., with discriminating against minority applicants). For several years, agencies were free to recruit and hire individuals for these positions without going through OPM (Ban and Ingraham, 1988). But the final result of several lawsuits was the reintroduction of centralized testing by OPM, using six different tests under the broad label of Administrative Careers with America (ACWA). Applicants who were tested were placed on a standing register (i.e., a ranked list of those who passed the test), and the top three names on the list were referred to agencies.

Although this sounds like a straightforward approach, and although the tests apparently had reasonably high validity, from the point of view of managers trying to hire, they were a disaster. Managers found the process of getting names to be very slow, and often the people whose names were sent were, in fact, not interested in the position that was offered. Further, managers who actively recruited found it very difficult to "reach" the people they wanted to hire from the ACWA lists. As a result, managers most frequently used a variety of other hiring methods—including the outstanding scholars program discussed above— or internal promotion, and avoided using ACWA (Ban, 1995; U.S. GAO, 1994). As a result the number of names on the ACWA lists continued to grow, and the chances of entering government employment via ACWA continued to decrease.

The OPM's solution to this dilemma was drastic. It abolished the standing registers and allowed agencies to use the ACWA as a screening tool for candidates if they wished. Candidates now apply to a specific job, either directly through the agency or at OPM. They complete a questionnaire on their training and experience, which is quickly scored, and the hiring official is given a list of the top three scorers from which to select. The proposed legal changes would allow agencies to control the recruitment and testing process even for common occupations, such as secretaries, accountants, or policy analysts.

Open Up and Streamline the Process.   The OPM has attempted to make it easier for people to apply for federal employment. First, the OPM abolished the mandatory use of a standard application form, known as SF-171, which was daunting and difficult to complete. New applicants can submit a resume or use a new optional form (OF-612). The OPM has attempted to maintain central information about job openings in the agencies and to make this available to applicants through a 900-number phone service.

The federal government has also gone further than the states in using new technology. The questionnaires that applicants complete on their training and experience are scored by computer to speed up the process. And for some occupations, such as nurses, the applicant can actually complete the questionnaire by phone, pressing buttons on a touch-tone phone to key in responses.

Increase Managerial Discretion.   It remains to be seen how much these reforms actually increase managers' freedom to participate actively in the process and to select the people they recruit. This will depend on the extent to which they play a role in designing the questionnaires used to screen applicants and on the extent to which they can name request (i.e., ask that if the person they wish to hire is eligible, his or her name would appear on the list). Just speeding up the process will make it easier for managers to hold on to good candidates who, in the past, might have grown tired of waiting for months for a decision and gone elsewhere.

Potential Problems with Federal Reforms

Many of the reforms being made by the federal government are long overdue. They are a genuine attempt to open up and streamline what has been a cumbersome and slow hiring process. But the sweeping nature of the reforms, coupled with changes in the OPM's role, have prompted some experts in the field to raise troubling questions. Some feel the reforms have gone too far; others feel that in critical areas, they have not gone far enough.

First, some question the appropriateness of abolishing the ACWA and maintain that the rating schedules being used have no predictive validity. If this is indeed the case, then the quality of new hires may decline. Further, the functions of the "reinvented" OPM have changed in ways that have direct effects on the hiring process. As Lane and Marshall point out, "OPM would be converted from a central management agency, with an emphasis on direction and regulation, to a commercial-style entrepreneurial agency that would hawk its wares to potential customers in the rest of the executive branch" (1995: 4). That change is already reflected in the requirement that henceforth, OPM would assist agencies in developing tests only on a "cost-reimbursable" basis. That is, OPM would start charging for its services. Small agencies, or those with low budgets, won't be able either to hire their own staffing specialists or to make use of OPM's. This would exacerbate the problems created by moving away from formal written tests. As one expert told me, "If agencies start using 'seat of the pants' approaches because they don't have the money to do it right or to pay OPM, productivity will go down."

Another potential problem is OPM's virtual abdication of its oversight function. Traditionally, OPM has not only established regulations for proper hiring procedures but has exercised its oversight role by making occasional visits to agencies to monitor whether the rules are actually being followed. Both the massive budget cuts at OPM and its redefined role mean that very little, if any, active oversight will remain (Lane and Marshall, 1995). The merit system was originally established to protect against wholesale abuses of the "spoils system." Although the absence of effective oversight probably won't lead to widespread abuse, there is ample evidence that, at least at some agencies, both the hiring of people because of political contacts and the hiring of cronies is still a problem (Ban and Redd, 1990). Without adequate controls, with maximum delegation and increased managerial discretion, abuse or the appearance of abuse may become an increasing problem.

Ironically, even though the federal government has taken some reforms much farther than the states have, it has lagged behind the states in one critical area: the rule of three. The federal government is still required by statute to provide hiring officials with the names of only the top three scorers on an examination. That includes such "unassembled" examinations as ratings of training and experience. As we saw above, many states have given managers far more discretion by expanding the numbers of people on the list from which the manager can hire. The U.S. Department of Agriculture has been conducting a demonstration project using category rating (i.e., zone scoring). As one MSPB report notes, "The importance and meaning of small differences in scores is questionable. . . . [T]he category rating process of the USDA demonstration project may be fairer than using specific scores to determine the order of candidates" (U.S. MSPB 1995: 33 of draft).

Further, the rule of three is narrowly defined in the federal government to mean three names, not three scores. When individuals are tied, the personnel staff applies a "tie-breaker." The first tie-breaker, by law, is veterans preference. If the hiring official has "name requested" a specific individual, he or she would go on the list ahead of others with the same score. Finally, personnel officials use random numbers to break ties among individuals. In contrast, even some states that still use the rule of three interpret it to mean the top three scores, which can yield far more than three names, and which does not require any discrimination against individuals with identical scores (U.S. MSPB, 1995).

The problems created by the rule of three are exacerbated by the federal government's long-standing policy of veterans preference. Veterans preference actually dates to the Civil War era, and the current law was enacted in 1944 during World War II. As the law currently works, veterans, their widows or widowers, or the spouses of disabled veterans or mothers of individuals who lost their lives while serving in the armed forces are all eligible for veterans preference under certain circumstances. Eligibles have points added to a passing score on an examination; disabled veterans have 10 points added. Further, disabled veterans with service-related disabilities of 10 percent or more "float to the top," that is, they are listed first on registers or lists of eligibles (U.S. MSPB, 1995, Appendix 2).

Veterans preference is not popular with managers or personnel specialists. In responding to a survey from the General Accounting Office, both managers and OPM and agency personnel staff were often critical of veterans preference. Particularly in conjunction with the rule of three, it was seen as "decreas[ing] their ability to obtain a quality pool of candidates" and as slowing down the process (U.S. GAO, 1995: 30). In fact, the GAO found that it sometimes played a role in managers' decision to return a list of candidates without making a selection, or in the decision to use alternative hiring mechanisms, such as the outstanding scholars program, which do not require application of veterans preference (U.S. GAO, 1995).

The unwillingness on the part of the NPR authors to take on veterans preference is understandable. Previous attempts to limit it have failed (Ingraham and Ban, 1983). Although politicians today attack affirmative action as undermining the merit system, veterans preference (which gives much greater advantages) does not come in for similar criticism. And effective lobbying by veterans groups has meant that veterans preference remains politically untouchable.

In sum, even though the federal reforms are addressing many of the factors that make the hiring system unwieldy from the point of view of managers, they do not touch the politically sensitive issues of veterans preference and the rule of three. Further, the pendulum is swinging so far in the direction of decentralization that agencies will lose the advantages of reasonable economies of scale, thereby increasing duplication of effort and costs. The absence of effective oversight by OPM is also troubling.

CONCLUSIONS

This chapter has explored the changing approaches to hiring in the federal and state governments. As we have seen, "expediency management"—that is, individual managers gaming the system—is still with us, but many jurisdictions have at least begun the effort of structural reform to address the underlying problems that make such gaming necessary in the eyes of managers.

If we compare the reforms recommended by the Winter Commission and the changes being implemented by some states with those called for by the NPR, we see two models: an evolutionary approach based on gradual reform, and revolutionary reform, that is, abrupt and drastic system changes (Palguta, 1993). Which approach to take will depend to a great extent on the diagnosis of the problem. If one thinks that civil service systems are basically sound but need technical fixes or moderate reforms to make them work better, then obviously the evolutionary approach will be seen as appropriate (Palguta, 1993). But if one concludes that the existing systems are causing serious problems, then one is more likely to agree with a former head of the New York State Civil Service Commission, who once said (probably only half in jest) that he had concluded that the system couldn't be reformed and that it should be blown up (Ban and Riccucci, 1994). The differences in approach at the federal and state levels may reflect different perceptions of the severity of the problem or different political environments providing different levels of support for radical change.

Whichever route to change is followed, there are several broad conclusions that can be drawn about the reform process. First, the process of change is usually slow. Formal change requires revising rules, passing new laws, and even amending the state constitution. Successful implementation also requires changing both the formal roles and the culture of the personnel office. It also requires a willingness on the part of managers to take on a broader responsibility in recruiting and selecting candidates (Ban, 1995). Without these changes, new systems may not work as expected.

Second, we will always have to struggle to find the proper balance between the need for control to prevent abuses and the need to give managers enough discretion to do their jobs well. In the area of hiring, the assumption of the reformers is that the values of a merit system are firmly planted, and that giving managers more discretion will not lead to widespread abuse. But even those who share that assumption (the author among them) recognize the need to maintain effective oversight of a decentralized hiring process to make sure new discretions are not abused. We need to recognize the risk that abuses will undercut the legitimacy of the merit system in the public's eyes (Masden, 1995).

Finally, attempts to reform hiring point, once again, to the importance of the political environment in personnel policy. At the federal level, the creation of the National Performance Review provided an environment where quiet revolutionary change was possible. Both at the federal and state levels, fiscal austerity has created problems but also opportunities to find ways to streamline processes. The political environment also limits what reforms are attempted. This is particularly true for veterans preference.

REFERENCES

Ban, Carolyn. 1991. "The Realities of the Merit System," in Carolyn Ban and Norma M. Riccucci, eds., *Public Personnel Management: Current Concerns—Future Challenges.* New York: Longman.

——— . 1995. How Do Public Managers Manage? Bureaucratic Constraints, Organizational Culture, and the Potential for Reform. San Francisco: Jossey-Bass.

Ban, Carolyn, and Patricia W. Ingraham. 1988. "Retaining Quality Federal Employees: Life after PACE." *Public Administration Review* 48, no. 3: 708-718.

Ban, Carolyn, and Toni Marzotto. 1984. "Delegations of Examining: Objectives and Implementation," in Patricia W. Ingraham and Carolyn Ban, eds., *Legislating Bureaucratic Change: The Civil Service Reform Act of 1978.* Albany: State University of New York Press.

Ban, Carolyn, and Harry Redd III. 1990. "The State of the Merit System: Perceptions of Abuse in the Federal Civil Service." *Review of Public Personnel Administration* 10, no. 3: 55–72.

Ban, Carolyn, and Norma Riccucci. 1993. "Personnel Systems and Labor Relations: Steps toward a Quiet Revitalization," in Frank Thompson, ed., *Revitalizing State and Local Public Service.* San Francisco: Jossey-Bass.

————. 1994. "New York State: Civil Service Reform in a Complex Political Environment." *Review of Public Personnel Administration* 14, no. 2: 28–39.

Harmon, Gloria (Executive Officer, California State Personnel Board). 1992. "Remarks to the National Association [*sic*] on the State and Local Public Service."

Ingraham, Patricia W., and Carolyn Ban. 1984. *Legislating Bureaucratic Change: The Civil Service Reform Act of 1978.* Albany: State University of New York Press.

Jensen, Cristy. 1992. "Briefing Paper: California State Government." Prepared for the National Commission on the State and Local Public Service.

Lane, Larry M., and Gary Marshall. 1995. "Reinventing OPM: Adventures, Issues, and Implications." Paper presented at ASPA Material Conference.

Lavigna, Robert (Administrator, Division of Merit Recruitment, Wisconsin Department of Employment Relations). 1995. Personal Interview.

Masden, Daniel. 1995. "Observations and Comments on Reinventing Government." *Public Personnel Management* 24, no. 1: 113–126.

Minnesota Department of Employee Relations. 1991. *Personnel Management and Affirmative Action; Management Development Core Program.* St. Paul: MDER.

————. 1994. *State of Minnesota Civil Service Pilot Projects.* St. Paul: MDER.

National Academy of Public Administration. 1983. *Revitalizing Federal Management: Managers and Their Overburdened Systems.* Washington, D.C.: National Academy of Public Administration.

National Commission on the Public Service [Volcker Commission]. 1990. *Leadership for America: Rebuilding the Public Service.* Lexington, Mass.: Lexington Books.

National Commission on the State and Local Public Service [Winter Commission]. 1993. *Hard Truths/Tough Choices: An Agenda for State and Local Reform.* Albany, N.Y.: Nelson A. Rockefeller Institute of Government.

National Performance Review. 1993a. *From Red Tape to Results: Creating a Government That Works Better and Costs Less.* Washington, D.C.: U.S. Government Printing Office.

————. 1993b. *Reinventing Human Resource Management.* Washington, D.C.: U.S. Government Printing Office.

Ospina, Sonia. 1992. " 'Expediency Management' in Public Service: A Dead-End Search for Managerial Discretion." *Public Productivity and Management Review* 15, no. 4: 405–421.

PA Times. 1995. "Personnel Department Eases Access to Best and Brightest." 18, no. 4 (April 1).

Palguta, John. 1993. "Federal Recruitment and Selection Methods: In Need of Evolution or Revolution?" Paper presented at the annual meeting of American Society for Public Administration.

Riccucci, Norma M. 1991. "Merit, Equity, and Test Validity: A New Look at an Old Problem." *Administration and Society* 23, no. 1: 74–93.

Rudner, Lawrence. M. 1992. "Pre-Employment Testing and Employee Productivity." *Public Personnel Management* 21, no. 2: 150.

Schnorf, Stephen (Director, Illinois Department of Central Management Services). 1994. Correspondence.

U.S. General Accounting Office. 1994. *Federal Hiring: Testing for Entry-Level Administrative Positions Falls Short of Expectations* (GAO/GGD-94-103). Washington, D.C.: USGAO.

———. 1995. *Federal Hiring: Reconciling Managerial Flexibility with Veterans' Preference* (GAO/GGD-95-102). Washington, D.C.: USGAO.

U.S. Merit Systems Protection Board. 1993. *Federal Personnel Offices: Time for Change?* Washington, D.C.: USMSPB.

———. 1994. *Entering Professional Positions in the Federal Government.* Washington, D.C.: USMSPB.

———. 1995. *The Rule of Three in Federal Hiring: Boon or Bane?* Washington, D.C.: USMSPB.

Wisconsin Department of Employment Relations. 1995. *Recruiting the Best and the Brightest: Reinventing Wisconsin's Civil Service Hiring System.* Madison: Wisconsin Department of Employment Relations.

chapter **13**

Employee Performance Appraisal: The Keystone Made of Clay

Charles J. Fox and Kurt A. Shirkey

INTRODUCTION: THE POLITICS OF PERFORMANCE APPRAISAL

Performance appraisal or evaluation is now ubiquitous in the public sector (Grider and Toombs, 1992; Murphy and Cleveland, 1995). It is mainstream management practice to install performance management systems that lead to performance evaluations. These are used in various ensembles to influence decisions on rewards, bonuses, compensation, promotion, transfer, discipline, discharge, and ranking for reductions in force (RIF) and for motivation, enhanced communication, training needs or potentials assessment, and criteria for selection procedure validation studies (Timmreck, 1989: 32). Performance appraisal, then, seems to be the centerpiece for virtually all aspects of the personnel function (England and Parle, 1987). One might reasonably assume that any such ubiquitous measure would be soundly based in unimpeachable theory arising from exhaustive empirical research and long practice. But alas, in this instance one would be mistaken (Landy and Farr, 1980). Banks and Murphy's (1985: 335) conclusion that "[E]ffective performance appraisal in organizations continues to be a compelling but unrealized goal" remains true.

Now, performance evaluation of a sort has long been practiced in the public sector. Many jurisdictions asked supervisors to fill out forms that listed desirable employee traits, such as promptness, friendly demeanor, good personal hygiene, and the ability to work well with others—Boy Scout virtues. These perfunctory exercises were tossed off, filed, and quickly forgotten; they were not the keystone of an entire managerial practice. Further, although this chapter is critical of performance appraisal, we recognize that at some level, judgments about the performance of everyone around us—from colleagues to sports heroes—are a major and unavoidable part of the flow and flux of everyday consciousness. We are constantly judging and being judged. To sermonize against performance appraisal in this sense is quixotic. The type of performance appraisal we have in mind is formal, "scientific," articulated by separate and nonoverlapping categories, aggregated numerically or adjectivally (e.g., "satisfactory"), comparative, written and filed as part of a permanent record, and used in a hierarchically ordered organization to allocate scarce or limited rewards.

It is important to the argument pursued here to realize that the more grandiloquent roles the performance appraisal process is now asked to play in government were cast politically, not scientifically. The watershed event was the passage of the Civil Service Reform Act of 1978.

Civil service reform had been on the agenda of executive-level reformers in and out of government since the Second Hoover Commission in the early 1950s. A major goal of civil service reform advocates was to bring the bureaucracy to bay by diminishing protective civil service regulations that hindered disciplining putatively recalcitrant public servants. The fortuitous confluence of economic recession (stagflation), tax revolt, and the diminished legitimacy of government institutions that accompanied the Watergate scandal, the policy failures of Vietnam, and the war on poverty created an accommodating climate for reform. Despite the fact that blame for these events can be more properly laid at the door of political elites, career civil servants were the ones targeted for retribution. Indeed, by 1978 bureaucrat bashing had become so much a part of the political campaign sport spectacle that in a Gallup poll over 60 percent of the American public agreed that "federal government employees do not work as hard as they would in nongovernment jobs," that "the federal government employs too many people," and that "federal workers are paid more than they would earn in nongovernmental jobs." Jimmy Carter, in proposing his legislation, opined: "The public suspects that there are too many government workers, that they are underworked, overpaid and insulated from the consequences of incompetence" (U.S. Congress, Senate Committee on Government Affairs, 1978: Appendix, 243-244).[1]

Although there were many aspects to civil service reform, performance appraisal was the most important in the sense that it embodied the punitive and scientistic aspects of that reform (Thayer, 1978). Simply put, performance appraisal was the key to enhanced managerial control. In one of its first publications, the newly established Office of Personnel Management made no bones about its goals:

> Perhaps the key problem in the past few years in public personnel administration has been the lack of responsiveness of career personnel to the needs of management. . . . [T]he dominant theme in public personnel reform is to improve the responsiveness of civil service personnel to management and hence to the general public to which

management [not the whole service] is ultimately accountable. (U.S. OPM, 1979: 1)

Resuscitated by the stroke of Carter's pen was the classical panoply of dubious assumptions about the nature of work and management in the public sector, including the intellectually tattered politics/administration dichotomy (compare Ban and Ingraham, 1984: 2).

Once it is understood that the coming of systematic performance appraisal to the public sector was politically motivated, it is easy to situate the practices in the conservative turn that the country experienced in the late 1970s and through the 1980s—exemplified by the Reagan administration's celebration of the simplistic tenets of "free enterprise" and its disparagement of most things governmental. In what follows we first demonstrate why appraising performance is so persuasive. Second, we show why the process is problematical. A final section suggests stances that human resource professionals might take with regard to employee performance evaluation.

THE PROMISE OF PERFORMANCE APPRAISAL

The ubiquity of performance appraisal is no accident. On first blush, it appeals to virtually all legitimate standpoints in organizational life. To some managers it offers direct control. To other managers it offers the capacity to coordinate individual aspirations to organizational objectives. To personnelists it offers rationality, consistency, and litigation avoidance. To employees it offers recognition and just deserts. It seems to be a "win, win, win, win" proposition. And it comports well with, indeed flows from, deeply held American cultural norms. Let us look briefly at each "win."

Appeal to Managers as Control Agents

Imagine for a moment, and this **is** *science* fiction, that as a manager you could know the true value of each of your employees. Value would include past and present performance and future potential. If you could know these things, you could be the consummate manager. You could reward, stroke, commend, discipline, admonish, promote, transfer, fire, motivate; you could deploy all of your human resources with complete confidence. It would be like a well-tuned piano and you the virtuoso—never a false or unanticipated note as you race through a score to your own promotion and bonus. Knowledge is power, and performance appraisal promises knowledge of human resources as perfect as it is possible to achieve. This promise is the same one that motivates social psychology in its quest to explain, predict, and *control* (Skinner, 1953: 6–7).

Furthermore, managers are likely to accept the most inflated validity claims of the purveyors of performance appraisal packages because their own success is likely based on a string of stellar performance appraisals (cf. Deming, 1982).

Appeal to Managers as Human Resource Development Facilitators

Caring, liberal-minded managers can also be seduced by the promise of performance appraisal. Identification of weaknesses can be used to "coach" the full development of human potential in one's charges; annual or semiannual appraisal sessions are opportunities for superior and subordinate to communicate their medium-term personal development goals. Organizational goals and personal fulfillment can then be coordinated (Tjosvold and Halco, 1992). Performance evaluation can be folded into organizational humanism and management by objectives (MBO) (Daley, 1988: 18).

Another advantage to the sensitive manager is that performance appraisal systems claim to "take administrators out of the role of playing God when they must take responsibility for judging the personal worth of their fellow employees" (Wiatrowski and Palkon, 1987: 71).

Appeal to Personnelists

Personnel people, in their staff function, are professional nags. They are called upon to keep the personnel system rationally consistent; compulsiveness is their stock in trade as they check and balance management tendencies toward impulsive decisions driven by pressing deadlines. Performance appraisal holds the promise of appropriate documentation for virtually all personnel actions, and it is this "paper trail" that increasing numbers of organizations believe (falsely, as we show below) will safeguard them from adverse legal action (Cleveland and Murphy, 1992).

Appeal to Employees

Employees have generally tended to support the concept of performance appraisal (Lovrich et al., 1980; Laumeyer and Beebe, 1988). This is counterintuitive because majorities rarely support performance appraisal once it has been implemented (Pearce and Porter, 1986; Rollins, 1988: 42). Although it may not immediately occur to employees that they are conceding to management a powerful tool of control, their later recognition of this circumstance reduces their support for the performance appraisal process and weakens its credibility (Roberts, 1994; Maroney and Buckley, 1992).

Two reasons lie behind employees' initial support for performance appraisals, and both stem from the fact that most workers think they are doing a good job. Estimates (Rollins, 1988) and research (Meyer, 1975) suggest that 90 percent to 75 percent of employees believe that their performance is "above average." Most workers want (positive) feedback, but management is often taciturn. Performance appraisal presents the face of requiring management to notice what a good job workers are doing. Second, most workers would like to be rewarded on the basis of their performance (Folger, cited in Roberts, 1992). So, if you ask someone:

"Do you think you should be judged and rewarded according to the worth of your achievements or your longevity in the job?" most would choose the former. After all, once the subject is brought up, isn't there some worthless piece of deadwood down the hall who is making as much or more than you are (Nalbandian, 1981: 394)?

CONGRUENCE WITH AMERICAN CULTURAL VALUES: PERFORMANCE APPRAISAL AS MARKET SURROGATE

That performance appraisal did not receive closer scrutiny before being imposed on the public sector, and that it persists despite growing evidence of its incoherence, is the result of its close fit with such American cultural values as individualism, merit, achievement, and material rewards.

Performance appraisal promises to isolate individual excellence. It will separate the wheat from the chaff. This is good because we believe that hard work and cleverness are what separate and should separate successful from unsuccessful people. In our culture merit is based on achievement, not on inherited wealth or status (ascription). We believe in equal opportunity to succeed and fail by our own efforts. For our efforts we expect to be rewarded individually and materially.

It may be postulated, then, that performance appraisal is a market surrogate. In the (partly mythical) past, American values of individual merit and material well-being through achievement could be secured in the untrammeled free market. Since the "invisible hand" of the market can no longer determine the merit of individuals who now work in large organizations, something else is needed to perform that role. In competitive capitalism, the market creates winners and losers; under corporate capitalism, tests and performance appraisals do.

FUNDAMENTAL FLAWS OF FORMAL EMPLOYEE PERFORMANCE APPRAISAL

What follows is an attempt to summarize the most telling critiques of performance appraisal. The case against formal performance appraisal is divided into two subcategories. First, it is one of today's most egregious examples of scientism/objectivism[2]—a reactionary throwback to scientific management facilely ignoring over 50 years of collective learning about human behavior in organizations. Second, it calls forth and exacerbates all the worst pathologies of hierarchy in organizations.

Scientism/Objectivism

Scientism/objectivism is a shorthand term by which we mean the fallacious faith in methods borrowed from natural science and, in this case, experimental psychology to measure and precisely identify living performance that transcends measurement and is inherently ambiguous. It is the attempt to break down holistic and reciprocally influencing dynamic relationships into atomistic units of concrete fixity—into things or objects (compare Nalbandian, 1981: 392-393).

Consider the pyramiding required for performance appraisal to be objective. Most contemporary organizations are not assembly lines with clear inputs and material outputs. The majority of occupations are office based and deal with intangible information exchanges. Especially in the public sector we serve diverse clientele, respond to requests, and communicate. Our days are varied; they vary by season, budget cycle, and externally generated deadlines. All these activities are somewhat artificially gathered up under the umbrella and named such and such unit, agency, or department. Such organizations are vastly complex macro-organisms made up of already extremely complex subgroups that are in turn made up of multifaceted, increasingly diverse individuals (Bretz, Milkovich, and Read, 1992). Out of this "primordial stew" we first evaluate jobs by breaking them down to minute components, attempting thereby to distill out the essential tasks by removing their human incumbents from consideration. We then articulate a position classification system that arrays clusters of tasks according to various criteria by which their comparative worth can be assessed (compare Quaid, 1993). We must then take *each* task or cluster of tasks and figure out precisely what level of performance, or what performance targets, may be termed *unsatisfactory, needs improvement, satisfactory, fully satisfactory,* or *outstanding.* Once all of this has been done we then ask a supervisor to semiannually or annually take the results of this fantastic series of abstract calculations, now reduced to a form, and use it to gauge the complex, interdependent, variegated activities of individual job incumbents. The end result of this process is to have objective data of sufficient validity to compare and reward or punish employees from across the entire organization.

The Misappropriation of Experimental Psychology. Faith that humans could successfully pull off such a feat of intersubjective judgment across the myriad of behaviors that make up an organization is empirically bolstered only by a misappropriation of the literature of experimental psychology. Two aspects of this literature make it inappropriate for ready transfer to personnel administration. First, it reports the rigorous testing of carefully controlled and *isolated* variables in laboratory settings for purposes of building scientific theory (Ilgen and Favero, 1985; Woehr and Feldman, 1993; Woehr and Huffcutt, 1994; but see Duarte, Goodson, and Klich, 1994). In other words, experiments are explicitly designed to avoid contamination of the isolated variables by anything remotely resembling organizational dynamics and the culture, history, mission, or anticipation of the future entailed thereby (Bretz, Milkovich, and Read, 1992). As Judge and Ferris note:

> Considerable research in the past ten years has investigated the role of cognitive processes in performance evaluation. However, researchers have called for more research on social and situational influences on

the performance-rating process. . . . Little empirical work has addressed those concerns, and the research that has been conducted has tended to investigate individual elements in isolation. (1993: 97)

Second, in order to study purely psychological aspects of situations, experi- mental psychology makes the operational assumption that stimuli are fixed and given so that they may concentrate their attention on the organism's responses to them. In the laboratory, where stimuli may indeed be controlled and fixed, psychologists talk about rater error, meaning that the rating subject has perceived stimuli in ways that the experimenter deems insufficiently precise. It is from these studies that the common errors that supervisors are said to make are derived: halo, central tendency, and leniency errors (Ilgen, Barnes-Farrell, and McKellin, 1993). The halo error, for instance, is described as the illegitimate carrying over of a positive impression of one aspect of a performance to a different aspect of performance. Now, it may be acceptable to break down behaviors to atomistic pieces in the laboratory (although we doubt even this) in order to identify rater processing errors with measurement devices such as halo indexes. It is quite another thing to say that these same errors lead to mistakes in judgment in the workplace, where behaviors simply do not come to us piecemeal, atom by atom (Funder, cited in Balzer and Sulsky, 1992). In their evaluations, separated by many months, supervisors are reporting com- pilations of a myriad of inseparable perceptions of well-known subordinates accumulated over time. In the workplace, "reductions in the presence of the typical rater errors . . . do not necessarily indicate greater accuracy" (Ilgen and Favero, 1985: 317). Besides, as Nalbandian (1981: 394) points out, supervisors generally believe that they know their employees well. Performance appraisal, then, is an extra duty imposed on them from above or from the personnel system. Their motivation is to get through it, not to meet some standard of scientific accuracy (Harris, 1994; Murphy and Cleveland, 1995).

Another unfortunate consequence of emphasizing rater error was the chimerical quest to eliminate it by improving the rating instrument (developing the perfect form) and then training raters in its use. But, as reported by Landy and Farr (1980: 84), after 30 years of experimenting with behaviorally anchored rating systems (BARS), "format differences accounted for trivial amounts of rat- ing variance (approximately 5 percent)." As a means of evaluating performance, time-consuming methods like BARS have offered high opportunity costs for relatively little return (Jacobs, Kafry, and Zedeck, 1980). Despite this, fortunes are still being made by personnel consultants on the basis of misleading claims of format superiority.

Regression to Taylorism.   As the above analysis demonstrates, performance appraisal seems, like the scientific management movement (Taylorism) of the early twentieth century, to neglect the human element of worker motivation. By focusing on individual task completion, it ignores and contravenes all that we have learned from the "human relations school" about informal organization and worker motivation. For (a very important) instance, performance appraisal would contradict the "job enrichment" movement (see Bockman, 1971). The measurement imperative would cause jobs to be narrowed, ever more precisely defined and thus delimited, so that performance of them can be more "objectively" gauged.

Pathologies of Hierarchy: Or, It's Being in the Army That Leads to Soldiering

Part of what makes performance appraisal so problematic is that it occurs within hierarchically ordered organizations. As was argued above, performance appraisal is the keystone to gaining more control over the bureaucracy. Superiors are given more power. Use or threat of power creates fear and undermines trust. It should not, then, come as a surprise that performance appraisal adversely diminishes organizational esprit de corps and carries with it punitive connotations. Resentment and dissatisfaction are the inevitable outcomes of a system that requires (at least from the ratee's standpoint) the relative failure of over half of a given work force. This section begins by showing that performance rating systems necessarily disappoint large portions of a work force. Evidence is then adduced for the proposition that those portions are precisely the ones that managers can least afford to discourage. We then suggest that combining performance appraisals with extrinsic motivational tools such as merit pay promotes dysfunctional competition in organizations. Finally, the phenomenon well enough known to have acquired several names (creaming, working to rule, perverse measurement, and goal displacement) is noted.

Cognitive Dissonance.   The law of averages seems to be a cruel piece of legislation. In Garrison Keillor's Lake Wobegon, it has been repealed because there all the children are above average. And consider, would you like to work for an organization where 50 percent of the work force was below average? Are you below average? The law seems also to have been repealed in the minds of many employees. Meyer (1975) found that 70 to 80 percent of the employees he surveyed at different firms rated their own performance as being in the top 25 percent. Other research indicates similar percentages (Rollins, 1988).

So most employees think they are doing a good or better-than-average job, and probably take some pride in it. One of the effects of performance appraisals is to disabuse employees of such notions. The effect on morale is predictable because, as Thompson and Dalton (1970: 150) have put it: "Performance appraisal touches on one of the most emotionally charged activities in business life—the assessment of a man's [*sic*] contribution and ability. The signals he receives about this assessment have a strong impact on his self-esteem *and* on his subsequent performance."

Matthew Effect.   Moreover, the pervasive effect of performance appraisal strikes at precisely that sector of the work force that the procedure was designed to reform. As Becker and Klimoski (1989: 356) have recently found, negative feedback from supervisors is related to lower performance: "[I]t is possible that [incidents of negative feedback] are disheartening and, as such, de-motivating; in fact, such events may build resentment on the part of the subordinate. Thus, negative expressions may not only stem from, but also lead to, poorer performance." Similarly, in their study of the federal work force, Pearce and Porter (1986: 211) found that "[t]here was a significant and stable drop in the organizational commitment of [merely] satisfactory employees after the introduction of formal appraisal."

Further, the discouragement and demotivation of satisfactory employees is in no way made up by a corresponding boost to outstanding performers (Becker and Klimoski, 1989; Perry, Petrakis, and Miller, 1989). After all, outstanding performers are already doing as well as can be expected. This relationship has been cleverly expressed by Gabris and Mitchell (1988: 369) as the Matthew effect: "For to him who has shall be given, and he shall have abundance: but from him who does not have, even that which he has shall be taken away" (Matthew 13:12).

War of All against All and Pay for Performance.   All along there has been skepticism about individual performance appraisal in organizations where team productivity is required (Deming, 1982; Gabris and Mitchell, 1988). Likewise, as early as 1957 we were warned by Douglas McGregor against tying appraisals to be used for employee development to appraisals to be used for reward/punishment (Cleveland and Murphy, 1992; Balfour, 1992). Yet rating individuals for simultaneously rewarding and developing is the essence of performance appraisal codified by CSRA for the federal government. Almost three-quarters of the cities surveyed by England and Parle (1987) do the same. Similar findings are reported for all sectors where studies have been conducted (Locher and Teel, 1988; Timmreck, 1989). The most obvious rewards/punishments are pay increases or the denial of them.

The traditional social contract between employees and employers is that longevity and seniority on the job entails higher pay. Seniority is associated with higher productivity, knowledge of organizational intricacies, and the ability to mentor, guide, and train junior employees. Step increments, cost of living adjustments, and labor's share in productivity increases were the norm. In a period when public employees are held in low regard, however, the argument that their pay should be incrementally adjusted upward for having survived to serve another year is one that no longer resonates with elected masters. The virtues of seniority when pejoratively viewed as time-serving and mindless pencil pushing are no longer obvious. Not years of service but excellence ought be rewarded.

It is difficult to argue against pay for performance in principle. It seems more equitable. Pay for mere seniority is a blunt instrument for rewarding experiential wisdom brought well to bear. But in practice equitable pay for performance requires precisely what we have been at pains to demonstrate is not possible: objective performance appraisals. Performance appraisals have served as the linchpin in virtually all public sector merit pay plans, including those first mandated by the federal Civil Service Reform Act of 1978 (CSRA) and the subsequent adjustments in 1984 known as the Performance Management and Recognition System (PMRS) (Condrey, 1994; Murphy and Cleveland, 1995), and state personnel systems (Ingraham, 1993).

Proponents of pay for performance in the public sector may well claim that its motivational qualities have never really been tested. In case after case at the federal (Perry, 1991) and state levels (Ingraham, 1993), funds sufficient to make performance pay a significant material incentive have fallen to the knife of public sector fiscal stringency. Employees are promised pay increases for excellence and then are denied them because legislative bodies fail to appropriate the money. To a public sector employee who entered service two decades ago, the following sequence of events has likely occurred. Automatic step increments were snatched away, but the promise of pay for meritorious service replaced them. Then superiors came around and did performance appraisals. If the employee exceeded expectations and now hoped to be rewarded, these came in measures smaller than, or equal to, the automatic step increments now proscribed. To the employee, the relationship between performance appraisal and reward for performance is at best obscure and at worst fraudulent; bait (more pay for good work) and switch (de-motivating performance appraisal).

Arguably, what the coming of performance appraisal has done is to artificially establish a state of psychic scarcity on top of what has already been, since at least the tax revolt of 1978, fiscal scarcity. It may be laid down as a general principle that scarcity creates more desperate and mean-spirited competition for that which has been limited. In this case of artificially delimited distinction or ego satisfaction, sharing and generosity are less likely as people concentrate more on the shortcomings of their colleagues than on their strengths. Fingers are pointed and negativity dominates. The atmosphere becomes poisoned by a thousand previously latent petty jealousies. Since human work performance is so variegated that no standpoint can be objective, to emphasize comparisons between group members in highly competitive situations is to invite invidious ones.

Closely related, setting up competition among co-workers establishes a reward structure that makes it irrational for them to cooperate. If one worker finds an easier way to do something, she or he is less likely to share it and lose the edge for superior performance appraisals. This is particularly true when there is a forced distribution system whereby individual performances must be arrayed along a bell-shaped curve.

Creaming, Working to Rule, Perverse Measurement, and Goal Displacement.   Performance appraisal can only enhance productivity if everything that contributes to organizational success can be specified (Nalbandian, 1981). To select particular tasks as performance targets to the neglect of other, perhaps more subtle, ones means that an employee knows what to aim at but also what he or she can safely ignore. Which corners to cut become obvious. If a certain number of cases are to be closed, then they will be closed whether entirely properly with attention to quality and detail, or not. The tendency will be to solve the easy cases and neglect the difficult ones. This phenomenon of goal displacement is well known in the literatures of criminal justice, social work, and program evaluation and need not be belabored here.

CONCLUSION: ABOLISH OR SUBVERT

As the discerning reader might intuit, we do not favor formal performance appraisals. They should be abolished or their use subverted. Three trends in labor force utilization strengthen this conclusion: (1) performance appraisal is deeply contradictory to the total quality management (TQM) movement; (2) jobs seem more and more to be professionalized; (3) we face a labor shortage in the very near future that will require more intelligent personnel policies. Each of these will be briefly treated, after which we will applaud the "vanishing performance appraisal" (Hall and Lawler, cited in Perry, Petrakis, and Miller, 1989).

TQM and Performance Appraisal

A recent development in management literature and training seminars is an orientation called "total quality management," or TQM (see Chapter 18 in this volume). Originally based on the teachings of W. Edwards Deming, TQM emphasizes customer service, teamwork, employee empowerment, systems design, and organizational commitment to continuous quality improvement. With TQM, faulty output—whether it be economic reports, zoning regulations, or customer service—is considered a result of faulty processes within the system, and it is the responsibility of management to identify and prevent these systemic dysfunctions (Eckes, 1994).

Individual employee performance, it follows, is seen as a function of systemic factors over which individual employees have little control (Boudreaux, 1994: 21; Dobbins, 1994). As Deming (1982: 110) observed, "apparent differences between people arise almost entirely from actions of the system [read "open" system] that they work in, not from the people themselves." Thus most of what workers do is simply reactive to the situations in which they find themselves. To distinguish between what is an "outstanding," "fully satisfactory," or "needs improvement" *reaction* and the web of systemic forces that individual employees are reacting *to* is impossible. From this point of view, performance appraisals make scapegoats of employees for management failures to address systemic deficiencies (Bowman, 1994).

Individual performance appraisal also contradicts the TQM emphasis on employee empowerment. Empowerment entails risk taking by line organizational members. As detailed above, performance appraisal dampens such behavior. Moreover, as Deming has taken great pains to point out, performance appraisals take away a worker's pride in his or her work; they are also destructive of quality production or service. Indeed, the persistence of managerial commitment to appraising worker performance may very well serve as a synecdoche for the fettering of the TQM movement.

Professionalism

If it is true that more occupations are being professionalized and that more professionals are working for public sector organizations, formal performance appraisals must wither away. Management is simply incapable of monitoring the exercise of professional expertise, particularly when the fields of expertise among management and professional employees do not coincide (Halachmi, 1993). Only peer evaluations make any sense in this type of environment, and increasing numbers of organizations (particularly in the private sector) are experimenting with variants of this approach (Norman and Zawacki, 1991). However, it remains to be seen if these new procedures will suffer from the same maladies that afflict the traditional methods of employee evaluation (Barclay and Harland, 1995).

Labor Shortage

If labor surpluses shift power toward management, labor shortages take the opposite direction. Organizations that wish to attract talented, educated, and skilled labor will be forced to make the workplace as pleasant and personally fulfilling as possible. Punitive performance monitoring systems that drive away even acceptable "below average" employees will have to be abolished or made meaningless. It is to this latter alternative that we now turn.

Vanishing Performance Appraisal

If, for public relations purposes, or to save face, the political powers that be feel the need to maintain some sort of performance appraisal system, let them have the shadow of one. They will, over time, probably become that anyway as organizations adjust to the human reality that full-blown, objective performance audits simply cannot be done. As reported by Perry, Petrakis, and Miller (1989), that seems to be the direction in which the federal government was heading as it switched from the extremely punitive Merit Pay System described by Thayer (1978), to the more lenient and flexible Performance Management and Recognition System in 1984. The state of Texas is moving in a similar direction.

A less complicated approach that we recommend in order to establish a defensible legal base for the occasionally needed adverse personnel action—firing or demoting, for example—is a simple form outlining position duties with only two rating categories: "unsatisfactory" and "fully satisfactory." This approach has recently gained support at the federal level, and the Office of Personnel Management is considering permitting agencies to use a two-level subjective rating system based on a pass-fail concept (U.S. Federal Register, 1995). As Barrett and Kernan (1987: 496) have convincingly argued in their review of court cases,

"Courts do not reject the subjective approach." You just have to be consistent in your subjectivity.

Whatever the strategy, we should work to abolish or mitigate formal performance appraisal as we know it.

NOTES

1. That those who had reform of the civil service on their minds took advantage of the confluence of events described here is affirmed by Alan K. "Scotty" Campbell, chief architect of the CSRA '78 and first director of the Office of Personnel Management created by the Act. In his words:

   > It is important to understand that we are living at a time characterized by a good deal of sentiment against government and against government employees—be they federal, state or local. We see this in many public opinion polls, as well as referenda such as Proposition 13. To the extent that our proposals were seen as an effort to make government more responsive and more efficient, we were in a position to use that public sentiment. (Campbell, 1979b)

   And the passing of CSRA

   > was certainly related to the mood in the country in which concern about the efficiency of government created an atmosphere that was receptive to changes that would increase efficiency and effectiveness. (Campbell, 1979a: 31)

2. Criticizing scientism in the social sciences is like trying to pull dandelions from one's lawn. You really should get to the root, which is the philosophy of science known as logical positivism. My own views on that are set out more meticulously in Fox (1980) and, in relation to policy studies, in Fox (1989).

REFERENCES

Balfour, Danny. 1992. "Impact of Agency Investment in the Implementation of Performance Appraisal." *Public Personnel Management* 21 (Spring): 1-15.

Balzer, William K., and Lorne M. Sulsky. 1992. "Halo and Performance Appraisal Research: A Critical Examination." *Journal of Applied Psychology* 77, no. 6 (December): 975-985.

Ban, Carolyn, and Patricia Ingraham. 1984. "Introduction," in Patricia Ingraham and Carolyn Ban, eds., *Legislating Bureaucratic Change: The Civil Service Reform Act of 1975,* pp. 1-10. Albany: State University of New York Press.

Banks, Cristina G., and Kevin R. Murphy. 1985. "Toward Narrowing the Research-Practice Gap in Performance Appraisal." *Personnel Psychology* 38, no. 2 (Summer): 335-345.

Barclay, Julie Houser, and Lynn K. Harland. 1995. "Peer Performance Appraisals." *Group and Organization Management* 20, no. 1 (March): 39-60.

Barrett, Gerald V., and Mary C. Kernan. 1987. "Performance Appraisal and Terminations: A Review of Court Decisions since *Brito v. Zia* with Implications for Personnel Practices." *Personnel Psychology* 40, no. 3 (Autumn): 489-503.

Becker, Thomas E., and Richard J. Klimoski. 1989. "A Field Study of the Relationship between the Organizational Feedback Environment and Performance." *Personnel Psychology* 42, no. 2 (Summer): 343-358.

Bockman, Valerie M. 1971. "The Herzberg Controversy," *Personnel Psychology* 24, no. 2 (Summer): 155-189.

Boudreaux, Greg. 1994. "What TQM Says about Performance Appraisal." *Compensation and Benefits Review* 26, no. 3 (May/June): 20-24.

Bowman, James S. 1994. "At Last, an Alternative to Performance Appraisal: Total Quality Management." *Public Administration Review* 54, no. 2 (March/April): 129-136.

Bretz, Robert D., Jr., George T. Milkovich, and Walter Read. 1992. "The Current State of Performance Appraisal Research and Practice: Concerns, Directions, and Implications." *Journal of Management* 18 no. 2 (June): 321-349.

Campbell, Alan K. 1979a. "Reflections on Reform" *Management* 1, no. 1 (September).
——— . 1979b. "The Politics and Substance of Civil Service Reform." Speech, University of Louisville (October).

Cleveland, Jeanette M., and Kevin R. Murphy. 1992. "Analyzing Performance Appraisal as Goal-Directed Behavior." *Research in Personnel and Human Resources Management* 10: 121-185.

Condrey, Stephen E. 1994. "Implications for Managerial Performance Appraisal Systems: Qualitative vs. Quantitative Performance." *Review of Public Personnel Administration* 14, no. 3 (Summer): 45-59.

Daley, Dennis. 1988. "Performance Appraisal and Organizational Success: Public Employee Perceptions in an MBO-Based Appraisal System." *Review of Public Personnel Administration* 9, no. 1 (Fall): 17-27.

Deming, W. Edwards. 1982. *Out of the Crisis.* Cambridge, Mass.: M.I.T. Press.

Dobbins, Cardy. 1994. *Performance Appraisal: Alternative Perspectives.* Cincinnati, Ohio: South-Western Publishing.

Duarte, Neville T., Jane R. Goodson, and Nancy R. Klich. 1994. "Effects of Dyadic Quality and Duration on Performance Appraisal." *Academy of Management Journal* 37, no. 3: 499-521.

Eckes, George. 1994. "Practical Alternatives to Performance Appraisals." *Quality Progress* 27, no. 11 (November): 57-60.

England, Robert E., and William M. Parle. 1987. "Nonmanagerial Performance Appraisal Practices in Large American Cities." *Public Administration Review* 47, no. 6 (November/December): 498-504.

Fox, Charles J. 1980. "The Existential-Phenomenological Alternative to Dichotomous Thought." *Western Political Quarterly* 33, no. 3 (September): 357-379.
——— . 1989. "Implementation Research: Why and How to Transcend Positivist Methodologies," in Dennis J. Palumbo and Donald J. Calista, eds., *Opening Up the Black Box: Implementation Research and the Policy Process.* Westport, Conn.: Praeger/Greenwood.

Gabris, Gerald T., and Kenneth Mitchell. 1988. "The Impact of Merit Raise Scores on Employee Attitudes: The Matthew Effect of Performance Appraisal." *Public Personnel Management* 17, no. 4 (Winter): 369-386.

Grider, Doug, and Leslie Toombs. 1993. "Current Practices of Performance Appraisal as a Linking Mechanism for Human Resources Decisions in State Government." *International Journal of Public Administration* 16 (Winter): 35-36.

Halachmi, Arie. 1993. "From Performance Appraisal to Performance Targeting." *Public Personnel Management* 22, no. 2 (Summer): 323-344.

Harris, Michael M. 1994. "Rater Motivation in the Performance Appraisal Context: A Theoretical Framework." *Journal of Management* 20, no. 4 (Winter): 737-756.

Ilgen, Daniel R., and Janet Favero. 1985. "Limits in Generalization from Psychological Research to Performance Appraisal Processes." *Academy of Management Review* 10, no. 2 (April): 311-321.

Ilgen, Daniel R., Janet L. Barnes-Farrell, and David B. McKellin. 1993. "Performance Appraisal Process Research in the 1980's: What Has It Contributed to Appraisals in Use?" *Organizational Behavior and Human Decision Processes* 54, no. 3 (April): 321-368.

Ingraham, Patricia W. 1993. "Pay for Performance in the States." *American Review of Public Administration* 23, no. 3 (September): 189-200.

Jacobs, Rick, Ditsa Kafry, and Sheldon Zedeck. 1980. "Expectations of Behaviorally Anchored Rating Scales." *Personnel Psychology* 33, no. 3 (Autumn): 595-640.

Judge, Timothy A., and Gerald R. Ferris. 1993. "Social Context of Performance Evaluation Decisions." *Academy of Management Journal* 36, no. 1 (February): 80-105.

Landy, Frank J., and James L. Farr. 1980. "Performance Rating." *Psychological Bulletin* 87, no. 1 (Winter): 72-107.

Laumeyer, Jim, and Tim Beebe. 1988. "Employees and Their Appraisal: How Do Workers Feel about the Company Grading Scale?" *Personnel Administrator* 33, no. 12 (December): 76-80.

Locher, Alan H., and Kenneth S. Teele. 1988. "Appraisal Trends." *Personnel Journal* 67, no. 9 (September): 139-145.

Lovrich, Nicholas, P. Shaffer, R. Hopkins, and D. Yale. 1980. "Public Employees and Performance Appraisal: Do Public Servants Welcome or Fear Merit Evaluation of Their Performance?" *Public Administration Review* 40, no. 3 (May/June): 214-222.

Maroney, Bernard Patrick, and M. Ronald Buckley. 1992. "Does Research in Performance Appraisal Influence the Practice of Performance Appraisal? Regretfully Not!" *Public Personnel Management* 21, no. 2 (Summer): 185-196.

McGregor, Douglas. 1957. "An Uneasy Look at Performance Appraisal." *Harvard Business Review* 35, no. 3 (May/June): 89-94.

Meyer, Herbert H. 1975. "The Pay-for-Performance Dilemma." *Organizational Dynamics* 3, no. 1 (Winter): 39-50.

Murphy, Kevin R., and Jeanette N. Cleveland. 1995. *Understanding Performance Appraisal.* Thousand Oaks, Calif.: Sage.

Nalbandian, John. 1981. "Performance Appraisal: If Only People Were Not Involved." *Public Administration Review* 41, no. 3 (May/June): 392-396.

Norman, Carol A., and Robert A. Zawacki. 1991. "Team Appraisals—Team Approach." *Personnel Journal* 70, no. 9 (September): 101-104.

Pearce, Jone L., and Lyman W. Porter. 1986. "Employee Responses to Formal Performance Appraisal Feedback." *Journal of Applied Psychology* 71, no. 2 (May): 211-218.

Perry, James L. 1991. "Linking Pay to Performance: The Controversy Continues," in Carolyn Ban and Norma M. Riccucci, eds. *Public Personnel Management: Current Concerns—Future Challenges.* White Plains, N.Y.: Longman.

Perry, James L., Beth Ann Petrakis, and Theodore K. Miller. 1989. "Federal Merit Pay, Round II: An Analysis of the Performance Management and Recognition System." *Public Administration Review* 49, no. 1 (January/February): 29-37.

Quaid, Maeve. 1993. *Job Evaluation: The Myth of Equitable Assessment.* Toronto: University of Toronto Press.

Roberts, Gary E. 1992. "Linkages between Performance Appraisal System Effectiveness and Rater and Ratee Acceptance." *Review of Public Personnel Administration* 12, no. 3 (Summer): 19–41.

——— . 1994. "Maximizing Performance Appraisal System Acceptance: Perspectives from Municipal Government Personnel Administrators." *Public Personnel Management* 23, no. 4 (Winter): 525–548.

Rollins, Thomas. 1988. "Pay for Performance: Is It Worth the Trouble?" *Personnel Administrator* (May): 42–46.

Skinner, B. F. 1953. *Science and Human Behavior.* New York: Free Press/Macmillan.

Thayer, Frederick C. 1978. "The President's Management 'Reforms': Theory X Triumphant." *Public Administration Review* 38, no. 4 (July/August): 309–314.

Thompson, Paul H., and Gene W. Dalton. 1970. "Performance Appraisal: Managers Beware." *Harvard Business Review* 48, no. 1 (January/February): 149–154.

Timmreck, Thomas C. 1989. "Performance Appraisal Systems in Rural Western Hospitals." *Health Care Management Review* 14, no. 2 (Spring): 31–43.

Tjosvold, Dean, and James A. Halco. 1992. "Performance Appraisal of Managers: Goal Interdependence, Ratings, and Outcomes." *Journal of Social Psychology* 132, no. 5 (October): 629–639.

U.S. Congress, Senate Committee on Government Affairs. 1978. *Hearings on S. 2604, S. 2707, and S. 2830, Appendix.* 95th Congress, 2d Sess.

U.S. Federal Register. 1995. Vol. 60, no. 18 (January 27): 5542–5556.

U.S. Office of Personnel Management. 1979. "Common Themes in Public Personnel Reform." *Personnel Management Reform* 1, no. 1 (September): 1–7.

Wiatrowski, Michael D., and Dennis S. Palkon. 1987. "Performance Appraisal Systems in Health Care Administration." *Health Care Management Review* 12, no. 1 (December): 71–80.

Woehr, David J., and Jack Feldman. 1993. "Processing Objective and Question Order Effects on the Causal Relation between Memory and Judgment in Performance Appraisal: The Tip of the Iceberg." *Journal of Applied Psychology* 78, no. 2 (April): 232–241.

Woehr, David J., and Allen I. Huffcutt. 1994. "Rater Training for Performance Appraisal: A Quantitative Review." *Journal of Occupational and Organizational Psychology* 67, no. 3 (September): 189–205.

chapter 14

Issues in Compensation and Benefits

N. Joseph Cayer

$\mathbf{F}$ew public sector human resource issues generate broader interest than compensation and benefits. Personnel specialists, employers, employees, the taxpaying public, and public policy makers all have reasons to be concerned about compensation and benefits. Because human resources usually represent 70 percent and more of the cost of governments, it is not surprising that expenditures on personnel attract a lot of interest, especially during this era of reinventing and downsizing government. Normally, legislative bodies have the final say on compensation issues. Although legislatures have delegated much of the responsibility for actually developing pay systems and any adjustments, they retain the final authority and, of course, have to budget the money for any increases in personnel costs.

Compensation in the public sector is immersed in the politics of public policy making. Because public employees are paid with public tax dollars, their compensation is subject to political debate. That debate often relates to what resources are available, the performance received for the pay and how fair the compensation is (both compared to the private sector and within the organization), and the role unions play in the process. Thus decision makers are confronted with the need to control costs while retaining the most capable personnel possible. In doing so, they are challenged constantly by changing demographics of the labor force. These concerns are addressed in this chapter around the themes of cost and cost containment, competitiveness and capability, and responsiveness to a changing work force.

COST AND COST CONTAINMENT

The personnel costs of government generate much political debate and concern. Campaigns for office often focus on the cost of government and particularly on the public bureaucracy. In 1994 congressional elections brought the role and cost of government to the forefront of public debate. The Republican majority elected to Congress promised major cuts in public programs and the elimination of many government agencies. All these proposals are supposed to save money and lead to reduction of the deficit as well as lower taxes.

As a way of defusing politics in setting pay for federal employees, Congress delegated the responsibility to the president through the Pay Comparability Act of 1970 and the Federal Employee Pay Comparability Act of 1990. The 1970 act authorized the president to establish a system for comparability. A comparability pay commission was established to survey employers across the country. The 1990 act formally established the Federal Salary Council, which now advises the president and the director of the Office of Personnel Management on comparability adjustments and other issues affecting compensation. The president may accept or reject the recommendations on adjustments or ask for modification. When the president accepts the recommendations, Congress then may vote to reject them. This system was established to depoliticize the process of adjusting pay to some extent, thereby relieving Congress of having to act affirmatively on pay adjustments, which usually engendered much political wrangling. Critics of the system argue, however, that this system results in fairly automatic pay increases, thereby raising costs, and also helps members of Congress, whose pay is included in the process. Thus, at election time, pay increases become central issues of political debate in many congressional districts. None of the goals of comparability, closing of the pay gap, depoliticization, or cost containment seem to have been met.

On some occasions, political considerations have been beneficial to public employees, at least in the short run. Especially in the area of benefits, some jurisdictions have been generous to public employees seemingly for purposes of currying political favor with strong unions. A common scenario would be for the jurisdiction to agree to increases in benefits that would have to be paid for at a later date in lieu of current direct pay increases. The elected public official would likely not have to be concerned about the long-term costs because of moving on to some other elected position. The financial difficulties of New York City during the mid-1970s were blamed, in part, on generous retirement benefits bestowed in such a way.

Personnel Costs

Pay. As noted earlier, upwards of 70 percent of the operating budgets of governments typically are spent on personnel. As a result, when budget cuts are necessary or politically expedient, personnel is affected. It is the major area for cutting. Since the 1970s, governments have found their revenues eroded or at least capped by either a lagging economy or taxpayer revolts or the current trend of reducing the size and role of government in people's lives. The result has been budget cuts or slowing of budget growth. Most jurisdictions have experienced both.

Governments have found it difficult to control costs because of numerous factors, including efforts to keep pay consistent with what is paid in the private sector to attract qualified applicants. Additionally, the public sector has become more unionized than the private sector, and collective bargaining results in pressure for increasing compensation. Research on the impact indicates that on average, unions make a difference of about 5 percent to 6 percent higher pay levels in state and local governments (Kearney, 1994). Many collective bargaining agreements and most retirement benefits have provisions indexing increases to the cost of living increase. Thus as the cost of living increases, pay and benefits rise.

Even without indexing, some benefits have increased significantly over the years. Between 1929 and 1989 the share of total payroll that supports benefits rose from 3 percent to 38 percent for U.S. employers (U.S. Chamber Research Center, 1990). Healthcare and retirement pensions represent the largest increases. These two benefits are examined here to illustrate benefits issues and approaches.

Healthcare Benefits. Healthcare costs have increased 35 percent more than cost increases for all other goods and services. Healthcare expenditures in 1989 represented 11 percent ($600 billion) of the gross national product (GNP), and it is estimated that they will reach 15 percent ($1.5 trillion) of GNP by the year 2000 (Brouder, 1992). The result has been rapidly increasing costs for healthcare benefits for all employers. Not surprisingly, employers search for ways of controlling those costs.

Despite many efforts to control healthcare costs in the public sector, there have been consistently spiraling increases (Cayer, 1995a; Handel, 1992). For traditional indemnity plans, average annual cost increases in recent years have hovered around 20 percent, whereas costs for health maintenance organization plans have averaged 8-12 percent increases. Increases for preferred provider organizations have ranged from 10 to 15 percent, and self-insured programs have experienced increases of 12-15 percent on average. For public jurisdictions, these cost increases lead to strain on budgets because most public jurisdictions tend to pay almost all of the cost of healthcare coverage. Virtually all cities and counties, for example, provide healthcare coverage and rarely require employee participation in paying for it (Cayer, 1995a). Twenty-six states pay full cost for the employee's coverage, and ten cover all the cost of the family as well. In those states that do not cover the full cost, the vast majority pay at least 80 percent of the employee premium, and half pay 80 percent of the family cost. Ten states also pay all the cost for retirees over age 65 (Handel, 1992).

The cost of healthcare services also relates to the types of coverage. Governments provide benefits for a wide variety of health care. Traditionally health insurance benefits covered medical care, but now mental health, dental, vision, employee assistance, and long-term nursing insurance are found in many public sector plans. Another feature that has cost implications is that some public sector jurisdictions also provide healthcare benefits to retirees. As people live longer, the cost impact is significant. With the cost increases and the addition of new benefits, most governments are moving slowly to cost sharing for healthcare coverage.

Retirement Benefits. In 1993, thirty million public employees and retirees were covered in public pension systems with assets of over $900 million (Cayer, 1995b). Public pension systems proliferated during the 1960s. Most were defined benefits plans in which the level of benefits was guaranteed to employees who met specified criteria for age and years of service. When people began retiring in large numbers during the late 1970s and 1980s, government jurisdictions came under severe financial strain. Most systems were pay-as-you go systems, meaning that benefits had to be funded out of current operating budgets as the pension benefits came due. Additionally, pension benefits typically are indexed to cost of living increases, thereby escalating the cost even more. There was little forward funding, although in recent years retirement funds have been established in most jurisdictions to provide for the payment of benefits. In recent years, because of the fiscal stress experienced by many public employers, they have moved increasingly to defined contributions pension plans, in which the employer sets aside a specified amount of money in an account in the employee's name that then pays benefits based on how much has been set aside in the employee's account and on how well investments of the fund have performed. Typically, employees also contribute some portion of their salary to the fund. Many jurisdictions, especially public colleges and universities, allow employees to put their retirement funds in optional plans allowing investment through private financial planners.

Controversies have arisen in recent years about the financing and management of pension funds. As has already been noted, in defined benefits plans (which still predominate in the public sector), payments had to come either from current operating budgets or from funds set up to forward fund the benefits. Investment of public pension funds traditionally has been very conservative, and returns have been low. As a result the actual pension benefits were meager as well, especially in the state systems. During the 1980s many of them shed their conservative investment strategies and began investing in speculative ventures. In addition, pressures for social investing and investing in home state or local corporations led to some major disasters for many public pension funds (Cayer, 1995b; Mactas, 1992).

Another issue for public pension funds has been the contribution the jurisdiction puts into them. Under increasing fiscal strain, many governments—especially states—saw the public pension fund as a good source of money to bail out budget problems. Many states began "raiding" the funds to cover operating costs of state government, leading many critics to complain that the security of the retirees or future retirees could be jeopardized (Zolkos, 1992).

The financial soundness of the systems also is affected by the contributions put into them. In defined benefits forward funding, actuarial standards are used to estimate how much money the fund needs to ensure the guaranteed benefits. Legislatures often adjust the actuarial assumptions in order to change the amount they need to contribute to the fund in any given year. Thus in a difficult budget year they can adjust the actuarial assumptions so that they can reduce the contribution to the system and then have the money to spend on other programs. The long-term viability of the systems can be imperiled in this way.

Strategies for Controlling Costs

Cost factors have been the driving force in recent efforts to reform compensation programs. The tight budgets experienced by most public sector employers in recent years, coupled with the increasing costs of everything, require employers to find ways of getting more for less. Because personnel costs are such a large part of public sector expenditures, they present the best opportunity for reining in costs. In this section we examine some strategies that have been tried in the public sector and some that might be tried.

Pay Strategies.   Strategies for controlling payroll costs include pay freezes, reductions in force, and contracting for services (privatization). Pay freezes accomplish short-term cost control by ensuring that payroll costs do not increase. In the long run, however, such a strategy may lead to even more cost as demoralized employees leave the organization and replacements have to be recruited and trained. The costs of recruitment and training often are not factored into the decision to freeze pay. Legislative bodies often view a pay freeze as a quick fix and also see it as a politically expedient approach, given that the voting public can understand the simple action of halting any increase in pay. With the public being generally cynical about the public service anyway, they are likely to support such action.

Equally easy to understand is the idea of reducing the number of employees on the public payroll. Thus cutting the size of the work force is a popular strategy. This can be accomplished either through layoffs (reductions in force, or RIFs) or through attrition (see Chapter 17 in this volume and Ban, 1995). Layoffs usually allow the managers of the organization some discretion concerning who is to be let go, although there may be some restrictions. In unionized settings, for example, negotiated agreements may use seniority as the sole basis for layoff. Attrition often represents the least stressful approach in that the organization just does not fill positions that become vacant. Attrition usually has less negative impact on employee morale because people do not fear losing their jobs. For the organization, however, the effect can be harmful because it may have no control over which positions will come open. Thus critical skills may be lost to the organization and/or the better employees may be the ones to leave.

Generally, RIFs may reduce costs, but long-run effects may not be positive for the organization. The increased work load for remaining employees may lead to lowered morale, increased stress, and less productivity. The ability of the organization to get its work done may suffer because of the particular employees who leave. Training costs also may increase.

Contracting for services (often referred to as privatization) is a popular approach to reducing costs, although the actual results also may not live up to promises. Popular lore has it that the private sector can provide services more cheaply than the public sector. Especially for small jurisdictions, the economies of scale of a private vendor may allow for less costly services because the private vendor may provide the service to many organizations and the private employer bears the overhead costs for maintaining its payroll. The public employer may avoid the long-term costs of benefits, especially retirement pensions. Sometimes contracting is done with other jurisdictions allowing for some of the same savings. The City of Phoenix introduced an innovative variation by allowing city departments and private vendors to compete for contracts for some services (e.g., trash collection and emergency medical services). The city department costs everything out, just as the private vendor does in the bid process.

Not everyone agrees that contracting for services is a way to control costs. The American Federation of State, County, and Municipal Employees (AFSCME), for example, believes that long-term costs of contracting for services are likely to be higher than if public employers staffed the operations with public employees (American Federation of State, County, and Municipal Employees, 1983, 1987). For the public employer, contracting for services leads to increased costs for monitoring contracts and protecting against potential abuse, including collusion between public officials and contractors. Training public managers for their new duties associated with supervising contractors leads to more cost as well. Clearly, contracting does not result in guaranteed savings unless it is carefully planned and implemented with realistic expectations (see Chapter 19 in this volume).

Benefits Strategies.   Strategies for controlling the costs of benefits programs are the primary focus in benefits management today. The spiraling costs have put heavy strain on public budgets, especially at the state and local level, resulting in efforts to reduce costs. Congress is considering adjustments to benefits programs of federal employees as well. Additionally, many jurisdictions attempt to control benefits costs by reducing the number of employees eligible for benefits.

Virtually every jurisdiction is struggling with healthcare costs. In recent years, most healthcare benefits plans have expanded to include health maintenance organizations and preferred providers organizations as options in addition to traditional indemnity plans for employees. Although the experience has not demonstrated decreases in costs, the level of cost increase probably has declined with these options. In addition to having these options, public employees increasingly are required to pay part of the premium for the options they choose.

Many jurisdictions find that they can decrease their costs through consortia that give them the benefit of larger numbers of participants. Thus many local governments (especially small jurisdictions) band together to purchase services (Cayer, 1995a). California has a number of alliances of counties and municipalities, and the state helps through its public employee retirement system for retirees, (Hackelman, 1994). In many areas, including Minnesota and New York, labor unions and public employers have established joint labor-management efforts to work together on developing alternatives to reduce costs.

Prevention is viewed as the best way of reducing costs and demands on the healthcare system. Thus wellness programs and various types of screening programs have become popular in recent years. The benefits to the employer are in catching potential problems early so that long-term effects can be diminished; for the employee, a healthier lifestyle is the result. Employee assistance plans also help, especially with substance abuse problems and their treatment. They also help in reducing employee stress, which can lead to many health problems.

To avoid some of the costs of benefits, employers increasingly employ part-time and temporary employees who are not eligible for benefits in most jurisdictions. Those employed less than half time generally do not qualify for benefits programs. Thus filling current full-time, permanent positions with part-time, temporary employees may save the jurisdiction significant resources. Another strategy adopted in recent years has been to develop a two-tiered system in which new employees may have lower levels of benefits than those employed at an earlier time. Because of contractual obligations, employers may not be able to change the levels of pay increase or long-term benefits of current employees, but they may more carefully control those items for new employees. Of course, morale problems may result, thus making such options less attractive.

COMPETITIVENESS AND CAPABILITY

In order to attract and retain capable employees, compensation must be competitive and must be considered fair by employees. Being competitive means being able to attract applicants for positions of the same or higher quality as other employers attract. Fairness is a subjective consideration, but it is important to individual employees in their decision to either take or keep a public sector position. Compensation often is viewed as an incentive for employees to perform. Traditional approaches to pay accepted this view with little question. However, with the human relations approach that emerged in the late 1920s, and its evolution into organizational humanism and behavioral science applications to organizations from the late 1950s onward, organization theorists and employers recognized that pay has limits as an instrument for motivation. It has become accepted as only one element in the matrix of factors that motivate people, and it also is recognized that it affects each individual in different ways. Nonetheless, it is important in establishing a foundation for attracting capable employees and keeping them productive.

Competitiveness

The total compensation package (pay and benefits) must be competitive with what other organizations pay for comparable positions in order to attract the type of employees desired. As noted earlier, the national government uses comparability studies to ensure that its pay levels are competitive. The idea behind comparability is that if government is to be competitive in recruiting and retaining quality employees, it must be competitive in pay.

The comparability pay system established by the Pay Comparability Act of 1970 and its refinement by the Federal Employee Pay Comparability Act of 1990 were aimed at making public sector pay competitive so that capable individuals would be attracted to government employment. Because pay comparability studies typically did not include benefits, government employees actually benefited by the comparisons to some extent. The level of the position within the civil service system affects whether it is likely to be competitive in pay with the private sector. At the higher-level positions, clearly the private sector has an advantage in that its benefits and perquisites often are very generous and go far beyond anything the government can do.

Benefits have become a major part of the total compensation package in government employment, thus helping to make public sector employment attractive. Benefits include mandated ones such as Social Security, unemployment compensation, disability, and family leave as well as discretionary benefits such as healthcare insurance and retirement pensions. Generally government has had generous benefits plans as compared to most employers, although large corporations have developed substantial plans over the years. Because pay was usually low in the public sector, generous benefits plans often were developed to provide security and thus retain employees.

During this era of budget cuts and downsizing, pay levels of the work force are affected negatively, thereby reducing the attractiveness of public employment. Lagging revenues usually mean that legislators are unlikely to approve meaningful pay increases. During the past two decades, many state and local government employees have gone years without pay increases or have received increases that come nowhere near covering inflation or the rising cost of living.

At the same time that resources are constrained, the costs of operating often go up, partly because service demand increases and partly because of the increased stress on and reduced morale of employees. Costs of benefits have been particularly vulnerable to cost increases. When people become stressed, use of some of the benefits (e.g., employee assistance plans and health care) is likely to increase. These increases in demand may have the added effect of forcing jurisdictions to find ways to trim costs and possibly to cut more staff.

Fairness of Compensation

Fairness of compensation is an important issue because it affects whether organizations will be successful in attracting the kinds of applicants they want and then whether they will be able to keep them. Fairness also affects morale and productivity, depending on whether employees feel that they are being paid according to their value to the organization and relative to others in the organization. Fairness may be categorized in terms of external equity and internal equity. External equity of compensation refers to the labor market, and internal equity relates to the comparable value of the job within the organization.

External Equity. Establishing competitive compensation levels so that high-quality applicants can be attracted requires knowledge of pay scales in organizations outside government. Thus comparability studies may be conducted, as is done in the national government, or other analyses might be done. State and local governments, for example, use U.S. Labor Department statistics and often check on what other jurisdictions are paying for a particular type of position. These data, along with internal analyses, are used to establish pay levels for the jurisdiction.

Problems in evaluating the external labor market arise as a result of several factors. Some government jobs do not have equivalents in the private sector. Police and fire services, for example, are almost universally public sector occupations, although some locales do contract for such services from private vendors. Firefighting, especially, is sometimes contracted for with private companies. Finding positions precisely comparable to those in a government organization can pose challenges and requires careful identification of jobs to be sampled. It also is necessary to compare the total compensation package. The tendency of governments to look only at direct pay sometimes leads to better total compensation because of the relatively better benefits packages that usually exist in government.

Comparability strategies also can have an escalating effect on compensation rates. When one jurisdiction increases its compensation to better compete with other jurisdictions in its labor market, other jurisdictions may then increase their compensation levels; the process repeats itself the next year and the cycle continues. What constitutes the appropriate labor market to examine also can be a problem. For example, in 1995 the governor of Arizona decided that he had to pay his staff higher salaries than states such as California and Texas, even though those states have vastly larger populations. His claim was that the higher salaries were necessary to attract and retain high-caliber staff who might be attracted to the private sector, although critics argued that he should have looked at the public sector market rather than the private sector.

Internal Equity. Public organizations traditionally have focused on internal equity to a greater extent than the private sector has. Internal equity relates to how the compensation for a position or individual in the organization compares to compensation for other positions or individuals. Since the public sector usually bases pay on position rather than on the individual employee, equity then focuses on how positions compare to one another. The classification plan and job analysis and job evaluation are used to help establish compensation for any given position. Based on the position description and qualifications required for the essential functions of the position, it can be given a value in the organization relative to other positions. Each job needs to be examined in terms of what the duties and responsibilities are and what specific skills, knowledge, and abilities (SKAs) are required to perform it. Positions that require similar duties and levels of responsibility as well as similar SKAs should be valued and paid at the same level. Most public sector employers have hundreds or even thousands of different job classifications; thus the task of comparing each on the criteria outlined above is a daunting one. Critics advocate reform of the classification and compensation systems to include fewer, broader classifications, and pay banding to increase the flexibility of managers to establish pay for an individual position or employee (Congressional Budget Office, 1991; National Academy of Public Administration, 1991).

In many local governments, parity is a major consideration reflecting internal equity concerns. Thus pay of all employees may be some ratio of pay for police officers, for example. Frequently, parity is a bargaining issue for police and fire employees. With the greater emphasis on internal equity, public sector compensation systems have been characterized by highly structured, inflexible pay plans focusing on the job or position. An aspect of public sector pay often missed in the focus on internal equity is that pay compression is a major problem in public sector compensation. The differences between the highest level employees and the rest of the organization are small in government as compared to the private sector. Whereas pay dispersion has widened in the private sector worldwide, it has not happened in the public sector (Katz and Krueger, 1993; Maguire, 1993). The private sector has been more likely to focus on the person in determining pay and thus has had more flexibility in adjusting pay to particular situations or needs.

In the federal government, for example, centralized and standardized compensation schedules are the tradition for white-collar workers, whereas blue-collar worker pay schedules have been sensitive to prevailing wages in given labor markets (Ingraham, 1993a). The result is that the vast majority of federal government workers were paid according to the same centralized schedule. Similarly, benefits have been standardized. The Federal Employees Pay Comparability Act of 1990 provides for locality pay in the federal government, thus allowing pay to be adjusted to reflect local labor market levels. This system has been in use for blue-collar workers historically but now has been introduced for all employees of the federal government, thereby decentralizing pay to a greater extent. State and local government jurisdictions typically follow the same approach used in the national government. As will be explained later, all levels of government have experimented with some decentralization in recent years. Some other nations (e.g., Australia, New Zealand, Sweden, and the United Kingdom) have decentralized their compensation systems to a much greater extent than the United States has (Maguire, 1993).

Comparable worth is another aspect of internal equity. Classes of positions dominated by women in organizations traditionally have been valued less and paid less than those dominated by males. The same is true of positions traditionally dominated by minorities. Comparable worth refers to equal pay for work of comparable value. Because discriminatory criteria were used in valuing jobs, discrimination in pay evolved. Pressure for comparable worth policies has come from women's organizations, collective bargaining, and litigation. Yet most jurisdictions have not actually adopted comparable worth as a policy. The Americans with Disabilities Act (ADA) is likely to have an impact, however, because it requires careful analysis of all aspects of the human resources system to ensure that discrimination does not exist. It should help in rectifying some of the inequities in the valuing of jobs in the organization. Job analysis is one instrument for examining the value of the job in the organization.

Capability

Employers assume the capability of employees to perform their jobs or quickly learn the job when they are hired. Keeping them motivated to perform, however, is another issue. In recent years, public sector employers have experimented with compensation plans as one way of motivating continued productivity.

Pay-for-performance or merit pay is a concept that has been used to reward high performance and thus motivate continued high performance. The idea behind pay-for-performance is an attractive one, especially for elected political officials who often denigrate public employees as part of their election campaigns. They often use public servants as scapegoats for the problems of government and suggest that they could be much more productive. Thus they suggest tying pay to the actual performance of the employee. The concept is one with which most people would agree. However, pay-for-performance systems have costs as well, and those same politicians usually are not willing to fund the systems to the point at which they will work.

Pay-for-performance assumes that we can accurately measure performance and the value of any given performance to the organization (see Chapter 13 in this volume). Although both are theoretically possible, they are fraught with controversy. Usually there is difficulty in agreeing on what is meritorious performance and how that performance contributes to the mission of the agency. Second, there is the morale problem associated with employees often feeling that their contributions are not really understood or valued as much as they should be. Finally, for pay-for-performance to work, employees have to feel that the rewards are significant enough to justify the effort both in being productive and in documenting performance and dealing with the morale problems. Unfortunately, most jurisdictions do not put the resources into making the rewards for distinctions in performance meaningful. Policy makers often seem to focus on the performance side of the system and forget the pay part of it. As a result, the promise of pay-for-performance has rarely been realized (Ingraham, 1993b; Siegel, 1992: Chap. 5). Nonetheless, the concept retains widespread popularity in the public sector (Kellough and Lu, 1993).

An alternative to pay-for-performance is the lump sum merit award paid in the form of bonuses on a one-time basis for exceptional performance. The city of Scottsdale, Arizona, adopted this approach after its pay-for-performance system failed, largely because of lack of adequate funding. The one-time bonus has the advantage of being tied directly to performance but does not get built into the permanent pay base of the employee. Thus the employee is rewarded for the performance at the time of the exceptional work and does not keep the reward forever, regardless of future performance. In most cases the employee would be eligible each year, so if performance remains exceptional, bonuses can continue to be awarded.

Pay banding is another approach that is being experimented with in the public sector, although it is much more common in the private sector (Ban, 1991; Bergel, 1994; National Academy of Public Administration, 1991). Pay banding allows flexibility to supervisors and managers to set pay for individuals, as opposed to the traditional system in which a position is slotted in a specific pay grade or range with limited steps. By allowing greater discretion and wider pay bands, it permits supervisors to reward outstanding employees and to shift around their pay resources to maximize the performance of their units. Although implemented experimentally in several federal agencies, pay banding has not yet been embraced by the public sector to any real extent (Risher and Schay, 1994). The politics of compensation issues probably inhibits its use because legislators and the public fear abuses. Similarly, unions and other employee organizations are fearful of too much supervisory or managerial discretion and help to inhibit its adoption. The need to control is strong among policy makers and many high-level executives, and it is difficult to change (Risher, 1994).

In the private sector, gainsharing, in which the work group or unit shares in the rewards for improved performance, has met with success. Suggestions for its use in the public sector often are heard, but the focus on individual performance is difficult to overcome (Siegel, 1994). Again, the political realities of the public sector are probably inhibitors of change to the approach. In the contemporary organization built upon teamwork, this approach would seem to be very appropriate.

RESPONSIVENESS TO A CHANGING WORK FORCE

Changing demographics mean that employers have work forces that are older, better educated, more diverse racially and ethnically, and more female. Because the public sector has been the leader in equal employment opportunity, it reflects these trends more than the private sector does. Implications for the public sector employer are many. For compensation policies the major impact is on benefits plans, although there are some direct pay implications as well.

The increasing diversity of the work force leads to greater scrutiny of pay systems to ensure that they are not discriminatory. The traditional focus has been on the experience of females and minorities. Now, with older and more educated employees, employers are challenged by employees who have few qualms about raising pay equity issues.

The changing demographics affect benefits packages in particular. Employers traditionally offered healthcare and retirement benefits. Now, however, work forces include many two-earner couples whose needs vary. Newer types of discretionary benefits are being offered to reflect these different needs (Ellis, 1993). The concept of life-cycle benefits encompasses the idea that all employees have different needs at different stages in their lives (Adolf, 1992). Thus, early in one's career, educational benefits (tuition reimbursement) and child care may be important benefits. At later stages, elder care, long-term care insurance, and pre-retirement counseling may be more important. By offering flexible, cafeteria-style benefits programs, employers allow their employees to choose the benefits most important to them. The employer may set aside a specific sum of money the employee can spend for benefits. Flexible plans allow the employee to get the best coverage for his or her situation and help hold down the overall cost of benefits plans for the employer. These plans require considerable effort to educate employees so that they understand the complex tradeoffs they face in choosing the best package of benefits for their needs.

Changing work-force demographics helped stimulate Congress to pass the Family and Medical Leave Act of 1993. The legislation is an attempt to balance work and family responsibilities (Crampton and Mishra, 1995). It requires employers with more than 50 employees to grant up to 12 weeks of unpaid leave during any 12-month period for employees to deal with ill family members, childbirth, or adoption. Clearly, there are implications for the employer's personnel costs and for the workload of other employees. At the same time, the Act recognizes the needs of individual employees to cope with their particular situations.

The aging of the work force also affects healthcare costs. Older employees tend to have more need for health care, and thus the use of healthcare plans increases. The plans pass on those costs to the employer, and the employer often requires sharing of the costs by the employee. Meeting the commitment to retirees is likely to become an even greater challenge with the aging of the work force (Elliott, 1995). The numbers of retirees are climbing steadily, and there are fewer young and middle-aged people in the work force. Retirement systems, especially early retirement, also affect the costs of healthcare programs. Longer life spans combined with early retirement programs lead to greater demand on healthcare systems. For those jurisdictions that provide healthcare benefits to retirees even after age 65, the increasing costs can be very significant.

As explained in Chapter 8 of this volume, domestic partnership benefits also reflect adjustment of benefits packages to a changing work force and society.

CONCLUSION

Compensation will continue to be a major concern for public sector human resource management and for government generally. The challenge for govern-ment is in balancing its needs in the labor market with controlling costs. The pressures in the political environment are intense. Voters have demonstrated little support for providing the revenue to support enhancement of public sector compensation. The mood is precisely the opposite, with the public showing a strong appetite for further cuts in government cost. The 1994 congressional elections produced a frenzied effort to cut most government programs, although the realities of the political process seem to have tempered the willingness of members of Congress to cut everything. Nonetheless, the public sector will continue to be under close scrutiny for some time.

Public sector compensation systems have been attempting to control growth through numerous approaches. The pressures for public sector pay restraint are likely to make it difficult for government to continue to recruit and retain high-quality employees. If the trends continue, a major crisis in public personnel is imminent. The public sector will not be competitive in compensation because the resources will not be there for either competitive direct pay or benefits. The implications for the public sector are many. The general public and political leaders will not be able to expect the quality or level of public services to be maintained without a change in attitude toward the public sector.

Even as the forces for reduction in government activity continue, the pressures resulting in increasing compensation costs are strong as well. As the economy continues to improve, competition for high-quality employees will increase and the public sector will need to offer competitive pay. Employee benefits costs appear to be on an unending upward spiral. Healthcare cost escalation, in particular, shows no signs of abating. If public employers do not provide coverage in the form of benefits, the likelihood is that taxpayers will have to bear the cost through public-supported health care, as the employees will not be able to bear the cost either.

Reforming the existing systems is a difficult challenge. Employee expectations are well ingrained and inhibit flexibility. It is almost impossible to change what has been promised. Facing such constraints, some jurisdictions have developed two-tiered systems. One represents the old system under which current employees serve; the second applies to newly hired employees. Such approaches are not helpful to morale but may be the cost of reform for some systems.

Managers also inhibit change as they hold on to old routines and approaches. They are supported by elected public officials who often fear giving up control in favor of experimentation and flexibility. Thus the forces of change conflict with inertia and the need to control.

REFERENCES

Adolf, Barbara P. 1992. "Life Cycle Benefits." *Employee Benefits Journal* 18 (March): 13–20.

American Federation of State, County, and Municipal Employees. 1983. *Passing the Bucks: Contracting Out of Public Services.* Washington, D.C.: American Federation of State, County, and Municipal Employees.

—————. 1987. *When Public Services Go Private: Not Always Better, Not Always Honest, There May Be a Better Way.* Washington, D.C.: American Federation of State, County, and Municipal Employees.

Ban, Carolyn. 1991. "The Navy Demonstration Project: An Experiment in Experimentation," in Carolyn Ban and Norma M. Riccucci, eds., *Public Personnel Management: Current Concerns—Future Challenges,* pp. 31-41. New York: Longman.

—————. 1995. *How Do Public Managers Manage? Bureaucratic Constraints, Organizational Culture, and the Potential for Reform.* San Francisco: Jossey-Bass.

Bergel, Gary I. 1994. "Choosing the Right Pay Delivery System to Fit Banding." *Compensation and Benefits Review* 26 (July/August): 34-38.

Brouder, John. 1992. "Labor-Management Cooperation Required to Address Health Care Costs," in Mary Jo Brzezinski, ed., *Public Employee Benefit Plans,* pp. 27-44. Brookfield, Wisc.: International Federation of Employee Benefit Plans.

Cayer, N. Joseph. 1995a. "Local Government Health Care Benefits," in *Municipal Yearbook 1995,* pp. 1-12. Washington, D.C.: International City/County Management Association.

—————. 1995b. "Pension Fund Management," in Jack Rabin, Thomas Vocino, W. Bartley Hildreth, and Gerald J. Miller, eds., *Handbook of Public Personnel Administration,* pp. 377-388. New York: Marcel Dekker.

Congressional Budget Office. 1991. *Changing the Classification of White-Collar Jobs: Potential Management and Budgetary Impacts.* Washington, D.C.: Congressional Budget Office.

Crampton, Suzanne M., and Jitendra M. Mishra. 1995. "Family and Medical Leave Legislation: Organizational Policies and Strategies." *Public Personnel Management* 24 (Fall): 271-289.

Elliott, Robert H. 1995. "Human Resource Management's Role in the Future Aging of the Workforce." *Review of Public Personnel Administration* 15 (Spring): 5-17.

Ellis, Wilson H. 1993. "Employee Benefits: Trends and Issues in the 1990s." *Compensation and Benefits Review* 25 (November–December): 37-41.

Hackelman, Paul. 1994. "Strategies in Controlling Health Care Costs for Public Employees." *Employee Benefits Journal* 19 (December): 8-12.

Handel, Bernard. 1992. "Financing Health Care Coverage in the Public Sector: Costs, Risks and Options," in Mary Jo Brzezinski, ed., *Public Employee Benefit Plans,* pp. 110-122. Brookfield, Wisc.: International Federation of Employee Benefit Plans.

Ingraham, Patricia W. 1993a. "Flexible Pay Systems in the United States Federal Government," in *Pay Flexibility in the Public Sector,* pp. 147-161. Paris: Organisation for Economic Co-operation and Development.

—————. 1993b. "Of Pigs in Pokes and Policy Diffusion: Another Look at Pay-for-Performance." *Public Administration Review* 53 (July/August): 348-356.

Katz, Lawrence F., and Alan B. Krueger. 1993. "Public Sector Pay Flexibility: Labour Market and Budgetary Considerations," in *Pay Flexibility in the Public Sector,* pp. 43-77. Paris: Organisation for Economic Co-operation and Development.

Kearney, Richard C. 1994. "Monetary Impacts of Collective Bargaining," in Jack Rabin, Thomas Vocino, W. Bartley Hildreth, and Gerald J. Miller, eds., *Handbook of Public Sector Labor Relations,* pp. 73-96. New York: Marcel Dekker.

Kellough, J.E., and Haoran Lu. 1993. "The Paradox of Merit Pay in the Public Sector: Persistence of a Problematic Procedure." *Review of Public Personnel Administration* 13 (Spring): 45-64.

Mactas, Mark V. 1992. "Is Your State Underfunding Your Pension Plan?" in Mary Jo Brzezinski, ed., *Public Employee Benefit Plans,* pp. 123-130. Brookfield, Wisc.: International Federation of Employee Benefit Plans.

Maguire, Maria. 1993. "Pay Flexibility in the Public Sector—An Overview," in *Pay Flexibility in the Public Sector,* pp. 9-17. Paris: Organisation for Economic Co-operation and Development.

National Academy of Public Administration. 1991. *Modernizing Federal Classification: An Opportunity for Excellence.* Washington, D.C.: National Academy of Public Administration.

Risher, Howard. 1994. "The Emerging Model for Salary Management in the Private Sector: Is It Relevant to Government?" *Public Personnel Management* 23 (Winter): 649-665.

Risher, Howard H., and Brigitte W. Schay. 1994. "Grade Banding: The Model for Future Salary Programs?" *Public Personnel Management* 23 (Summer): 187-199.

Siegel, Gilbert B. 1992. *Public Employee Compensation and Its Role in Public Sector Strategic Management.* New York: Quorum.

——— . 1994. "Three Federal Demonstration Projects: Using Monetary Performance Awards." *Public Personnel Management* 23 (Spring): 153-164.

U.S. Chamber Research Center. 1990. "Employee Benefits—Survey Data from Benefit Year 1989." Washington, D.C.: U.S. Chamber of Commerce.

Zolkos, R. 1992. "Guvs Eye Pensions, City Taxes." *City and State* (June 1-14): 1, 21.

chapter **15**

Public Employees' Liability for "Constitutional Torts"

David H. Rosenbloom

> *Every person who, under color of any statute, ordinance, regulation, custom, or usage, of any State or Territory or the District of Columbia, subjects, or causes to be subjected, any citizen of the United States or other person within the jurisdiction thereof to the deprivation of any rights, privileges, or immunities secured by the Constitution and laws, shall be liable to the party injured in an action at law, suit in equity, or other proper proceeding for redress. For the purposes of this section, any Act of Congress applicable exclusively to the District of Columbia shall be considered to be a statute of the District of Columbia.*
>
> *Civil Rights Act of 1871, as amended and codified in 42 U.S. Code, Section 1983 (1982)*

Ever since the establishment of the Republic, public employment in the United States has been considered to be a "public trust." Historically, this concept of the special obligations of public employees has led to a variety of restrictions on the constitutional rights they could otherwise exercise as citizens. For instance, the Constitution prohibits federal employees from being electors in the Electoral College and from accepting gifts, offices, emoluments, or titles from foreign governments without the consent of Congress. The document also requires them to swear or affirm their support for it. As early as 1801, President Jefferson sought to restrict the rights of federal employees to engage in electioneering because he deemed such activities "inconsistent with the spirit of the Constitution and his duties to it" (Rosenbloom, 1971: 39–40). Over the years, public employees have faced limitations not only on their political and economic activities but also on their residency, privacy, speech and association, and general liberties (Rosenbloom, 1971; Rosenbloom and Carroll, 1995). Beginning in the 1970s they also became potentially liable for "constitutional torts," which has had the effect of requiring public administration to comport more fully with constitutional law and values. The development of this relatively new legal obligation, its scope, and its implications for public personnel management in the United States are the subjects of this chapter.

Constitutional torts are actions taken by public officials or employees, within the frameworks of their jobs, that violate individuals' constitutional rights in ways that can be appropriately remedied by civil suits for money damages. For instance, the violation of an individual's right to privacy through an unconstitutional search or seizure is such a tort. Civil liability for money damages for constitutional torts can now be potentially attached to most federal, state, and local government employees. The Eleventh Amendment prevents suits in federal court against state governments for money damages for constitutional torts. By extension, state employees cannot be sued as surrogates for state governments in such actions (*Will v. Michigan Department of State Police,* 1989). However, state employees can be sued in their personal capacities for constitutional torts committed within the framework of their jobs (*Hefer v. Melo,* 1991). Local governments can also be sued for compensatory damages for constitutional torts (*Pembaur v. City of Cincinnati,* 1986). By contrast, federal agencies cannot be sued for money damages for their constitutional torts (*FDIC v. Meyer,* 1994). Even public employees who never deal directly with members of the public may face liabilities for violations of their subordinates' constitutional rights.

This chapter focuses on public employees' personal liability for constitutional torts because such liability has had a profound effect on American public administration at all levels of government. It gives every public administrator a direct incentive to know the constitutional law governing his or her job. In the case of public personnelists, personal liability for constitutional torts requires knowing how the Constitution pertains to public employment and building constitutional protections into administrative systems for recruitment, selection, employee development, promotion, adverse actions, reductions in force, equal opportunity, and labor relations. At the outset, however, it should be noted that as important as constitutional torts are for public personnel administration, they are but one remedy for breaches of law by public employees, agencies, or governments. Unconstitutional actions can also be remedied through injunctive relief, administrative appeals systems, and special constitutional doctrines such as the "exclusionary rule" (which prevents much illegally seized evidence from being introduced in criminal trials). Under the Federal Tort Compensation Act of 1988, the federal government is solely responsible for the negligent and wrongful acts of its employees—that is, for ordinary torts committed within the scope of their employment. In drafting the Act, Congress purposefully did not attempt to modify federal employees' responsibilities for their constitutional torts. State and local public employees' liability for ordinary torts varies, but under the statute quoted in the chapter's opening epigraph they are expressly liable for violations of individuals' federally protected statutory and constitutional rights. Violations of these rights can also trigger criminal punishment, but such cases are relatively rare.

PUBLIC OFFICIALS' ABSOLUTE IMMUNITY: THE TRADITIONAL APPROACH

Until the 1970s, under federal law and judicial interpretations, public employees at all levels of government generally held absolute immunity from civil suits arising out of the exercise of their official functions. Under this approach, when a public officer is acting within the outer perimeter of his or her authority, an individual harmed by his or her actions cannot recover damages even if the action taken clearly violates the individual's constitutional rights. For example, in *Stump v. Sparkman* (1978) a state judge enjoying absolute immunity was shielded from a damage suit even though he authorized the sterilization of a "mildly retarded" female high school student under circumstances that failed to protect her constitutional right to due process of law. Moreover, the judge acted without specific legal authorization, but not beyond the ultimate scope of his office. The rationales for granting legislators, judges, executive branch officials, and rank-and-file employees absolute immunity are all somewhat different. But at their root is the belief, developed in common law interpretations, that the activities of government functionaries should not be controlled by individuals' lawsuits or by threats of such actions. As the Supreme Court stated the principle in *Spalding v. Vilas* (1896), the first case on official executive immunity to reach it:

> In exercising the functions of his office, the head of an Executive Department, keeping within the limits of his authority, should not be under an apprehension that the motives that control his official conduct may, at any time, become the subject of inquiry in a civil suit for damages. It would seriously cripple the proper and effective administration of public affairs as entrusted to the executive branch of the government, if he were subjected to any such restraint. (*Spalding v. Vilas*, 1896: 498)

This approach also drew some of its legal strength from the principle of "sovereign immunity," derived from the notion that "the king can do no wrong," that still prevents the federal government from being sued without its own permission and has application to state governments as well. However, the premises behind the application of sovereign immunity in American law are relatively weak, and in practice the principle has waned substantially since the 1940s. In fact, in *United States v. Lee* (1882: 207) the Supreme Court admitted that "while the exemption of the United States and of the several states from being subjected as defendants to ordinary actions in the courts has . . . been repeatedly asserted here, the principle has never been discussed or the reasons for it given, but it has always been treated as an established doctrine."

GENERAL LEGAL TRENDS RELATED
TO OFFICIAL LIABILITY

Whatever the strength of the legal rationales for public employees' absolute immunity, by the 1970s judicial support for the idea had clearly weakened, apparently as a result of two major legal trends. First, there had been an expansion of legal liability generally throughout the American legal system. As Peter Schuck (1988: 4) observes, "On almost all fronts and in almost all jurisdictions, liability has dramatically expanded. It does not seem to matter what kind of party is being sued. Doctor or public official, landlord or social host, government agency or product manufacturer—all are more likely to be held liable today." Although the number of suits initiated per capita may be no larger at present than in colonial times and other periods in U.S. history (Galanter, 1988: 19), plaintiffs appear more apt to win or receive satisfactory settlements because of contemporary judicial interpretations. Schuck, a leading student of "suing government" (1982), concludes:

> Although the new judicial ideology of tort law is complex and multi-faceted, four elements stand out: (1) a profound skepticism about the role of markets in allocating risk; (2) a shift in the dominant paradigm of causation [from determinant to probabilistic causal relationships]; (3) a tendency to broaden jury discretion; and (4) a preoccupation with achieving broad social goals instead of the narrower, more traditional purpose of corrective justice between the litigants. (Schuck, 1988: 6)

Not all of these elements apply directly to liability suits against public employees for constitutional torts. However, there are some broad parallels. For instance, if private individuals can be held liable for conditions in private mental health facilities, why exempt government employees for similar conditions prevailing in public facilities? If private power companies are liable for radioactive leaks, why exempt the U.S. Department of Energy from liability for similar leakage from nuclear weapons plants? If liability is seen as a way of promoting social reforms such as greater safety in the workplace, why not view it as also having the capacity to reform public administrative operations such as the management of prisons? Liability is a powerful tool with many applications. Restricting its use to the private sector—or to the public sector, for that matter—would be impractical.

The second trend toward greater liability for public administrators is rooted in the vast changes in constitutional doctrines initiated by the Warren Court (1953-1969). Beginning in the 1950s, the federal judiciary demonstrated a continuing propensity to afford individuals greater constitutional protections vis-a-vis public administrative action (Rosenbloom, 1983). Whole categories of persons who formerly had very few constitutional protections when interacting with public bureaucracies were granted greater substantive, procedural, and equal protection rights under the First, Fourth, Fifth, Eighth, and Fourteenth Amendments. For instance, public employees were afforded much greater due process protections in dismissals, greater freedom of speech and association (including such activities as whistleblowing and joining labor unions), and equal protection rights. Clients, such as those receiving welfare or public housing, found their interests in these benefits to be clearly protected by due process for the first time. The courts reinterpreted the equal protection clause to overturn the "separate but equal" doctrine that had previously permitted public services, such as education, to be racially segregated. Prisons were also desegregated under the Fourteenth Amendment and were drastically reformed to reduce over-crowding and brutal conditions under the Eighth and Fourteenth Amendments. Individuals confined to public mental health facilities were granted a con-stitutional right to treatment or habilitation. The constitutional rights of persons accused of crimes were expanded to include "Miranda warnings" (*Miranda v. Arizona*, 1966) and other safeguards. The privacy and due process rights of those individuals engaged in "street-level" encounters (Lipsky, 1980; *Terry v. Ohio*, 1968) were also enhanced (see, for example, *Delaware v. Prouse*, 1979; *Kolender v. Lawson*, 1983). More recently, property rights have been strengthened against administrative "takings" by zoning regulations (*Dolan v. City of Tigard*, 1994) and forfeitures (*United States v. Good Real Property*, 1994). Taken together, these developments brought about a revolution in the relation of federal courts to public administration at all levels of government. It is no longer unusual to find a federal court deeply involved in the management of a state or county prison or local school system. A substantial "juridical" element has been added to federalism (Carroll, 1982), and judges have become far more involved in such public administrative matters as budgeting and personnel (Rosenbloom, 1983; Horowitz, 1983; *Missouri v. Jenkins*, 1990).

When individuals possessed few constitutional rights regarding their encounters with public administrators, constitutional torts would necessarily be limited in number. Certainly, police brutality or violations of the Fifteenth Amendment's guarantee of the right to vote regardless of race might have been the basis of suits, but by and large it was difficult for public administrators to violate individuals' constitutional rights simply because individuals held so few sub-stantive, procedural, and equal protection guarantees in the context of their encounters with public agencies. However, once the courts articulate rights for public employees, clients, prisoners, public mental health patients, persons engaged in street-level encounters, and property owners, the potential number and scope of violations becomes substantial. Consequently, some enforcement mechanism is necessary to enable individuals to preserve and vindicate their new protections against administrative action. Enter liability.

FROM ABSOLUTE TO QUALIFIED IMMUNITY: THE RISE OF LIABILITY

As late as 1959, a plurality on the Supreme Court continued to adhere to the principle that:

> It has been thought important that officials of government should be free to exercise their duties unembarrassed by the fear of damage suits in respect of acts done in the course of those duties—suits which would consume time and energies which would otherwise be devoted to governmental service and the threat of which might appreciably inhibit the . . . administration of policies of government. (*Barr v. Matteo,* 1959: 571)

However, after the judiciary had articulated new rights for individuals vis-a-vis public administrators and as liability actions expanded throughout the legal system, the courts sought to establish a better balance between the needs of the government for efficient and effective administration on the one hand and those of individuals for protection of their rights and compensation for injuries to them on the other. In fact, so remarkable had the changes in liability and constitutional law been that by the 1970s the concept of "absolute" immunity for most public officials was clearly out of place.

During that decade, the Supreme Court used two legal vehicles to redefine the liability of public administrators. First, in *Bivens v. Six Unknown Named Federal Narcotics Agents* (1971), the Court held that federal officials could be liable, directly under the Constitution, for breaches of individuals' Fourth Amendment rights. In essence, the Court reasoned that the Fourth Amendment gives individuals harmed by unconstitutional federal searches and seizures a constitutional right to sue the officials involved for monetary damages. Subsequently the Court ruled that similar rights to redress exist under the Fifth and Eighth Amendments (*Davis v. Passman,* 1979; *Carlson v. Green,* 1980). Under ordinary circumstances, individuals can bring suits against federal officials under the First Amendment as well (see *Bush v. Lucas,* 1983, for an exception).

Second, the Supreme Court dramatically reinterpreted the standards for liability regarding local public administrators and officials. The Court permitted—indeed, invited—attorneys to resurrect the Civil Rights Act of 1871, which is now codified as 42 U.S.C. Section 1983. The relevant section of the Act is quoted in the epigraph at the beginning of this chapter. Although well conceived in the Reconstruction era as a means of providing federal judicial protection to former slaves, the Act was rendered virtually moribund by a number of judicial interpretations and doctrines that drastically restricted its coverage (Rosenbloom, 1983; "Section 1983 and Federalism," 1977). In terms of liability, the courts refused to interpret literally the Act's explicit application to "every person who." Instead, the judiciary reasoned that in writing "every person," Congress could not have intended to override the long-standing absolute immunity at common law enjoyed by many state and local government officials, such as legislators and judges, from civil suits for damages. Consequently, even though such officials might be directly responsible for the violation of individuals' federally protected rights, they could not be effectively sued under the Act. It was through the redefinition of official immunity during the 1970s that the Act became a major force in public administration and American law.

The Supreme Court broke away from past interpretations in *Scheuer v. Rhodes* (1974) when it abandoned the concept of absolute immunity for officials exercising executive functions, opting instead for a "qualified immunity":

> In varying scope, a qualified immunity is available to officers of the executive branch of government, the variation being dependent upon the scope of discretion and responsibilities of the office and all the circumstances as they reasonably appeared at the time of the action on which liability is sought to be based. It is the existence of reasonable grounds for the belief formed at the time and in light of all the circumstances, coupled with good-faith belief, that affords a basis for qualified immunity of executive officers for acts performed in the course of official conduct. (*Scheuer v. Rhodes,* 1974: 247-248)

Under this standard, many public officials would be immune from civil suits for money damages if they acted in good faith and reasonably. A year later, in *Wood v. Strickland* (1975: 321-322), reasonability was interpreted to mean whether the official "knew or reasonably should have known that the action he took within his sphere of official responsibility would violate the constitutional rights" of the individuals affected.

Bivens, Scheuer, and *Wood* opened the door to many suits against public administrators by individuals seeking money damages. Under the standard for qualified immunity they relied upon, these suits could allege that the administrators acted without good faith, that is, with malice or reckless disregard of individuals' protected rights. In practice, defending against such a charge proved burdensome for the public officials involved. The issue of "good faith" is considered a matter of fact that may be submitted to juries for determination. Consequently, suits could be drawn out and very expensive to defend. Under such conditions, the process itself was punishment, and public officials were consequently under substantial pressure to settle out of court, without strict regard to the merits of the charges against them. In an age of crowded dockets, elaborate trials in liability suits against public officials also took a toll on the courts. The Supreme Court sought to reduce these pressures in *Harlow v. Fitzgerald* (1982), which established the current standard for public administrators' qualified immunity and liability.

The *Harlow* decision "completely reformulated qualified immunity along principles not at all embodied in the common law" (*Anderson v. Creighton,* 1987: 645). The standard for qualified immunity eliminated the issue of good faith from suits for compensatory damages: "government officials performing discretionary functions, generally are shielded from liability for civil damages insofar as their conduct does not violate clearly established statutory or constitutional rights of which a reasonable person would have known" (*Harlow v. Fitzgerald*, 1982: 818). Motives become irrelevant, as the sole issue is whether the conduct violated individuals' rights of which the administrator should reasonably have known. As a result, many suits no longer have a factual dispute for resolution by a jury. Instead, at issue is a question of law—Did the conduct violate clearly established rights of which a reasonable person would have known?—that can be submitted to a judge for summary judgment. Jury trials are unnecessary, and cases can be resolved more quickly with less expense. The immunity is from suit, not just a defense against liability (*Mitchell v. Forsyth*, 1985). The *Harlow* construction applies to federal officials directly under the Constitution and to local officials through judicial extension.

THE LOGIC OF LIABILITY: DETERRENCE AND JUDICIAL INFLUENCE ON PUBLIC ADMINISTRATION

When the courts do something as dramatic as overturning the effects of centuries of common law, one is impelled to search for their rationale and to assess the effects of the change. The logic of rejecting absolute immunity in favor of qualified immunity (or liability) is clear. First, the liability under prime consideration here is personal liability, not the liability of agencies or government entities. Personal liability is viewed by the Supreme Court as an excellent enforcement mechanism. In the Court's words, "the *Bivens* remedy [i.e., official liability], in addition to compensating victims, serves a deterrent purpose" (*Carlson v. Green*, 1980: 21), and the general point has been to "create an incentive for officials who may harbor doubts about the lawfulness of their intended actions to err on the side of protecting citizens' constitutional rights" (*Owen v. City of Independence*, 1980: 651–652).

The deterrent effect of liability is magnified greatly by the potential assessment of punitive damages against public administrators. In *Smith v. Wade* (1983) the Supreme Court had an opportunity to require the federal courts to apply a tough standard for subjecting public administrators to punitive or exemplary damages. Historically, there have been two standards for such damages generally. One is whether the individual found liable acted with malice in violating the other party's rights, that is, displayed "ill will, spite, or intent to injure" (*Smith v. Wade*, 1983: 37). Recklessness, or a "callous disregard of, or indifference to, the rights or safety of others," is the other standard (*Smith v. Wade*, 1983: 37). In allowing lower courts to use the weaker of the two—recklessness—the High Court reasoned that "the conscientious officer who desires . . . [to] avoid lawsuits can and should look to the standard for actionability in the first instance" (*Smith v. Wade*, 1983: 50), that is, the standard of whether the conduct at issue violated clearly established rights of which a reasonable person would have known. In other words, a finding that compensatory damages are appropriate will often support the assessment of punitive damages as well, because the behavior at issue will manifest at least an indifference to the rights of the injured party. Reliance on recklessness rather than malice makes it easier to use punitive damages to punish public administrators financially and to deter similar illegal behavior on the part of others. Although punitive damages may trigger due process concerns (*Pacific Mutual Life Insurance Co. v. Haslip,* 1991), they are largely open-ended and not technically required to bear a direct relationship to the injury involved. Consequently, plaintiffs may in some cases also allege malice in the hope of recovering more.

A second aspect of the logic of liability is more complex. The courts have constructed public officials' liability so as to enable the judiciary to exercise considerable direction over public administration. In effect, the Supreme Court has made knowledge of constitutional law a matter of job competence for public administrators. As it stated in the *Harlow* case (1982: 819), "a reasonably competent public official should know the law governing his conduct." But what is that law? In the words of former Supreme Court Justice Lewis Powell, "Constitutional law is what the courts say it is" (*Owen v. City of Independence,* 1980: 669). Consequently, public administrators are in effect responsible for understanding the judicial decisions that bear upon their jobs. Moreover, despite the qualifier in *Harlow* that the rights involved must be "clearly established," the Supreme Court has not limited liability to situations in which those "clearly established" rights were specifically articulated in a previous case (*Pembaur v. City of Cincinnati,* 1986). Rather, the concept of "clearly established" extends to constitutional values and principles that should be known by a reasonably competent public official. In other words, even if the constitutionality of some particular act has never been litigated, a public administrator engaging in it may be liable because he or she reasonably should have understood the applicable constitutional concerns.

Overall, therefore, public administrators' liability promotes two objectives apparently held by the judiciary. It is a strong enforcement mechanism for the rights newly granted to individuals vis-a-vis public administration. It also enables the courts to exercise greater direction over public administration. The latter judicial concern has also been manifested in the courts' willingness to entertain suits seeking very broad reforms of administrative institutions or processes, such as public mental health facilities, public schools, and public personnel systems (Rosenbloom, 1983; Chayes, 1976; Horowitz, 1977, 1983; *Missouri v. Jenkins,* 1990).

THE IMPACT OF LIABILITY

It is difficult to assess comprehensively the impact of the change from absolute to qualified immunity. Available analysis suggests that between 1977 and 1983 approximately 3,000 liability suits against government officials and government entities were litigated in the federal courts (Lee, 1987).[1] The majority of these were brought by private individuals (37%), public employees (26%), and prisoners (21%), with businesses (7%), interest groups (5%), and recipients of public assistance (4%) making up the remainder (Lee, 1987: 163, Table 2). The main targets of the suits were public employment practices (27%), alleged violations of due process (26%), invalid statutes (16%), police misconduct (15%), and conditions of confinement (8%). In 1989, over 5,000 suits were pending against federal officials (Farley, 1989: 3). These data indicate that liability suits are a viable option for individuals unconstitutionally or illegally harmed by public administrators' conduct. Presumably a large number of cases are settled before reaching court, and others are resolved by the parties after being docketed or heard. Judging from public administrators' concern with liability and the amounts of money paid out in damages and defense, the impact of such suits has been substantial even though the likelihood of receiving an adverse verdict and personally paying such costs appears to be relatively slim.[2]

Even if more were known about case resolutions, settlements, and damages, however, it would still be very difficult to assess the overall impact of liability upon public administrative practices. Part of the intent of liability is to change public administrators' behavior so as to ensure that it always comports with constitutional requirements. To the extent that the new standard of liability has been successful, public administration is more constitutional and, therefore, the basis for suits is more limited. For example, police today routinely do recite "Miranda warnings," and social service and personnel agencies have built constitutional due process into their standard operating practices. Nevertheless, there are surely many instances in which individuals whose rights are violated by public administrators fail, for one reason or another, to bring cases. Thus only limited inferences can be drawn from the number of cases filed, the absence of more filings, and the outcomes of cases. But clearly liability law is a very active area of adjudication, and public officials are aware that they may face liabilities growing out of their performance on the job.

EXCEPTIONS TO THE GENERAL PATTERN OF PUBLIC OFFICIALS' LIABILITY

There are some exceptions to the current standard for qualified immunity and to the availability of compensatory damages as a remedy for injuries. Employees engaged in adjudicatory or quasi-judicial functions continue to enjoy virtually absolute immunity. In *Butz v. Economou* (1978: 514-517) the Supreme Court held that at least insofar as other remedies or avenues of redress were available, persons "performing adjudicatory functions within a federal agency are entitled to absolute immunity from damages liability for their judicial acts." Included in this category are "those officials who are responsible for the decision to initiate or continue a proceeding" and "an agency attorney who arranges for the presentation of evidence on the record." In *Tower v. Glover* (1984), however, a closely divided Supreme Court refused to convey blanket absolute immunity to public defenders. In *Cleavinger v. Saxner* (1985) the Court likewise refused to extend absolute immunity to members of a prison disciplinary committee.

Because absolute immunity depends on the public official's functions rather than title, a judge can be liable for violations of individuals' constitutional rights in the context of nonjudicial acts, such as hiring clerks or other staff (*Forrester v. White,* 1987). In *Burns v. Reed* (1991) the Supreme Court held that a public prosecutor was entitled to absolute immunity regarding his participation in a probable cause hearing but had only qualified immunity for legal advice he gave to police concerning an investigation. One exception to this functional approach is the U.S. president, whose office conveys absolute immunity (*Nixon v. Fitzgerald,* 1982).

In *Bush v. Lucas* (1983) the Supreme Court held that liability suits were inappropriate remedies in cases brought by federal employees alleging that they had been subjected to illegal or unconstitutional personnel actions. The Court reasoned that federal personnel law provides for elaborate remedies, including hearings before the Merit Systems Protection Board, for such employees. There-fore, in the Court's view, since Congress explicitly created these remedies, it would be improper for the judiciary to fashion additional ones through con-stitutional interpretation. The *Bush* ruling does nothing, however, to prevent nonfederal government employees from using 42 U.S.C. Section 1983 as a means of seeking compensatory damages for personnel actions taken against them in violation of their federally protected constitutional or statutory rights.

THE CONSTITUTIONAL RIGHT TO DISOBEY

Public administrators' potential liability for constitutional torts has generated a concomitant nascent constitutional right to disobey unconstitutional directives. In *Harley v. Schuylkill County* (1979) a federal district court explained that:

> The duty to refrain from acting in a manner which would deprive another of constitutional rights is a duty created and imposed by the Constitution itself. It is logical to believe that the concurrent right is also one which is created and secured by the Constitution. Therefore, we hold that the right to refuse to perform an unconstitutional act is a right "secured by the Constitution . . ." (*Harley v. Schuylkill County,* 1979: 194)

The Supreme Court has not had occasion to consider the constitutional right of public employees to disobey unconstitutional orders. However, the district court's conclusion appears to be supported by strong policy reasons as well as by constitutional imperative. As Robert Vaughn (1977: 294–295), a leading legal scholar in the area of public employees' rights, points out, "Congress and the courts have already adopted the concept of personal responsibility by providing penalties for the wrongful acts of public employees. The courts now have the opportunity to vindicate the concept of personal responsibility by accepting the right of public employees to disobey under appropriate circumstances." To pre-vail in asserting a constitutional right to disobey unconstitutional directives, the employee may have to show (1) that the refusal to obey was based on a sincere belief that the action at issue was unconstitutional, and (2) that he or she is correct in his or her legal analysis.

In practice, of course, disobedience is likely to be a last resort. Public employees also have a constitutional right to seek to eliminate unconstitutional practices through whistleblowing (*Pickering v. Board of Education*, 1968; *Givhan v. Western Line Consolidated School District*, 1979). In modern personnel and management systems, employees will also have the opportunity to discuss their reasons for not wanting to carry out an order with a supervisor, and some resolution short of litigation is highly likely.

IMPLICATIONS FOR PUBLIC PERSONNEL ADMINISTRATION

Public employees' relatively new liabilities for constitutional torts have several important implications for public personnel administration. First, although such liability conveys great benefits by helping to protect constitutional rights, it also adds to the cost of government. Liability makes public employment less desirable. In some areas, including human services and corrections, the risk of personal liability may be among the barriers to recruiting and retaining personnel. Public personnel management, too, is infused with constitutional law and potential liability. In the past decade or so, the Supreme Court has decided several cases involving public employee challenges to personnel actions allegedly violating freedom of speech or association, Fourth Amendment privacy rights, procedural due process, and equal protection.[3] The government plainly could have avoided some of the suits it lost by paying greater attention to clear constitutional doctrine in the first place.[4] Many public personnel systems have sought to protect their employees from liability suits by providing them with legal representation, legal insurance, and/or indemnification. These approaches go a long way toward eliminating the risk of being harmed financially in a lawsuit arising out of one's performance in public office. However, insurance is expensive, the availability of legal representation may depend upon the specific circumstances involved, and indemnification may be unavailable for punitive damages or otherwise incomplete. Moreover, although these measures assuage the psychological anxiety of being sued, they are not likely to eliminate it altogether. Consequently, liability remains an aspect of the public service that may be viewed as a drawback by prospective and current public employees.

Second, public personnel systems will have to take greater responsibility for teaching public servants to be constitutionally competent (Rosenbloom and Carroll, 1990). The public administrator's best defense against liability for constitutional torts is reasonable knowledge of the constitutional rights of those individuals upon whom his or her official actions bear. Universities can teach broad constitutional principles, values, and reasoning in their Master of Public Administration programs, but they are not well suited for teaching the detailed constitutional law that controls specific jobs, such as that of a social worker, police officer, or prison guard. Constance Horner, former director of the U.S. Office of Personnel Management, recognized the important role that personnel agencies can play in constitutional education by calling for "constitutional literacy" among higher-level federal employees (Horner, 1988). Even in the absence of a commitment by personnel agencies, greater training in constitutional matters is virtually certain because, under the Supreme Court's decision in *City of Canton v. Harris* (1989: 390), a local government may be held liable for violations of constitutional rights caused by its failure to take "reasonable steps to train its employees."

Third, education and training in personnel and human resources management for the public sector should cover comprehensively the constitutional rights of public employees and applicants. Public servants have extensive constitutional rights to freedom of speech, association, privacy, due process, equal protection, and liberty (Rosenbloom, 1971, 1983; Rosenbloom and Carroll, 1995). Therefore, virtually any public administrator who engages in hiring, promoting, disciplining, or evaluating subordinates may potentially violate an individual employee's constitutional rights. Traditional personnel policies based on managerial values, such as efficiency as "axiom number one" (Gulick and Urwick, 1937: 192), must now be revised substantially or even abandoned in favor of policies that recognize the importance of public employees' constitutional rights. Personnelists who are poorly trained in the constitutional aspects of public employment will not be in a good position to develop policies that secure the due process, equal protection, privacy, and other constitutional rights of public employees.

Fourth, government agencies and contractors should pay attention to the possibility that privatizing public functions will make private individuals liable for constitutional torts (*West v. Adkins,* 1988). Further, private individuals engaged in state action may lack any immunity at all from liability for their constitutional torts committed under color of law (*Wyatt v. Cole and Robbins,* 1992).

By way of conclusion it should be said that although liability for constitutional torts complicates public administration and public personnel management considerably, it also points toward a public administration that is in greater harmony with constitutional principles and values. The latter has been a goal ever since the adoption of the Constitution in 1789; the rise of liability for constitutional torts at long last makes constitutional values, principles, and reasoning central to the day-to-day practice of public administration.

NOTES

1. Yong Lee (1987) identified approximately 1,700 cases in the odd years from 1977 to 1983, for an average of 425 cases per year. I have assumed that the even years during the period would witness the same number of cases. My figure, like Lee's, pertains only to those cases that were reported. The number of unreported federal district court decisions in official liability cases is unknown, but presumably substantial.

2. Lee (1987: 169) lists the mean awards as follows: 1977, $48,552; 1979, $14,711; 1981, $63,031; 1983, $92,411. The mean for attorneys' fees in 1983 was $33,149. Farley (1989: 3) noted that as of 1989 there were only 44 known adverse verdicts against federal employees, only 6 of which resulted in actual payments by the defendants. However, he points out that the Department of Justice was receiving about 80 requests for representation in such suits each month.
3. Successful First Amendment challenges include: *Chicago Teachers Union v. Hudson,* 1986 (non-union employees in bargaining unit have right not to pay for union's nonrepresentational activities, including political activities, and a procedure for resolving amounts in dispute is required); *Rankin v. McPherson,* 1987 (remark by probationary employee in constable's office expressing hope that next assassination attempt on President Ronald Reagan is successful is constitutionally protected and cannot be the basis for dismissal); *Rutan v. Republican Party of Illinois,* 1990 (partisan affiliation or support is an unconstitutional basis for personnel actions involving ordinary public employees' promotion, training, assignment, and similar actions, as well as hiring and firing); *Waters v. Churchill,* 1994 (speech-related dismissal requires reasonable belief that employee made alleged remarks); *United States v. National Treasury Employees Union,* 1995 (provision banning federal employee acceptance of pay for non–job-related published and other expression violates free speech/press). Fourth Amendment decisions include: *O'Connor v. Ortega,* 1987 (administrative searches and seizures in public workplace must be reasonable in inception and scope if employee meets threshold test of having a reasonable expectation of privacy under the circumstances involved); *National Treasury Employees Union v. Von Raab,* 1989 (suspicionless drug testing of some categories of customs employees is constitutional). For case involving a violation of procedural due process because of dismissal from civil service job without prior notice and opportunity to respond see *Cleveland Board of Education v. Loudermill,* 1985. For case on Equal Protection Clause prohibiting dismissal of non-minority in violation of seniority rights to further equal employment opportunity/affirmative action see *Wygant v. Jackson,* 1986.
4. *Cleveland Board of Education v. Loudermill* (1985) is the clearest example of an instance in which a minimal, almost costless procedure could have obviated a suit. *Wygant v. Jackson* (1986) occurred because a school board agreed to race-based dismissals that would almost certainly result in litigtion and, in high probability, loss as well. The statutory ban in *United States v. National Treasury Employees Union* (1995) was exceptionally broad and the administrative rules pursuant to it were so complex as to appear irrational and arbitrary.

REFERENCES

Anderson v. Creighton, 483 U.S. 635 (1987).
Barr v. Matteo, 360 U.S. 564 (1959).
Bivens v. Six Unknown Named Federal Narcotics Agents, 403 U.S. 388 (1971).
Burns v. Reed, 114 L.Ed. 2d 547 (1991).
Bush v. Lucas, 462 U.S. 367 (1983).
Butz v. Economou, 438 U.S. 478 (1978).
Carlson v. Green, 446 U.S. 14 (1980).

Carroll, James D. 1982. "The New Juridical Federalism and the Alienation of Public Policy and Administration." *American Review of Public Administration* 16 (Spring): 89-105.

Chayes, Abram. 1976. "The Role of the Judge in Public Law Litigation." *Harvard Law Review* 89: 1281-1316.

Chicago Teachers Union v. Hudson, 475 U.S. 292 (1986).

City of Canton v. Harris, 489 U.S. 378 (1989).

Cleavinger v. Saxner, 106 S.Ct. 496 (1985).

Cleveland Board of Education v. Loudermill, 470 U.S. 532 (1985).

Davis v. Passman, 422 U.S. 228 (1979).

Delaware v. Prouse, 440 U.S. 648 (1979).

Dolan v. City of Tigard, 114 S.Ct. 2039 (1994).

Farley, John J. 1989. "The Representation and Defense of the Federal Employee by the Department of Justice." Washington, D.C.: U.S. Department of Justice, Spring (mimeograph).

FDIC v. Meyer, 127 L.Ed. 2d 308 (1994).

Forrester v. White, 108 S.Ct. 538 (1987).

Galanter, Marc. 1988. "Beyond the Litigation Panic," in Walter Olson, ed., *New Directions in Liability Law,* pp. 18-30. New York: Academy of Political Science.

Givhan v. Western Line Consolidated School District, 349 U.S. 410 (1979).

Gulick, Luther, and L. Urwick, eds. 1937. *Papers on the Science of Administration.* New York: Institute of Public Administration.

Harley v. Schuylkill County, 476 F. Supp. 191 (1979).

Harlow v. Fitzgerald, 457 U.S. 800 (1982).

Hefer v. Melo, 116 L.Ed. 2d 301 (1991).

Horner, Constance. 1988. "Remarks on FEI's [Federal Executive Institute's] 20th Anniversary Dinner." Charlottesville, Va., October 14, p. 14.

Horowitz, Donald. 1977. *The Courts and Social Policy.* Washington, D.C.: Brookings Institution.

———. 1983. "Decreeing Organizational Change: Judicial Supervision of Public Institutions." *Duke Law Journal* 88, no. 3: 1265-1307.

Kolender v. Lawson, 461 U.S. 352 (1983).

Lee, Yong. 1987. "Civil Liability of State and Local Governments: Myths and Reality." *Public Administration Review* 47 (March/April): 160-170.

Lipsky, Michael. 1980. *Street-Level Bureaucracy.* New York: Russell Sage.

Miranda v. Arizona, 384 U.S. 436 (1966).

Missouri v. Jenkins, 110 S.Ct. 1651 (1990).

Mitchell v. Forsyth, 472 U.S. 511 (1985).

National Treasury Employees Union v. Von Raab, 489 U.S. 656 (1989).

Nixon v. Fitzgerald, 457 U.S. 731 (1982).

O'Connor v. Ortega, 480 U.S. 709 (1987).

Owen v. City of Independence, 445 U.S. 622 (1980).

Pacific Mutual Life Insurance Co. v. Haslip, 111 S.Ct. 1032 (1991).

Pembaur v. City of Cincinnati, 89 L.Ed. 2d 452 (1986).

Pickering v. Board of Education, 391 U.S. 563 (1968).

Rankin v. McPherson, 483 U.S. 378 (1987).

Rosenbloom, David H. 1971. *Federal Service and the Constitution.* Ithaca, N.Y.: Cornell University Press.

———. 1983. Public Administration and Law. New York: Marcel Dekker.

Rosenbloom, David H., and James D. Carroll. 1990. *Toward Constitutional Competence: A Casebook for Public Administrators.* Englewood Cliffs, N.J.: Prentice-Hall.

———— . 1995. "Public Personnel Administration and Law," in Jack Rabin, Thomas Vocino, W.B. Hildreth, and Gerald Miller, eds., *Handbook of Public Personnel Administration,* pp. 71–113. New York: Marcel Dekker.

Rutan v. Republican Party of Illinois, 497 U.S. 62 (1990).

Scheuer v. Rhodes, 416 U.S. 232 (1974).

Schuck, Peter. 1982. *Suing Government: Citizen Remedies for Official Wrongs.* New Haven, Conn.: Yale University Press.

———— . 1988. "The New Judicial Ideology of Tort Law," in Walter Olson, ed., *New Directions in Liability Law,* pp. 4–14. New York: Academy of Political Science.

"Section 1983 and Federalism." 1977. *Harvard Law Review* 90: 1133–1361.

Smith v. Wade, 461 U.S. 31 (1983).

Spalding v. Vilas, 161 U.S. 483 (1896).

Stump v. Sparkman, 435 U.S. 349 (1978).

Terry v. Ohio, 392 U.S. I (1968).

Tower v. Glover, 467 U.S. 914 (1984).

United States v. Good Real Property, 126 L.Ed. 2d 490 (1994).

United States v. Lee, 106 U.S. 196 (1882).

United States v. National Treasury Employees Union, 63 USLW 4133 (1995).

Vaughn, Robert. 1977. "Public Employees and the Right to Disobey." *Hastings Law Journal* 29: 261–295.

Waters v. Churchill, 62 USLW 4397 (1994).

West v. Adkins, 108 S.Ct. 2250 (1988).

Will v. Michigan Department of State Police, l09 S.Ct. 2304 (1989).

Wood v. Strickland, 420 U.S. 308 (1975).

Wyatt v. Cole and Robbins, 118 L.Ed. 2d 504 (1992).

Wygant v. Jackson, 478 U.S. 267 (1986).

chapter **16**

Oppositional and Connectional Paradigms: Ways to Study and Practice Employee Discipline

Willa Marie Bruce

Current estimates indicate that at any one time, from 10 to 20 percent of the work force are not performing up to capacity, and that those 10 to 20 percent will consume from 80 to 90 percent of supervisory time and effort (Bruce, 1990: 1). In fact,

> problem employees cost North American companies as much as $100 billion a year in worker's compensation, health insurance and benefit costs . . . and that's not including the costs brought on by poor decision making, safety violations, lowered morale, and equipment damage. (Boyd, 1994: 64)

Although comparable data is not available for the public sector, one can suspect that nonproductive employees in government are equally costly. This suspicion is supported by a 1995 U.S. Merit Systems Protection Board (MSPB) report that acknowledges that "misperceptions and disincentives . . . work in combination to keep supervisors from firing their poor performers" (U.S. MSPB, 1995: 9). Yet, there is a dearth of research on the subject of problem employees. A few publications provide checklists of do's and don'ts or give advice about how to remove a problem employee (see, for example, Garnett, 1989; Reeves, 1989; Jerris, 1992; Kruger and McEachern, 1993; Bohlander, 1994; Boyd, 1994; U.S. MSPB, 1995). Fewer still relate successful discipline to good management practices (see, for example, Hollman, 1979; Bryant, 1984; Campbell et al., 1985; Riccucci and Wheeler, 1987; Bruce, 1990; Raper and Myaya, 1993).

Indeed, neither studying nor practicing successful employee discipline is easy. Yet being able to understand and manage the disciplinary process is especially important in the public sector where citizen scrutiny is intense, where due process is mandated, and where removing a poorly performing employee is difficult. This chapter sheds light on the topic of employee discipline by defining the term *discipline* and describing the special requirements of the public sector. It identifies and critiques two paradigms that inform both research and action in the area of employee discipline, describes the practical implications of the two paradigms, deplores the paucity of scholarly research about employee discipline, and offers suggestions for practice and further research.

DISCIPLINE DEFINED

Discipline is a complex concept. Published materials that discuss discipline in the context of managing employees most frequently equate it with *punishment* and *correction.* The term *discipline,* however, also describes the strength of character that comes from self-control, moderation, restraint, and participation in a regimen of self-development—as in "she is a disciplined person." The definitional differences suggest that discipline can be imposed upon someone from without or can emerge from within.

> Punishment refers to an undesirable event that follows an unacceptable behavior and is intended to decrease the frequency of that behavior. . . . Discipline is a broader term. It has three meanings:
>
> • punishment for violations of rules, standards, and direct orders;
> • training that molds, strengthens, improves, or corrects behavior;
> • control gained by enforced obedience.
>
> In other words, discipline has a training and education aspect as well as an enforcement and punishment side. The former is preventative. . . . The latter is corrective. (Cline and Seibert, 1993: 21)

In this chapter the preventative approach to discipline is identified with what Follett (1926) calls "the law of the situation," what Riccucci and Wheeler (1987) and Bryant (1984) designate as "positive discipline," and what Argyris (1993) labels "Model II"—a dynamic approach to organizational problem solving that is connectional and that fosters learning and personal change.

Positive discipline "focuses on coaching, individual responsibility and an adult-to-adult problem solving method" (Bryant, 1984: 79). Here, the worker is viewed as co-creator of the work situation and of problem resolution. Positive discipline is discipline without punishment in which employees are encouraged to solve problems, set their own standards, agree to them, and take personal responsibility for performance. In this approach to discipline the supervisor's role is one of "coach" rather than "judge" (Campbell et al., 1985: 164).

The opposite of positive discipline is the litigious, procedure-driven approach to discipline so often found in the public sector. This is an oppositional method that pits worker against supervisor in a win-lose interaction that is alienating and confrontational. Called "punitive" by Campbell et al. (1985), "traditional" by Bruce (1990), and "industrial" by Riccucci and Wheeler (1987), this approach to discipline is akin to Argyris's (1993) "Model I." It emphasizes a "'here's what you get for what you did' posture, smacks of retribution, and tends to provoke resentment, hostility or apathy in the wrongdoer" (Bryant, 1984: 79).

The structure and process for externally imposed disciplinary actions in the public sector include policies and procedures designed to ensure due process—a formal requirement in government employment (see, for example, Reeves, 1989; U.S. MSPB, 1995). The U.S. Supreme Court described the characteristics of due process when it declared in *Cleveland Board of Education v. James Loudermill et al.* (1985: 1493) that:

> The essential requirements of due process . . . are notice and an opportunity to respond. The opportunity to present reasons, either in person or in writing, why a proposed action should not be taken is a fundamental due process requirement. . . . [T]he tenured public employee is entitled to oral or written notice of the charges against him, an explanation of the employer's evidence and an opportunity to present his side of the story.

Because of due process requirements, public sector supervisors faced with disciplinary decisions must make certain to follow all established procedures completely and to talk with their own immediate supervisor and with the agency or installation's personnel officer. The discussion about styles and paradigms of employee discipline in this chapter is meant to promote due process, not negate it. Indeed, due process provides protective insurance for both employer and employees. In this latter part of the twentieth century, however, those who manage the people in organizations are coming to recognize that discipline is more than procedural justice. Rather, it can be a way of organizational life.

The next section describes Models I and II, which depict the types and effects of organizational assumptions upon manager-worker interactions and illustrate the thought processes that generate ideas about what is appropriate and effective discipline.

MODEL I AND MODEL II

In introducing Models I and II, Argyris (1993: 50) argues that two very different "theories of action" subconsciously govern decisions about the kinds of strategies that will be used to bring about change, whether in people or in organizations. He found that the most prevalent is Model I, which he describes as follows:

> Model I theory-in-use . . . has four governing values:

1. Achieve your intended purpose.
2. Maximize winning and minimize losing.
3. Suppress negative feelings.
4. Behave according to what you consider rational. (Argyris, 1993: 52)

Argyris argues that the consequences of these values are likely to be "defensiveness, misunderstanding, and self-fulfilling and self-sealing prophecies." Model I creates an oppositional environment in which one person can be pitted against another. It is the stuff of which traditional-punitive-industrial approaches to discipline are made.

Argyris offers Model II as an alternative and better approach to managing change. "The governing values of Model II are valid information, informed choice, and vigilant monitoring of the choice in order to detect and correct error" (p. 55). Effects of these values are very different from those of Model I. Because Model II values encourage productive reasoning, the consequences of internalizing its values are openness, understanding, and process learning. Model II creates a collaborative environment of shared problem solving in which activities such as positive discipline can flourish.

In the next section, Models I and II are integrated into two paradigms for understanding employee discipline. I call these paradigms the *oppositional* and the *connectional*, to reflect the pattern of beliefs that they represent.

PARADIGMS FOR UNDERSTANDING EMPLOYEE DISCIPLINE

Although not previously identified in the literature on employee discipline, two paradigms have informed inquiry and practice. I have named them the *oppositional* and the *connectional*. Even though, theoretically, paradigms are value-neutral, I argue that the oppositional paradigm contains the traditional, punitive approaches to employee discipline and is, therefore, not adequate for successful human resource management. I suggest that the connectional paradigm is a normative approach representative of what might be called "good management" and, therefore, able to contribute to effective and sustained learning and positive change.

The oppositional paradigm and the connectional paradigm are opposite ways of knowing and doing, as well as opposite belief systems about employees in the disciplinary process. Thinking about employee discipline from the standpoint of the oppositional paradigm will result in different research design, different observations, different expectations, *and* different solutions than will that same thinking if it originates in the connectional paradigm. Clearly the ontological and epistemological assumptions on which one bases inquiry influence the results of that inquiry. The next two subsections describe how the two different paradigms shape the study and practice of employee discipline.

The Oppositional Paradigm

In the oppositional paradigm, employee discipline is viewed as action or forces outside the employee that affect what the employee does, and employees are seen as persons who are products of what happens around them. They are expected to need disciplining. In describing employees' behavior in an environment where punitive discipline was a part of organizational norms, Riccucci and Wheeler (1987: 50) say that employees "were acting rebelliously toward this system of discipline because they were treated as disobedient children." Raper and Myaya (1993) suggest that under norms of opposition, employees are seen as replaceable and expendable resources to be manipulated, rather than engaged. In other words, the oppositional paradigm can be likened to McGregor's Theory X managerial assumptions that people will not perform consistently and satisfactorily unless they are made to in some way. Behavior is thought to be deterministic and able to be manipulated.

Those who share the assumptions of the oppositional paradigm will explain employee discipline by suggesting ways in which a supervisor can "make" a problem employee perform through use of some external set of behaviors directed toward that employee. Here a supervisor is expected to take corrective action, impose a set of penalties, document certain types of behavior, and rely on the personnel system to motivate or eliminate the nonperforming employee. Thinking in the oppositional paradigm places the burden of success or failure on the shoulders of the one designated to impose discipline.

Disciplinary actions in this paradigm are fraught with suspicion and resentment by the employees to whom they are directed. The account presented in Box 16.1 illustrates the kind of personal and professional trauma that punitive actions can generate.

In the oppositional paradigm, leadership might be viewed as "transactional" (Raper and Myaya, 1993) or "contractual-instrumental" (Barnard, 1938). The employee-employer relationship is seen as one of exchange—a quid pro quo arrangement in which supervisor and employee are both separate and unequal, engaged in a parent-to-child interaction where the supervisor represents authority.

Research questions that might emerge from the oppositional paradigm are: "What are the rules and how do I enforce them?" "What is the effect of a supervisor's actions (or of identified policies and procedures) on employee performance?" "Does using the disciplinary process change an employee's behavior?" "What can I do to reduce absenteeism?" Whatever the question, methodology will be nomothetic and empirical understanding through measurement, analysis, and explanation will be sought.

Managerial practice in the oppositional paradigm consists of techniques for identifying performance problems and lists of methods for prodding, nudging, correcting, and punishing. So that the reader will be cognizant of these traditional approaches to employee discipline, the next section describes the oppositional approach to discipline as punishment.

BOX 16.1   "You Can't Tell Me What to Do."

Steve (not his real name) refused to be told what to do. Because he did not agree with a decision his supervisor made, he prepared and distributed a flyer criticizing his supervisor. When he was suspended for this, he filed a grievance. During the grievance procedure, he shouted that he despised the supervisor and called him a "pompous ass" and a "baby." Then Steve grabbed the supervisor's files and threw them at him; next he took the supervisor's keys and threw them in a wastebasket; then he ended the performance by grabbing a pencil from behind his supervisor's ear and throwing it across the room.

"Who do you think you are? You can't tell me what to do!" he shouted.

SOURCE: Willa Bruce, *Problem Employee Management* (Westport, Conn.: Quorum, 1990): 9-10.

Discipline as Punishment.   The oppositional paradigm has largely governed the thinking on employee discipline in the public sector. Frequent usage, however, does not make it the most effective way to approach discipline, only the most common. Traditionally, the term *employee discipline* has been synonymous with *punishment, chastisement,* or *corrective action.* Discipline is what happens to employees who fail to perform or who do not follow stated policies and procedures. Indeed, the terms *discipline* and *punishment* are often used interchangeably.

Because of this, employee discipline is often viewed as a set of difficult and uncomfortable activities that most supervisors don't want to do. For example, the MSPB (1995) study of the federal workplace found that of the 78 percent of supervisors who have had an employee with a performance problem, only 23 percent took action to demote or remove the employee. The employee's "negative attitude" discouraged 55 percent of the supervisors from acting, and legal requirements in due process legislation discouraged 34 percent of them.

A recent report of the International City County Managers Association (Siegle, 1994) is representative of the oppositional paradigm. It advises that supervisors can recognize performance problems in the early stages by watching for decreased productivity, changes in mood, unusual absenteeism or tardiness, frequent or prolonged absences from the work area, and/or preoccupation with personal problems.

When these signs appear, the advice typically given recommends imposition of punitive action of some sort. It includes (1) accepting that the employee has a problem that is not likely to disappear, (2) documenting his or her failing job performance, (3) confronting the employee, and (4) suggesting that the employee seek the help of a counselor or accept disciplinary action (Bruce, 1990: 47).

All this advice places the burden of getting a worker to perform on the shoulders of a supervisor. It suggests that "good management" involves identifying and solving problems; and, unfortunately, it ensures that the employee who has failed to perform or is conducting him- or herself in an unacceptable manner will consume approximately 80 to 90 percent of the supervisor's time and energy. That's a very discouraging prospect, but it can be a reality for the supervisors who view themselves as oppositional to their workers.

Working under the assumptions of the oppositional paradigm, supervisors seem not to think about discipline until a work-related crisis occurs. Then they latch on to the punitive disciplinary process in order to "solve the problem" or "fix the employee." In my experience this is as apt to complicate the problem as it is to resolve it, for it underscores the oppositional underpinnings that pit worker against management. It instigates a "fight" and "fight back" mentality that often leads to discharge, appeal, arbitration, retribution, and restitution.

Recent research indicates that of the eight to nine thousand rights arbitration cases that come before the American Arbitration Association each year, about half come from public sector employees, and "discipline and discharge constitute almost 30 percent of all public sector rights arbitration" (Bohlander, 1994: 73). In this clearly oppositional environment, the top ten reasons given for over-turning disciplinary actions in order by number of cases are: (1) the evidence did not support the charge, (2) evidence supports the charge but there are mitigating circumstances, (3) management committed procedural errors, (4) punishment was harsh, (5) management was partly at fault, (6) the rule was applied unreasonably, (7) there were no rules, (8) there was inconsistent enforcement of rules, (9) the employee did not know he or she was violating a rule, and (10) the employee's right to due process was violated.

Research also indicates that supervisors who base their actions within the oppositional paradigm often feel helpless when faced with disciplining an employee. They take the burden of their assumed responsibility seriously, yet somehow they hope that if they ignore the problem it will go away. Other employees often contribute to a supervisor's procrastination by forming a "conspiracy of silence" in which they cover up for someone's poor performance or inappropriate conduct (Hollman, 1979). Even supervisors participate in the conspiracy. When they do, the behavior that calls for discipline can escalate and accumulate.

Timing of discipline is a critical component in the oppositional paradigm. Policies and procedures, as well as advice of those who have supervised employees, indicate that discipline must begin at the first suspicion of misconduct or poor performance. Supervisors who postpone action inhibit and weaken their power over employees, but the concomitant failure to interact with employees does nothing to change employee behavior.

Following an oppositional disciplinary process in the public sector is a complex set of activities, because public employees have more rights than those who work in private industry. They are protected from arbitrary and capricious disciplinary actions of supervisory and managerial personnel, since "firmly embedded in statutory and case law is the principle that a worker, protected by civil service, cannot be disciplined (i.e., punished) except for 'cause'"

(Garnett, 1989: 30). Proving cause is not easy. Garnett, who is a labor law attorney, argues that civil service law "may have the operational effect of tolerating an incompetent work force" (p. 30). That, of course, is not its intent. Rather, the intent of the law is to protect the rights of public employees who otherwise might be victims of political maneuvering.

Supervisors in the public sector must understand legal constraints and civil service definitions and requirements. Further complicating performance management in the public sector is the societal expectation that government employees be exemplary individuals both on and off the job. Yet determining whether or not off-duty behavior is cause for disciplinary action is not simple. For off-duty behavior to be the cause of disciplinary actions, it must have a detrimental effect on the employing agency and be so inappropriate that discipline does not constitute an unwarranted intrusion into the employee's personal life (Kruger and McEachern, 1993: 30).

Traditionally, the personnel office has been viewed as the repository of knowledge about legislative and procedural mandates, as well as about policies that emerge from court or arbitration decisions. Personnel officers, with their responsibilities to ensure compliance with the legal requirements of the personnel process, have been put in an oppositional mode that requires focus on procedural development and oversight (Ross, 1984: 15).

The evidence indicates that the assumptions of the oppositional paradigm have become deeply ingrained in the personnel management process. These Model I theories tell "individuals to craft their positions, evaluations, and attributions in ways that inhibit inquiries into them and tests of them with others' logic" (Argyris, 1993: 52). Thus managerial personnel at all levels are caught up in a win-lose mentality that is difficult to challenge.

Clearly, discipline is a complex process with many nuanced issues. Within the oppositional paradigm, worker and supervisor are pitted against one another with each seemingly trying to outsmart or out-act the other. This relationship is very different in the connectional paradigm, as are the assumptions that govern the practice and understanding of discipline.

The Connectional Paradigm

In the connectional paradigm, discipline is conceptualized as inner strength that produces actions. Employees are seen as persons who are co-creators of their work environment. Within this paradigm employees are not assumed to be in need of discipline; rather, they are viewed as disciplined. They are seen as valuable resources to be nurtured and empowered. Here the organizational culture is itself integral to the development of the person, because it is viewed as "a direct purveyor of influence and values, of hopes and aspirations, dreams and desires" (Denhardt, 1993: 40).

In other words, the connectional paradigm can be likened to McGregor's Theory Y managerial assumptions that employees are capable and interested persons who find work as natural as play. Although they may need encouragement, job skills training, and necessary tools to perform their jobs, they do not need coercion or adversarial interactions. Even when something goes wrong at home or at work and performance suffers, those operating within the connectional paradigm would suggest that employees can be challenged and strengthened by engaging in "productive reasoning" (Argyris, 1993: 55) or "adult-to-adult problem solving" (Bryant, 1984: 79).

The connectional paradigm is reminiscent of Follett's (1926; cited in Shafritz and Ott, 1992: 151) "law of the situation" in which "the giving and receiving of orders ought to be a matter of integration through circular behavior." Speaking against what I have called the oppositional paradigm, Follett observes that "the more you are 'bossed,' the more your activity of thought will take place in the bossing-pattern, and your part in that pattern seems usually to be opposition to the bossing" (p. 153).

Practice in the connectional paradigm is not described in print as often as that which is embedded in the oppositional paradigm. In published works, scholars are apt to cite surveys and practitioners are apt to provide checklists. Research in the connectional paradigm, like other forms of interpretive studies, is scarce. Box 16.2 provides a manager's story to illustrate how the paradigm can inform both learning and action. The reader will want to contrast this account with that in Box 16.1 to see the different kinds of results a manager might engender from the assumptions of each paradigm.

In the account presented in Box 16.2, one can picture the situation and contrast the results of the oppositional and connectional approaches to supervision. One can also see how a potential "discipline problem" with a "problem employee" was averted simply by replacing opposition with connection. Whether that outcome will always hold is, of course, unknown. But the fact that the outcome did occur once is enough to suggest that it might again; and when it does, questions about employee discipline in similar situations become relevant.

Those who share the assumptions of the connectional paradigm explain employee discipline by suggesting that discipline is personal responsibility shared by both employee and supervisor, who can plan together for the mutual betterment of themselves, their clients, and the organization as a whole. Proponents of the connectional paradigm assume that people accept what they help to create. Supervisors and employees are co-creators. Decision making is participative. There's a commitment to one another and to the organization that transcends the traditional contractual-instrumental, quid pro quo, workplace value system. And there's a critical distinction in the fundamental philosophy of management concerning the employer-employee relationship that replaces transactions with transformation (Raper and Myaya, 1993).

Research questions that emerge from the connectional paradigm might be: "How does the employee or the supervisor feel about the work setting?" "How do shared values affect the disciplinary process?" "What are the norms about working late, or leaving early, or problem solving, or dealing with emergencies?" "What are the shared concerns of employees?" "How are people working together or problem solving or helping one another?" Whatever the question, the methodology will be idiographic

BOX 16.2 Learning the Law of the Situation.

Two months ago I began a new job. For the first time in my professional life, I am responsible for the supervision of an employee. Developing effective supervisory skills as well as becoming a "good supervisor" is my top goal in my new position.

My position includes supervision of an administrative aide. The administrative aide started two weeks before me. In this time she had developed ways of coping with situations and tasks that came up in her day-to-day routine. When I started, I realized that some of the ways in which she was handling her workload were decreasing her efficiency and she was not using good time management techniques. Our first one-on-one meeting was the perfect opportunity for me to point out these inefficiencies and tell her my ideas about how to remedy them. I set up ways for her to transfer phone calls and times for her to leave the reception area to do filing. I instructed her to use her computer to set up address lists to merge with documents.

The meeting was a success, I thought, and I assumed immediate implementation of the new and efficient practices. Instead the orders were not carried out, or they were in a diluted form and did not have the effect I intended. In our next weekly meeting I pointed this out to her. The administrative aide told me that she did not know how to merge address lists with documents on her computer. Also transferring calls was a problem because of individual voice mail systems, and the times I had given her to work on filing were wrong. I had told her to file in the morning, but mail did not come till afternoon.

Then I realized what I was doing wrong. I was not looking at the whole picture and circumstances surrounding each activity. The orders should have flowed from the situation, rather than me trying to dictate the situation with orders. Also, I did not bring my employee into the decision process. Her involvement was crucial. Equally important was my lack of teaching. Orders do not replace teaching.

At our next meeting, I asked my employee for ideas on how we could improve things. We brainstormed ideas. She suggested a new time to file. We now have a message center and I taught her to use the merge/mail feature on her computer. I have reformed my "order giving." That has helped me become a better supervisor.

SOURCE: Kristi Farmer, "Learning the Law of the Situation" (unpublished paper, 1995).

and the answer will be understood to be different, based on who is asked the question, and the way that person experiences the organization.

Here, persons are not considered products of what happens around them; rather, they are believed to be creators of shared vision and shared experiences. In other words, behavior is thought to be voluntaristic and the employee to be the "controller rather than the controlled, the master rather than the marionette" (Burrell and Morgan, 1980: 2).

A self-conscious commitment to the assumptions and behaviors of the connectional paradigm can be expected to generate a productive, participative work setting in which discipline is not something to be dreaded but, rather, is a way of organizational life. Practically, discipline is seen as positive, shared action. This perspective to discipline is discussed in the next section.

Discipline as Positive Action. Actions within the connectional paradigm might be called "just good management," for "good management" occurs when workers are empowered rather than overpowered. These actions can, however, be theoretically grounded in the work of Follett (1926), Riccucci and Wheeler (1987), and Argyris (1993). Follett argues for the value of the "face-to-face suggestion" and a "joint study of the problem" (p. 154). Riccucci and Wheeler describe a process of "positive employee discipline" that is participative, enhances employer-employee relations, and can prevent costly litigation. Argyris suggests that people generally lack the skills necessary to engage in learning. His book, *Knowledge for Action* (1993), is a description of his teaching those skills within what I call the *connectional paradigm* and his bringing about effective change by engaging organizational members in ongoing, learning-oriented conversations.

Within the connectional paradigm, "discipline is seen as involving self-control and a sense of personal responsibility for conduct, behavior, and performance" (Tracey, 1991: 95). Here, discipline can be understood as a mutual undertaking by both supervisor and employee in which both develop the inner strength to take responsibility for personal actions and share a commitment to learning from their interactions.

In their description of the PEP (Positive Employee Performance) process in Pinellas County, Florida, Riccucci and Wheeler (1987: 50) explain, "A positive approach incorporates coaching and counseling sessions, and these three formal PEP steps—an oral reminder, a written reminder and a paid decision-making leave." Through this process, it is expected that employees who engage with their managers in participative problem solving will arrive at mutually acceptable solutions that can be implemented without further ado. As Campbell et al. (1985: 164) note, "Once employees set their own standards and agree to them, it's a lot more difficult for them to say they didn't understand the rules."

However, shared problem solving is only the first step in positive discipline. In Pinellas County, Florida, for example, in the event that the employee does not implement the agreed-upon solution, the supervisor offers an oral reminder (not a reprimand) about the previously shared agreement and documents the conversation in the employee's personnel file. If, after three months, the problem is corrected, the reminder record is purged from the file. If the problem is not resolved, a written reminder is provided and documented. It remains active for a longer period of time. If that too is ineffective, the employee is offered a "decision-making leave," which is a leave without pay to demonstrate a good-faith effort to enable the employee to think through the consequences of a decision to change or to not change the problem behavior (see Riccucci and Wheeler, 1987).

> By confronting the issue from this different, more adult perspective, managers perceive the entire issue of discipline from a different angle. No longer caught up in trying to determine the punishment that fits the crime, managers now explore positive ways to build commitment, generate self-discipline, and ensure individual responsibility. (Campbell et al., 1985: 164)

Although it is true that the punitive approach to discipline is very much a part of the public personnel practice, the emergence of cooperative and generative activities (such as that in Pinellas County) opens the way for non-punitive, creative approaches to discipline in the best connotation of the word— a sense of personal responsibility for conduct, behavior, and performance.

For those who might wonder about the sustained effectiveness of discipline without punishment, the following figures are important. When the Texas Department of Mental Health and Mental Retardation instituted a nonpunitive discipline system for its 26,000 employees, in the first quarter alone "the change to a nonpunitive system saved the department more than 1.7 million (dollars)" (Campbell et al., 1985: 164). Thus the practice of discipline as positive action can be a powerful organizational asset.

CONCLUSIONS

This chapter has demonstrated that employee discipline is studied and practiced from the perspectives of two dichotomous paradigms. One is *oppositional* and transactional. The other is *connectional* and transformational. Although the latter paradigm is not so firmly ingrained in the personnel management literature as is the former, it is firmly rooted in the classical work of Follett and the contemporary ideas of Riccucci, Argyris, and Denhardt. It deserves more attention in the research and philosophical discussions about employee discipline than it has received.

The paucity of research in the specialized area of employee discipline in the public sector is deplorable. Most of what exists is a "how-to" approach consisting of checklists and advice with little or no acknowledgement of the underlying assumptions that spawned the commentary. What's needed are comprehensive studies with paradigmatic assumptions clearly articulated. In the oppositional paradigm, research will be empirical, systematic, and explanatory.

In the connectional paradigm, research will be interpretive and heuristic. Discovery of new knowledge using both paradigms will inform and enhance the practice of employee discipline.

Traditionally, employee discipline has not been a part of mainstream inquiry into issues of personnel management. Scholars seem almost to have assumed it away by preoccupation with the grander challenges such as motivation, pay-for-performance, diversity management, and challenging work. Yet discipline is an issue that continues to plague practitioners. Scholarship is needed to understand, inform, and improve their practice. This chapter has laid a foundation for that scholarship by identifying and describing two paradigms from which it might emerge. Perhaps there are others. Perhaps in the process of examining employee discipline, new ways of being together in organizations will be discovered.

REFERENCES

Argyris, Chris. 1993. *Knowledge for Action.* San Francisco: Jossey-Bass.

Barnard, Chester. 1938. *The Functions of the Executive.* Cambridge, Mass: Harvard University Press.

Bohlander, George. 1994. "Why Arbitrators Overturn Managers in Employee Suspension and Discharge Cases." *Journal of Collective Negotiations* 23, no. 1: 73-89.

Boyd, Malia. 1994. "One Bad Apple." *Incentive* (August): 64-69.

Bruce, Willa. 1990. *Problem Employee Management.* Westport, Conn.: Quorum.

Bryant, Alan. 1984. "Replacing Punitive Discipline with a Positive Approach." *Personnel Administrator* 29, no. 2 (February): 79-98.

Burrell, Gibson, and Gareth Morgan. 1980. *Sociological Paradigms and Organizational Analysis.* London: Exeter.

Campbell, David, R. L. Fleming, and Richard Grote. 1985. "Special Report: Discipline without Punishment—At Last." *Harvard Business Review* 63, no. 4 (July–August): 162-178.

Cleveland Board of Education v. James Loudermill et al. 1985. 84 L.Ed. 2d 506.

Cline, Erik, and Pennie Seibert. 1993. "Help for Discipline Dodgers." *Training and Development* 47, no. 5 (May): 19-22.

Denhardt, Robert. 1993. *Theories of Public Management.* Belmont, Calif.: Wadsworth.

Farmer, Kristi. 1995. "Learning the Law of the Situation." Unpublished paper.

Follett, Mary. [1926] 1992. "The Giving of Orders," in Jay Shafritz and J. Steven Ott, eds., *Classics of Organization Theory,* pp. 150-158. Pacific Grove, Calif.: Brooks/Cole.

Garnett, William. 1989. "Incompetence in Civil Service Cases. *New York State Bar Journal* (April): 30-35.

Hollman, Robert. 1979. "Managing Troubled Employees: Meeting the Challenge." *Journal of Contemporary Business* 8, no. 4 (October): 43-57.

Jerris, Linda. 1992. *Solving Employee Discipline and Grievance Problems: Special Report.* New York: Panel Publishers.

Kruger, Daniel, and Michael McEachern. 1993. "An Analysis of Arbitration Decisions Involving Off-Duty Conduct of Public Employees." *Government Union Review* 14, no. 4 (Fall): 29-55.

Kuhn, T. 1970. *The Structure of Scientific Revolution,* 2nd ed. Chicago: University of Chicago Press.

Raper, James, and Susan Myaya. 1993. "Employee Discipline, a Changing Paradigm." *Health Care Supervisor* 12, no. 2 (December): 67–77.

Reeves, T. Zane. 1989. "Due Process before Discipline: What Public Employers Need to Provide." *Employee Responsibilities and Rights Journal* 2, no. 3 (Spring): 163–171.

Riccucci, Norma, and Gary Wheeler. 1987. "Positive Employee Performance: An Innovative Approach to Employee Discipline." *Review of Public Personnel Administration* 8, no. 1 (Fall): 49–63.

Ross, Joyce. 1984. "A Definition of Human Resources Management," in J. Matzer, ed., *Creative Personnel Practices: New Ideas for Local Government,* pp. 13-17. Washington, D.C.: International City-County Manager's Association.

Siegle, Elizabeth. 1994. "Disciplining Difficult Employees—Progressive Approaches." *ICMA Management Information Service.* Washington, D.C.: ICMA.

Tracey, William. 1991. *The Human Resources Glossary.* New York: AMACOM.

U.S. Merit Systems Protection Board. 1995. "Removing Poor Performers in the Federal Government." Issue Paper. Washington, D.C.: MSPB Office of Policy and Evaluation.

Williams, T. Hensley. 1995. "How to Discipline Your Staff without Getting Sued." *Medical Economics* (January 23): 63–67.

Current and Future Challenges

$\mathbf{T}$he final section of this book addresses issues that are more explicitly political. All levels of government are struggling not only with fiscal problems but also with debates over the proper role and structures for government. These debates concern both the size of government and the appropriate management styles.

In Chapter 17, Carolyn Ban addresses both the political and management challenges of cutback management. She stresses the need to plan carefully the downsizing effort to ensure the minimum damage to the organization and its employees.

Evan Berman, in Chapter 18, explores the challenge of total quality management (TQM) from several perspectives. He looks both at the role of personnel staff in implementing TQM throughout the organization and at the issues raised by applying TQM to the human resources function itself.

Privatization continues to be a controversial issue. In Chapter 19, Donald Kettl critically examines the effects of privatization on public employees, unions, and civil service systems. He concludes that privatization, although having some advantages, is hardly a "magic bullet" for improving government.

Finally, in Chapter 20, "Political/Career Relationships in Public Management: The Good, the Bad, and the Possibilities," Patricia Ingraham looks at the complex and changing relationships between political and career executives in government and the broader issues of the relationship between politics and merit. As she points out, the creation of the Senior Executive Service gave presidents tools with which to control the bureaucracy. But "reinventing government," with its emphasis on decentralization and deregulation, may weaken executive control of the career service.

chapter **17**

The Challenges of Cutback Management

Carolyn Ban

Some government reform efforts have reflected the goal of improving public management (see, for example, Chapters 1 and 12 of this volume). But the current environment of reform is also driven by financial and political forces. First, governments at all levels are facing real fiscal constraints. Second, reformers are responding to widespread negative images of government and to the continued perception of government as too large, too intrusive, and too inefficient. These forces, combined, have been a powerful incentive for cutting the size of government—not just government budgets, but also government work forces. These pressures have been particularly strong at the federal level (Kettl and DiIulio, 1995), but they have also been evident in many state and local governments.

This chapter examines the human resource issues involved in cutback management. It explores both the technical issues involved in managing cuts and the broad challenges that public sector managers face in trying to manage organizations and programs in the difficult cutback environment.

MANAGING THE CUTS: DECIDING WHOM TO CUT AND HOW TO CUT

Managers of an organization confronted with shrinking budgets face a series of difficult choices, chief among them deciding where to make the cuts and selecting the techniques for effecting cuts. Although the focus in this discussion is primarily on the human resource (HR) issues involved in this process, it is an area where HR policy and budget policy are inextricably linked. Indeed, the organization's success in downsizing will depend to a large extent on the ability

269

of top management, the budget staff, and the HR staff to work together to find the least damaging ways to make cuts.

Whom to Cut: Across-the-Board versus Targeted Cuts

One of the most basic decisions any organization facing cuts must make is where to take the cuts. Certainly the easiest way to cope with cuts is simply to require all parts of the organization to absorb the losses equally. This has two obvious advantages: It is simplest to manage, since it requires virtually no analysis or planning; and it is likely to be perceived as equitable by most organization members. As Biller put it, "It is a device by which all members of the community or organization can come to believe in the fairness with which the matter is being handled. [The message is] 'We are all being asked to shoulder some responsibility in this matter'" (1980: 607).

But across-the-board cuts have major shortcomings as well. First, the sense of equity is more apparent than real. In fact, such cuts penalize the more efficient organizations and reward those that have maintained slack resources. Levine (1979) labels this the "efficiency paradox." The biggest problem with across-the-board cuts is that, in Levine's words, "it is not responsible management." That is, the organization's leadership has failed to take advantage of (or even abdicated the responsibility for) the opportunity to manage the organization strategically. That means deciding what are the core organizational functions, those central to the mission, and protecting them. It also means taking a hard look at the organization and identifying functions that are no longer necessary or parts of the organization that are, at least relatively, overstaffed. The pressure to cut can be used as an opportunity to make needed changes that might have encountered more resistance in flusher times. Indeed, the National Academy of Public Administration (1995: ix) cites as one of the "key lessons learned" by organizations that have undergone downsizing the need to "restructure the organization to reflect the changed mission, staffing levels, and performance expectations before determining staff reductions."

Deciding where to take cuts is not just a matter of rational planning, however. It is also a political process in which the concerns of outside actors, from the legislature to relevant interest groups, must be considered (McTighe, 1979). Senior managers may need to consult with legislative leaders to make sure they "buy in" to the reduction strategy. In highly charged political situations, the legislature may give managers little leeway; the legislators may explicitly require that cuts be taken in certain programs or may dictate how the cutback process should be managed.

In sum, making intelligent decisions about where to take cuts requires serious strategic planning, based on policy priorities and involving both the budget office and the human resources office working together to analyze staffing needs. If the organization has in place a work force–planning capacity, projections can be made about the size of staff cuts needed, given normal attrition rates, and about the need to reallocate staff to meet the needs of high-priority functions. Unfortunately, this ideal is not often met. In spite of repeated calls for strategic human resource management (see Chapter 2 of this volume), human resource staff are often left out of the initial planning and are brought in only later, when decisions are being made about how to implement cutback plans made elsewhere.

Scholars studying organizational strategies report mixed findings. On the one hand, MacManus (1993: 299), studying local governments in Florida, found that the most commonly reported reduction strategy for jurisdictions facing general budget shortfalls was across-the-board cuts, "whereas programmatic cuts or elimination are more likely to follow major statutory changes, particularly those of an intergovernmental nature." The preference for across-the-board cuts appeared to reflect a belief that the fiscal stress would only be temporary. In contrast, when Lewis (1988) examined employment changes in 154 large cities, he found that cuts did not come across-the board; rather, cities tended to focus their cuts on their less efficient organizations.

How to Cut: RIFs versus Attrition

Once managers have decided where cuts should be taken, the next strategic choice is how to go about making the cuts. Many organizations, faced with relatively small budget cuts, will first cut or delay as many nonpayroll expenses as possible. Travel and training are often the first expense categories to be frozen. Organizations may delay purchases of new equipment; cities may postpone capital improvements or repair (MacManus, 1993; MacManus and Pammer, 1990). But, given that salaries and benefits are a huge proportion of most public organizations' budgets, large cuts almost invariably mean at least considering either reducing the size of the work force or finding other ways to cut personnel costs. The two main options for downsizing organizations are layoffs (generally referred to in the public sector as reductions in force, or RIFs) and attrition, with or without incentives to leave. In some cases, organizations have also attempted to cut costs without reducing the size of the work force, via "give-backs" such as reduced benefits or via furloughs (i.e., temporary layoffs). Each of these approaches has advantages and disadvantages.

RIFs: Only as a Last Resort? The common wisdom is, indeed, that RIFS should only be used as a last resort, because actually laying people off is the most expensive and traumatic option, at least in the short term. Studies comparing the financial cost to the organization show that RIFs are quite expensive, both because of administrative costs and because of immediate expenses, such as unemployment chargebacks and the need to pay departing employees for accrued leave time. Cost-benefit analysis of RIFs also can include such indirect costs as lost productivity, because of the widespread disruption caused by a RIF; costs of administering the RIF, including outplacement and counseling services (NAPA, 1995); and even loss of state income tax revenues and losses due to increased alcohol abuse (Greenhalgh and McKersie, 1980).

Not all the costs of RIFs are financial. RIFs invariably are a traumatic event for the whole organization. The psychological pain, even for those who retain their jobs, is severe. As we see in more detail below, the impact on morale may be drastic.

The organizational trauma is greatly exacerbated by the rules that govern RIFs in the public sector. They are remarkably complex and arcane. And they are clearly designed to protect individuals, rather than to serve the needs of the organization (Kingsbury, 1995). RIF rules permit organizations to target positions, not individuals. The organization is divided into competitive levels and competitive areas. The individual occupying the position that is eliminated may be able to bump people at the same competitive level who have lower seniority or to retreat to a job held previously, or one very similar, at a lower level. Individuals are ranked in a complex formula that factors in employment status, veterans status, seniority, and performance. Taken to its extreme, the provision of bump and retreat rights means that for each position eliminated, four or even more people may be moved out of their jobs into positions that, for various reasons, may be less desirable to them. The results are sometimes ludicrous; a RIF at the Office of Personnel Management in 1982 resulted in a Ph.D. psychologist being assigned to work in the mail room. Given the long chain of bumping, the person who was actually "RIFfed out the door" was the mail room clerk. Since the Ph.D., who bumped down, retained his salary (which was considerably higher than the clerk's) for two years, one can see that the salary savings were far from immediate. Retreating may also place people in positions they have not occupied for years, for which their skills are, at best, rusty. These people will need training or retraining and may have serious morale problems (Ban, 1995).

The federal government moved in 1986 to mitigate somewhat the disruption caused by RIFs. The revised RIF rules weighted performance more heavily by adding additional years of service based on an average of the last four years' performance appraisals. In addition, bumping and retreating were limited to three grades or three grade intervals (for jobs where people normally move up two grades at a time)[1] (Ban, 1995).

Nonetheless, factors designed to maximize individual protections worsen costs to the organization. Among these is the fact that regulations encourage agencies to draw competitive areas as large as possible, which gives affected individuals more opportunities to bump or retreat, thereby worsening the disruption (Kingsbury, 1995).

RIFs pose another dilemma for organizations, particularly those that have made serious affirmative action efforts. Because seniority plays such a large role in deciding who actually leaves, RIFs are likely to fall disproportionately on women and people of color, who are often the last hired and thus the first fired (NAPA, 1995). Attempts to protect these groups by circumventing the seniority system have not been successful; indeed, the Supreme Court has upheld the use of bona fide seniority systems in conducting RIFs (see Chapter 4 in this volume and Roberts, 1981).

This bleak picture certainly explains why many experts feel that RIFs should be a last resort. But organizations still do, on occasion, conduct RIFs. Why? First, if the cuts the organization faces are huge enough, and if it is clear that they are permanent, the organization may have no choice. For example, the Defense Department has been forced to use RIFs on several occasions, reflecting both the massive budget cuts and sharply changing mission as a result of the end of the cold war. Furthermore, a RIF is like drastic surgery—painful but over with relatively quickly, whereas, as we shall see, attrition is a slow, drawn-out process. Sometimes it may be better to simply take the cuts, get it over with, and then allow the agency to get on with its work. Further, RIFs have one significant advantage over attrition: It is easier to use the RIF process strategically by targeting those parts of the organization that are nonessential or that are relatively overstaffed.

Finally, and most troubling, RIFs may be used politically or symbolically. Political leaders who are elected by campaigning against "big government" tend to focus not on reducing the size of the budget but on cutting the size of the work force. Indeed, RIFs are a powerful symbol. Although stories on TV with interviews of sad employees packing up their offices may tug at the heartstrings, they may be just the message that a conservative administration is trying to get across to the public. Clearly, the RIFs run by President Reagan in 1982 were not cost-based. Rather, they conveyed a clear political message. Such politically motivated RIFs, when not tied to changes in agency mission, may force agencies to turn to contractors to cover essential functions. The inclusion of specific targets for cutting the size of the federal work force in the National Performance Review appears to be similar political symbolism (Kettl, 1995).

Attrition: A Kinder, Gentler Way to Cut?   As we saw above, RIFs often feel as traumatic as major surgery. In contrast, shrinking a work force via attrition feels more like being on a long-term diet, with low-level discomfort over a long period of time, and with the pain worsening the longer the process drags on. Even when budgets are not shrinking, Congress micromanages federal agencies' work-force levels through the mechanism of personnel ceilings (Ban, 1995). State agencies' ceilings are often controlled by the state budget office. When the size of the work force must actually be reduced, then agencies turn to hiring freezes, counting on normal attrition to reduce gradually the number of employees. When results are needed more quickly, the agency may, if permitted, offer separation incentives, such as early retirement or "buyouts" (i.e., severance payments) to encourage people to leave. For instance, to meet the personnel targets set by the National Performance Review, federal agencies were permitted to pay buyouts of up to $25,000 per employee. The General Accounting Office estimated that agencies would pay buyouts to over 100,000 employees in fiscal year 1995 (U.S. General Accounting Office, 1995).

Certainly, using attrition is a more humane way to make cuts; most people who leave do so voluntarily (although recent cuts in New York State government were taken in part by forcing some people to take early retirement). It is also usually less expensive in the short run, although offering "sweeteners" such as buyouts obviously raises the costs. But attrition creates difficult problems for management, because it is hard to manage both equitably and strategically. Simply put, the people who leave are often not those whom the organization wants to lose (Ropp, 1987; NAPA, 1995). Those who are most mobile are the high achievers and the ones in such sought-after specialties as computer programming or nursing. These people must, often, be replaced in order to fulfill critical functions. For example, an overly broad early retirement offer in New York State in the 1980s led to the departure of many doctors from state mental hospitals.

Further, people don't always leave from the parts of the organization that are overstaffed. Indeed, the progressive effects of attrition may exacerbate these imbalances, as work is piled on to people in understaffed divisions, thereby harming morale and increasing turnover in a downward spiral.

To avoid these problems, senior management must actively plan and manage the attrition process. This requires, first, accurate work-force planning data so that critical skills can be identified and staffing levels can be examined across the organization. Then it requires hard choices. For example, buyout or early retirement offers should be targeted carefully to occupations or parts of the organization where reductions are desired. The harder choices come as attrition starts to take hold. Strategic management of the process requires holding some positions in a central pool to be allocated to parts of the organization that are experiencing real shortage (Rubin, 1980). The inevitable effect is to centralize decision making at a high level in the organization, often in the budget office. Such reforms as the National Performance Review and Total Quality Management call for delegating authority and empowering both workers and line managers. But the "bean-counting" mentality and need for control that accompany downsizing drive power up the hierarchy, leading to frustrated and disenfranchised managers (Ban, 1995).

In sum, attrition, too, has its drawbacks. Not only is it hard to manage, but it has a gradually corrosive effect on morale and productivity as a culture of scarcity permeates the organization. Further, attrition, precisely because it is a more humane approach, makes less of a political splash. The Clinton administration has, in fact, shrunk the federal work force far more drastically than did the Reagan administration, actually bringing the federal work force under two million for the first time since the mid-1960s (*Federal Times,* 1996), but it is not clear, absent the drama of a major RIF, that the media or the voters have noticed.

Cutting Costs without Cutting People: A Stop-Gap Approach.   Ideally, managers would like to avoid permanently separating staff, particularly when they suspect that the budget problems may be only temporary. Although large cuts will probably force a certain degree of downsizing of the work force, some jurisdictions have explored other possibilities. One is to utilize reductions in the level of pay and benefits. As Chapter 14 of this volume makes clear, benefits costs have been rising sharply. Tight fiscal constraints can lead management to use the collective bargaining process, where the work force is union-ized, to ask for "givebacks," that is, to try to convince the union that it must make concessions, agreeing to no pay raise or even a cut in pay, or bargaining to reduce benefit levels or to change work rules in order to cut costs. Indeed, management may actually threaten layoffs to try to extract financial concessions from unions (Rich, 1983). Unions in some jurisdictions have resisted this strat-egy (Roberts, 1981), but in others they have actually formed partnerships with management to try to craft strategies for saving money or even for downsizing. Druker and Robinson (1992) report on one such effort in Maine, in which labor and management utilized a quality of work life (QWL) process to devise cutback approaches.

Other stop-gap measures focus on temporary or voluntary reductions in working hours as a way to reduce payrolls. These include furloughs, reduced working hours, job sharing, or voluntary leave policies (Robinson and Druker, 1992).

Research on recent state practice (Robinson and Druker, 1992) shows that in fact the most popular method for making cuts was attrition, or freezing hiring (used by 34 of the 47 states surveyed). The second most frequent approach was to provide inducements for retirement (used by 18 states). Several states utilized voluntary approaches to reduce work hours or attempted to reduce costs, and 13 states actually laid off workers. It is clear that at the federal level as well, organizations see RIFs as a strategy of last resort (NAPA, 1995).

MANAGING DURING AND AFTER CUTS

Whatever method the organization chooses for making cuts, the result will be a series of difficult challenges both for the organization as a whole and for individual managers. Briefly, they include coping with the process itself, particularly for RIFs, and coping with the impact of cuts on morale and on the related issue of productivity.

Managing during a RIF

Whereas attrition causes organizational stress, RIFs are in a class by themselves for creating trauma throughout an organization. Indeed, Williams (1994) classes them as a form of "organizational violence." Among the predictable responses are widespread anxiety during the RIF process, since it is often unclear who will be affected and in what way. Rumors abound, and new rumors spread almost daily (Hirschhorn et al., 1983). Those who do lose their jobs often display open anger and hostility (Ban, 1995). Organizations that have been most successful in conducting RIFs attempt to manage the rumor mill by releasing as much information as possible. They often provide concrete support to those being RIFfed, including outplacement services, counseling, and courses on such topics as job search skills and stress management (Ban, 1995).

Strategic choices in how the RIF is managed will have differential effects on different populations. For example, drawing the competitive area narrowly may provide fewer opportunities for some people—even those with many years of seniority—to bump or retreat to other positions. But, conversely, it may mean less dislocation and less organizational adjustment for those who remain.

Maintaining Morale

Although it is obvious that RIFs are traumatic for those who lose their jobs, both RIFs and attrition are also likely to affect the morale of those who remain. In fact, one recent study found that "to our surprise, some of the saddest people we talked with are those who remain inside, settling in in the reengineered organization and hoping the old days will return. Some of the happiest and most successful people we interviewed were those who left or were laid off and built new lives" (Johansen and Swigart, 1994: xii–xiii).

The survivors of a RIF have already lived through months of anxiety and uncertainty. Even if they knew they were unlikely to go out the door, they worried about who might bump them and where they might end up. Long after the process has taken place, feelings of anxiety may remain. Survivors may feel anger and show lower levels of organizational commitment, in response to what they perceive as the breaking of an implicit contract that guaranteed employees job security as long as their work was adequate. By breaking this implicit contract (i.e., by letting others go), the organization has made it clear to its members that this might happen again.

That decreased sense of security may be combined with some level of "survivor's guilt" (Brockner et al., 1986) or what Noer (1993) calls "layoff survivor sickness." According to Noer, the symptoms of layoff survivor sickness are anger, depression, fear, distrust, and guilt. These symptoms may be quite long-term. The problem is that organizations tend to give support and counseling to those who leave, not to those who stay (Noer, 1993).

Although attrition is not as dramatic or traumatic, the message given employees by early retirement or buyout offers is not that they are valued but that the organization wants to push them out the door. And the older they are (and, usually, the deeper their commitment to the organization), the more aggressively they will be pushed.

One clear lesson is that cutback has powerful emotional meaning (Hirschhorn et al., 1983). The way both RIFs and attrition are presented to the organization and the language used carry important symbolic messages. Noer goes so far as to refer to "the language of layoffs as the language of assassination" with its references to "taking out" or "terminating" people. Other managers use intentionally abstract language, talking about "restructuring" or "rightsizing" (Noer, 1993: 23–24). Withholding information about the process or providing misleading information increases the loss of trust (Williams, 1994).

The uncertainty about the future affects all those who remain. It may also affect the organization's ability to rebuild, when the need arises, or to replace those with critical skills, because the fact that the organization had recently cut back (particularly if a RIF was conducted) will make it less attractive as an employer in the future.

In short, individual managers will be concerned about how to maintain both morale and organizational commitment. This will be even more challenging than usual because most monetary rewards are likely to dry up. Although some organizations may maintain some pay-for-performance plan, both salary increases and money for bonuses are unlikely to be available. Opportunities for travel and training, often used as "perks," are also likely to have been cut or eliminated. And the opportunity to take on challenging new assignments, which might have been seen as a positive in the past, will be looked at more skeptically by employees being asked to take on the work of those who have left. Further, taking on new work or additional work is far less likely to lead to promotion in the new leaner, flatter organizations.

In this environment, all kinds of positive reinforcement become very important. Employees need to know that their skills and their work continue to be valued. Reward ceremonies and plaques, even though little or no money is attached, convey the message that the individual manager and the organization recognize the contribution that an individual or group is making. Organizational ceremonies and social events are important ways of reestablishing employees' sense of identity with the organization (Noer, 1993). The increasing use of teams as a way to structure work poses a number of dilemmas, one of which is that many organizations have not yet figured out how to reward the work of teams (Johansen and Swigart, 1994; see also Chapter 18 in this volume).

At an organizational level, there is often a need to rebuild trust. Some organizations focus on improving communication with employees or on surveying employees to try to assess the nature and level of morale problems (Luce, 1983). But, as Luce makes clear, this is a slow process: "Morale has to be painstakingly rebuilt" (p. 70).

Maintaining Productivity

At the same time that cutbacks are wreaking havoc with morale, they are making it harder for managers to manage their programs and to deliver the work or services for which they are responsible. Unless the organization has approached the cutback process strategically and "reengineered" its operations, often the remaining work force is expected to do the same amount of work, in the same way, with fewer people. Clearly, if some of those people have been bumped down to jobs they don't want and perhaps haven't done for years (if ever), productivity problems will be compounded. The obvious answer is that these "new" employees need training; but in a cutback environment, the training budgets may already have been slashed, and production pressures may be so great that managers are hesitant to release employees from work for training.

The underlying dilemma for managers is that the multiple stresses of managing in a downsized organization create role strain for them. In the terms of the competing values model of management roles (Quinn, 1984; Quinn, et al. 1990; Ban, 1995), on the one hand, they need to play the roles of "producer," "director," and "monitor," focusing on setting tasks and making sure the work of the organization gets done, at the same time that they are asked to focus more on the human relations aspect of the job, as "mentor" and "facilitator," providing emotional support and guidance to individual employees or groups. At the same time, since the organization is short-handed, first-line supervisors are under increasing pressure to pick up some of the work that would normally be done by their subordinates, in order to meet deadlines—in other words, they become what I have called elsewhere "worker-managers" (Ban, 1995).

In sum, the pressures created by managing in a cutback environment are difficult for all workers, but perhaps most for supervisors, who face the tough challenge of simultaneously addressing production demands and the need to maintain morale in difficult circumstances.

CONCLUSIONS

This brief introduction to some of the difficult challenges posed by cutback management leads to certain conclusions for managers. First, critical to successful downsizing is the capacity to target the cuts. Doing so requires the organization to engage in strategic planning to decide what functions are core and thus must be protected, and to redesign the organization to reflect current priorities. In choosing how to take cuts, managers face a dilemma: The most humane ways of cutting are the hardest to use strategically. Management sends very powerful messages about its values both through the means it chooses for cutting and through the choice of which units bear the brunt of cuts (Luce, 1983).

A critical concern for management has to be attempting to maintain morale and productivity among the workers who remain. Involving employees in the decision process, either through their unions or through other consultative mechanisms, increases the perceived fairness of the process and the odds of "buy-in."

Even with such consultation, and even if cuts are well managed, severe cuts can lead to declining capacity and to decreases in services to the public. Contrary to popular perception, many government organizations are not operating with large slack capacity. On the contrary, many already come close to being "hollow organizations" that are unable to fulfill their missions as defined by law because of inadequate capacity. Sharp cuts will inevitably create even more such "hollow" organizations (Milward, 1994), which are forced to hire temporary employees or contract out work to meet their statutory obligations.

Finally, cutback situations are a two-edged sword when it comes to organizational change. Such situations may force organizations to restructure or to try new approaches. They may force management to deal with issues that could safely be ignored when budgets were more generous. But individuals coping with the uncertainty of a cutback environment may become more rigid, more self-protective, and more resistant to reform precisely because they feel so vulnerable. This dilemma is particularly relevant for those attempting to implement the National Performance Review (see Chapter 1 in this volume). The increasing focus of that effort on major cuts may undermine the attempts to implement other parts of the NPR proposals, particularly deregulation and use of more participative management techniques.

NOTE

1. The only exception is for veterans with a 30 percent or greater "service-connected compensable disability," who can retreat as many as five grades or grade levels (U.S. Merit Systems Protection Board, 1987).

REFERENCES

Ban, Carolyn. 1995. *How Do Public Managers Manage? Bureaucratic Constraints, Organizational Culture, and the Potential for Reform.* San Francisco: Jossey-Bass.

Biller, Robert P. 1980. "Leadership Tactics for Retrenchment." *Public Administration Review* 40, no. 6: 604-609.

Brockner, Joel, et al. 1986. "Layoffs, Equity Theory, and Work Performance: Further Evidence of the Impact of Survivor Guilt." *Academy of Management Journal* 29, no. 2: 373-384.

Druker, Marvin, and Betty Robinson. 1992. "Offsetting the Downside of Downsizing: Implementing QWL Options." *Journal of Health and Human Resources Administration* 15: 183-208.

Federal Times. 1996. "Streamlining Government." April 8: 2.

Greenhalgh, Leonard, and Robert B. McKersie. 1980. "Cost-Effectiveness of Alternative Strategies for Cut-Back Management." *Public Administration Review* 40, no. 6: 575-584.

Hirschhorn, Larry, et al. 1983. *Cutting Back: Retrenchment and Redevelopment in Human and Community Services.* San Francisco: Jossey-Bass.

Johansen, Robert, and Rob Swigart. 1994. *Upsizing the Individual in the Downsized Organization.* Reading, Mass.: Addison-Wesley.

Kettl, Donald, 1995. "Building Lasting Reform: Enduring Questions, Missing Answers," in Donald F. Kettl and John J. DiIulio Jr., eds., *Inside the Reinvention Machine: Appraising Governmental Reform.* Washington, D.C.: Brookings Institution.

Kettl, Donald F., and John J. DiIulio Jr. 1995. *Cutting Government.* Washington, D.C.: Center for Public Management, Brookings Institution.

Kingsbury, Nancy. 1995. "Smaller Government: New Paradigms for Reductions-in-Force." *Public Manager* (Summer): 13-16.

Levine, Charles H. 1979. "More on Cutback Management: Hard Questions for Hard Times." *Public Administration Review* 39, no. 2: 179-183.

Lewis, Gregory B. 1988. "The Consequences of Fiscal Stress: Cutback Management and Municipal Employment." *State and Local Government Review* 20: 64-71.

Luce, Sally R. 1983. *Retrenchment and Beyond: The Acid Test of Human Resource Management.* Ottawa, Canada: Compensation Research Centre of the Conference Board of Canada.

MacManus, Susan. 1993. "Budget Battles: Strategies of Local Government Officers during Recession." *Journal of Urban Affairs* 15, no. 3: 293-307.

MacManus, Susan, and William J. Pammer Jr. 1990. "Cutbacks in the 'Country': Retrenchment in Rural Villages, Townships, and Counties." *Public Administration Quarterly* 14: 302-323.

McTighe, John J. 1979. "Management Strategies to Deal with Shrinking Resources." *Public Administration Review* 39, no. 1: 86-90.

Milward, H. Brinton. 1994. "Implications of Contracting Out: New Roles for the Hollow State," in Patricia W. Ingraham and Barbara S. Romzek, eds., *New Paradigms for Government.* San Francisco: Jossey-Bass.

National Academy of Public Administration. 1995. *Effective Downsizing: A Compendium of Lessons Learned for Government Organizations.* Washington, D.C.: NAPA.

Noer, David M. 1993. *Healing the Wounds: Overcoming the Trauma of Layoffs and Revitalizing Downsized Organizations.* San Francisco: Jossey-Bass.

Quinn, Robert E. 1984. "Applying the Competing Values Approach to Leadership toward an Integrative Framework," in J. Hunt et al., eds., *Managerial Work and Leadership: International Perspectives.* Elmsford, N.Y.: Pergamon Press.

Quinn, Robert E., Sue R. Faerman, Michael P. Thompson, and Michael R. McGrath. 1990. *Becoming a Master Manager: A Competency Framework.* New York: Wiley.

Rich, Wilbur. 1983. "Bumping, Blocking and Bargaining: The Effect of Layoffs on Employees and Unions." *Review of Public Personnel Administration* 4, no. 1: 27-43.

Roberts, Robert N. 1981. " 'Last Hired, First Fired' and Public Employee Layoffs: The Equal Employment Opportunity Dilemma." *Review of Public Personnel Administration* 2, no. 1: 29-48.

Robinson, Betty D., and Marvin Druker. 1992. "A Contextual Model for Public-Sector Downsizing." *Sociological Practice Review* 13: 73-82.

Ropp, Kirkland. 1987. "Downsizing Strategies." *Personnel Administrator* 32: 61-64.

Rubin, Irene. 1980. "Retrenchment and Flexibility in Public Organizations," in Charles H. Levine and Irene Rubin, eds., *Fiscal Stress and Public Policy.* Beverly Hills: Sage.

U.S. General Accounting Office. 1995. *Federal Downsizing: Observations on Agencies' Implementation of the Buyout Authority.* Testimony before the Subcommittee on Civil Service, Committee on Government Reform and Oversight, House of Representatives (GAO/T-GGD-95-164). Washington, D.C.: U.S. General Accounting Office.

U.S. Merit Systems Protection Board. 1987. *Reductions in Force: The Evolving Ground Rules.* Washington, D.C.: U.S. Merit Systems Protection Board.

Williams, Lloyd C. 1994. *Organizational Violence: Creating a Prescription for Change.* Westport, Conn.: Quorum Books.

chapter **18**

The Challenge of Total Quality Management

Evan Berman

INTRODUCTION

In recent years, Total Quality Management (TQM) has become a popular productivity improvement strategy (Berman and West, 1995a, 1995b; Cohen and
Brand, 1993; Milakovich, 1991, 1995b; Garrity 1993; West, 1995). Applications
of TQM in government often aim to improve service quality, to increase alignment
between citizen needs and government services, and to decrease service cost,
time, and errors. This increasing use of TQM in the public sector poses three
distinct challenges to public personnel management. *First,* it must ensure that
organizational personnel policies are consistent with the practice of TQM:
Applying TQM may require the review of existing policies for performance
appraisal, compensation, selection, and other traditional concerns of public
personnel managers (see, for example, Hyde, 1993; Siegel, 1993; Carnevale, 1995;
West, Berman, and Milakovich, 1994a). *Second,* public personnel managers must
be credible experts in the implementation of TQM. This is because they are often
called on to provide employee training in TQM skills, as well as advice to
management on implementation strategies (see, for example, Reynolds, 1994;
Brown, Hitchcock and Willard, 1994). *Third,* TQM has profound implications for
the public personnel function: Personnel departments that apply TQM to themselves expand their range of services, emphasize quality services to a multitude
of clients or stakeholders, and use employee empowerment, continuous improvement, and benchmarking as key service delivery paradigms. This chapter discusses these challenges and focuses on progress that public personnel managers
have made toward addressing them.

What Is TQM?

TQM is a productivity improvement philosophy and strategy whose principal tenet is to serve customer (i.e., stakeholder) needs. TQM is characterized by (1) a commitment to customer-driven quality; (2) employee participation in quality improvement; (3) a bias toward taking actions based on facts, data, and analysis; (4) a commitment to continuous improvement; and (5) developing a systemic perspective on service means and ends (Berman and West, 1995a, 1995b; Barzelay, 1992). TQM applications vary widely because organizations emphasize different stakeholder needs, and because organizations differ in the extent to which they make use of empowerment and quantitative measures for benchmarking and continuous improvement (Berry, 1991). Organizations that implement TQM tend to be flatter, more empowered, and more focused on outcomes (rather than on processes), and they experience greater communication than traditional hierarchical organizations. Employee empowerment (i.e., increased decision making by employees) is especially important in TQM, because empowerment allows employees to respond to client needs in a timely and customized way (Berman, 1995a).

Historical Development

The origins of TQM in public organizations are based on past experiences of TQM in large U.S. manufacturing companies. These organizations adopted and adapted TQM in response to Japanese competition in automobiles and consumer electronics in the 1970s. Initial TQM applications, in the early 1980s, resulted in increased product quality and reduced manufacturing time and costs. Applications in the late 1980s emphasized increased cross-functional teamwork to reduce product development time. TQM was popularized by the writings of Deming (1986), Juran (1980), Crosby (1979), and Ishikawa (1985). Awareness of TQM in U.S. industry has also been increased by the prestigious Malcolm Baldrige National Quality Award (Hunt, 1993). This annual award is given by the federal government to firms that achieve high standards of quality. Past winners include Cadillac, Xerox, Ritz-Carlton, and AT&T. Since the late 1980s, TQM has been increasingly applied in medium-size firms and hospitals. Government and nonprofit organizations are the latest frontiers in TQM implementation.

Implementing TQM in the public sector poses some distinct challenges as compared to the private sector. Public sector TQM applications are often committed to serving a broader set of stakeholders. Typical stakeholders include clients, taxpayers, voters, and legislators. When the needs of these stakeholders conflict, differences are resolved in public arenas—which constitutes another difference between the sectors. A third difference is that public managers experience greater oversight from elected officials than do private managers from board members.

TQM is increasingly being used by public managers (see, for example, Berman and West, 1995a; GAO, 1992). In general, TQM is attractive to public managers because it provides them with a strategy for redirecting agency priorities by focusing on new stakeholder needs, for improving the performance of public agencies, and for reducing citizen and client complaints (Berman,

1994). Implementing TQM is also consistent with notions of professional competence, and expertise in TQM may increase a public manager's marketability: Many state and local government positions now require familiarity with quality improvement (ICMA, 1995). To further promote TQM in government, the federal government established the Federal Quality Institute, which provides TQM training and support for federal agencies (FQI, 1991). Due to budget cuts, the Office of Personnel Management abolished FQI in 1995, but some training functions were taken over by OPM (*Federal Times,* 1995). Many state and local governments have also made quality an important productivity priority (Milakovich, 1995a). In addition, many graduate public administration programs now offer coursework in "quality improvement," and many textbooks discuss TQM as a productivity improvement strategy. These developments should help ensure that future public managers are familiar with TQM.

Despite the growing use of TQM, a persistent concern is its "staying power" (Bleakley, 1993). Past productivity improvement strategies—such as Excellence in the 1980s and Organizational Development in the 1970s—have often been short-lived. The concern is that TQM may be a fad. However, the lack of staying power may reflect problems of implementation rather than questions about the "merit" of meeting stakeholder needs. Important barriers are tradition, employee cynicism, competing demands on employee time, inadequate rewards for employees, traditional hierarchical structures, inadequate funding for training, employee resistance to change, inadequate support from top management, competing demands on leadership, inadequate team-building skills, and disconnect between productivity and strategic goals (Berman, West, and Milakovich, 1996). These barriers were also present in past productivity improvement efforts, some of which are now part of TQM (e.g., empowerment). Many of the above-mentioned problems suggest an increased role for public personnel management, because of its potential contributions to overcoming employee resistance and helping leaders to select effective change strategies.[1]

WHAT ARE THE "RIGHT" PERSONNEL POLICIES FOR TQM?

The use of TQM presents challenges to existing human resources (HR) policies in such traditional areas as performance appraisal, training, and labor-management relations. Specifically, existing policies are often inadequate and impede the application of TQM. Although other chapters in this book discuss some of these areas generally, the following concerns are related to TQM.

Performance Appraisal

In recent years, the issue of using performance appraisal in organizations that use TQM has been widely discussed. The chief concern is that the use of performance appraisals creates a climate that is damaging to the installation of

TQM. The following concerns have been raised. First, whereas performance appraisals aim to increase organizational performance by improving the performance of individuals, a core TQM tenet is that systems, not individuals, are the cause of most organizational underperformance (Hyde, 1993; Halachmi, 1993). The reasons for poor organizational performance in TQM are often postulated to be inadequate focus on client needs and satisfaction, and insufficient employee empowerment; these conditions are not addressed by individual performance appraisal. In addition, performance appraisal focuses on individual performance and often excludes elements of teamwork that are required for TQM.

Second, the use of performance appraisals introduces divisiveness between individuals, because differences between employees are magnified in a zero-sum competition for merit awards (Daley, 1992). Although these awards are often small, they have important symbolic value for both employees and organizations. Such divisiveness and competition is contrary to TQM, which relies on cooperation and teamwork in order to improve productivity.

Third, performance appraisals involve assessments of work behaviors and interpersonal communication measures that, despite the appearance of objectivity, are often subjective and produce a climate of fear. Bowman (1994) suggests that performance appraisals are a tool through which managers control the workers and enforce conformity. This chokes off intrinsic motivation, self-esteem, and, hence, the possibility of innovation (Moen, 1989). TQM organizations, however, depend on employee creativity and initiative to identify and meet stakeholder needs.

In spite of these problems, performance appraisals are difficult to abolish. One reason is that employees want to know how well they have done and what is expected of them. Another reason is that managers like performance appraisals, in part because they help keep workers under control (Bowman, 1994). Thus the challenge is to adapt performance appraisals to the requirements of TQM. Daley (1992) believes that the above-mentioned objections can be overcome by developing more objective rating methods. He also recommends using "developmental appraisals," which link performance appraisals to training needs rather than merit increases. Hyde (1994) suggests using an annual "performance review" in which employees and supervisors are asked to complete an annual assessment of work processes, communications, planning processes, and other "systems"-level activities. Another possibility is reducing the importance of annual performance appraisals by emphasizing ongoing feedback from co-workers, supervisors, and customers. It is plausible to suggest that frequent feedback and formal development planning increase organizational performance more than formal but infrequent feedback and informal, inadequate development planning.

Some organizations have begun to adapt their performance appraisals in response to the above-mentioned concerns and suggestions. West and Berman (1993) find that contributions to team performance are an important criterion in performance appraisals used by local governments, and that "quality of work performed" is now the most important criterion. Pollack and Pollack (1994) describe how the U.S. Office of Personnel Management incorporates feedback from subordinates in evaluations of the performance of entry-level career managers. Some organizations also obtain feedback from team members. However, according to Brown, Hitchcock, and Willard (1994), incorporating client feedback in standard performance appraisals is very burdensome, and team feedback is sometimes resisted by employees to avoid "ratting" on co-workers. A problem with team-based appraisals is that very little is known about the reliability of team feedback (Seidler, 1994). Another adjustment is that many organizations now require that employees formulate a "development plan" in which they indicate future development and training objectives. However, it is unclear whether such plans are given much weight in most organizations. Moreover, few organizations have developed "performance review" approaches that balance employee performance and organizational structures and processes.

Employee Training and Development

TQM places a good deal of emphasis on training. In traditional organizations, employees are assumed to have appropriate skills and training for their given level and rank; but in organizations that use TQM, skills and knowledge training are assumed to be constantly on the verge of obsolescence because of changes in technology and stakeholder needs. TQM organizations must adapt rapidly to changes in their environment, and employees need increased ability and authority to bring their skills to bear on problems. According to Carnevale (1992), employees and organizations need to be supported through appropriate training and development policies, an approach which he calls the "Learning Support Model" and that is associated with high performance in organizations. The implication is that TQM organizations need to reexamine their training and development policies, and that most will need to increase their efforts. The challenge for public personnel management is to ensure that training is given high priority. In this regard, the National Commission on the Public Service (1989) notes that whereas progressive firms often spend 5 to 10 percent of their payroll on training, the federal government spends only 0.8 percent. An additional challenge is that the discretionary nature of training budgets makes them vulnerable to reductions when budget shortfalls occur.

Training and development policies must target employees as well as managers, and they must focus on interpersonal skills and behaviors as well as technical expertise. For example, in traditional bureaucracies the supervisors are assumed to have superior knowledge of workers' jobs, and they may use directive communication in dealing with employees. However, in organizations that use TQM the supervisors must be supportive "coaches" of workers and teams. Supervisors need to share their knowledge with workers and help workers to learn more, faster, and better. Training must be provided that supports managers in developing their communication and interpersonal abilities, as well as appropriate values. The development of interpersonal skill and teamwork competencies is also relevant for employees. The development of employees' values, commitments, character traits, and motivations is necessary and appropriate for well-functioning teams and interactions with clients (Siegel, 1993).

Employee training and development in TQM organizations is also linked to reward structures. Traditional reward structures emphasize hierarchical advancement and monetary rewards, even though some studies question the effectiveness of pay-for-performance schemes (see, for example, Perry, Petrakis, and Miller, 1989), and organizations are becoming flatter and are downsizing. The traditional rewards are often no longer available; instead, rewards for accomplishment are increasingly sought in assignment to other, more challenging work as well as in nonfinancial rewards such as recognition. An additional reward, which is consistent with the use of TQM, involves making employees and managers eligible for training programs. Doing so enables employees to develop their skills and ensure their competitiveness. Thus training is seen as a reward rather than as a punishment for failure.

Labor-Management Relations

Finally, TQM challenges traditional labor-management relations, which are often legalistic and adversarial. Current federal policies aim to transform labor-management relations into cooperative partnerships (Loney, 1993). If TQM implementation is to succeed, labor must cooperate (or acquiesce) with management in order to ensure worker empowerment (i.e., increased responsibilities) and reassignment (due to process reengineering and streamlining). In this regard Ban (1995) discusses Executive Order 12871 (October 1, 1993), which established the National Partnership Council (NPC), a unit composed of representatives of labor, management, and organizations charged with resolving labor-management disputes such as the Federal Mediation and Conciliation Service. The purpose of the NPC is to develop proposals for labor law reform and thereby assist the implementation of the National Performance Review (NPR), with its emphasis on issues of empowerment, streamlining, and TQM. By involving the unions, NPR managers sought to head off resistance by unions, which are often suspicious of "schemes" such as TQM. In the short run, some unions appear to have accepted work-force reductions in exchange for a greater role in decision making. However, it is unclear whether in the long run labor-management relations will be cooperative in light of further federal personnel reductions and increased responsibilities for those remaining. It is also unclear whether some unions have the capacity to accept greater partnership responsibilities. Thus the challenge to ensure labor-management cooperation continues (Ban, 1995).

IMPLEMENTING TQM

Whereas the preceding section focuses on the implications of TQM for personnel policy, in many agencies TQM is already under way. This section discusses the experiences and issues of personnel departments in providing training and support for TQM. The increased use of TQM has been a growth industry for public personnelists. In some agencies, as many as 1,500 managers and 8,000 employees have received TQM training (see, for example, FQI, 1991; Quality Oklahoma, 1994). In addition, senior agency managers look to personnel administrators for general support in managing TQM implementation strategies (West, Berman, and Milakovich, 1994b).

Training Emphases

TQM requires training in a broad range of conceptual and technical skills (Chang, 1993). Conceptual skills involve understanding the nature of quality and TQM, as well as know-how and practice in the application of these concepts to specific quality problems. Quality is defined as a multifaceted concept that includes such aspects as performance, conformance, accuracy, reliability and timeliness as well as durability, the range and nature of features, serviceability, and aesthetic appearance (see, for example, Berman and West, 1995a; Garvin, 1987). Training is needed to help employees and managers apply these concepts to their areas of expertise.

In addition, TQM involves certain statistical and analytical tools that help to assess the causes of poor quality. These tools include workflow and systems analysis (which identifies redundancies that increase costs and reduce timeliness), cause-and-effect or fishbone diagrams (which identify the causes of poor quality), pareto charts (which identify the frequency of problems or complaints in order to distinguish the vital few from the trivial many), scatter diagrams (which show the relationship between variables), control charts (which monitor delivery processes in order to discern performance patterns and to identify outliers), and histograms (which display the spread of data under consideration). The use of these tools provides diagnosis, baseline data, and opportunities for monitoring and benchmarking progress. Hunt (1993) discusses these tools in further detail.

As discussed, TQM also requires training in team skills, interpersonal competencies, and empowerment practices. To this end, instruments such as the Myers-Briggs Type Indicator (MBTI) and Adjective Check List (ACL) tests are increasingly being used in the private sector, as well as by the U.S. Internal Revenue Service in its leadership development programs (Mani, 1993; Brull, 1994). These tests assist aspiring managers in the development of needed values and skills before they are selected for management positions. In addition, training and support is needed to create a "quality" culture, that is, one in which employees and managers use creativity, open communication, employee empowerment, collaboration and shared decision making. To this end, some HR departments emphasize team building (see, for example, Toppert and DeSantis, 1993), whereas other departments assist their agencies in applying the Malcolm Baldrige Award criteria (the federal awards program for quality improvement efforts). These criteria encompass a comprehensive set of transformational, culture-changing efforts in employee and team training, senior executive leadership, policy development and strategic planning, analysis of stakeholder needs and delivery processes, strengthening of customer relationships, and redesigning of existing delivery processes.

Public personnel managers can also play a more strategic role in TQM implementation by ensuring that critical expertise and know-how about organizational transformation exists among senior managers. Specifically, studies suggest that successful efforts require (1) consensus regarding the reason for implementation (usually a threat or crisis), (2) commitment from top management, (3) knowledge of successful implementation strategies (e.g., use of "shadow organizations," "ripe apple/domino"; see, for example, Reynolds, 1994), (4) elimination of employee and middle management fears, and (5) an implementation plan (Hunt, 1993; FQI, 1991). In addition, management must be perceived by employees as being competent and honest in managing change. When these conditions are lacking, implementation cannot be successful. Various authors have proposed "implementation readiness" or awareness checklists that assess these conditions (see, for example, Berry, 1990). Some of the lists imply that the ethical climate in an organization is a relevant factor in determining the suitability of implementing TQM.

Results from a 1993 survey on the use of TQM in local government show that personnel organizations provide a wide range of TQM-related training activities. HR provides employee development programs, training in team skills, coaching for supervisors, assessment of employee skills, surveys of employee and customer satisfaction, and training in statistical skills. These efforts are found to be positively associated with the use and diffusion of TQM in city governments (West, Berman, and Milakovich, 1994b).

Barriers

Experience to date suggests that there have been many problems with TQM training. For example, there has been inadequate or ineffective training in team leadership and participation skills. Technical training has sometimes been irrelevant to actual job situations, and concept training has not been followed through with applications and experience. This may cause employees to doubt the agency's commitment to TQM. Performance appraisals have also not been adapted to TQM and teamwork (Brown, Hitchcock, and Willard, 1994). To make training more effective, it should be conducted on-the-job, with real examples, with unambiguous support and participation from senior managers, and with progressive applications and reinforcement. In addition, trainer-coaches should be made available to support quality teams in applying TQM concepts and practices.

Another problem is ensuring long-term support for TQM training and development efforts. At state and local levels, turnover among senior executives has hurt the continuity of TQM implementation efforts, especially when supportive leaders have been replaced by those who are indifferent or antagonistic toward TQM (Berman, 1994). But long-term support is also needed from legislatures. According to Kettl (1995), various laws associated with NPR were passed by Congress on the premise of short-term cost savings. Similarly, at the local level, city councils often approve requests for increased training when short-term cost savings are foreseen (Hequet, 1995). The problem, or fear, is that legislatures may cut off future requests of financial support for TQM after initial cost savings have been realized, and thereby reduce training. Thus a fundamental challenge is to get elected officials to take a long-term view, and the implementation of TQM includes the political task of obtaining such support. Public personnel managers who contribute to overcoming these challenges must blend their knowledge of human resources with expertise in broader issues affecting organizations.

"WALKING THE TALK": APPLYING TQM TO HUMAN RESOURCES MANAGEMENT

At the same time that HR departments help other units to implement TQM, a third area of concern is the application of TQM to the personnel function itself. Personnel departments that are serious about TQM may begin by conducting a customer satisfaction survey of their client departments and by eliciting client feedback for developing customer-defined measures of quality. Not surprisingly, initial TQM efforts often focus on reducing the cycle time of HR paperwork and on decreasing the number of errors in processing. Such problems are often major irritants to the customers of personnel services.

These improvements are just the beginning, however. TQM-oriented personnel departments must fully develop their support roles in such areas as management succession, employee selection, employee training, individual and organizational career development, strategic human resource planning, employee retention, employee relations, and employee-support services. Although these concerns are not new, TQM suggests that personnel departments go about developing activities in these areas through interaction with their customers. For example, employees may desire greater support in fully developing their skills, as well as in career counseling and planning. Studies show that there is a great need for these programs and that these activities contribute to both employee and organizational effectiveness (West and Berman, 1993). Also, the objectives of existing employee support programs are frequently changed. Examples include extended day-care services as well as support in meeting elder care needs and even the delivery of groceries and dry cleaning to office buildings. Listening to the voice of management is also important and may increase the fit between strategic human resource planning activities and the needs of management.

A recent study shows that TQM is used in only about 8 percent of personnel departments in cities with populations greater than 25,000 (West, Berman, and Milakovich, 1994b). At the state level, TQM is used in about 40 percent of personnel departments in transportation, corrections, education, health, and welfare agencies (Berman, 1995b). However, follow-up interviews suggest that many HR departments are just beginning to implement TQM and that many implement only parts of it. In other cases, HR departments provide TQM training and support for agencies but do not much use TQM themselves.

Challenges

The challenges of implementing TQM in HR departments are broadly similar to those of other departments, but with some differences that are unique to support functions such as HR. First, implementing TQM in personnel management suggests that stakeholders (i.e., customers) should also set priorities among these activities based on their needs. Rather than building up new bureaucratic fiefdoms for personnel departments, stakeholders might be given an "HR budget" that they can spend as they wish, and where they wish, for either internally or externally provided personnel services. TQM-oriented personnel departments are increasingly developing their roles as providers of just-in-time, quality personnel services, as well as their strategic role for helping the organization to ensure quality human resources.

Second, personnel departments that implement TQM must train their employees to be empowered in dealing with customers and in developing new services. This is often difficult, given the extent to which personnel procedures are constrained by legal and regulatory requirements. Personnel departments must provide a broader range of services, and employees must be evaluated, in part, on the basis of customer feedback. TQM also has implications for supervision in HR departments. In the TQM environment, personnel managers must adopt team-style forms of management rather than traditional styles of directive, top-down management, which are common in routine services associated with compliance. However, many TQM-oriented personnel functions have yet to develop new assessment and evaluation procedures or to use quantitative, customer-based measures of quality.

Third, the transformation of personnel departments may require support from legislators, chief executives, and agency directors. These actors provide resources, legislation, and cover from those who oppose such changes. To this end, personnel departments must carefully manage their stakeholder relations. Some departments may even develop informal partnerships and coalitions for the purpose of ensuring broad-based support for their services. As discussed above, these actors may exact promises of short-term results in return. Studies show that support from political actors is associated with increased effectiveness of TQM implementation efforts and results (Berman and West, 1995a).

CONCLUSION

TQM poses challenges to public personnel in three different ways: in developing personnel policies that are congruent with TQM, in supporting the implementation of TQM in public agencies, and in applying the principles of TQM to the personnel function. This chapter has shown that although a knowledge base exists to assist public managers in overcoming these three challenges, and although some jurisdictions are making progress in implementing TQM, in many public agencies much work remains to be done.

A critical ingredient is leadership. However, willpower alone is not enough: Action must be combined with insight. TQM is less about "storming the beach" than about carefully surveying the land and scoring victories where progress can be made. Competent public managers lay the groundwork for successful TQM implementation by artfully raising awareness about the need for change, by developing their capacity (and organizational reputation) for change management, by orchestrating necessary resources and commitments for TQM, and by developing plans for phased implementation and successes. These axioms have many implications, one of which is that initial TQM efforts are often so careful and low key that they are not even called TQM (or anything else).

Finally, although TQM aims to increase trust between agencies and the users of public services, it is paradoxical that TQM requires a climate of internal trust in order to be implemented. Many employees (and unions) are rightfully fearful of change, because they have been burned by past implementation strategies that have been incompetent and inadequate. The loyalty of employees has been severely tested by unkept promises, too. Based on these experiences, it is rational for many employees and managers to hope that TQM will pass them by. In view of these concerns, the possible failure of TQM poses a double tragedy: the lost opportunity to improve public services and, hence, public confidence, and the likelihood of heightened employee cynicism. Public personnel managers, by virtue of their responsibility and expertise in managing human resources, have a special responsibility in furthering TQM efforts: to provide necessary TQM training, to ensure that their organization does not undertake incompetent and ill-advised implementation efforts, and to adequately prepare and support leaders in their efforts to improve organizational performance.

NOTE

1. A confounding problem is that the introduction of new productivity improvement strategies frequently receives substantial media attention, which, by its nature, is short-lived. Some managers also cash in by giving lip service to hot productivity efforts and then rejecting them when it becomes fashionable to do so. These realities obscure the ongoing efforts of progressive public organizations and managers to improve their services. The existence and endurance of progressive efforts surprises many skeptics (Walters, 1992, 1994).

REFERENCES

Ban, Carolyn. 1995. "Unions, Management and the NPR," in Donald Kettl and John DiIulio, eds., *Inside the Reinvention Machine: Appraising Governmental Reform.* Washington, D.C.: Brookings Institution.

Barzelay, Michael. 1992. *Breaking through Bureaucracy*. Los Angeles: University of California Press.

Berman, Evan M. 1994. "Implementing Total Quality Management in State Governments: A Survey of Recent Progress." *State and Local Government Review* 26, no. 1: 46-53.

———. 1995a. "Employee Empowerment in State Agencies: A Survey of Progress." *International Journal of Public Administration* 18, no. 5: 833-850.

———. 1995b. "TQM in State and Local Personnel Operations." *Periscope* 15, no. 3: 6.

Berman, Evan M., and Jonathan P. West. 1995a. "Municipal Commitment to Total Quality Management: A Survey of Recent Progress." *Public Administration Review* 55, no. 1: 57-66.

———. 1995b. "TQM in American Cities: Commitment and Impact." *Journal of Public Administration Research and Theory* 5, no. 2: 213-230.

Berman, Evan M., Jonathan P. West, and Michael E. Milakovich. 1996. "Implementing TQM in State Health Service Agencies." *Journal of Health and Human Resources Administration* (forthcoming).

Berry, Thomas H. 1991. *Managing the Total Quality Transformation*. New York: McGraw-Hill.

Bleakley, F.R. 1993. "Many Companies Try Management Fads, Only to See Them Flop." *Wall Street Journal,* July 6: 1.

Bowman, James S. 1994. "At Last, an Alternative to Performance Appraisal: Total Quality Management." *Public Administration Review* 54, no. 2: 129-136.

Brown, Mark G., Darcy E. Hitchcock, and Marsha L. Willard. 1994. *Why TQM Fails and What to Do about It.* New York: Irwin.

Brull, Harold P. 1994. "Selection in the TQM Environment: What's Needed and How Do We Know Who's Got It?" Paper presented at the International Personnel Management Association Assessment Council Conference, Charleston, S.C., June 26-30.

Carnevale, David G. 1992. "The Learning Support Model: Personnel Policy beyond the Traditional Model." *American Review of Public Administration* 22 (March): 19-34.

———. 1995. *Trustworthy Government: Leadership and Management Strategies for Building Trust and High Performance*. San Francisco: Jossey-Bass.

Chang, R.Y. 1993. "When TQM Goes Nowhere." *Training & Development* 47 (January): 23-29.

Cohen, S., and R. Brand. 1993. *Total Quality Management in Government*. San Francisco: Jossey-Bass.

Crosby, Philip B. 1979. *Quality Is Free*. New York: Mentor.

Daley, Dennis M. 1992. "Pay for Performance, Performance Appraisal, and Total Quality Management." *Public Productivity and Management Review* 16, no. 1: 39-51.

Deming, W. Edwards. 1986. *Out of the Crisis*. Cambridge, Mass.: MIT Press.

Federal Quality Institute. 1991. *Introduction to Total Quality Management*. Washington, D.C.: FQI.

Federal Times. 1995. "Quality Institute Axed." July 24: 20.

Garrity, R.B. 1993. "Total Quality Management: An Opportunity for High Performance in Federal Organizations." *Public Administration Quarterly* 17 (Winter): 430-459.

Garvin, David A. 1987. "Competing on the Eight Dimensions of Quality." *Harvard Business Review* 65 (November/December): 101-109.

General Accounting Office. 1992. "Quality Management: Survey of Federal Organizations." Washington, D.C.: U.S. Government Printing Office.

Halachmi, Arie. 1993. "Total Quality Management, Performance Appraisal and Training: Selected Issues and Implications." Paper presented at the 54th National Training Conference of the American Society for Public Administration, San Francisco.

Hequet, Mark. 1995. "TQM at City Hall." *Training* 32 (March): 58–64.

Hunt, V. Daniel. 1993. *Quality Management in Government: A Guide to Federal, State and Local Implementation.* Milwaukee: ASQC Press.

Hyde, Al C. 1993. "Barriers in Implementing Quality Management." *Public Manager* 22 (Spring): 33–37.

———. 1994. "Total Quality Management: A Quality Perspective," in Steven Hays and Richard Kearney, eds., *Public Personnel Administration.* Englewood Cliffs, N.J.: Prentice-Hall.

International City and County Management Association. 1995. *Job Bulletin,* various issues.

Ishikawa, Kaoru. 1985. *What Is Total Quality Control?* Englewood Cliffs, N.J.: Prentice-Hall.

Juran, Joseph M. 1980. *Quality Planning and Analysis.* New York: McGraw-Hill.

Kettl, Donald. 1995. "Building Lasting Reform: Enduring Questions, Missing Answers," in Donald Kettl and John DiIulio, eds., *Inside the Reinvention Machine: Appraising Governmental Reform.* Washington, D.C.: Brookings Institution.

Loney, Timothy J. 1993. "TQM and Labor Relations Cooperation." Paper presented at the 54th National Training Conference of the American Society for Public Administration, San Francisco.

Mani, Bonnie G. 1993. "Total Quality Organization Development in Bureaucracies: Increasing Awareness of Creativity, Change, Conformity, Judging and Perceiving." Working paper.

Milakovich, Michael E. 1991. "Total Quality Management in the Public Sector." *National Productivity Review* 10, no. 2: 195–213.

———. 1995a. "How Quality-Oriented Have State and Local Governments Really Become?" *National Productivity Review* 14, no. 1: 73–84.

———. 1995b. *Improving Service Quality: Achieving High Performance in the Public and Private Sectors.* Delray Beach, Fla.: St. Lucie Press.

Moen, Ronald D. 1989. "The Performance Appraisal System: Deming's Deadly Disease." *Quality Progress* 22 (November): 62–66.

National Commission on the Public Service. 1989. *Leadership for America: Rebuilding the Public Service.* Washington, D.C.: National Commission on the Public Service.

Perry, James L., B.A. Petrakis, and T.K. Miller. 1989. "Federal Merit Pay Round II: An Analysis of the Performance Management and Recognition System." *Public Administration Review* 49, no. 1: 29–37.

Pollack, Leslie J., and David M. Pollack. 1994. "Using 360 Degree Feedback in Performance Appraisal." Paper presented at the International Personnel Management Association Assessment Council Conference, Charleston, S.C., June 26–30.

Quality Oklahoma. 1994. *Implementation Model Training.* Oklahoma City: State of Oklahoma.

Reynolds, Larry. 1994. *Beyond Total Quality Management.* London, U.K.: Sheldon.

Seidler, Edward. 1994. "Discipline and Deselection in the TQM Environment." Paper presented at the International Personnel Management Association Assessment Council Conference, Charleston, S.C., June 26–30.

Siegel, Gilbert B. 1993. "Job Analysis in the TQM Environment." Paper presented at the 54th National Training Conference of the American Society for Public Administration, San Francisco.

Toppert, Bethany, and Melanie DeSantis. 1993. "Using Teams to Create a Quality Culture." Paper presented at the 54th National Training Conference of the American Society for Public Administration, San Francisco.

Walters, Jonathan. 1992. "The Cult of Total Quality." *Governing* 5 (May): 38–42.

―――― . 1994. "TQM: Surviving the Cynics." *Governing* 7 (September): 40-45.

West, Jonathan P., ed. 1995. *Quality Management Today.* Washington, D.C.: International City Management Association.

West, Jonathan P., and Evan M. Berman. 1993. "Human Resource Strategies in Local Government: A Survey of Progress and Future Directions." *American Review of Public Administration* 23 (September): 279-297.

West, Jonathan P., Evan M. Berman, and Michael E. Milakovich. 1994a. "HRM, TQM and Organizational Policies: The Need for Alignment," in *Proceedings of the Academy of Business Administration: Public Sector Studies,* 923-929. London, U.K.: ABA.

―――― . 1994b. "Implementing TQM in Local Government: The Leadership Challenge." *Public Productivity and Management Review* 17 (Winter): 175-190.

chapter **19**

Privatization: Implications
for the Public Work Force

Donald F. Kettl

Privatization has become the buzzword of reformers in the 1990s. Advocates press it as a strategy to shrink the size of government, to improve its efficiency, and to satisfy citizens better. Sometimes, in fact, its advocates oversell it as an answer to virtually anything that ails government. The movement gathers under its tent a diagnosis of popular dissatisfaction with government (government is inherently inefficient) and a prescription to cure its ills (private provision of public services, especially because of competitive markets, is more efficient and effective).

The privatization debate has evoked such visceral reactions because of its implicit agenda. Since the government-reduction movement began during the late 1970s in California, elected officials and citizens alike have argued the need to shrink government and improve its performance by turning more of its functions over to the private sector (Lipset and Schneider, 1987; National Commission on the Public Service, 1989). The theoretical roots of privatization lie buried in public-choice theory, generated by economists to analyze how governments behave. Individuals seek to maximize their utility, the theorists argue; that is, they attempt to secure the greatest possible amount of desired ends for them-selves. This assumption, of course, undergirds most of economic theory, and the famous supply-demand curves are simply elaborations on this basic notion. What happens, public-choice theorists asked, when utility-maximizing individuals become public officials? Their response, the theorists argued, is naturally to maximize their utility, to increase to the extent possible their personal and organizational power, money, and prestige. As economist William Niskanen put it, "the beginning of wisdom is the recognition that bureaucrats are people who are, at least, not entirely motivated by the general welfare or the interests of the state" (Niskanen, 1971: 36; see also Downs, 1967; Buchanan, 1977; Savas,

1987). Government and the administration of public programs thus becomes transformed from an opportunity to serve the public interest into a chance to promote one's individual interests. In the process, the public-choice theorists concluded, government efficiency and effectiveness suffer.

How can the public defend itself? The answer that many reformers propose is privatization: relying on the self-correcting behavior of competitive markets instead of the self-serving behavior of public officials. If individuals in corporations attempted to use organizations to promote their own interests, the market would recognize the inefficiencies that resulted and would punish them—ultimately, by driving them out of business. The presumed superiority of private-sector organizations over government led to three tactics for improving public programs.

First, government could simply get out of the business of providing a service. In 1987, for example, the federal government sold Conrail, the government-owned national railroad freight system, for $1.6 billion. The argument: Government has no place in providing many services; the private sector can often deliver better services more cheaply.

Second, government could supply citizens with vouchers, which they could in turn spend to buy services from suppliers of their choice, instead of having government supply it. For example, the Department of Housing and Urban Development in 1985 began supplying poor people with vouchers to subsidize their homes instead of building low-income housing. The argument: Government has no incentive to provide low-cost, high-quality services if it has a monopoly over the services. If citizens can choose, they will choose the service provider that gives them the most for their money.

Third, government could contract with private sector organizations for services. Instead of running a prison or providing social services, government could arrange for some private sector organization to do so. The argument: Government would say what it wanted done, but not how. Private sector organizations would compete to produce the services as cheaply as possible to win the government's contract. The result, privatization advocates argue, would be better services at lower costs. Of the three principal forms of privatization, contracting out is the most widespread and important (Oakersen, 1987).

Although privatization is certainly not a new idea—the federal government has been contracting for services and supplies since the very beginning of its history—its application became much more widespread during the 1980s and dramatically expanded during the 1990s (Rehfuss, 1989; Fixler and Poole, 1987; Smith, 1987; Ferris and Graddy, 1986; Colman, 1989). Virtually no part of local government operations has been untouched by contracting out. Among many other services, some local governments contract out library operations, tree trimming, data processing, parking lot operations, garbage collections, and even fire services. State governments are contracting for hospitals and prisons. In Florida, for example, one out of five public services involves privatization in some form (Carlson and Fixler, undated). At the federal level, contracting out accounts for 20 percent of all spending through 20 million contracts per year.

Complicating the debate is the fact that privatization is not one approach but many. It is an umbrella term for a grab-bag of very different tactics. But what they all share is strong reliance on competitive markets, either by turning government functions directly over to the private sector or by relying on market-like strategies within government programs.

The growth of privatization raises three important questions for the public work force: Just how has the privatization movement affected public employees? What new management issues has the movement created? How has the nature of public sector work been changed by the movement?

EFFECTS ON PUBLIC EMPLOYEES

Public employees, naturally, lie at the center of the privatization debate. Although a host of reasons have been advanced for contracting out, most of them boil down to saving money and increasing flexibility. Many public employees and their union leaders have seen in these slogans codewords for bypassing public employee unions and civil service regulations, as well as procurement rules that restrict public actions. Labor costs account for about three-fourths of most municipal budgets (Rehfuss, 1989), so the contracting-out debate soon boils down to the issue of public employees. Problems of public employee morale thus quickly seize the agenda.

Morale

The argument for privatization is always implicitly, and sometimes explicitly, anti-bureaucratic. The reason government has problems, the theory goes, is because all individuals are utility maximizers; when government bureaucrats maximize their utility, they subvert the public's interest. As a former economist for the president's Council of Economic Advisers succinctly put the argument, "public ownership without public waste is a myth" (Steven H. Hanke, quoted in Fitzgerald, 1988: 215).

Not all the complaints tag public sector employees as selfish workers with narrow visions. Some critics suggest that public employees really cannot help themselves. No matter how noble their intentions, they cannot "transcend their bureaucratic restraints" because the "competition and profit incentives" of the private sector "are far stronger efficiency tools than any bureaucratic management ploy, except perhaps the threat of death, that government has ever devised." They simply have to work with "straitjackets imposed by the institutional surroundings" (Fitzgerald, 1988: 17,18). Public officials like to expand their programs, not only because the programs supply their livelihood but also because they have concluded that their programs were critical to solving the nation's problems (Butler, 1987; Savas, 1987). On top of that, Savas from his experience in government contended, "It's *fun* spending other people's money!" (Savas, 1982: 84).

Not all the pro-privatization writings are so provocative. Nevertheless, it is impossible to escape the implication that the movement is, at its core, anti-bureaucratic. Privatization advocates see the self-serving behavior of bureaucrats as the core of public sector problems. They argue that transferring work from government bureaucrats to the private sector promotes efficiency. The privatization movement thus adds greater fuel to the anti-government fire on which many candidates for public office have capitalized. The tasks of rebuilding public confidence in the public service and of motivating public employees thus become markedly greater.

Union-Busting and Civil Service Restrictions

Many proponents of contracting out believe, furthermore, that a central reason why public sector costs are so great is the power of public employee unions. Critics complain that unions place too many restrictions on how their members can work, force governments to hire more workers than are needed to do the job, win fringe benefits that are too generous, and use their power to withhold services to extort higher salaries than are justified. Even worse, public employee unions supply endorsements, campaign contributions, and campaign workers to candidates for office. In return for this, Savas argues, "they expect—and frequently obtain—a quid pro quo in the form of greater expenditures for the service their union produces, pay raises, and collective bargaining rules that will lead to more favorable outcomes of labor negotiations" (Savas, 1982: 84). Some of the cost savings that privatization advocates hope to realize thus come from breaking the power of public employee unions and reducing their salaries and fringe benefits (AFSCME, 1987, 1984).

Even in the absence of unions, critics often complain that civil service rules restrict the flexibility that managers need to operate efficiently. A management study performed for Nashville, Tennessee, for example, concluded, "the Civil Service rules and regulations have been so extensively modified that management's rights are now virtually nonexistent." The study's authors concluded that many services could be purchased from private contractors for half what public agencies cost (Metropolitan Government of Nashville and Davidson County, 1989: 3).

The study reported, for example, that garbage collection crews were paid to work four 10-hour days per week. Their work rules, however, contain an incentive clause that allows them to go home when they complete their work. "Department records reveal," the report said, "that although many routes are completed by noon and almost all before 2:00 PM crews were paid until 5:00 PM." On days after a holiday, workers were able to collect two days' worth of garbage in an extra one and a half hours. Contracting out the service, the study estimated, would save $3 million per year (Metropolitan Government of Nashville and Davidson County, 1989: 92-93). Instead of arguing for new rules, the study's authors simply concluded that services should be privatized wherever possible (Metropolitan Government of Nashville and Davidson County, 1989: 3).

Reduce the Number of Public Employees

Privatizers see reducing the number of public employees as the key to reducing government costs and improving efficiency. They contend that public sector organizations tend to hire too many employees because larger staffs mean more power and greater success in winning larger budgets. "All too often, agency or department heads see their task as providing employment rather than delivering the particular service in the most cost-efficient manner" (Poole, 1987). (Of course, most of these perks are only available to top political appointees, whom elected officials can replace at their pleasure, not the legions of civil servants whose behavior allegedly lies at the bottom of government's performance problems. The cynical views of many privatization advocates thus reflect on the authors' own experiences as high government officials, not the everyday work lives of the vast majority of public sector workers!)

In fact, the key savings that privatizers hope to realize is in reducing the number of employees required to deliver a service. They believe that public sector enterprises "tend to be overstaffed" and that contracting out, therefore, lowers costs (Poole, 1987: 38). At least implicitly, arguments for more contracting out are arguments for fewer public-sector employees. Since 1955, for example, the federal government has followed the policy to contract out work that could be done more efficiently in the private sector. The policy, formalized as Office and Management and Budget Circular A-76 in 1966, has been revised frequently. During the Reagan administration, OMB revised A-76 to require that all new activities that could be performed by the private sector must be contracted out, except when private sector costs are unreasonable or when national security needs dictate otherwise. Furthermore, government employees must compete for their jobs by calculating their costs to perform a given job; if a contractor can beat the cost by at least 10 percent, the activity is contracted out. During the Reagan years the government studied "commercial activities," from data processing to laundry services, performed by over 72,000 government employees. The process produced a cost savings of $2.8 billion over seven years, largely by reducing the number of government positions by more than 45,000. Prodded by congressional Republicans, the Clinton administration then considered expanding the contracting process even more aggressively.

The competition process produces many hard feelings among government employees because they do not believe that the game is played on a level playing field. The federal ground rules under which the cost savings have been calculated have regularly changed, especially in determining government employees' fringe benefits. The cost base for fringe benefits changed three times in fifteen months, during 1976 and 1977, from 7.0 to 24.7 percent of wages, back down to 14.1 percent and then up to 20.4 percent. The higher the rate, of course, the harder it would be for government employees to compete for their jobs. As one commentator noted, "three changes in fifteen months probably destroyed any belief in the figure's reliability, regardless of how carefully it might have been calculated" (Rehfuss, 1989: 202–203.) Public employees bitterly complained that the system was being rigged against them, because no matter how hard they worked the fringe benefit figure could be set to give private sector competitors an advantage.

The process, furthermore, upsets traditional management styles. Public sector managers must set output measures, analyze how each employee contributes to that output, and calculate how costs might be saved so the government agency can retain the project. With "measurable performance standards," OMB concludes, "the employees finally have something to work towards." OMB concedes that "Initially, the workers are resistant to this kind of change but once they get over the initial hurdle of adopting the clearly defined goals, managers tend to find the employees happier, better adjusted and more productive" (U.S. Office of Management and Budget, 1988: 15). That conclusion presumably applies to employees who were able to keep their jobs, since the A-76 process inevitably means that some employees will lose their positions even if the federal agency successfully competes for the operation. A General Accounting Office survey of 2,535 government employees who lost their jobs through the A-76 process found that 74 percent obtained other government positions. Only 5 percent were fired; the remainder decided to retire, resign, or go to work for the contractor (U.S. Office of Management and Budget, 1988: 15).

For some government employees, the competition process can have drastic effects. But more important, it is helping establish a new managerial philosophy. No employee involved in any activity that can be contracted out can assume that he or she can keep the position indefinitely. Moreover, the process creates far stronger pressures on government officials to manage for results: to identify program goals and provide feedback to employees about how well they are doing. The contracting-out process thus is far more than a way to save money by shrinking the size of government. It is having important effects on the behavior of government officials who continue to provide public services.

Assessment

The argument that self-interested bureaucrats produce inefficient government programs is neat and powerful. Public choice theory flows, almost inexorably, from the initial assumption about maximization of utility by public officials. There are, however, three major flaws in the logic.

First, government spending has indeed grown, but it is hard to argue that power-seeking bureaucrats are responsible. Spending by all levels of government has increased from 30 percent of the gross domestic product in 1978 to about 34 percent in 1995. However, the government's expenditures for goods and services has actually remained relatively stable since the early 1960s, at about 20 percent of GDP. Most of the growth in government spending, especially at the federal level, is not accounted for by the goods and services that government employees provide but by income transfer programs, especially Social Security and Medicare (Kettl, 1989). Administration of these programs actually requires relatively few government employees.

Second, the real constituency for these programs is the public, not the bureaucrats. Continuing budget battles over Medicare and Social Security have demonstrated just how hard it is to trim spending for them. "Despite widespread anti-spending rhetoric, the fact is that most citizens like most of the programs on which government spends money" (Starr, 1987: 127).

Third, it is not always clear that the private sector is more efficient than the public sector. Every tale of waste and abuse in government can be matched by another in the private sector. In fact, many of the most popular government "horror stories" of the 1980s—from influence peddling in the Department of Housing and Urban Development to overcharging in defense contracts—involved unscrupulous behavior by private sector individuals.

Finally, the central argument of the privatization debate circles around to catch contracting-out proponents by surprise. Contracting out, they argue, is superior because it reduces self-interested behavior on the part of government bureaucrats. The rest of the story, of course, is that contracting out increases the number of people and organizations in the *private* sector with a direct stake in the size of government budgets. In fact, as one critic points out, "Contracting out expands the set of claimants on the public treasury" (Starr, 1987: 128). Thus if the logic of the public choice movement holds, contracting out might increase, not decrease, public spending. And indeed, lobbying by contractors is a powerful engine behind spending for space, nuclear energy, and defense programs.

If the privatization logic is not always consistent, the movement nonetheless is powerful. There are many good arguments—including obtaining expertise and operating flexibility that the government does not have—that also drive contracting out. For all these reasons, privatization has become an important part of American government.

NEW TACTICS

The logic of privatization has led, in turn, to new tactics "beyond the margins of government," as two experts describe it (Moe and Stanton, 1989). Public choice theorists argued on principle that private organizations are inherently more effective; public decision makers, in turn, have harnessed that broad argument to serve more pragmatic interests. When budget restraints make it hard to create new government programs or when civil service rules restrict flexibility, government at all levels has turned to quasi-private organizations and government-sponsored enterprises to do the public's work. These organizations fit neither the neat administrative theories of public administration nor the logic of privatization. They nevertheless are irresistible to public officials seeking flexible responses to new problems. Working in a world in which the organization is privately owned yet publicly accountable poses enormous new challenges to personnel policy in the twilight zone (Moe, 1995).

Meanwhile, several local governments, led by Phoenix and Indianapolis, have developed a new competitive process to decide whether government workers or private contractors ought to deliver public services. Since 1979, for example, the city of Phoenix has held competitions between city departments and interested contractors for 56 different service decisions in 13 different areas. The services ranged from data entry and fuel distribution to senior citizen housing management and street sweeping. In 34 cases, private contractors submitted low bids; in the other 22 competitions, city workers won the work because they offered to perform it more cheaply. In the process, the city saved $27 million as compared with the cost under the previous system (Flanagan and Perkins, 1995).

City officials say that in addition to lowering costs, they have increased citizens' happiness with the services they receive. "Customer satisfaction" surveys show dramatic improvements in the rating citizens give the quality of services. Officials also claim that the focus on customer service has improved management.

> Discussions of unit costs, customer complaints, down time, and other production-line events occur with interest and energy. There is no need to build bureaucratic reporting, regulatory, and oversight devices. Internal and external studies, citizen committees, cheerleading, and other public management tools are weak mechanisms when compared to the capability of real competition to sustain self-directed attention. (Flanagan and Perkins, 1995: 7)

Such strategies are new, but they are spreading. Governments struggling to maintain high-quality services at lower costs often leap at any option. The Phoenix case is intriguing. Its experience is substantial and its gains real. But they have not come easily or for free. The city has had to develop new management expertise. Bid specifications must be prepared carefully for a new range of services. Good cost analysis is critical, and city managers must carefully monitor the quality of work, regardless of who performs it. That, in turn, has required the creation of a management information system beyond what most governments use.

Moreover, the system has created important managerial issues. The competitive process has upset existing routines and forced some employees to move to new jobs. Everyone involved has had to develop a fresh focus on cost and quality and to adapt their work to new processes. Where some departments have not had their work subjected to the competitive process, conflicts sometimes have developed with other departments that have had to build new strategies. The potential gains, in both cost savings and service improvements, are significant. But even more significant are the ways in which workers and managers have to change to meet the challenges that competition creates. Moreover, competition means very different things in the public and private sectors (Kelman, 1990).

EQUAL PROTECTION

Privatization, in all its forms, also raises important questions about how best to ensure equal protection: both of government employees, who stand potentially to lose their jobs, and of citizens, whose services are provided under an increasingly mixed system.

Protection of Employees

The very rationale for the creation and continuing existence of the civil service is to provide fair treatment for government employees. We have come to believe and expect that no one should have a stronger claim on any government good, including employment, because of political favoritism. We believe that employees ought to be hired and promoted on the basis of merit.

Likewise, when the government established new contracting-out procedures, it mandated basic protections for government employees. One broad issue is what equality means when two people, one a government employee and the other working for a contractor, do the same job within the same organization. A more narrow but much more contentious issue is how to ensure public employees' rights in the decision to contract out. The technical questions that arise in public-private cost comparisons often are surprisingly complicated; and regardless of the technical complexity, the political drive toward contracting out can sweep technical issues aside, as the dispute over setting federal employees' fringe benefit rates demonstrates. Several presidents ran for office against Washington and, when they came to town, devoted themselves to reducing government in any way they could. It is little wonder, then, that government employees worry that the contracting-out movement threatens the integrity of the hiring, retention, and promotion processes.

These basic issues of rights are difficult enough. Complicating personnel management are the grievance procedures that the contracting-out process creates. A-76, for example, requires each agency conducting a public-private cost comparison to create an appeals process. Everyone involved, from public employee groups to unsuccessful private bidders, has the right of appeal. Public employees have complained that they often receive little advance notice of impending cost competitions, that they have little time to prepare their appeals, and that their unions have little access to important information (Ketler, 1986). Furthermore, drawing the line between administrators' rights to exercise their managerial authority and employees' rights to have that authority exercised in a procedurally fair way is extraordinarily difficult. Often, in fact, the issues must be determined on a case-by-case basis. The result is a complicated mix of arbitration and review of contracting-out decisions by the General Accounting Office (Ketler, 1986). Thus the move to privatization not only raises predictable problems—how to deal with public employees' natural fear of losing their jobs—but also some unexpected ones—how to manage the surprisingly difficult appeals process that results (Shenk, 1995).

Protection of Citizens

Since the mid-1960s, the federal courts have expanded citizens' rights to be treated fairly by government and, if they are entitled to public services, to receive them promptly. Furthermore, the courts have more generously granted standing to sue to aggrieved citizens, and claimants on public services have more aggressively sued in the federal courts for benefits they believe they ought to receive (Brown, 1981; Kettl, 1988a, 1988b).

Many of these guarantees, however, do not apply to services provided by contractors. The Supreme Court's doctrine of "state action," which holds that private organizations are responsible for guaranteeing constitutional rights only when they operate on the government's direct authority, greatly reduces citizens' rights under privatized programs. Harold J. Sullivan argues, "By turning production of public services over to private agencies, government can effectively evade most constitutional restraints." He concludes, "In the end, privatization and protection of civil liberties may prove to be mutually exclusive goals" (Sullivan, 1987: 464, 466).

The issue of the public's right to basic services is heightened in privatized programs. Some communities have privatized their fire protection services, for example, and the private fire service has stood by watching a house whose owner had not contracted for fire protection burn to the ground. The issue of constitutional rights is even more problematic, especially in privatized state prisons where the protecting of inmates from "cruel and unusual punishment" by privatized jailers is a difficult issue.

The point is not that privatization violates basic rights, because this need not be the case. Rather, regardless of what economic savings privatization may bring, it also inevitably raises new and profound problems.

THE CHANGING NATURE OF PUBLIC WORK

Privatization not only reduces the public work force but significantly alters its character. The number of blue-collar workers has dramatically fallen. In 1955 blue-collar employees—such as maintenance, cafeteria, and factory workers—accounted for 30.7 percent of all federal employees. By 1984 their share was less than half that amount, or 15.3 percent. (Over the same period, the blue-collar work force in the overall economy dropped by less than one-fourth to about 48 percent of all workers.)

As federal employment has become more white-collar, it has also become higher-paid and higher-level. According to the U.S. Office of Personnel Management, *Pay Structure of the Federal Civil Service,* for various years, the share of federal employees at the GS-9 level (the professional entrance level) and above increased from 40.8 percent in 1967 to 50.4 percent in 1983. Public choice advocates, in fact, have long complained that "grade creep" (a tendency of civil service grades to increase over time) is a natural result of government employees' utility-maximizing behavior (President's Private Sector Survey on Cost Control, 1984: iii, 243; Downs, 1967). Such a pattern, however, is just what one would expect when more services are privatized. The government needs to employ fewer service providers, located principally at lower levels of the bureaucracy, and more service managers at upper levels (Durst, Patterson, and Ramsden, 1989).

The nature of federal work has changed slowly but markedly since World War II. Federal employees are performing fewer front-line functions. Indeed, with the exception of workers in Social Security offices, few Americans encounter federal service providers on a regular basis. In most federal agencies except the Social Security Administration, the job of federal employees is now principally one of studying and planning what policies ought to be undertaken, supervising others (especially contractors and grantees) who implement the policies, and monitoring what in fact has happened (Bailey, 1987). This is not necessarily a worse collection of jobs, but it certainly is much different from that in the past.

Assessing such changes at the state and local level is harder, in part because statistical record keeping is not uniform and in part because privatization has not spread as far. When governments provide education, police, fire, and prison services, government employees still are in the front lines almost everywhere. Nevertheless, similar trends are at work there as well. More privatization means more employees supervising others outside government who themselves provide the services (Kettl, 1988a, 1988b). And the spread of strategies like the Phoenix competition approach subjects everyone to very different expectations and standards of work.

Finally, it requires only modest imagination to think about third parties in the private and nonprofit world as partners with government employees in providing public services. It is becoming harder not only to draw the line between the public and private sectors but also to differentiate between the jobs performed by many public and private sector workers. These trends suggest three important implications for public service education.

First, traditional approaches to public administration and public personnel do not begin to satisfy the managerial demands of privatized programs. Traditional training in public administration is hierarchy-based, whereas privatized programs are nonhierarchical. More recent changes in public administration education emphasize decision making, whereas privatized programs place heavy emphasis on program implementation and monitoring. Thus education for future public servants who will be working in a privatized world needs to focus more on the broad public-private environment of public programs; on the difficulties of setting performance standards and negotiating contracts; on the techniques of monitoring contracts, measuring performance, and auditing expenditures; and on maintaining control when control is, at best, indirect (Rehfuss, 1989; Cigler, 1989). There is a body of knowledge to deal with these problems, but it lies principally under the rubric of "management control," which is rarely explored in public administration education (Anthony, 1988; Swiss, 1991).

Second, the job of public servants varies by their level and role within the bureaucracy. Most government employees are initially hired for their technical skill: as chemists, physicists, economists, policy analysts, accountants, and lawyers, among the many specialties that governments require. These skills serve them well in dealing with the technical issues that confront government employees in their first years on the job. Technical experts who perform well are often promoted to managerial positions, but the skills required in these managerial positions are much different. Being a good chemist, or even a good policy analyst, does not mean that one will be a good manager. Hence there is a need for emerging managers to acquire new managerial skills as they rise in the bureaucracy. That, in turn, suggests that training public servants for entry-level jobs does not finish the task. Continuing education for public managers is critical in helping them make the transition from technical expert to generalist manager.

Third, much of the training that public sector employees require is needed by government's proxies as well. Workers in nonprofit and private sector organizations need to know how to negotiate and to comply with government contracts as the law requires; how to keep records as government needs to have them kept; how to protect the rights of employees and service recipients as federal law requires; and how to deal with the many other administrative aspects of privatization. In short, this suggests that education for the public service need not be limited to public servants.

CONCLUSION

The advocates of privatization offer it as a magic bullet to solve government's problems of efficiency and performance. In fact, privatization in its various forms, especially contracting out and other competition strategies, does offer substantial opportunities for greater flexibility, lower costs, and better performance than do the more traditional government management strategies.

Privatization is scarcely a magic bullet, however. Its advocates promote it as a largely self-administering, self-regulating tactic, but the lesson of American experience to date is that privatized programs require careful management by government. Indeed, where it has worked best, smart management has been just as important as competition. Privatization makes many of the old issues, such as accountability, harder to solve and raises many new ones, such as how to control government-sponsored enterprises.

A second lesson also suggests itself: that privatization, if anything, requires an even more highly skilled work force, one trained in skills that are much different from traditional approaches to public administration. The techniques of supervision, motivation, and control that predominate in most public administration and public management programs do not begin to deal with the complications that arise when the persons to be supervised, motivated, and controlled work outside a government agency. The competition-based approaches require dramatically increased abilities to define public services, measure their costs, and assess their performance. Moreover, the technical skills that work for entry-level positions do not serve the manager's needs well. With promotions comes the need for retraining in management skills and rethinking the manager's roles and responsibilities. To date, however, privatization has grown more rapidly than government's capacity to manage it.

REFERENCES

AFSCME (American Federation of State, County, and Municipal Employees). 1984. *Passing the Bucks: The Contracting Out of Public Services.* Washington: D.C.: AFSCME.
——— . 1987. When Public Services Go Private: Not Always Better, Not Always Honest, There May Be a Better Way. Washington, D.C.: AFSCME.
Anthony, Robert N. 1988. *The Management Control Function.* Boston: Harvard Business School Press.
Bailey, Robert W. 1987. "Uses and Misuses of Privatization," in Steve H. Hanke, ed., *Prospects for Privatization,* pp. 138-152. New York: Academy of Political Science.
Brown, George D. 1981. "The Courts and Grant Reform: A Time for Action." *Intergovernmental Perspective* 7 (Fall): 6-14.
Buchanan, James M. 1977. "Why Does Government Grow?" in Thomas E. Borcherding, ed., *Budgets and Bureaucrats: The Sources of Government Growth,* pp. 3-18. Durham, N.C.: Duke University Press.
Butler, Stuart. 1987. "Changing the Political Dynamics of Government," in Steve H. Hanke, *Prospects for Privatization,* pp. 4-13. New York: Academy of Political Science.
Carlson, Kenneth W., and Philip E. Fixler Jr. Undated. *The Role of Privatization in Florida's Growth.* Miami: Law and Economics Center, University of Miami.
Cigler, Beverly A. 1989. "Trends Affecting Local Administrators," in James L. Perry, ed., *Handbook of Public Administration,* pp. 40-53. San Francisco: Jossey-Bass.
Colman, William C. 1989. *State and Local Government and Public-Private Partnerships: A Policy Issues Handbook.* New York: Greenwood Press.
Downs, Anthony. 1967. *Inside Bureaucracy.* Boston: Little, Brown.
Durst, Samantha L., Patricia M. Patterson, and John J. Ramsden. 1989. "Impacts of Traditional Explanatory Factors on Average Grade Increases in U.S. Cabinet-Level Departments." *Public Administration Review* 49 (July/August): 362-371.
Ferris, James, and Elizabeth Graddy. 1986. "Contracting Out: For What? With Whom?" *Public Administration Review* 46 (July/August): 332-344.
Fitzgerald, Randall. 1988. *When Government Goes Private: Successful Alternatives to Public Services.* New York: Universe Books.
Fixler, Philip E., Jr., and Robert W. Poole Jr. 1987. "Status of State and Local Privatization," in Steve H. Hanke, ed., *Prospects for Privatization,* pp. 164-178. New York: Academy of Political Science.
Flanagan, Jim, and Susan Perkins. 1995. "Public/Private Competition in the City of Phoenix, Arizona." *Government Finance Review* (June): 7-12.
Hanke, Steve H., ed. 1987a. *Prospects for Privatization* (Proceedings of the Academy of Political Science). New York: Academy of Political Science.
——— . 1987b. *Privatization and Development.* San Francisco: Institute for Contemporary Studies.
Kelman, Steven. 1990. *Procurement and Public Management: The Fear of Discretion and the Quality of Government Performance.* Washington: AEI Press.

Ketler, Richard K. 1986. "Federal Employee Challenges to Contracting Out: Is There a Viable Forum?" *Military Law Review* 111 (Winter): 103-166.

Kettl, Donald F. 1988a. "Government by Proxy and the Public Service." *International Review of Administrative Sciences* 54 (December): 501-516.

———. 1988b. *Government by Proxy: (Mis?)Managing Federal Programs.* Washington, D.C.: Congressional Quarterly Press.

———. 1989. "Trends and Traditions in the Budgetary Process." *Public Administration Review* 49 (May/June): 231-239.

———. 1993. *Sharing Power: Public Governance and Private Markets.* Washington, D.C.: Brookings Institution.

Lipset, Seymour Martin, and William Schneider. 1987. *The Confidence Gap: Business, Labor, and Government in the Public Mind,* rev. ed. Baltimore: Johns Hopkins University Press.

Metropolitan Government of Nashville and Davidson County. 1989. *Efficiency in Metropolitan Government: Task Force Report, 1989.*

Moe, Ronald C., 1995. *Managing the Public's Business: Federal Government Corporations.* United States Senate, Committee on Governmental Affairs, Senate Print 104-18. Washington, D.C.: U.S. Government Printing Office.

Moe, Ronald C., and Thomas H. Stanton. 1989. "Government-Sponsored Enterprises as Federal Instrumentalities: Reconciling Private Management with Public Accountability." *Public Administration Review* 49 (July/August): 321-329.

Mosher, Frederick C. 1979. *The GAO: The Quest for Accountability in American Government.* Boulder, Colo.: Westview Press.

National Commission on the Public Service. 1989. "Public Perceptions of the Public Service." *Task Force Reports.* Washington, D.C.: National Commission on the Public Service.

Niskanen, William A., Jr., 1971. *Bureaucracy and Representative Government.* Chicago: Aldine, Atherton.

Oakerson, Ronald J. 1987. "Local Public Economies: Provision, Production and Governance." *Intergovernmental Perspective* 13 (Summer/Fall): 20-25.

Poole, Robert. 1987. "The Political Obstacles to Privatization," in Steve H. Hanke, ed., *Prospects for Privatization,* pp. 33-45. New York: Academy of Political Science.

President's Commission on Privatization. 1988. *Privatization: Toward More Effective Government.* Washington, D.C.: U.S. Government Printing Office.

President's Private Sector Survey on Cost Control (Grace Commission). 1984. *A Report to the President.* Washington, D.C.: U.S. Government Printing Office.

Rehfuss, John A. 1989. *Contracting Out in Government.* San Francisco: Jossey-Bass.

Savas, E.S. 1982. *Privatizing the Public Sector.* Chatham, N.J.: Chatham House.

———. 1987. *Privatization: The Key to Better Government.* Chatham, N.J.: Chatham House.

Seidman, Harold. 1988. "The Quasi World of the Federal Government." *Brookings Review* 6 (Summer): 23-27.

Seidman, Harold, and Robert Gilmour. 1986. *Politics, Position, and Power,* 4th ed. New York: Oxford University Press.

Shenk, Joshua Wolf. 1995. "The Perils of Privatization." *Washington Monthly* (May): 16-23.

Smith, Fred L., Jr. 1987. "Privatization at the Federal Level," in Steve H. Hanke, ed., *Prospects for Privatization,* pp. 179-189. New York: Academy of Political Science.

Starr, Paul. 1987. "The Limits of Privatization," in Steve H. Hanke, ed., *Prospects for Privatization,* pp. 124-137. New York: Academy of Political Science.

Sullivan, Harold J. 1987. "Privatization of Public Services: A Growing Threat to Constitutional Rights." *Public Administration Review* 47 (November/December): 461-467.

Swiss, James E. 1991. *Public Management Systems: Monitoring and Managing Government Performance.* Englewood Cliffs, N.J.: Prentice-Hall.

U.S. Office of Management and Budget. 1988. *Enhancing Governmental Productivity through Competition.* Washington, D.C.: U.S. Government Printing Office.

chapter **20**

Political/Career Relationships in Public Management: The Good, the Bad, and the Possibilities

Patricia W. Ingraham

American public organizations and their management structures are notable for an unusual organizational characteristic: a truncated structure in which the larger part of the organization is composed of members appointed through civil service or merit processes, whereas the top of the organization—the leadership structure—is appointed through political processes by elected officials. This odd configuration was created to meet both the need for a permanent and professional public service and the need to provide political and policy direction to that service. Although this structure is found at all levels of government, it is most pronounced at the national level. The American federal government has more political appointees than any other modern democracy. The ability of the president to fill all available slots, the quality of the appointees, and the willingness of the appointees to stay in their positions long enough to really lead public organizations have become issues of critical significance for both public management and public policy.

Historically the political management system that the truncated structures permit is a relative newcomer. Prior to the passage of the federal Pendleton Act in 1883 and the state civil service laws that followed, public jobs were filled by patronage. Under a patronage system, political affiliation and connections are the most important job qualifications. Patronage is also referred to as "spoils," as in "to the victor belong the spoils." Such a system was in place for the first century of American government; indeed, the spoils system continued well after passage of the Pendleton Act because that legislation initially covered only 10 percent of the federal work force.

Unlimited patronage became problematic very early in its development. Public jobs were bought and sold; presidents and other elected officials were assailed by job seekers; the capacity of government was diminished as waves of employees moved in and out after every election. Nearly 40 years after the Pendleton Act created a federal merit system, President Woodrow Wilson declared that patronage was "a thorny path that daily made [him] wish [he] had never been born" (Ingraham, 1995: 37). The merit system grew at the expense of patronage; every job covered by merit examination or appointment was no longer available to elected officials for a patronage appointment. As a result, the growth of the merit system was incremental and disjointed; the political management system developed in tandem.

The relationship between politics and merit is, therefore, close but troubled. The merit system is to provide a professional, stable, and neutral public service. The political appointee management system is to provide for policy change and for political direction. There are obvious tensions. Dwight Waldo has argued, in fact, that nearly all contemporary public problems can be related to the difficulties inherent in relating political matters and values to those of administration (Waldo, 1981). In the United States, these difficulties have been exacerbated by a deep-seated distrust of bureaucracy and centralized power. These tensions and disparities come together on a daily basis in the relationships between political appointees and career civil servants in public organizations. A history of the management of public organizations is very much a review of the recurring cycle of problems created by institutionalizing these tensions. Yet an effective partnership between political executives and the career service is fundamental to effective government. A brief review of efforts to create a workable solution is useful in understanding the complexity of creating that partnership.

MERIT, NEUTRALITY, AND GOOD GOVERNMENT

Despite the longevity of the politics/administration debate, and the changed political, social, and economic conditions in which it has recurred, there is remarkable continuity in its component parts. The values of responsiveness, effectiveness, and neutrality have always been present but have assumed different priorities at different times (Kaufman, 1956). Since the time of the Brownlow Committee Report in 1937, the role of the president as manager of the executive branch has been a part of the debate. Since the report of the Second Hoover Commission in 1955, the role of the higher civil service and the critical role it could play in interfacing between political appointees and lower levels of the organization has been included. The issue of centralized direction and control versus decentralization has been notable for its endurance. The role of Congress, and the balance of authority between Congress and the president, has emerged consistently but less frequently. Political appointees have most often been viewed as emissaries of the president; Congress and its staff have resorted to other means for ensuring responsiveness to their interests.

A number of "models," or conceptual descriptions, have attempted to impose clarity and coherence—and, to some extent, legitimacy—on the relationship between elected and appointed officials and the members of the career civil service. The model with the greatest longevity is the "science of administration." The ideas and assumptions in this model rely heavily on the politics/administration dichotomy and its foundation concept that the "worlds" of politics and administration are different and separable. If, in Wilson's terms, the "hurry and strife" of the political world are removed from administration, it is possible for it to operate in a neutral, efficient, and even scientific manner (Wilson, 1887).

In this view of the relationship, the role of politics is not diminished by the separation; rather, administration responds to political directions and objectives, but clarifies them, and "straightens their path" in the process (Wilson, 1887). The broader model that this view of the relationship implies is very bureaucratic and Weberian: a clear hierarchical organizational structure, neutral application of expertise and skills, and long-term stability for both the organization and the employees within it. At the height of its acceptance, the idea of a science of administration for members of the career bureaucracy led to efforts to identify the single most efficient way to perform a task and to standardize such performance across government. Efficiency was highly prized; Luther Gulick declared it to be "the number one value" in democratic government (Gulick and Urwick, 1937).

The simplicity of this perspective and the neatness that it implies for the politics/administration relationship are very compelling. As the range of government activities expanded, however, and as government became more complex, the disjuncture between the simple model and the real world became ever more jarring. Competing models were devised; most focused on the extent to which the complex reality of modern problems and programs precluded simple responsiveness on the part of the career civil service; their expertise was inevitably a part of the problem-solving process—and therefore the policy-making process—as well (Appleby, 1949). This view provided greater insight into the nature of political direction and management: Traditionally, policy was the purview of politics; increasingly, policy making was dependent on skills and abilities that elected officials and their appointees did not necessarily have. Institutional memory, technical and scientific expertise, and a longer view of both problems and their potential solutions assumed greater significance. As they did, both the nature of the relationship between appointees and the career service, and the long-term emphasis on efficiency changed.

The reality of administrative power also became evident; this caused additional tensions within public organizations. As government grew, and as the role of the permanent bureaucracy became more central to it, the potential for career civil servants to develop a power base independent from that of elected officials and appointees grew as well. The need to curb this power, as well as to manage public organizations effectively, created a new equation for political executives and the elected officials who appointed them. Again, this was particularly true in the federal government, where there was a pronounced tendency for members of the career civil service to be viewed as the problem, rather than as problem solvers.

As political management systems have evolved, then, a relationship that was always somewhat tendentious encountered both new responsibilities and new difficulties. Presidents, governors, and other elected officials have devised different strategies for managing, for directing, and often for controlling. It is useful to examine key resources available to them as they implement these strategies, as well as to note characteristics of political appointees that bear directly on their ability to carry out the tasks suggested by the various strategies.

POLITICAL APPOINTMENTS
AND POLITICAL APPOINTEES

A variety of appointment authorities are available to elected officials wishing to fill their management cadres. Only the top level—in the federal government called "PAS" (presidential appointment; Senate approval)—must have their credentials examined and approved by the legislature. These top-level appointees are the equivalent of the chief executive officers for each major department or agency. They must have excellent management skills but also policy expertise and a good working relationship with the president (or governor). Most often, they are appointed for their political affiliation as well.

Other appointment authorities are also available in the federal government. In 1955, President Dwight D. Eisenhower created Schedule C authority by executive order. The purpose of Schedule C is to provide the president and his top appointees the opportunity to fill lower-level slots with policy significance— or with substantial access to policy-sensitive information—with sympathetic partisans. Eisenhower argued that special assistants or executive secretaries, for example, needed to be "policy confidential." This is how the Schedule C positions were initially utilized. To the end of the Ford presidency, Schedule C authority was used in a limited way. Beginning with the Carter presidency, and continuing to the present time, however, larger numbers of Schedule C appointees have been placed in mid-level management positions; the total number of such appointees has doubled in the last 20 years, to about 1,800 (Ingraham, 1987; Ingraham, Thompson, and Eisenberg, 1995). Schedule C appointees are generally not chosen for their management or policy skills but for their partisan affiliation or party service.

Finally, in the federal government and in several states, some members of the Senior Executive Service (SES) may also be political appointees. The Senior Executive Service was created for the federal government in 1978, by the Civil Service Reform Act. Fully 90 percent of its members were the highest ranking executives in the career service; the other 10 percent were to be political appointees, with potential placement essentially throughout the organization. The SES is an interesting part of the political/career puzzle; its members have the greatest potential to work closely together, given their similar status in the organization. However, there is little evidence that the SES has worked in this way.

Political appointees share common characteristics that have important implications for the role they are able to play in public management and for the relationships they are able to build while holding their appointive positions. One of the most significant is that they stay in position for relatively short periods of time (MacKenzie, 1987; Ban and Ingraham, 1990). The average time in position for the very highest level of appointees is about two years; it is lower for both political members of the SES and for Schedule C appointees. The short tenure is due partly to pay constraints in the public sector; it is also attributable to the desire of lower-ranking appointees to move on to other, higher-ranking or more visible appointments. Roberts (1994) reports this problem to be less severe for state governments, but for the federal government it is a long-term and substantial issue.

The tenure problem is directly related to two other appointee characteristics: They come to government generally distrusting career employees, and they come with limited confidence in their ability to manage the "politics" of public positions (MacKenzie, 1987). Both of these problems tend to be alleviated over time. Of those political appointees who do stay longer than two years, a large majority report that as they came to know career employees, they grew to trust them and to respect their expertise. Short tenure in position does not allow that to happen.

The problems caused by short tenure among appointees are exacerbated by the much longer tenure and intensive program experience and expertise of the career executives with whom they work most closely. Most career members of the SES have at least 12 to 14 years of experience—often with the same program. From their perspective, political appointees can be viewed as short-timers who are prone to shooting themselves in the foot. Efforts by career executives to deter such bodily harm may be viewed by appointees as resistance to their initiatives.

PRESIDENTIAL MANAGEMENT STRATEGIES AND POLITICAL/CAREER RELATIONSHIPS

Despite the problems noted above, every president since Lyndon Johnson, and many governors, have devised political management strategies around the increased use of political appointees. The strategies are founded on two common assumptions: Career bureaucrats will resist political initiatives, and political appointees will be able to carry out the directives of the elected official. The first assumption was the guiding principle for Presidents Nixon and Reagan. Presidents Carter and Bush placed explanations for resistance on the premise that members of the career bureaucracy were essentially good people but were trapped in "bad systems." Whatever the differences in emphasis, there were remarkable commonalities in the components of the political management strategies.

President Nixon's strategy was comprehensive and included structural reorganizations in the executive branch, as well as block grants, budget cuts, and withholding of funds already approved by Congress. For our purposes here, it is most important to note the emphasis on political/career relationships. Both the block grants and the reorganizations were intended to limit the influence and discretion of the permanent bureaucracy; the fear that even carefully selected appointees would "go native" led to careful directives from the White House on how to avoid that fate. The infamous "Malek Manual," prepared by President Nixon's White House Personnel Office, provided instructions on ways to bypass and subvert the merit system. To paraphrase the manual's theme, it argued that good management was fine but that political control was better (Thompson, 1979). The strategy led to both political excess and illegal activities, but key components of the "Administrative Presidency," in Nathan's (1983) terms, became an integral part of political/career relationships in the federal government.

President Carter emphasized comprehensive reform of the civil service system. The legislation that his administration successfully designed and passed—the Civil Service Reform Act of 1978—abolished the Civil Service Commission, created pay-for-performance for mid-level and upper-level managers, and created the Senior Executive Service, among other things. Each of these three provisions altered the relationship between political appointees and the career civil service. Abolishing the Civil Service Commission and replacing it with the Office of Personnel Management eliminated a bipartisan board in favor of one director, who was a presidential appointee. Pay-for-performance created a system in which performance bonuses were based on performance appraisals and ratings; for the higher civil service—the SES—those evaluations and appraisals were most often conducted by political appointees. The Senior Executive Service contained provisions for reassignment and other forms of mobility that gave political appointees new and potentially powerful tools for moving members of the career service to less influential positions.

The Carter strategy was also notable for its dramatically increased reliance on the Schedule C appointment authority. During Carter's administration the number of these appointees nearly doubled; significantly, the greatest increase occurred at the GS13–GS15 levels, those of mid-level managers. This permitted much greater direction of lower-level decision points, which had traditionally been the purview of career managers. Succeeding presidencies continued to build on the high Carter numbers, and Schedule C appointments became a much more significant component of presidential management strategies.

President Reagan pursued a different and much more punitive strategy toward the career service. His appointees were carefully screened for ideological compatibility with the president and his top advisors, as well as for policy skills. Ninety-three percent of Reagan's initial appointees were Republicans; 47 percent of them opposed an activist role for government (Aberbach, 1991). Part of a broader strategy to reduce both the size and the scope of government, Reagan's tactics included special targeting of agencies and departments such as the Environmental Protection Agency and the Department of Education, and special efforts to achieve tighter control of the central management agencies—the Office of Personnel Management, the Office of Management and Budget, and the

General Services Administration. In all these agencies the total numbers of political appointees increased significantly, whereas the total numbers of career civil servants declined (Ingraham, Thompson, and Eisenberg, 1995).

The tools of the Civil Service Reform Act, particularly the Senior Executive Service, proved to be very useful in the hands of a president determined to cut back government. In some agencies all political SES slots were filled, whereas available career slots were not; in other agencies the SES mobility provisions permitted "dumping" of career SES in small and less powerful offices, whereas political SES and other political appointees filled the "plum" slots. When Aberbach and Rockman studied the higher civil service in 1980, nearly half of those they interviewed reported that they had "a great deal" of policy influence. In their subsequent study in 1986, that number had dropped to below 20 percent (Aberbach, 1991). Although the impact of this aggressive strategy varied from agency to agency, it clearly did shift the balance of the political/career relationship from one of modest joint participation in decision making and policy making to one of clear political direction.

The Bush administration was a sharp contrast to that of President Reagan. Perhaps reflecting his own long career in the public service, Bush's statements early in his term supported the career civil service and the Senior Executive Service. At least partially because he had great difficulty recruiting appointees, Bush also relied to a greater extent on the SES for top management positions. The total number of filled SES positions increased by nearly 1,000 during the Bush term; political SES appointments decreased from 9.3 percent to 8.7 percent (Ingraham, Thompson, and Eisenberg, 1995). Michaels reports that Bush appointees were "primed to work cooperatively with careerists," either through the president's example or through their own previous experience (Michaels, 1995: 279).

Finally, the Clinton administration evidenced no clear strategy in its first three years. Coming into power after 12 years of Republican control and the inevitable "blanketing" of political appointees to career positions, Clinton appointees demonstrated some of the traditional lack of trust. The Clinton appointment process was extremely slow; some agencies went well into the second year of the Clinton presidency without key appointees. Others (notably the Department of Commerce, whose Secretary, the late Ronald Brown, was the former director of the Democratic National Committee) apparently reverted to a traditional patronage model and filled nearly all available appointee slots very quickly.

It was clear that despite the lack of a clear strategy, there was not really a backing away from the higher numbers of politicals found in previous presidencies. The Clinton administration's Reinventing Government initiative—which advocated cutting the total size of government employment by 272,000 positions, or 12 percent—did not even mention reducing the size of the political appointee cadre. President Clinton did, however, initiate a new practice in political management: He created performance contracts between himself and the top political appointee in each of the major departments and agencies. These contracts specified particular program and policy objectives; in some cases, performance

TABLE 20.1 Number of political appointees, 1980–1992; Schedule C and Political SES.

Type of Appointee	1980	1986	1992
Schedule C	1456	1643	1699
Political SES	582	658	704
TOTAL	2038	2301	2403

SOURCE: Adapted from Patricia W. Ingraham, James Thompson, and Elliot Eisenberg, "Political Management Strategies and Political/Career Relationships: Where Are We Now in the Federal Government?" *Public Administration Review* 55 (May/June 1995).

measures were included. The contracts are notable in the political/career relationship because they strengthen the relationship between the Executive Office of the President and top political appointees. As a result, they have the potential of clarifying what is expected of the political/career relationships inside the agencies.

Overall, then, nearly 30 years of presidential management strategies have had two notable effects on the political/career relationships in the federal bureaucracy: They have increased the total numbers of political appointees, and they have clarified the tenuous equilibrium that defines an effective working relationship. As Table 20.1 demonstrates, the largest increases have come in the Schedule C ranks—that level of appointment that does not require legislative examination or approval. How larger numbers of essentially patronage appointments impact working relationships inside public organizations is not completely clear, but it does not improve either management or organizational efficiency. In many cases it adds another, confounding management level (Light, 1995).

REINVENTING GOVERNMENT: APPLYING THE ISSUES TO A REAL PROBLEM

There are several lessons to be drawn from the preceding discussion of the political/career relationship in modern American government. The first is the remarkable endurance of the issues surrounding it. The extent to which career civil servants simply respond to the directives of political appointees, versus the extent to which they legitimately "argue back" on the basis of their longer tenure and specialized expertise, is one example. The extent to which efficiency—however defined—should be a primary consideration is another. Equally enduring, however, is the need for an effective partnership to be molded. A contemporary example, the Clinton administration's efforts to reinvent government, provides striking evidence.

Reinvention: The Process and the Strategy

The Clinton administration's position on government and the career bureaucracy is somewhat equivocal. According to the president and the vice-president, government can be an effective problem solver—but only if it is reinvented first.

Based on the analysis published in the National Performance Review's *Creating a Government That Works Better and Costs Less* (1991), President Clinton argues that public organizations and their employees have become trapped in overly regulated and controlled systems of rules and regulations.

Layers of regulators—budget analysts, personnel specialists, and the like—need to be removed. Executive and managerial discretion need to be increased. Attention to product, rather than process, must be emphasized. Employees at all levels of the organization must be empowered and must participate in problem solving. As organizations become smaller, flatter, and more decentralized, the role of middle management will be dramatically altered and reshaped. The total number of middle managers will decrease significantly.

It is important to note that most of the analysis that informed the NPR report was done by career civil servants. The accompanying reports to the main volume outline both problems and proposed solutions in specific detail. This process and level of involvement for career staff is very similar to the process that designed the Civil Service Reform Act of 1978. The difference with reinvention is that it proposes much more extensive decentralization, the elimination of many more rules and regulations, and the delegation of much more flexibility and discretion to career managers and executives than did CSRA. So what? Very clearly, such discretion and flexibility will decrease the ability of political executives to direct and control the career service. These lines of authority are further attenuated by the NPR's and reinvention's emphasis on customer satisfaction. A brief examination of these and other issues clarifies the centrality of effective political/career partnerships to reinvention and other reforms.

Responsiveness Revisited

In traditional models of political/career relationships, responsiveness is viewed in simple, hierarchical terms. Members of the career service respond as fully as possible to the authority and direction of political executives, both as managers of the organization and as spokespersons for perceived electoral mandates. This view of the relationship has always been problematic in terms of the role of Congress. Responsiveness in the context of a reinvented government, however, increases the problem exponentially. DiIulio, Garvey, and Kettl have noted the multidimensional nature of the role of citizens in this regard: as consumers, as taxpayers, sometimes as partners in service provision, and always as overseers of general performance (DiIulio, Garvey, and Kettl, 1993). Each of these roles suggests a different component of responsiveness and different values by which responsiveness will be assessed. It is very possible—indeed, likely—that responsiveness to one or more of these citizen dimensions will conflict with, or directly contradict, political executive direction. Add to that the role of Congress or the legislature, the responsiveness to the teams and other employee groups within the organization, and—unless major systemic changes occur—the continuing need to respond to the laws, rules, and regulations that govern the organization and its programs. This is an enormously complex undertaking; unless there is a firm partnership between political and career executives at the top of the organization, and firm joint commitment to overall goals, it will be impossible to juggle competing demands and expectations. The traditional hierarchical model of responsiveness is not only hopelessly outdated, it will be a major obstacle to effective action.

Without Rules, What?

The issues of increased flexibility and discretion are closely related to the preceding discussion. The NPR recommended eliminating unnecessary rules and regulations and unnecessary layers of organizational regulators. In response, the entire Federal Personnel Manual was ceremoniously dumped. There was widespread agreement that many of the rules and regulations were absurd; there is far less agreement about alternative means of ensuring accountability and external direction of public bureaucracies.

There is no tradition in the American public service that values flexibility and discretion for public employees. Quite to the contrary, there is deep-seated distrust of both the bureaucracy and the persons it employs. Rules and regulations governing every aspect of organizational life were adopted precisely because elected officials and citizens believed they were necessary to ensure appropriate bureaucratic behavior.

Reinvention not only values, but mandates, considerable *individual* autonomy and discretion; one of its major unexplored assumptions is that individual accountability will be an adequate and widely accepted replacement for rules and regulations. What does all this have to do with political/career relationships? A great deal. As noted earlier, there has always been a suspicious and distrustful relationship between new appointees and the members of the career service with whom they will work. The hierarchical control model of neutral responsiveness provided some comfort in that regard. But if that model cannot work in the reformed organizations, and if rules are more flexible—and less controlling— as well, both political and career executives must find some new ground for effective collaboration.

Downsizing and Managing Change

Most public agencies involved in reinvention are managing other change activities as well. The most common accompaniment is downsizing the organization. As noted above, a reinvented government will have smaller and flatter organizations. The combined activities create very difficult management problems on a number of levels. Many members of the career service will be asked to manage themselves out of a job. Others, particularly middle managers, face an extremely uncertain future in the organization. At the same time it is necessary to manage the change activities, to maintain employee morale in the face of organizational turbulence, and, of course, to continue to deliver program services at the same or higher levels of productivity. In some agencies, managing just the change activities is essentially a full-time job. One career executive, who considers himself "onboard" with reinvention, reported no fewer than 12 reinvention initiatives in his office. Political executives cannot do these things; they must rely on the career service to implement the day-to-day changes that reinvention and other reforms require. The political/career relationship must be one that provides rewards for the career managers and executives who deal with the daily pain of managing change. If the career executives who support political initiatives such as reinvention are not clearly rewarded—or worse, if they are not supported by political leadership in the risks they obviously take—the potential for effective change is very limited. We are only beginning to understand the difficulty of managing multidimensional change in public organizations, but it is already clear that a mutually supportive political/career partnership will be one component of success. One commonality in a recent study of successful performance of high-ranking careerists—execucrats—was a good working relationship with political appointees (Riccucci, 1995). Successfully managing change is an area in which the mutual dependency is very high.

An additional argument for partnership is the long-term nature of organizational change. The differences in political and career perspectives in this regard are dramatic. Political executives operate with a narrow window of opportunity and a short timeline for seeing success. The next election is a compelling deadline. The short tenure of political executives exacerbates the demand for rapid results. Career civil servants, on the other hand, have a much longer time frame for both reference and results. A common fear on the part of political executives is that careerists will "wait them out" rather than change. The structure of the system makes that possible, if the career executives are so inclined.

Creating a bridge between these disparate time frames is critically important to effective public change. That change is a lengthy process; the best estimates for institutionalizing the change objectives and achieving some measure of success in meeting them is five to seven years. Even in the best of circumstances (a two-term president or governor), most of the political executives who initiated the change will be long gone. Most of the career executives who worked with them will remain. They are absolutely key to the success or failure of the change activity.

Finally, in this regard, political/career cooperation is important to provide an effective "shield" for the change activities. Public organizations are remarkably open; virtually every activity is subject to public and legislative scrutiny. Evidence from existing efforts to reinvent, restructure, and reengineer public organizations demonstrates that some ability to protect the early stages of these activities from external intervention is important (Thompson and Ingraham, 1996). Early analysis of the activities in reinvention laboratories supports that conclusion. The career civil servants who are actually managing the reinvention efforts are often at the edge of existing practice and wisdom; they need protection if they are to be willing to take the risks this entails. Political executives can provide a shield, as well as a cushion of support and trust.

CONCLUSION

The political/career relationship at all levels of government has long been a troubling issue in American government; the problem has been most contentious at the federal level. In efforts to "solve" this thorny problem, several alternative models of control versus cooperation have been advanced. The most widely accepted has been that of responsive competence: Members of the career service utilize their skills and expertise in a neutral way to respond to the directives of political executives. Although the need to be responsive is not in doubt, however, other components of this model are either outdated or seriously questioned by current reform and reinvention activities, as well as by the realities of modern government.

Both political and career executives bring special skills and abilities to public management. Political appointees bring new policy ideas, a force for change, and the authority of electoral choices and top elected officials. Career executives bring program and policy expertise, institutional history, and a keen knowledge of managing in a public context. Both sets of these skills are important to the abilities of public organizations to change effectively. For that to happen, however, the skills of both political and career executives must be used constructively, so that each enhances and strengthens the other. Unfortunately, for much of the history of public management that has not been the case.

There is no doubt that public organizations will face ever-increasing demands for change. Economic constraints will mandate that, but there are other reasons as well. The changing nature of public problems, the unpredictable nature of those changes, dissatisfaction with past performance, and new expectations place public organizations and their managers in a turbulent environment. The Perot campaign, Reinventing Government, and the Contract with America are all a part of the turbulence. Effectively managing public organizations through these changes requires strong and committed leadership in those organizations; neither political executives nor career managers can provide that leadership alone. A full partnership will be required.

REFERENCES

Aberbach, Joel. 1991. "The President and the Executive Branch," in Colin Campbell and Bert Rockman, eds., *The Bush Presidency: First Appraisals.* Chatham, N.J.: Chatham House, pp. 223-247.

Appleby, Paul. 1949. *Policy and Administration.* University: University of Alabama Press.

Ban, Carolyn, and Patricia W. Ingraham. 1990. "Short-Timers: Political Appointee Mobility and Its Impact on Political/Career Relations in the Reagan Administration." *Administration and Society* 22 (May): 106-124.

DiIulio, John, Gerald Garvey, and Donald Kettl. 1993. *Improving Government Performance: An Owner's Manual.* Washington, D.C.: Brookings Institution.

Gulick, Luther, and Lyndall Urwick, eds. 1937. *Papers on the Science of Administration.* New York: Institute of Public Administration.

Ingraham, Patricia W. 1987. "Building Bridges or Burning Them? The President, the Appointees and the Bureaucracy." *Public Administration Review* 47 (September/October): 425-435.

————. 1995. *The Foundation of Merit: Public Service in American Democracy.* Baltimore: Johns Hopkins University Press.

Ingraham, Patricia W., James Thompson, and Elliot Eisenberg. 1995. "Political Management Strategies and Political/Career Relationships: Where Are We Now in the Federal Government?" *Public Administration Review* 55 (May/June): 263-273.

Kaufman, Herbert. 1956. "Emerging Conflicts in the Doctrine of Public Administration," American Political Science Review (December): 1057-1073.

Light, Paul C. 1995. *Thickening Government.* Washington, D.C.: Brookings Institution.

MacKenzie, G. Calvin. 1987. *The In and Outers.* Baltimore: Johns Hopkins University Press.

Michaels, Judith E. 1995. "A View from the Top: Reflections of Bush Presidential Appointees." *Public Administration Review* 55 (May/June): 273-284.

Nathan, Richard P. 1983. *The Administrative Presidency.* New York: John Wiley and Sons.

National Performance Review. 1991. *Reinventing Government: Creating a Government That Works Better and Costs Less.* Washington, D.C.: U.S. Government Printing Office.

Riccucci, Norma M. 1995. "Execucrats, Politics, and Public Policy: What Are the Ingredients for Successful Performance in the Federal Government?" *Public Administration Review* 55 (May/June): 219-231.

Roberts, Deborah D. 1993. "The Governor as Leader: Strengthening Public Service Through Executive Leadership," in Frank J. Thompson, ed., *Revitalizing State and Local Public Service.* San Francisco: Jossey-Bass.

Thompson, Frank J., ed. 1979. *Classics of Public Personnel Policy.* Oak Park, Ill.: Moore Publishing.

Thompson, James, and Patricia W. Ingraham. 1996. "Organizational Redesign: The Reality of Public Sector Change," in Donald F. Kettl and H. Brinton Milward, eds., *New Issues for Public Management.* Baltimore: Johns Hopkins University Press.

Waldo, Dwight. 1981. *The Enterprise of Public Administration.* Novato, Calif.: Chandler and Sharp.

Wilson, Woodrow. 1887. "The Study of Administration." *American Political Science Review* 2 (June).

Index